**Wm. C. Brown
Communications, Inc.**

David J. Flick
Sales Representative

**Wm. C. Brown
Communications, Inc.**
District Office
142 Foster Avenue
London, Ontario N6H 2L1
519-438-8585

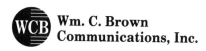 **A Times Mirror
Company**

LEISURE AND SOCIETY:

A Comparative Approach

LEISURE AND SOCIETY:

A Comparative Approach

Hilmi Ibrahim
Whittier College

 WCB Wm. C. Brown Publishers

Book Team

Editor *Chris Rogers*
Production Coordinator *Carla D. Arnold*

WCB **Wm. C. Brown Publishers**

President *G. Franklin Lewis*
Vice President, Publisher *George Wm. Bergquist*
Vice President, Publisher *Thomas E. Doran*
Vice President, Operations and Production *Beverly Kolz*
National Sales Manager *Virginia S. Moffat*
Advertising Manager *Ann M. Knepper*
Marketing Manager *Kathy Law Laube*
Managing Editor, Production *Colleen A. Yonda*
Production Editorial Manager *Julie A. Kennedy*
Production Editorial Manager *Ann Fuerste*
Publishing Services Manager *Karen J. Slaght*
Manager of Visuals and Design *Faye M. Schilling*

Cover design by Carol V. Hall

Cover images: top and right—Aneal Vohra, bottom—Kimberly
Burnham, left—Chris Boyla; all from Unicorn Stock Photos

Library of Congress Catalog Card Number: 89–82466

ISBN 0–697–05374–1

Printed in the United States of America by Wm. C. Brown Publishers,
2460 Kerper Boulevard, Dubuque, IA 52001

10 9 8 7 6 5 4 3 2 1

Dedicated to
Harry and Leona Nerhood

CONTENTS

PART FOUR

THE SHAPING OF LEISURE BEHAVIOR

PREFACE

We live in a time in which a global perspective is imperative. We have begun to look outward in areas such as economy and technology. So it is only natural that when we consider leisure, we consider its role in the various cultures of the globe.

This text looks at leisure practices throughout the world and compares them. It explains the role of the ritual and the ways in which rituals have determined the role leisure has played in countries around the world.

The text is designed for Leisure and Recreation majors, as well as for general college students interested in studying society's use of its free time. Students are invited to bring their own thoughts to the course and to draw their own conclusions as to the future of leisure. It is, after all, the students of today who will decide the role of leisure tomorrow.

The book is divided into four parts and fourteen chapters. Following the Preface, Part One deals with the sociocultural bases of leisure. Chapter 1 presents the evolution of play, ritual, and society. Chapter 2 discusses the physical, biological, psychological, and social elements of time as they relate to leisure behavior. Chapter 3 discusses the macrocultural and physical variables acting on leisure.

Part Two is concerned with the potentiality of certain activities in the ritualistic lives of "primitive" people (chap. 4), which evolved into recreative and amusive activities catering, in many instances, to a growing leisure class. This change is present to a greater extent in the stage of intermediate society (chaps. 5 and 6).

As human society evolves into what is termed a modern society, ritualized and class leisure evolve as well, for sociological and sociotechnological reasons, into mass leisure (Part Three). Chapter 7 presents these changes in four Third-World countries, chapter 8 in four Communist bloc countries, chapter 9 in three Western European countries, chapter 10 in Canada, and chapter 11 in the United States.

Part Four is devoted to factors that shape leisure behavior, the agents of socialization, into leisure pursuits (chap. 12), and the places where these pursuits take place (chap. 13). The mass leisure witnessed in the modern society is not without problems, and these are presented in the last chapter, chapter 14.

The evolutionary perspective is the most suitable one for both the pedagogical and the scholarly understanding of leisure in society. For today's student, living at the threshold of the twenty-first century, change is not just probable but inevitable. He or she is living through change. To understand the mechanism of change is to understand the future.

Hilmi Ibrahim
Whittier College

ACKNOWLEDGMENTS

I am grateful to my wife, Cynthia, for her unwavering support and for her involvement in every phase of this project. My two research fellows, Mike Montgomery and Amy Green, gave many hours of hard work towards its completion. The technical ability of C. J. Hines, Jean Ettinger, Cathy George, and Robert Olsabeck is greatly appreciated. I would like to thank the Whittier College faculty for the grant that I received over the four-year period that it took to finish this project.

I also wish to thank Chris Rogers, editor of *Recreation,* for having faith in this project and for seeing it through to its successful conclusion.

Cindy Kurhasch, the development editor in charge, provided support and encouragement throughout the development of the manuscript. Also, the constructive criticism of the following reviewers was of great help in putting the volume in its final form: Michael J. Leitner, California State University, Chico; Sandra L. Little, Illinois State University; Francis A. McGuire, Clemson University; James F. Murphy, San Francisco State University; Larry L. Neal, University of Oregon; Mounir G. Ragheb, Florida State University; Howard D. Richardson, Indiana State University; S. Harold Smith, Brigham Young University; and Carl Yoshioka, Arizona State University.

INTRODUCTION

This book treats leisure as a universal phenomenon. Leisure activities are seen in every society today, yet they vary in quality and quantity. Given the prevalence of leisure activities today, the question arises, What about previous societies? This question leads to another: Did previous societies have the same or similar activities? Still more questions come to mind. If these activities vary, why? What makes them change over the years? And under what conditions do they begin to change? Why are certain activities dominant in one society and not another?

The affect-effect relationship between leisure and society is the pivotal point in seeking answers to these questions. The need for a sociohistorical treatment of the leisure phenomenon is evident. This new perspective investigates the leisure phenomenon without attachment to one historical time or geographical place, defining it as *a state of mind or being that allows a person to choose contemplative, recreative, or amusive activities at the time in which he or she is relatively freed from work, civil, or familial obligations.*

The existence of relative freedom to pursue leisure activity has its basis in two evolutionary principles. The first is differentiation, in which a simple, extrinsically motivated activity in the life of early humans evolves over time into an intrinsically motivated one. A good example of this is hunting. Done for survival purposes in early and medieval societies, today it is basically recreational. The second evolutionary principle is that a simple activity becomes increasingly complex over the years. An example is American football, which was played at its inception by a team of 11 men who constituted both the defense and the offense. Today, a college team may include up to 44 players, divided into offense, defense, and other specialized units for kicking and receiving. The coaching staff has grown likewise, from one to over ten.

Such is the evolution in leisure activities as affected by the accompanying societal evolution. An approach to the evolution of society was needed, and this led to the adoption of Talcott Parsons' schema (1966). It divides the evolution of society into three stages: "primitive," intermediate, and modern. Regardless of its level on the evolutionary scale, a society has control over a wide range of human activities. It is therefore self-sufficient, which means that it has adequate control over motivation and commitment to human activities, including leisure activities. Since social life is surrounded by many envelopes, one of which is culture, understanding culture is a necessity, because culture tells us the way in which things should be done. Ultimate reality stands above the cultural system, which, in turn, stands above the social system. The social system is affected by and, in turn, affects the behavioral system. All of these are a part of a particular physical environment and are affected by it (fig. I.1).

As I compiled data from sources over 150 years old (Lane 1836, Wood 1871) and from recent sources as well, it became clear that the activities observed in the past are similar, and sometimes identical to, some of today's leisure activities. Yet the societal niche allowed for leisure activities in the sociocultural milieu is different from the one these activities occupy today. In fact they were placed in a very powerful niche: the ritual. Further research showed that a transformation has taken place, led in many instances by the wealthy elite who were freed from many obligations, including work and ritual. That group was labelled by Veblen as the leisure class (1953).

Systematic arrangement of leisure activities showed that there are basically three types: ritualized activities that take place during collective rituals, class activities that are enjoyed by certain privileged people, and mass leisure that is enjoyed

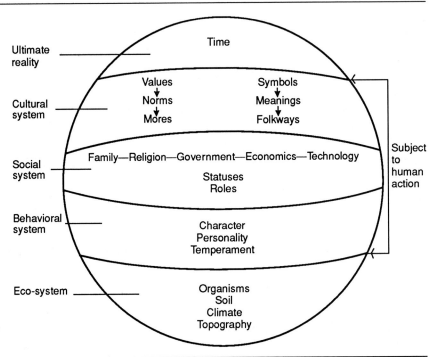

FIGURE I.1 *Society in its environment*

by most members of the society. Ritualized leisure and class leisure can be considered the bases for many of today's leisure activities.

Further research showed that play is the common denominator in all three types of leisure activities. Does this mean that play is universal? If so, how? Clearly a section on play was needed, but it has been kept within the parameters of the evolutionary perspective.

These three types also correspond to the three levels of society. Ritualized leisure is dominant in the stage of "primitive" society; the activities of the leisure class are dominant in the intermediate society; and mass leisure is dominant in the modern society. Despite all the advantages and the gains of the modern society in the area of leisure offerings and services, a number of problems are present in the leisure sphere of modern society.

Inherent in the evolutionary perspective is the comparative approach, which facilitates understanding in many social sciences. For instance, Rostow's stages of economic growth describe the conditions through which a given society moves from primitive to intermediate to an advanced economic stage (1960). Service describes how the formation of state helps, or hinders, the advance of culture in a given society (1975). Much other work, using either the evolutionary perspective or the comparative approach, has advanced our understanding of the social system and its subsystems: family, religion, government, economics, and technology. Since the leisure sphere is becoming increasingly important for many people around the globe, the comparative approach should be applied to it.

Stone Age

Paleolithic   Old Stone Age—Perhaps 1,000,000 Years Ago

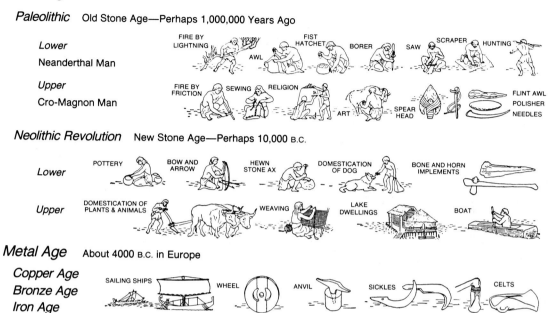

FIGURE I.2 *The development of early humans. From* CIVILIZATION: Past and Present, 3/e *by T. Walter Wallbank and Alastair M. Taylor. Copyright © 1954 by Scott, Foresman and Company. Reprinted by permission of Harper Collins, Publishers.*

PART ONE

SOCIOCULTURAL BASES OF LEISURE

1 EVOLUTION, PLAY, AND RITUAL
2 ON TIME
3 LEISURE, CULTURE, AND NATURE

Part One lays the foundations for an evolutionary perspective of leisure. Play and ritual had an important role in the initiation of leisure activities and their development over the years. Play is traced from lower animals to man, and the rise of ritual is analyzed as it relates to leisure. Since time is an important feature in any leisure activity, it becomes essential to explain it from physical, biological, psychological, and social points of view. Also, differences in how cultures view time have a direct bearing on the type of leisure activities practiced in them.

Culture is viewed as an envelope that surrounds the society and its ideals, values, norms, meanings, and symbols. While the society socializes its members to play certain roles, these roles tend to cluster into institutions that seem to be universal: family, religion, government, economics, and technology. All these, along with the other envelope that surrounds the society, the ecosystem, have an affect-effect relationship with leisure behavior.

1

EVOLUTION, PLAY, AND RITUAL

Human evolution is a process through which individuals who are the "most fit" survive. But "most fit" does not necessarily mean the strongest and most aggressive; "most fit" also depends on resistance to disease, choice of food, and care for the young. Cultural evolution, on the other hand, deals with changes in societies that arise from differentiation and adaptation. To reconstruct evolutionary history, archaeological records are utilized. Fossils give us an idea of human evolution, while other archaeological records help us to understand cultural evolution.

Another way to reconstruct the human and cultural past is to employ the comparative method, which utilizes samples from human groups that are extant today yet are varied enough for valid comparisons. A third method involves examining our closest relatives in the animal kingdom—the Old World monkeys and apes. But between the early primates and human beings, there must have existed some intermediate groups that we should consider.

This chapter discusses the evolution of the human brain with its concomitant impact on the tendency to play, the propensity to ritualization, and the relationship between them. The chapter also presents the role of culture in the utilization of the tendency to play and the propensity to ritualization, along with the evolution of leisure.

HUMAN EVOLUTION AND THE BRAIN

Humans are classified under the phylum Chordata, which includes animals characterized by an internal skeleton that encloses a spinal cord, a brain, and a well-developed nervous system that contributes to our excellent kinetic ability. Evolutionary changes led to efficient systems, particularly in mammals and especially in the primates. The highly developed hands, digits, and opposable thumbs of primates allow them to grasp and manipulate objects. The primates also have the largest brain of the mammals, which is accompanied by a more complex nervous system and a greater mental ability. This increase in brain size has been largely in the motor areas and is to be correlated with a high degree of muscular coordination. Primates' brains, including the human brain, have gone through four stages of evolution, each related to play, ritualization, and leisure.

The first stage took place when the bilaterally symmetrical creature's frontal nerve tissues evolved into two brains. One was closer to the body for internal control, and the other was for external affairs. That elementary device became the basis for today's human brain. It is also the reptilian brain that determines the general level of alertness, warns the organism of incoming information, and handles basic functions of self-preservation and preservation of the species. Paul McLean has shown that the reptilian brain contains programs responsible for hunting, homing, mating, fighting, and territoriality (Restak 1984:136).

Surrounding the reptilian brain is the limbic system, or the "old mammalian brain," which represents the second evolutionary stage in the human brain. It serves a creature that is more alert, sensitive to condition, and can make more decisions—freezing, fleeing, climbing a tree, or playing dead. More choice means more switches in the brain, and a larger brain was needed. Along with it came emotional feelings that guide behavior. McLean stated that three behaviors are identified with the limbic system: mothering, audiovocal communication, and play (fig. 1.1).

Capping the reptilian and the "old mammalian" brains is the neocortex, the third of the four stages in the evolution of the brain. The neocortex is, in turn, divided into two hemispheres, each responsible for the opposite half of the body. The two hemispheres are connected by a band of nerve fibers called corpus callosum.

According to Ornstein and Thompson (1984:34), between 400,000 and 1 million years ago, hemispheric specialization took place around the time that humans became bipedal. This meant becoming less reliant on smell and more reliant on vision. Also, humans began to use their front limbs in toolmaking. Immediately thereafter, humans made and used symbols (fig. 1.2). With its enlarged capacity, the human brain became capable of handling more mental processes, which can be roughly divided into processes that pertain to the social order and to human expression.

THE EVOLUTION OF PLAY

In its simplest form, play refers to an activity participated in for its own sake, not for survival and not for the purpose of achieving collectivity. Granted, play does not remain at such a simple level. Nonetheless, this definition keeps discussion within the confines of simple animal life. Paul McLean proved that when he severed the limbic system of some small animals, they reverted to reptilian behavior that is void of play. Also, the destruction of the cingulate gyrus of the limbic system led to the demise of play in experimental animals (Hooper and Teresi 1986:48).

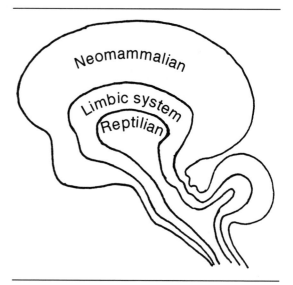

FIGURE 1.1 *Evolution of the human brain*

No wonder then that the more advanced the mammal, the greater the tendency to play. The primates have, relatively speaking, the largest brain among the mammals, a more complex nervous system, and greater mental ability. Increase in brain size has been largely in the motor areas and is correlated to the higher degree of muscular coordination primates exhibit. This allows them a greater variability in play than mammals of a lower order.

Young chimpanzees spend over 50% of their time in play. This includes mock-fighting and hanging by their arms from a branch and kicking wildly at each other. Acrobatics, wrestling, and boxing are also observed. Some chimps play at building nests by pulling small branches toward them and sitting on them. Male infants tend to engage in more rough-and-tumble activities than do females. They also tend to threaten and attack others and generally practice more aggressive behavior than do the females (deVore 1965:529).

Play observed among the baboons includes play-climbing, play-manipulating, running, and somersaulting. Play is the first behavior seen at their sleeping places and the last thing to be observed before they retire. The developmental

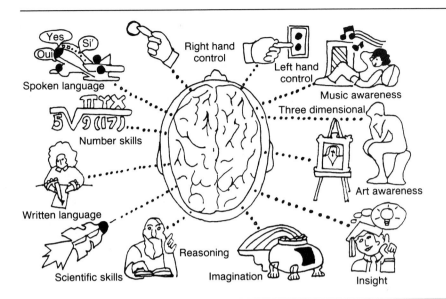

Yes Si'
Oui

Spoken language

Number skills

Written language

Scientific skills

Right hand control

Left hand control

Music awareness

Three dimensional

Art awareness

Reasoning

Imagination

Insight

FIGURE 1.2 *Hemispheric specialization*

trend appears to be a progression toward play-manipulating of particular objects, with earlier random efforts. Social play among these monkeys is a kind of trial-and-error experience that determines adult dominance and the patterns of adult sexuality (deVore 1965:87).

Bonnet macaque infants will hop together at the age of one month, chase each other at two months, and wrestle at six months. As the wrestling becomes wilder, females and the very young withdraw. The lack of threatening gestures, biting, growling, or screeching shows that this is play. Chasing, as such, is usually limited to infants.

Among the young howlers, play takes most of waking time. Their play is not only disorganized, it is chaotic, varying from wrestling on branches to chasing each other, to sometimes a group ganging up on an individual. Young howlers switch roles from chasing to being chased and from charging to being charged after. There seems to be some element of competition in these play activities. Peer interaction among them is second only to their interaction with mothers, giving play a very signifi-

cant place. deVore believes that aside from the development of perceptual motor skills, play helps the young howlers to learn roles and statuses. Without this knowledge, he may become "maladjusted" or excluded from the group (deVore 1965:283).

The play of rhesus monkeys is classified into three categories: rough-and-tumble play, approach-withdraw play, and activity play (deVore 1965:528). The least playful of the primates, the mountain gorilla, pairs up, chasing, wrestling, and engaging in a "follow-the-leader" type game.

It is a difficult comparison to make, but it appears that the chimpanzee is the most playful primate of all. Many activities, such as climbing, swinging, and jumping, are often incorporated into social games of chasing, dodging, and wrestling. Sometimes, they are performed for their own sake, even if playmates are present (deVore 1965:529). According to Lancaster, play, like other behaviors, varies from species to species. She states, however, that all field workers "have been impressed with the amount of time and energy spent every day in play by juvenile primates" (Lancaster 1975:49).

Play and the Child

Of the many attempts at explaining the play of children in the nineteenth century, most were scholarly efforts of a speculative nature. In this century, there has been systematic research on the nature of play, particularly its function in the life of a growing child. Two nineteenth-century speculations were that one plays in order to expand or channel excess energy (Spencer 1873), and to prepare for the future (Groos 1908). In 1940, brain research led to the assumption that a drive for arousal in man and animal helps in avoiding boredom (Berlyne 1961). Recently, advances in the neurosciences have helped to show the role of the brain in the play of both man and animal. It is commonly agreed that the brain regulates our behavior "caught" between our external and internal worlds. Eisen has suggested connections between such diverse factors as territoriality, social hierarchies, ritual, and play location in a structural complex on the brain. If one gives serious consideration to recent discoveries in neurology and endocrinology, one is almost compelled to believe in a "hormonal code" or "genetic programming," which can initiate, propel, and, to a limited degree, regulate play. There is no greater evidence than in the sequence of play forms that can be described as follows (1988).

The young of the hominids, including humans, share with all young mammals *leaping,* or attempts to free oneself from the confines of gravity. But in the developmental sequence, it occurs much later in humans, which may be the result of the bipedal position that freed the hands and increased the size of the neocortex. Accordingly, manipulative play dominates during early infancy in humans (Wolf 1984:176) since locomotion, a necessary step for leaping, is delayed until balance and coordination are acquired.

Leaping is followed by repetitive play, which is seen in all hominids. In repetitive play, a specific act or gesture is repeated again and again. For example, A chases B, B stops and threatens A, then chases A. A then stops and threatens B, chases B, and so on.

Another form of play observed among human infants and some primates that requires the use of the hands is relational play. Relational play finds the young trying to combine objects. By age two, the human infant participates in a form of play that is uniquely human—symbolic play. Here, the young child re-enacts familiar schemes out of context. Examples of this are drinking from an empty cup or combing a teddy bear's hair. At age five, the young child begins to make-believe in preparation for rule-governed play, a form of play that is strictly human.

What is intriguing is that this sequence of play-forms among humans (manipulative, repetitive, relational, make-believe, and rule-governed play) is remarkably stable across diverse populations (Wolf 1984:178). Humans share forms of play with animals, and all humans share forms of play. The evolution of play was accompanied by another evolution, the evolution of free time into leisure.

EVOLUTION AND LEISURE

Humans are primates, and the only human species we have to observe are modern humans. Other species have vanished; only their fossil remains are left. These remains indicate their morphological traits, but they tell us nothing about their play and work habits. We can, however, use the fossil remains to make some deductions about the life-style of pre-modern humans.

It is believed that an earlier human species, *Ramapithecus,* lacked powerful teeth to defend itself and therefore vanished. *Ramapithecus* was primarily arboreal, but foraged for food on the forest floor over a vast territorial range that included India, Kenya, China, Germany, and Spain. Shivers (1979:5) has suggested that since this species made some primitive tools, it must have had some time free from the continual struggle to survive. But more free time was provided for man's real ancestor. It is believed that ten million years passed after *Ramapithecus*, a time of which little is known, before it was possible for the genus *Homo* to evolve. The genus *Homo* must have existed with other hominids, but contemporary man comes from *Australopithecus*, who lived about nine million years ago.

The "pebble culture" of East Africa, as shown by the artifacts found at Olduvai Gorge in Kenya, suggests that *Australopithecus* was capable of toolmaking—a process that filled time freed from the struggle of survival (Leakey and Isaac 1972:128–41). It is also believed that the early hominid groups were formed from families composed of a dominant male, his harem, and offspring. When several families of the same ancestry lived together, they formed a clan, and a group composed of more than one clan became a tribe.

Shivers (1979:14) asserts that attempts at trial and error in making tools required time off from the struggle for survival. While such time could not be labeled "leisure", it did provide the freedom that is the *sine qua non* of leisure. In the earlier discussion of play we saw that higher mammals have young with a great tendency for play. Man could have been *faber* (toolmaker) and *luden* (player) at the same time. In addition, he had become *erectus* (bipedal). The interplay of these three characteristics was significant in the evolution of culture and human society, which includes a nucleus for leisure. *Homo erectus* acquired freedom of his hands and an enlarged brain. *Homo faber* utilized free hands to create tools, and stored some of the knowledge that was gained in a newly enlarged brain. The toolmaking skills and the ability to store information helped create for premodern humans some time free from obligatory work. This was time used to express the tendency as a higher mammal to play. Thus, humans became *luden*, player. The word *luden* is derived from *ludus*, which refers not just to children's games but also contests, liturgical and theatrical representation, games of chance, and recreation in general (Huizinga 1950:35).

But did humans have time to participate in all these activities as they struggled to survive? Probably not. Very early in our appearance on earth (some 600,000 years ago), our *ludus*, derived from and based on play, must have been very limited. Free time was used in an activity essential to our well-being—ritualization.

The term *ritualization* describes the phylogenetically performed ceremonial acts of animals, such as the penguins' reception of males returning from long expeditions beyond the seas. Such ritualized interplay is an affirmation of a bond. Ritualization is related to a biological factor, rhythmicity.

Researchers have amassed evidence suggesting that humans and other animals have several oscillators in the brain, along with a master clock. Rhythmicity, essential to biological life, is observed on all levels of biological organization, from cell, tissue, and organs to organisms and species. Examples are the alternation of systole and diastole and the cycle of wakefulness and sleep (Ibrahim 1988b).

Another biological factor, the tendency to formalization, to impose order and repetition on bodily movement, springs from emotional impulses. It may have paved the way, with rhythmicity, for the acts we now call ritualization.

To Erikson (1977:79) the first signs of ritualization among humans occur between the newborn and its mother. The newborn awakens in the mother a whole repertoire of emotive, verbal, and manipulative behaviors, and it involves the limbic system.

Susanne Langer (1972:302) believes that the communion that takes place between mother and infant hominids spreads into other forms. The simple impulse to groom, cling, or to go to sleep in each other's arms is gradually replaced by symbolic collective acts. In other words, the need for contact between individuals undergoes a change from bodily to mental contact.

Ritualization becomes a viable cultural setting represented by creative forms that help to avoid impulsive excess and compulsive self-restriction in young and old alike. To Erikson (1977:82), ritualization accomplishes a formidable number of things for humans and society:

1. It elevates the satisfaction of basic needs, such as hunger, into the context of a communal actuality.
2. It can transfer the infantile sense of omnipotence into a joint sense shared with parents, clan, and tribe.
3. It helps discriminate between prescribed good behavior and shameful guilty acts.
4. It puts emerging cognitive patterns in the service of a general vision shared by the community.
5. It provides the psychological foundation for a gradual shift from one status to another.

There is much to suggest that humans are born with the need for regular and mutual affirmation and certification. Such needs extend into all face-to-face recognitions and many social and cultural settings. All such settings, although formalized, include a playful element—that of surprise. Ritualized affirmation extends beyond daily life into religious and secular activities, and into the full ritual that will be discussed later.

It is believed that the utilization of fire, which may have taken place among *Homo neanderthalensis,* changed their life-style. *Neanderthalensis* used fire for cooking, which softened food and led to the reduction in the musculature of the jaw. This in turn led to cranial expansion and further enlargement of the brain. These early humans occupied caves and felt safe in them, adjusting their biological clock to tend the fire at night. This may have given them the requisite time to develop more ritualized activities. It also allowed them to contemplate the kinds of tools they needed to enhance their chances for survival.

Improvements in communication and in tool-making occurred in Cro-Magnon's life-style, and can be seen in the caves inhabited by them between 20,000 and 15,000 years ago. These improvements ultimately led to more rituals. Cro-Magnon worshipped cave bears, made images of them in clay or painted them on walls, danced for them, and stuck spears in them, a ritual designed to ensure a future supply of food (Rodnick 1966:29). All these activities required freedom from time spent on survival. Free time came with a revolution.

The first great revolution for man was the development of agriculture, which led to settlement around water. The first of these settlements was around Jericho some 9,000 years ago. A new age dawned, characterized not only by agriculture but by stone implements, pottery, weaving, and domesticated animals. In carrying out these activities, humans sought the help of supernatural powers, using the mode of ritual.

THE NATURE OF RITUAL

Ritual is defined as a set or series of acts, originally involving religion or magic, with sequence established by tradition and stemming from the daily life of a people. Perhaps the most significant aspect of ritual is that it evokes some kind of collective behavior, to the extent that Emile Durkheim (1915) asserts that religion is actually a product of collective behavior.

Grimes (1982:36) states that when meaning, communication, or performance becomes more important than function and pragmatic end, ritualization has begun. Such indicators of ritual are also indicators of leisure: being autotelic, having meaning in itself with no pragmatic end sought.

Grimes (1982) went on to distinguish six modes of ritual sensibility: ritualization, decorum, ceremony, liturgy, magic, and celebration. These are not types of ritual but rather sensibilities. If one of them dominates, then one has a "ritual of" one of the following:

1. **Ritualization.** According to Grimes (1982:37), ritualization presupposes the other ritual modes. It is usually used to designate the stylized, repeated gestures and posturing of animals, yet humans show that they have their own ritualizations. The rain and fertility dances are examples of dances and rhythms that show interaction with the ecosystem. The rain dance is an interaction between humans and the physical setting; the fertility dance, between humans and their bodies. Is it possible that our biorhythms are responsible for our "repetition-compulsions," which are the basis of ritualization?

   Granted, not every pattern constitutes ritualization, but all ritualizations are patterned. The pattern is rhythmic, but it is also to a great extent (at least originally) seasonal. Thus, the element of time is as crucial to ritualization as it is to leisure.

2. **Decorum.** While ritualization grows out of our organic and biological nature, decorum grows out of our social life. Erving Goffman uses the term *interaction ritual* (1959:1967) to discuss this type of behavior. Decorum is inessential, as is decoration, but it is practiced because it facilitates interaction. It is not essential because it is not psychobiologically based. Yet, there is still a rhythm of sorts in decorum. For example, response to greetings must come within a specified time. Walking with a person requires an adjustment to his rhythm. A specific example of decorum is the Japanese tea party. Here, a single invitation to have tea in ancient Zen monasteries became laden with over one hundred rules for interaction between host and guest, and both host and guest need a specific amount of free time to engage in such a prolonged interaction.

3. **Ceremony.** In contrast to decorum, which is not "essential," ceremony requires that one surrenders to the offices, histories, or causes of the ceremony (Grimes 1982:42). Sometimes the ceremony is competitive and conflict-laden, such as in military and parliamentary parades. Ceremonies are not face-processes like decorum; accordingly, power becomes the central consideration. The Communist party's October Day and the Muslim Haj are examples of ceremonies.

4. **Liturgy.** Liturgy, etymologically, means "people work." Here, power is also central. Such work is directed spiritually and not organically, as is the case in ritualization. The participants act so they can be acted upon. Examples of liturgy include the Christian Eucharist, the Sufi twirlings, and Shamanic dance. But in many instances, liturgy is meditative or contemplative, the form of leisure considered highest by Aristotle. Another characteristic of liturgy emphasized by Grimes is its "full emptiness, a monotony without boredom, a reverent waiting without expectation, a vacuum plenum" (1982:44). This is akin to the concept of leisure.

5. **Magic.** Magic uses a transcendent frame of reference to effect change in a social relationship or interaction (Grimes 1982:96). While ceremony is political, magic is transcendental and associated with trickery. It shares the element of play with celebration.

6. **Celebration.** According to Grimes, celebration has its roots in play, because it seems unmotivated and spontaneous (1982:47). The first five forms of ritual arise from concatenation of some force or another: ritualization is compelled, decorum is expected, ceremony is enforced, liturgy is a cosmic necessity, and magic is desired. Yet all of these include an element of play. Even in liturgy there is a note of playfulness, and when this note is fully sounded, celebration begins. To Grimes, play is at once a root of the ritual and a fruit of the same (1982:48). Celebration is ritualized play, the inverse of magic, which is ritualized work. In celebration, one does what one does to no external end. This is also characteristic of leisure, play, and contemplation. According to Pieper, the soul of leisure lies in celebration, where "the three points of leisure come to a focus: relaxation, effortlessness and the superiority of active leisure to all functions" (1964:44).

Yet it is obvious from the above that all six sensibilities include a great deal of play and, in some way, contemplation. The combination of play and contemplation forms the rudimentary elements of leisure. When humans play, some participate and others watch; participation has led to recreation, and watching has led to amusement. Thus we have the three forms of leisure suggested by Aristotle: contemplative, recreative, and amusive. Chapters 4–11 will provide examples of these activities in different human societies, be they primitive, intermediate, or modern.

Components of Ritual

One of the most important works on ritual is Arnold van Gennep's *The Rites of Passage* (1960). Gennep gave this name to the ceremonies surrounding the arrival of key periods in one's life, such as birth, puberty, marriage, and death. These rites develop an emotional state of being that facilitates bridging the gap between old and new. Gennep suggests a tripartite classification:

1. Rites that separate a person from previous associations.
2. Rites that prepare a person for a marginal period.
3. Rites of aggregation that incorporate the person into his or her new experience.

Turner (1982a), states that a person goes through *limen,* meaning "threshold" in Latin, in the second type of rites, and in the transitory phase that is characteristic of all rituals. The marginal period is a sort of social limbo, but this limbo is not altogether negative. According to Gennep:

The novices are outside society, and society has no power over them, especially since they are actually sacred and holy, and therefore, untouchable (1960:114).

In other words, the novices are beyond the normative social order. According to Turner, such liminality may involve a complex sequence of episodes in sacred time-space, and may also include subversive and ludic, or playful, events (1982a:27). Limen to Turner is a long threshold or corridor, almost a tunnel that may, indeed, become a set way of life, a state like that of the anchorite or monk. Is it also the state of contemplation, the first of Aristotle's three states of leisure?

To Turner, the sphere of liminality allows those who go through it, those he calls liminaries, to proceed between the established social structures. Leisure is likewise a betwixt-and-between, a neither-this-nor-that domain—a lodgment between work and civil/familial activities (1977:43). This is corroborated by the very root of the word, old French *leisir,* itself derived from the Latin *licere,* which means "to be permitted, to be in an in-between state." The Latin word comes from the Indo-European base *leik,* which means to "to offer for sale," which refers to the liminal sphere of the market with its variation and exchange. In other words, liminality lends itself to play in addition to providing an atmosphere for contemplation.

There are two directions for the evolution of leisure that derive from liminality: from earnestness comes contemplative leisure, and through the ludic comes recreative and amusive leisure. The two directions may separate and one become dominant, but sometimes they come together. This is the case with some Eastern religions, in which creation is not only the work of the gods but also their play. At the other extreme, the three religions of The Book, Judaism, Christianity, and Islam, have stressed the solemn at the expense of the festive during liturgy and in celebration. Societies vary in their treatment of ritual, and the evolution of ritual becomes subject to multiple factors, as will be seen in the next section.

SOCIETAL EVOLUTION AND LEISURE

A society in the first instance is politically organized (Parsons 1966:2). Both Aristotle and Ibn Khaldun agree with this (Barnes 1984, Mahdi 1964). The society must have some form of loyalty, both to a sense of community and to a corporate agency that we call government. It must establish a normative order within territorial area. This does not necessarily mean that all societies are similar; in fact, they vary a great deal. Perhaps this is because societies, like organisms, go through an evolutionary process. Sociocultural evolution, like organic evolution, proceeds through variation and differentiation. It moves from simple to complex, but not necessarily in a linear direction.

Society is a special kind of a social system, a concept that is applicable to a family as well as to a society. A society, however, has a greater control over a wider range of human activities than does a family; so it is considered a mega-social system. It is therefore self-sufficient, which means that it has adequate control over motivation and commitment to human activities. Sociologists use the term *human action* to refer to the patterning of human behavior. While psychologists may be interested in physical aspects of behavior for their own sake (such as psychological and emotional responses to leisure), sociologists are more interested in social factors that lead to the patterns of leisure behavior. That is, leisure is investigated as a social phenomenon. Since culture is one of the envelopes that surrounds social life, understanding culture is a must.

As shown in figure I.1, ultimate reality stands above the cultural system, which in turn stands above the social system, which has an affect-effect relationship with the behavioral system, standing below it in a cybernetic hierarchy. The behavioral system involves learning, developing, and maintaining through the life cycle of a member of society the motivation necessary to join human action. In return the member gains satisfaction and reward. For example, the "average" American becomes involved in the World Series each October. Below the behavioral system lies the organism, and below that the physical setting. Initially the main concern here is the provision of food and shelter. But as technology advances, the physical environment may provide a surplus that allows for more free time, an important ingredient of leisure.

Structural Components of Society

How does a group of people get together and develop a social system and its environment? Even if the members were born into the system, how is it maintained? Sociologists believe that a number of structural components come into play. The first of these are *values*, which can be distinguished from *norms* in that values primarily hold together the cultural system, while norms are primarily social. But within the social system itself, there are *groups* whose members play certain *roles*.

According to Parsons (1966:19), these four structural categories—values, norms, groups, and roles—may serve certain social functions:

1. Values serve the pattern-maintenance function.
2. Norms serve the integrative function.
3. Groups serve the goal-attainment function.
4. Roles serve the adaptive function.

We must point out that these four structural components of society are very much interrelated, for there is no group without members' roles, and there is no role that is not regulated by the norms and characterized by a commitment to certain values. Perhaps the fundamental question to raise at this point is, "Where does leisure fit into all of this?" One might also ask: "Do leisure activities lead to maintaining social pattern? Integrating these patterns? Attainment of societal goals? Adaptation of the individual to society?" Let us see what these four functions mean in a society.

Subsystems and Society

There are four primary subsystems in society, derived from the four functions mentioned above:

1. The integrative subsystem, which is considered the core of the social system because of society's need for normative coherence, harmony, and coordination. Does the leisure activity meet some of these needs?
2. The goal-attainment subsystem, or the policy, which is concerned with the relations of society to the personalities of individual members. Are the members allowed to play?
3. The adaptive subsystem, or the economy, which is concerned with the relations of the society to the physical setting. Is there a surplus that allows for free time?
4. A pattern-maintenance subsystem, which is concerned with the relations of the society to the cultural system, and, through that, to ultimate reality. An important variable to consider is time, as an element of reality and as a component of leisure. How much is time valued? What are the sources of its value?

Evolutionary Change

For evolutionary change to take place in a society, its adaptive capacity must be enhanced, leading to a new type of social structure. This can occur either through internal organization or through cultural diffusion. For actual change to occur, a number of processes are needed.

First is the process of differentiation, which takes place when a single, relatively well-defined place in the society divides into two or more places, and in turn, the roles and/or the groups involved become differentiated.

For example, a nature group may split into hikers and rock climbers. For differentiation to become significant, the new subgroups must go through another process—adaptive upgrading—which means, in the example above, that the level of enjoyment of the activity increases. Thus the hiker enjoys not only nature but the physical exertion that comes with hiking in nature. The rock climber enjoys not only nature but the feeling of vertigo.

The example shows that differentiation and adaptive upgrading of an activity will affect how it is valued. Another value may be added to appreciation of nature: the value of the fitness. The new values must now be part of a new pattern that accommodates the wider variety that is now beginning to appear. Such expansion may be met by severe resistance from the fundamentalists who believe the original value is the real one, the only one. Such resistance may lead to strict conformity that renders change impossible. In fact a revived fundamentalism may bring a "backward" change. Today's Iran is a good example of such a society.

Evolutionary Structures

This author agrees with Parsons in distinguishing the evolutionary process as neither continuous nor linear. Parsons argues that the transition from "primitive" to intermediate society is in the language, which is part of the cultural system. When and if a written language is developed, primitiveness subsides and intermediacy begins. This is because a written language increases the differentiation between the social and the cultural system, extending the power of the latter. Cultural diffusion increases both in space and in time, and greater audiences are reached over a longer period.

The role of language in the evolution of man and society has been given a central place by Huizinga's assertion that play is the basis of culture

(1950:4). He believes that in making speech and language, there is a continual sparking between matter and mind. For behind every abstract expression there lies the boldest of metaphors, and every metaphor is a play on words. Written language and the availability of documents act to stabilize many relations. This in turn may help develop a single primary normative order (one moral, legal code). Norms, as previously stated, serve an integrative function. They are derived from values, which serve a pattern-maintenance function. If most members of the society follow the same values and norms, a single normative order will stand for the whole society, which should be placed above even the governing authority. If for some reason a separate normative order is practiced by a minority that is also the ruling group, the loyalty and commitment of the majority would be doubtful. A good example of this is the Roman Empire, which failed to develop a single normative order above the governing elite. Indeed, there was one government ruling from the Atlantic to the Arabian Gulf, but there was no single normative order covering all, including Caesar. Here is one reason for "the fall of the Roman Empire." In fact, most of the intermediate societies of the past—for example, the Islamic, Persian, and Mongolian empires—suffered from the same fate. No single normative order was practiced then; for it comes about only when the society's code is institutionalized into a single legal-moral system. This is a necessary step for an intermediate society to become a modern one (Parsons 1971:27).

The evolutionary perspective of society dates back to the second half of the nineteenth century when Herbert Spencer introduced the concept and was backed by a number of eminent social scientists. The term *evolution* should be differentiated from *revolution*. *Evolution* refers to alterations in society that are lawful, orderly, and gradual; *revolution* connotes a sudden and far-reaching change. In evolution, the society and its institutions may be viewed as having evolved from the uniform to the multiform. For example, simple societies consisting of families may evolve into clans, tribes, and nations, and experience an increase in size that perpetuates structural and functional differentiation. Evolution is not unilinear but rather a branching-out process. The earlier dimensions do not disappear when new dimensions emerge, as the process of social differentiation takes place along each dimension.

Societal differentiation is sometimes defined as a process whereby roles change. Roles are the things we are obliged to do in return for some reward. For example, a teacher who plays his or her role right is paid, praised, and selected teacher of the year. Roles are dynamic and change over the years. The classroom teacher of the recent past has become many teachers of many subjects. In fact there has evolved a new role in today's schools, that of a teacher's aide.

The present work assumes that technology lies at the core of societal differentiation. Technology is not limited to tools and instruments; it may include technical know-how, information, education, and communication. Technology pervades all aspects of life. The important point is that technical development has increased the number of roles.

Granted, sustaining life was the first order of social life, and still is. To ensure survival, collective living became necessary, and another form of societal differentiation took place. Human action concentrated on goals pertaining to these two adaptive processes: survival and collectivity. Our biosocial nature has been put into use to buttress these two processes. If and when technology ensures survival and collectivity, our biosocial nature is called on as follows:

1. **Adaptation to the external environment.** For any group to survive, it must have an adequate technology to provide for the minimum of food, clothing, and shelter appropriate to its size, geographical setting, climate, and so on. Such requirements should meet both short-term and long-term survival needs. This also includes provisions for the protection of young against all predators. Maintaining control over the

Table 1.1 **Societal development and level of leisure participation**

Goldschmidt:	Five categories of development	Parsons' classification	Ibrahim's trichotomy
	E: Industrial/urban society	Modern societies	Mass leisure
	D: Agriculture state society	Intermediate societies	Class leisure
	C: Horticulture village & tribal society B: Settling/hunting/food gathering A1 A2: Nomadic/hunting/food gathering	Primitive societies	Ritualized leisure

environment required the assistance of supernatural powers and a commitment from the members. Both of these were acquired through ritual in ceremony, liturgy, and magic.

2. **Adaptation to collective living.** Some social scientists say that man is driven to collective living to satisfy psychic needs. Humans who live together must coordinate and integrate their actions to some degree to avoid chaos and confusion. While the coordination of activities among animals is almost instinctive, it is totally social among humans. Once a society establishes a system of collective living, it has to endure; otherwise, every generation will have to go through the same thing again. In other words, humans had to develop a culture, defined as the grand total of all objects, habits, values, and knowledge that can be transmitted through generations. Ritualization, decorum, and ceremony were useful in this respect.

3. **Adaptation to human biosocial nature.** A society should cater to the individual needs of its members, which may include the need for companionship, status, exercise, and expression. Expressive needs manifest themselves in leisure pursuits such as drama, art, music, dance, games, and sports. Ritual provided the stage for many of these activities.

The conditions that lead to such manifestations will vary from society to society. The conditions and the types of manifestations have been of interest to sociologists for a great number of years, beginning with Ibn Khaldun, who suggested that societies move from tribal to urban living. Similarly, Tonnies' Gemeinschaft-Gessellschaft, Durkheim's Mechanical-Organic, and Becker's sacred-secular dichotomies are descriptions of societal differentiation.

These classifications are limiting since they are, first of all, dichotomies, and secondly, always pertain to preindustrial societies. Other classifications include the preindustrial-transitional-industrial complex. Goldschmidt's outline (1959) includes five categories representing a sequence of development from nomadic to urban-industrial societies. It corresponds, to some degree, to Parson's classification. These two, along with this author's classification of leisure, are shown in table 1.1.

Table 1.1 suggests the following:

1. **Ritualized leisure** is practiced in what Parsons describes as "primitive" societies, which are (a) nomadic/hunting/food gathering, (b) settling/hunting/food gathering, or (c) horticultural/tribal societies.

2. **Class leisure** is practiced in what Parsons describes as intermediate societies. It must be emphasized that ritualized leisure exists in these societies and continues on among the commoners at this level.

3. **Mass leisure** appears in industrial/urbanized societies, but not to the demise of class leisure or ritualized leisure.

In other words, these three types of leisure are like three strata. While the first stratum exists in primitive societies, the second is found to be above it in intermediate societies; and the third layer, mass leisure, covers these two in modern societies.

While the above describes three types of leisure (ritualized, class, and mass), three forms of leisure—contemplative, recreative, and amusive leisure—may exist in all three types. One important variable in this respect that needs be discussed before embarking upon a discussion of the types and levels of leisure is time. Time is an important ingredient of leisure.

SUMMARY

The tendency to play is related to the evolution of the brain. When it is coupled with the propensity to ritualize, a niche for some human activities is established. As humans evolved, they were able to acquire more free time from the demands for survival and collective living. Freed time was possibly used in ritualization, a mechanism of mutual affirmation and affirmation found in all societies regardless of their degree of sophistication. But the meaning of some rituals changed over the years, and the performance of the ritual became more important than the function and the purpose of the ritual. Play activities found their way into human life, particularly in rituals of celebration.

As the human society evolved, the necessity to adapt to the physical environment and to enhance collective living waned. More attention was paid to the human tendency to play and the propensity to ritualize. Activities of certain rituals evolved into what is termed *ritualized leisure,* which is witnessed in preliterate "primitive" societies. As a society evolved into an intermediate stage, another form of leisure took place: class leisure, with its emphasis on spectating over participating, particularly among the ruling class. Mass leisure, leisure activities for everyone, came about in advanced, modern society. But such a step necessitated allocation of time to these activities, the subject of the next chapter.

REVIEW QUESTIONS

1. In what way could there be "a blueprint" in the human brain that makes one engage in play activities?
2. Were play and leisure subject to evolution? How?
3. Why is it important to study ritual's relation to leisure?
4. In what sense could leisure be related to the evolution of society?

SUGGESTED READINGS

deVore, I. 1965. *Primate behavior.* New York: Holt, Rinehart and Winston.

Erikson, E. 1977. *Toys and reason: Stages in the ritualization of experience.* New York: Norton.

Grimes, R. 1982. *Beginnings in ritual studies.* Lanham, MD: University Press of America.

Smith, P., ed. 1984. *Play in animals and humans.* London: Basil Blackwell.

2

ON TIME

Time is not an easy phenomenon to tackle. It is so interrelated with other phenomena that few, if any, scholars dare to declare that it is understood. Despite this elusiveness, descriptions of time and attempts at understanding it can be revealing and rewarding.

It was Aristotle in his *Physics* (Barnes 1984:369) who asked the question, "In what sense, if any, can time be said to exist?" The answer, which is yet to be found, must deal with the problem of the reality and nonreality of time. Before Aristotle, there was a concern with the measurement of time rather than with its definition. Ancient astronomers used "natural clocks," provided by recurrent natural phenomena such as the periodic passage of the sun across the meridian. Human-made devices that produce repetitive phenomena, such as a dial with a rotating pointer that passes over a mark, were used for clocks. Both natural and human-constructed clocks would proceed at that same rate if the natural phenomenon recurred regularly. So the human race began to measure time without really defining it.

In this chapter the components of time, whether physical, organic, biological, psychological, or social, will be presented. The cultural aspects of time in both non-Western and Western culture will be discussed. The attitudes toward utilization of time from the Middle Ages to today's America will follow. Measuring time as a research technique in understanding leisure behavior is also discussed.

TIME AND THE UNIVERSE

Isaac Newton's edict that there is an "absolute, true and mathematical time, of itself and of its nature, flowing equably without relation to anything external" had enormous impact on Western life-style. Western people coordinated their lives to this clock rather than the clock to their daily activities. Newton also suggested that the universe is infinite, for he believed that if the universe were not infinite then gravity would cause all its matter to collect at its center. If the universe were infinite, extending into space, might it be possible that time also is infinite, extending indefinitely into the past as well as the future? A universe without spatial limits has neither a beginning nor an end. This contradicted widely held Christian doctrine.

Lyell, in his *Principles of Geology* (Morris 1985:87) argued that strict adherence to biblical chronology was untenable. According to Christian doctrine, the world was created some 7,000 years ago. About this same time, William Thomson (Lord Kelvin), considered the greatest physicist of the nineteenth century, criticized the concept of the infinite universe. He based his criticism on the second law of thermodynamics. The first law states that energy can be converted from one form to another, and can neither be created nor destroyed. The second law, however, can be stated in many different ways. In our case, it simply states that any process that converts energy from one form to another will always dissipate some of that energy as heat. This process is very inefficient. Accordingly, the universe does not have the infinite supply of energy necessary to keep it going indefinitely.

Early in the twentieth century, scientists discovered radioactivity, and realized that such emissions are accompanied by the release of heat. A few years later, an accurate radioactive dating method was invented. Radioactive elements on earth are between 11 and 17 billion years old. Spectroscopic analysis of the light emitted by far away stars indicates that their age is no more than 18 billion years. Thus the age of the universe can be expressed as a range rather than a definite figure. Some scholars accept 15–18 billion years as the possible range; others have concluded that it is between 7 and 10 billion years. Despite the disagreement on the age of the universe, scientists in general agree that the universe began with what is termed the "big bang." We must point out that the big bang theory does not use the word "beginning." It tells us that at a particular point called Planck Time, the universe was in an extremely hot, dense state. Planck Time is the point beyond which all of our known physical laws break down. Whatever happened before then is a subject for philosophy and/or theology.

Leibniz, the "father of calculus," tried to avoid the dilemma of defining time by stating that time is simply the order in which events happen. His theory that events are more fundamental than moments is known as the relational theory of time. We do determine time from events and not the other way around. However, Newton's ideas were so dominant at this time that, for example, the introduction of daylight savings time was met with great protest. "How could we play with the natural flow of time?" people asked. Einstein put an end to the Newtonian notion with his theory of relativity. Einstein tried to visualize himself traveling within the stationary medium through which light moves, at the same velocity as light. He concluded that he would observe the spatially oscillating electromagnetic field at rest. Does this mean that no time is passing?

The classical theory of time had assumed that the connection between event A and event B and their simultaneity is observed by all. Einstein found, mathematically, that two observers in uniform relative motion would assign two different times to the same event. While this is negligible in everyday life, it is significant in the long run. In other words, if we look at time in a subjective way, we can say that "now" does not extend beyond "here." If two events take place in space and no signal traveling at the speed of light can possibly get from A to B before B takes place, then their time order is ambiguous. Some observers will conclude that A happens first, others that B was earlier in time. Yet this does not contradict the ordinary ideas of causality. No observer will ever see a basketball go through a hoop before the player has shot.

TIME AND ORGANIC EVOLUTION

The idea of evolution arose from the discovery of fossils that were left behind by plants and animals unknown to us. Evolution implies linearity—that occurrence A took place before occurrence B and so on. Originally, sediments and fossils were thought to be life in a relative sequence with no absolute age. The natural history of the earth's surface and of life itself was pieced together and was thought to be compatible with biblical history. Now, however, earth is estimated to be close to one billion years old. The earth's surface evolved over time, allowing for life to emerge as follows:

ERA	PERIOD	EPOCH	TIME
	Quaternary	Recent	10,000 years
	Pleistocene		2 million years
Cenozoic	Pliocene		12 million years
	Miocene		25 million years
	Tertiary	Oligocene	35 million years
	Eocene		50 million years
	Paleocene		62 million years
	Cretaceous		128 million years
Mesozoic	Jurassic		180 million years
	Triassic		225 million years
	Permian		265 million years
	Carboniferous		310 million years
Paleozoic	Devonian		405 million years
	Silurian		465 million years
	Ordovician		518 million years
	Cambrian		611 million years
Precambrian			

One way of visualizing geologic time is through scale reduction. If we compact all existence, starting with the big bang, to a single year, the following picture emerges:

The world began on January 1st. Then conditions in which life could have arisen developed in early August. The oldest known fossils, life of the past imprinted in the rocks, were living things about mid-October, and life was abundant, most of it in the seas, by the end of the month. In mid-December, dinosaurs and other reptiles dominated the scene. Mammals, with hairy covering and suckling their young, only appeared in time for Christmas, and on New Year's Eve, at about five minutes to midnight, from amongst them stumbled man. Of these five minutes of man's existence, recorded history represents about the time the clock takes to strike twelve (Klamus 1981:332).

Evolutionary changes are measured in three different ways. In genus formation, an organism living in a stable environment will change rather slowly in comparison to an organism living in a changing environment (these are changes in the dimensions or shapes of solid organs, such as teeth, shells, or bones). Finally, there are changes in gene frequency in species that cannot adapt to environmental changes and become extinct. Those that survived, adapted, and changed over time created a wide variety of biological creatures, which led scientists to develop a classificatory scheme. Of interest to us is the animal kingdom to which we belong. The classification of the animal kingdom, using humans as an example, is divided up as follows, from most specific to most general:

Species: *erectus, faber, sapiens, luden*?
Genus: *Homo*
Suborder: Anthropoid
Order: Primate
Subclass: Placential
Class: Mammals
Subphylum: Vertebrate
Phylum: Chordata

While humans belong to the genus *Homo,* where do they belong as a species? Are they indeed *erectus*? Maybe in the past. Are they *faber*? Jane

Goodall has proved that chimps are also tool-makers. Are humans *sapiens*? With all the destruction we bring upon ourselves, we are far from being wise. The concept of *Homo luden* has its appeal. It was forwarded by Dutch historian Johan Huizinga about forty years ago (1950). Huizinga was convinced that human civilizations arise and unfold through play. He saw human beings as sharing a higher form of play; thus the designation *Homo luden.*

BIOLOGICAL TIME

Biological time refers to an organism's awareness of time duration and its own location. Observations of plants and animals led scientists to discover that the sense of time comes from many sources. The first source, photoperiodism, refers to a plant's sensitivity and response to the daylight-darkness polarity. Secondly, celestial orientation is observed in birds and insects. Thirdly, endogenous rhythm is witnessed in many plants and animals, including humans; thus a circadian rhythm (based on 24-hour intervals) is exhibited by almost all living things. Exogenous factors such as light, temperature, gravity, humidity, and barometric pressure exert their effects on the circadian rhythm.

Many experiments have been conducted on lower and higher animals, and it appears that endogenous rhythm persists after the removal of many parts of the animal. This suggests that cells may be involved in biorhythm. This does not necessarily mean that all bodily rhythms are in complete phase with one another. In fact, we tend to get out of phase rather easily, in illness and accidents, while traveling, and during emotional upheavals. These out-of-phase rhythms become synchronized with a physical reaction, which leads to pain. When our internal clock becomes synchronized with a new exogenous factor or factors, it makes us suffer, as in the case of jet and space travel.

It is believed that the cerebral cortex of the central nervous system acts as our master internal clock, since damage there leads to loss of timing.

It seems that nerve impulses are filtered and sequenced. If they arrive at the brain in a disorderly manner, they produce sensations of pain and discomfort; rhythmic flow is associated with comfort, even pleasure. We appreciate things that are essentially rhythmic: light, color, music, and poetry.

In a study on the impact of jet travel on metabolic rate, reaction time and simple decision-making skills were checked every two hours on subjects in flight. When these factors were checked on a flight from Washington, D.C., to Santiago, Chile, within a one-hour time zone, no change occurred. In the flight from Oklahoma City to Rome, Italy, with a seven-hour time zone difference, reaction time was the most impaired. Both reaction time and temperature needed four days to return to normal. In a longer flight, from Oklahoma City to Manila, the Philippines, with a ten-hour time zone difference, in addition to the above, the subjects suffered from mental dullness for 24 hours (Blatt and Quinlan 1972:510). Studies of this sort are important in understanding and planning leisure travel.

Wade (1985:7) suggested that biorhythmic behaviors are significant components of leisure because leisure is self-paced, which is significant to periodicity. Periodicity is a function of the interaction between physiological and psychological processes. Evidence suggests that children exhibit periodic behaviors of both a physiological and a psychological nature (work/rest and habituation). The same could apply to adults.

EXPERIENCING TIME

Time is experienced in two fundamental ways (Shallis 1981:14). First, it seems to flow like an endless stream. Secondly, it is perceived as a succession of moments with clear distinctions between past, present, and future. Consequently, time seems a linear process, in the sense that events seem to come and go, then come again.

One can experience time in terms of quality as well as quantity. One area in which time's quality can be felt is the time of day. For instance, early morning has a distinct quality, different from the quality of the evening. The Sabbath has its own quality. Seasons bring about their own qualities: autumn has its falling leaves, winter its coziness, spring its flowers, and summer its pleasant balmy evenings. Eras also have their own qualities: the handle bar moustaches of the early 1900s, the Roaring Twenties, the crew cut of the 50s, the long hair of the 60s, and the punk look of the 80s.

Understanding time may help a person transcend his or her biological and/or cultural time. Biological time is a burden we have to live with; cultural time is a burden we place on ourselves in support of society. Contemplation, a forgotten art that belongs in the domain of leisure, may help to explain time. Aristotle placed contemplation as the highest form of leisure, along with rhythm. In the hurried pace at the end of the twentieth century, we miss the joy of contemplation and meditation. This is the price we pay for the agricultural, industrial, scientific, economic, and electronic revolutions of the last few centuries.

Experiencing time is very much related to how the brain works. Biologically, we are able to orient ourselves to time in the absence of external stimuli. On the other hand, there are agents that disturb our sense of time, such as body temperature and oxidation of nerve cells in the brain. Outside of these biological factors, the unconscious aspect of our mind plays a very important part in the experience of time (Elton and Messel 1978:90).

It is known that the unconscious reveals itself in "Freudian slips" and in dreams. But the most interesting aspect of the unconscious as related to time are the sudden flashes of insight that are the essence of the creative process. Freud stipulated that in the unconscious there is no before or after. This unidirectionality is observed in much artistic, mathematical, and scientific thinking. Many a scholar has reported that after a long, exhausting process of thought on a problem, which has led to no solution, a flash of insight suddenly presented itself—a whole answer appeared in a way quite unrelated to the earlier process. The simultaneity with which the complex solution arrives in the conscious mind indicates the timeless nature of the unconscious.

Is this phenomenon, the timelessness of the unconscious, linked to stepping outside time? By stepping outside time, one may experience the repetition of time known as "deja vu." In this experience, one is reliving a part of one's life, not predicting or sensing a remote incident. Also, by stepping outside time, one may see through time into the future. Precognition is the ability to perceive a future event. Precognition should not be equated with prediction, which entails the conscious ability to speculate about the future. Nor should it be equated with premonition, which involves an emotional response to possible future events.

SOCIAL AND CULTURAL TIME

Pitrim Sorokin was one of the first sociologists to pay attention to temporality and its impact on social life. He believed that social life has a two-phase rhythm. For example, the business world may go into a depression-prosperity cycle, and ethical relationships may go into an idealism-materialism cycle (1937:618). In the prosperity side of the first cycle, leisure may flourish.

Another sociologist who was philosophically oriented, Georges Gurvitch, suggested that eight kinds of time permeate social life: enduring time, deceptive time, erratic time, cyclical time, retarded time, alternating time, time-in-advance-of-itself time, and explosive time (1964:30–33). Leisure behavior may be affected by all these categories, particularly enduring time. Gray and Ibrahim (1985) conducted in-depth interviews with twenty subjects and found that most memorable experiences go back many years, up to fifty years.

A third sociologist, Wilber Moore, believed that time presents itself to human beings as a scarce resource and as a mode for ordering life. In ordering life, three elements are necessary (1963:5):

1. Synchronization or the necessity for simultaneous actions.
2. Sequencing, which refers to the fact that certain actions require specific ordering.
3. Rating, which indicates the frequency of the event at hand.

All human activities, including leisure, whether contemplative, recreative, or amusive, require synchronization, sequencing, and rating. But who or what determines that contemplation will be rated, or done with more frequency than another human activity, such as attending to the gods of ancient Athens? Since Aristotle decidedly listed contemplation as the highest form of leisure, was it he who placed leisure above any other activity participated in by the ancient Athenians? The answer to these questions lies with the culture and its values, particularly the values placed on time, for time, and in time. A review of the cultural views of time is necessary at this point.

Two "simple," preliterate societies will provide examples of the ancient views of time. To the Navajos of North America, real time, like real space, is that which is here and now, for there is so little reality to the future (Lauer 1981:36). In such a culture as the Navajo's, to organize, let us say, an athletic tournament, would be extremely difficult. Amusement may prevail over recreation or contemplation, since these two are future-oriented. Contemplation of past events, however, may take place.

Something similar is witnessed among the Balinese, who view the day as composed of discrete periods of time for which there are appropriate activities, but without any progression to an end. In other words, there is no climax to the process (Geertz 1973:396). Clearly, organized recreational activities would not evolve in such a culture.

Furthermore, the Balinese believe that there are good and bad days on which to conduct events—for instance, have a puppet show.

In contrast to the Balinese, the Hindus view time, space, and causality as illusory. Accordingly, the reality of the "tangible universe is only apparent and derivative." The empirical reality of things is derived from the "absolute reality of Brahman, as the apparent reality of a mirage is derived from the reality of the desert" (Nikhilananda 1949:39). Lauer suggests, then, that Hindus would seek freedom by withdrawing into their inner being rather than by actively striving to manipulate the external world (1981:9). In our terms, they would be inclined to spend their leisure contemplating rather than recreating or being amused.

Further east, the Chinese, although the first to invent the clock, were never subject to the Western obsession to maximize activity in a minimum of time (Lauer 1981:129). In the nineteenth century, Arthur Smith in his book on Chinese characteristics entitled one chapter "Disregard Of Time." He states that the Chinese were free from the feeling that to us has become second nature, that "time is money" (1894:29).

Lauer suggests that the Chinese belief in the cyclical nature of the temporal process led to reminiscing over a past Golden Age, and a neglect of the present. In fact, the present is treated as degraded and corrupt. Consequently, the tempo of change, of accepting new ideas, is extremely slow in such an environment (1981:135). Marcus stated that when Chinese peasants shifted their attitude from resignation to expectation of progress, the Communists were the beneficiaries, for Mao had provided a blueprint for the future (1961:138).

Originally, the Japanese people, like the Chinese people, were not coerced by time as are the people in the West. But beyond this, the Japanese people are strikingly different when it comes to their view of time. It seems that around the 1700s the view of time changed drastically in Japan. Instead of seeing time as cyclical, as was the case in China, the Japanese began to view it as linear. Moreover, the adoption of the Zen philosophy in Japan added a new dimension to time.

An ever-changing, incessant temporal flux is identified with the Ultimate Being Itself (Nakamura 1981:87). The kind of thinking that recognizes absolute significance in the temporal, phenomenal world seems to be culturally related to the traditional Japanese love of nature. Love of mountains, rivers, flowers, birds, and so on made some of their recreational activities rather unique and their recreation places exquisite—flower arrangement, for example, and Japanese gardens.

TIME IN JUDEO-CHRISTIAN THOUGHT

According to Herchel, Judaism is a religion of time, aiming at its sanctification:

Judaism teaches us to be attached to holiness in time, to be attached to secret events, to learn how to consecrate sanctuaries that emerge from the magnificent stream of a year. The sabbaths are our great cathedrals; and our Holy of Holies is a shrine that neither the Romans nor the Germans were able to burn; a shrine that even apostasy cannot easily obliterate: the Day of Atonement— Jewish ritual may be characterized as the art of significant form in time, as architecture of time (1951:28).

Kaplan (1960:49) states that time in this case is accompanied by strong ritual, whose strength arises from repetition and brings continuity between past, present, and future. Such sanctification of time may have been one of the reasons why leisure came extremely slowly into Jewish life. Another factor may be the fact that a negative attitude toward leisure started early, when the Jews lived in bondage in Egypt. Psalm 137: "How shall we sing the Lord's song in foreign land?"

Although the right to the Sabbath was one of the six rights in the life of the early Israelites, the Sabbath was not intended to be a day of leisure, but rather a holy day, a day of rest and worship. Other holy days included three primary ones that were agricultural in origin: Passover (unleavened bread in spring), Pentecost (first fruits of summer), and In-gathering (tabernacles in fall) (Ibrahim 1979:55). Khunkkhah and Purim were added as feasts around the second century before the Common Era.

Although all these holy days, including the Sabbath, were intended to ensure rest, unity, and devotion to the one God, eventually some forms of music and dance emanated from the ritual. However, a distinction was made to make these activities sacred and holy vis-à-vis the activities of the pagans surrounding the Israelites.

In Christian thought, time began with man in a fallen state, caught up in the toils of his sin. But there was promise for restoration when a son of Adam would crush the head of the serpent that caused the Fall. Those who would serve Him would end in a Promised Land and receive a Messiah who would lead the world. "When the fullness of time was come, God sent his son" (Galatians 4:4). The Incarnation was the focal point in time, with the Fall as its beginning. Things will come to an end with the Second Coming of Christ and the Last Judgment (Russell 1981:63). Since the end may come any time, the individual Christian should "watch and pray, for you know not when the time is" (Mark 13:33). "Behold, now is the acceptable time; Behold, now is the day of Salvation" (Corinthians 6:2).

According to Russell (1981:70), the biblical teaching limited the extent to which the Greek view of time could be accepted. The idea of progress, either cosmic or human, was rejected. Humans and the universe were in steady states, not evolving ones. Saint Augustine expounded on the concept of time as being created by God. The Bible states that "In the beginning, God created heaven and earth" (Genesis I). A beginning is attributed to every creature, and since time is by definition change, it is also a creature by God. It has a beginning, a deviation, and is not eternal (Gilson 1960:190). According to Augustine, God, being eternal, has created everything—even time.

For early Christians, eternity was an extension of time (Le Goff 1980:31). This meant that the early Christians were to use their time to arrive at its extension by using it in the service of God. Not only was time freed from work, all forms of *negotium* (secular activity) were condemned, and a certain type of *otium* (leisure) that showed confidence in Providence was encouraged (Le Goff 1980:61). The early Christians kept well in mind what Jesus Christ said about the birds of the air: "They sow not, neither do they reap nor gather into barns; yet your Heavenly Father feedeth them. Are ye not much better than they?" (Matthew 6:26). Work was to be done in one's free time; most time was to be devoted to contemplation, the focus of which was obligatory and unitary. The focus was God and nothing else, for this was determined to be the way to true happiness (Kretzmann et al. 1982:673). Clearly, this was not the high form of leisure that Aristotle had exalted so long ago.

But if the early Christians had to work, Saint Augustine suggested handwork, tilling, or small business, for elaborate work might easily distract them from God. This constituted the life of monks, such as the Benedictines: simple work, along with pure contemplation, meditation on the Divine (de Grazia 1962:25). This practice became known as *otium monasticum.* But by the twelfth century, as work hours became longer, the term became *otium negotiosum* (Le Goff 1980:75).

In fact, monks not only did work with their hands, they constructed machines (Le Goff, 1980:80) to make themselves available for a more essential thing—the contemplative life. The monks' engagement in labor raised the position of labor, which was important to establishing a new era in medieval Europe.

In the meantime, with the legalization of Christianity by Constantine, the Christian church began to develop its own holy days. Christmas on December 25 and Epiphany on January 6 were the primary days that were celebrated during the fourth century. Eventually, the number of holy days increased to 115 days (Lee 1964:137). It was this excess of holy days that led to objections by Wycliffe and Luther.

THE MIDDLE AGES AND TIME

Time belonged to God. But medieval merchants became suspected of selling it, since their profits sometimes implied a mortgage on time. The merchants were barred from asking for greater payments from clients who could not settle their accounts immediately. According to Le Goff (1980:30), the conflict between Church's time and merchant's time took place during the deteriorating conditions of the Middle Ages and became one of the major events of that period.

As conditions improved and commodities were moved to far places, trip time had to be included by merchants and the conflict between Church's time and merchant's time grew wider. Eventually, urban centers in Europe adopted an approach to time that differed from the Church's, which dominated the countryside.

Labor time was measured in the urban centers by the day, which started at sunrise and ended at sundown. Since the workers were paid per day, they tried their best to reduce it. But employers used a bell, different from that of the church, to start and end the day. When a worker needed a pause, he took it at None, which eventually became Noon. This led to the concept of half day, and another measurement of time was added.

Eventually, the general view of time changed. Such a change can be observed in the poetry of Dante (born 1265) and Petrarch (born 1304). Although both were from about the same era, they had widely different views on time. A comparison of their work shows that Dante had a preoccupation with eternity, while Petrarch viewed time as a commodity (Morris 1985:31).

But it was the Protestant movement that sanctified time. This movement began in the early sixteenth century when a group of small principalities protested the Church's refusal to grant princes of the empire the right to determine the religion of their territories. A formal protest was filed. Eventually, the supporters of the Reformatio ‹ doctrines came to be called Protestants. With the sponsorship of Henry VIII, Protestantism became strong in England and spread to the New World.

Max Weber suggested that capitalism, as an ideology, emerged from the Protestant movement. He showed how early Christian writings preached that wealth is a great danger, its temptation never-ending, and its pursuits ungodly. Although possession was acceptable to the Protestants, their moral objection was to what possession might do to Christians, including enjoyment of wealth, temptation of the flesh, and distraction from the pursuit of the right path (1930:157).

Some early Protestant teachings proclaim that neither leisure nor enjoyment should be pursued. Such is a waste of time, the deadliest of sins. Only the activity that would serve His glory should be pursued.

> *Loss of time, through sociability, idle talk, luxury, even more sleep than is necessary are worthy of absolute moral condemnation. . . . Thus inactive contemplation is also valueless, or even directly reprehensible if it is at the expense of one's daily work (Weber 1930:157–58).*

This was the attitude toward time brought to America with the early settlers, particularly in New England. There, between 1620 and 1650, the initial settlers were Puritans. This name was given to a dissident party within the Church of England around 1570. The Puritans sought to reform the whole liturgy of the church so that it would have a greater theological integrity. Puritans followed strictly controlled habits with great zeal in order to regulate everything in life, including time. The Puritans became much like spiritual athletes who practice, with zeal, every aspect of their life according to certain rules, and appeal to God at particular times. Dulles notes (1965:9) that the Puritans resented the amusive life-style of the wealthy leisure class in England.

The influence of the Puritans on America was such that in 1619 Virginia's Assembly decreed that any person found idle should be bound over to compulsory work. All activities that were deemed nonwork were prohibited: dice, cards, bowls, dancing, and drama. These prohibitive laws were meant to promote industry and frugality (Dulles 1965:5–6). The Puritans were obsessed with interpretation of the meaning of the Sabbath in the Old Testament and took it upon themselves to condemn any free activity on the Lord's Day.

THE MEASUREMENT OF TIME

To keep track of time, the ancient Egyptians used shadow clocks. A shadow clock was a T-shaped instrument lying flat on the ground, with the cross of the T elevated and placed in an East-West direction. These clocks were the forerunners of the sundial, which came to be used in the eastern Mediterranean and Europe. Outflow or inflow of water was also used to tell time. In ancient Egypt, a *clepsydra,* or water clock, was used. In a water clock, a measuring rod is fixed to a float with a pointer moving about a scale. These simple clocks were used in law courts in Greece and in Rome to limit the length of speeches. Various time-telling devices were used in China between the eighth and eleventh centuries (Lloyd 1981:388–89).

It was the medieval Europeans who created clocks that used weight-driven devices instead of water, oil, and sand, although attempts at mechanical clocks started in China as early as the eleventh century. These early attempts were not completely successful because the weight-driven clock would eventually run down. Something had to be invented to stop the running down, produce an indication, then allow the clock to start running down again, and so on. An unknown person in the thirteenth century invented the verge escapement, which did just that.

Mechanical clocks were used by the monks, as were the clepsydra and the hourglass. Equal periods of 24 segments were established, each of which was divided equally into 60 minutes, which, in turn, was broken down into increments of 60 seconds. These divisions were based on Babylonian/Greek astronomy.

However, it was Galileo's diagnostic instrument that helped to count a patient's pulse that revolutionized the clock. To construct this device, he used a board with a peg and a string with a dangling weight. This was a sort of pendulum, which he transferred to time machines (Lloyd 1981:393).

In 1843, a Scottish scientist, Alexander Bain, sank carbon and zinc plates into the ground where moisture provided the electrolyte that drove the pendulum of the first electric clock (Lloyd 1981:396). Now time could be measured in hours instead of days, weeks, months, or years. Before 1800, labor groups asked that workers not be forced to work longer than 12-hour days. Immediately thereafter they asked for ten-hour days, with American government workers leading the way. In 1884, the Federation of Organized Traders and Labor Unions resolved that after May 1, 1886, workers should refuse to work more than eight hours a day, but it was not until the turn of the century that they were able to realize their demand.

TIME-BUDGET STUDIES

With the advent of the industrial society and its emphasis on production, time became an important commodity. In fact, even in the preindustrial era there were traces of this concept, which Ben Franklin summed up, brilliantly and succinctly, in the maxim "time is money." Consequently, time was counted in the same fashion that people count money.

Time-budget studies began with attempts to report on the life-style of the working class before the turn of the century. The labor movement then adopted as a password "3 × 8," claiming eight hours of sleep, eight hours of work, and eight hours of leisure as the rightful daily schedule for all toiling people. Social scientists began to use time-budget measurement to depict the life-styles of different groups.

Data were collected on simple forms. The respondent was asked to remember, or guess, the average duration or frequency of an activity during the day, week, or month. Leisure, or the lack of it, became the central theme of an incredible number of time-budget studies carried out after World War II, in practically every country where social research had matured. In fact, cross-cultural comparisons used a somewhat sophisticated time-budget technique with a combined questionaire-diary-interview technique. Time, one of the three components of leisure, is easier to submit to objective scrutiny than the other two components, activity and state of mind. Consequently, time-budget technique was used in leisure research (Szalai 1972, Ibrahim 1981).

Some leisure researchers have shown skepticism about the accuracy of self-reported participation rates. Chase and Godbey (1983) expressed concern that an "expressed" recreation need is often predicated on information gathered through interviews and mailed surveys that require recall on the part of the respondent. This is a weak basis for recreation planning.

Other leisure researchers have defended this method as both needed and accurate. Boothy suggested that "objective and complete measurement of participant is a counsel of perfection which will be difficult at least at this stage in the development of leisure studies" (1987:102). Perhaps no recreation planning—national, regional, or local—should be based on the results of one study, and only one study.

This does not mean that the time-budget technique lacks validity. Robinson tested the validity of a diary approach with more detailed observational records for the same period. These observations included having respondents keep beepers that alerted them to random movement so they would record what they were doing, and have them record as much detail during the day (1977). Also, Cosper and Shaw (1985) compared data from a recall questionnaire, which measured the number of times respondents participated in 12 leisure activities and the amount of time spent in each, to data obtained from a previous study in which the respondents kept a diary of all their activities for a 24-hour period. Both studies included categories for television watching, radio listening, leisure reading, arts and hobbies, active sports and exercise, and performing arts. Although there were some statistically significant differences in the scores obtained from these two techniques, absolute differences were not large, and on the whole, results were very similar. The authors conclude that confidence can be placed in the validity of time-budget studies. Consequently, time-budget studies will be used in this volume for comparative purposes whenever applicable.

SUMMARY

Most of the components of time have a direct bearing on leisure behavior. While the physical and organic components do not directly affect such behavior, the biological component does. For example, humans suffer when they change time zones. With pleasure travel at its peak, understanding what brings about such change is important. Also, it seems that nerve impulses are filtered and sequenced to arrive in the brain in an orderly manner. Thus rhythmic flow, music, poetry, color, and light make us comfortable. Leisure planners should know that.

In terms of psychology, leisure planners could maximize our experience of time by enhancing the quality of time. Time of day, season, year, even era should be considered. Socially we are subject to synchronizing, sequencing, and rating time. What are the sources of these practices? The dominant values of the culture play an essential role here. Leisure providers should be aware of that role.

REVIEW QUESTIONS

1. How is biological time related to leisure?
2. Does experiencing time enhance one's leisure attitude?
3. In what way does culture affect one's view of time?
4. How valid are time-budget studies as tools for understanding leisure behavior?

SUGGESTED READINGS

Lauer, R. 1981. *Temporal man: The meaning and the uses of social time.* New York: Praeger.

Morris, R. 1985. *Time's arrow: Scientific attitudes toward time.* New York: Simon & Schuster.

Shallis, M. 1981. *On time: An investigation into scientific knowledge and human experience.* New York: Schocken Books.

Wade, M., ed. 1985. *Constraints on leisure.* Springfield, IL: Ch. Thomas.

3

LEISURE, CULTURE, AND NATURE

This chapter expands the discussion of the nature of society, and will describe the relationship between the cultural and social systems, and their affect-effect relationship to leisure. It includes a discussion of the role that values and norms play in determining leisure behavior. The chapter also presents the subsystems of the social system, mainly family, religion, political structure, the economy, and technology, as they relate to leisure behavior. Elements of the ecosystem topography, land forms, climate, vegetation, water resources, and wildlife are introduced to prepare for a discussion of their impact on leisure behavior in the different societies examined later.

LEISURE AND CULTURE

The cultural system of any society includes all its historically created designs, explicit and implicit, rational and irrational, that are used as potential guides for behavior. These designs emerge from shared social life, although they may spread from one society to another. For example, the cross was taken as a symbol of Christianity by early Christians, passed from that society to others, and survived many social orders. Consequently, culture may remain virtually unchanged over time, despite drastic alterations in the underlying patterns of social order. Perhaps the reason for this is that it is culture that gives meaning to both actions and objects.

A meaning is, primarily, a property of the actor's behavior and secondarily, a property of his or her act. Getting a cup of coffee and writing a book are acts that vary considerably, but both have a process and a product. Walking, pouring, drinking; thinking and typing; here acts tend to cluster to form an activity. However, a meaning may become detached from its corresponding act or activity. This explains why some activities may be consummated vicariously, yet still be meaningful. A good example of a vicarious activity is watching sports on television, which has tremendous meaning to the millions who are glued to the set on New Year's Day in the United States. One doubts that a Tibetan monk could find much meaning in sport.

Meanings are given to fictional subjects such as Santa Claus, and to nonfictional subjects such as great athletes. Activities that tend to have similar meaning may cluster together to form a category. This satisfies human perception by presenting the world in an orderly manner. In fact, some meanings become so inflexible that the meaning of an activity may become fixed—for example, leisure activities being a waste of time among the early settlers of New England. Meanings vary in their degree of complexity, in the extent of their stability, and in the way humans are consciously aware of them.

Meanings are generally shared by the members of society. This does not imply that all members are able to share the meanings of all actions and objects within a particular society. There is always the possibility of what is termed a *subculture*. Also, membership in a society does not necessarily mean automatic membership in its cultural system. For instance, an alien who responds to the meanings of actions and objects in a different cultural system may continue being a member in this society by paying taxes, driving on the right side of the road, speaking in the native tongue, and becoming a citizen. Regardless of that, he may be culturally alien—favoring soccer over American football, engaging in "outlawed" cockfighting, and so on.

Humans make use of symbols to refer to meanings. Yet the meaning of a symbol cannot be derived from an examination of the symbol itself, for it is the particular value that has been assigned to that symbol that makes it what it is. A medal, for instance, is a symbol that has particular meaning; it is not the piece of metal that is meaningful, for there is nothing intrinsically valuable in it. It is what the medal represents that is meaningful.

In general, symbols and meanings are abstractions that are affirmed in social interaction. They can be either private or conventional, and they are products of communication rather than direct experiences. The clarity of one's conception of one's world rests with the adequacy of one's stock of symbols. Consequently, one's social world is the result of effective communication, which provides one with a set of symbols. Human conduct, then, is the outcome of one's participation in the social world, including the leisure world. For example, giving a "T" signal by hand has been borrowed from basketball and is now used in daily life in the United States to mean "time-out" from any activity that generally has no time-out.

As stated before, values give both symbols and their meanings the social and cultural weight they carry within a society. A discussion on values and leisure is appropriate at this time.

LEISURE AND VALUES

Values are agreements among social actors about what is desirable (or undesirable) in social life. Values become sentiments associated with desires for certain ends and objects. Valuation becomes identified with the articulation of such a desire. Agreements among social actors are points of understanding called norms. While norms are specific rules of behavior, values are general principles of behavior.

Feather (1975:5) argues that there are two types of values, according to dominant beliefs. The first type refers to modes of conduct; so these are *instrumental values*. The second type refers to end-states of existence; so they are *terminal values*. Instrumental values encompass such concepts as honesty, love, responsibility, and courage. Terminal values include concepts such as freedom, equality, peace, and harmony. We would like to think of leisure as a terminal value, although this is not always the case.

Values have received little attention from scholars in comparison to other related concepts: attitudes, needs, and desires. Rokeach (1973:17–23) suggests that this has happened because of the variety of methods that have been developed to measure attitudes, compared with the limited number of procedures available for assessing values. This is true in leisure studies where tools to measure leisure attitudes were developed (Crandall and Slivken 1979, Beard and Ragheb 1980). The fact that we can measure something does not necessarily mean that it is more important than something we cannot measure.

In other areas of social science, the terms *values* and *attitudes* have been used interchangeably. According to Rokeach, these two should and can be easily distinguished (1973:13–33). An attitude involves an organization of beliefs focused upon a single subject or situation. In contrast, value refers to single belief about a desirable mode of conduct (instrumental value) or a desirable end-state of existence (terminal value).

Values and needs have also been confused. Values should be looked upon as representing societal and institutional demands placed on needs, as well as the cognition and transformations of these needs. In other words, there could be no corresponding similarity between need and value. For instance, sexual need can be channeled in many directions, according to societal values. Sex is satisfied only through marriage in some societies, through out-of-wedlock relations in others, and through both in certain societies.

Parker (1976:149) states that the question of values underlies the treatment of leisure throughout his book. He proposes that four sets of value questions must be faced when treating leisure:

1. Questions concerning the meaning of leisure, and the relationship of meaning to activity.
2. Questions concerning the appropriate role of leisure in the life of the individual, and of society.
3. Questions concerning the paradox of planning for leisure versus the freedom of leisure.
4. Questions concerning the nature of sociology of leisure in light of the answers to the above.

In answering the first set of questions, Parker alludes to the fact that leisure delivery systems in modern societies determine to a great extent, through programming, the type of activity in which one participates. Granted, some activities provided may not be meaningful to an individual or two; but they are, by the nature of things, meaningful to most members of a given society. No recreation department in the United States would schedule bullfighting as part of its program, nor would a sports council in Great Britain schedule baseball, and no youth center in Saudi Arabia would dare offer social dance!

As to the appropriate role of leisure in society, Parker states that two parallel extremes of leisure may take place. The first extreme utilizes leisure as the highest expression of culture. Clearly, if and when leisure becomes a means of social control, it ceases to be leisure. Time freed without the right to choose or reject an activity or to change from one activity to another defies the basic definition of leisure. At the other extreme, leisure by itself cannot be the highest expression of culture. The great soprano who works hard on her aria is not at leisure. Her audience is at leisure, though. She alone does not create culture, and they alone do not either. It is the two together who create the highest expression of culture.

Does planning for leisure deprive it of its basic characteristic, freedom? It may, particularly if the delivery system is politically controlled. But such a condition applies to only one form of leisure: recreation. The other two, contemplation and amusement, remain relatively free of this type of structure.

LEISURE, NORMS, AND SOCIAL INSTITUTIONS

How is it that a number of independently motivated human beings are able to coordinate their respective activities? This depends upon the degree of consensus that exists among them. Such common understanding may be referred to as a norm. Common understanding is an ongoing process and can be linked to the functional unit of analysis referred to earlier, the human act. An act that is likely to elicit adverse reactions from others may be inhibited or redirected; otherwise, the actor may be subject to negative sanction by the group. The type of sanction concerning a particular act is a function of norms. It is believed that self-control, which includes the giving up of certain acts, helps concerted action proceed smoothly. Some acts may be meaningful to the actor but not to the group, and these acts may have to be given up. Enhancement of an act may include a positive sanction, which requires a common understanding (norm).

Norms do not exist in a vacuum and tend to cluster into a specific order. They may be clustered into customs that are standardized practices enforced by informal societal control. When formal control is applied, the set of norms is called laws. While norms are relatively fixed for customs and laws, they are not so much fixed for fads. It is believed that fads are rehearsals for social change. Unfortunately, faddish behavior takes place during freed time, which gives leisure a black eye because fads are departures from the ordinary.

The formation of human groups is controlled by norms derived from values. In all human groups, roles are played according to the adopted norms. Could these groups be considered "societies"? The answer is no, for the mere grouping of humans does not lead to the formation of a society—not until the group occupies a definite territory. Even societies labeled nomadic hunting/food gathering groups by Goldschmidt (1959) have a territory within which they move. Also, it is essential to make a distinction between a community of households and a society. A society is expected to exist longer than the life span of its members, who are "recruited" mainly through reproduction. Moreover, society has a system that controls all aspects of life; community control over its members is rather limited.

Once a society is formed, it begins to look as if it is made of a system of roles. A role is the part that an actor is expected to perform and the services he or she is supposed to receive from other actors in recognition of his or her contributions. A role can be seen in terms of the rights and obligations of an individual actor. The term was once confined to those behaviors associated with a position. Today such a definition is seen as very restrictive. Behavior as such may be a good criterion for allocating a position in social life. Some roles, however, are played strictly on the basis of non-behavioral criteria, for example, sex and age. Many important roles are derived from physical distinctions between people; consequently, some roles may be ascribed. On the other hand, many roles are achieved, such as that of the "storyteller" of an ancient society, the court jester of the Middle Ages, or the Olympian of today.

Roles may also be differentiated as basic, general, or independent. For instance, basic roles are ascribed to people at birth, while general roles are usually allocated in accordance with qualifications (occupational roles). Independent roles are allocated in accordance with one's merit and have few implications for other roles (leisure roles). Certain roles carry with them a status. Status is a position

in a pattern of social relationships that together encompass a collection of rights and obligations. Statuses may be regarded as bundles of norms, and societies may be regarded as bundles of statuses. A status is meaningless without reference to other statuses in the system. Thus, it may be ranked as higher or lower than another. For instance, a world-class athlete has a greater status than a college athlete. The typical reward for a high status is prestige.

All these are functions of values. If a society does not value a particular role, it will not last long, and if it does last, it will probably have a low status with no prestige. A role may also become devalued. For example, the athlete was highly valued in ancient Greece but not among the early Christians.

Custom is a broad term that embraces all of the norms classified as folkways and mores. But custom does not include the inner sense of obligation—morality does. Among the many Western customs is the Christmas celebration. This has become a part of Western folkways. Yet folkways also include durable patterns that apply to everyday behavior. Examples of these are the coffee break, the happy hour, and the pep rally. Mores differ from folkways in that they are supported by some extremely strong sanction. Maltreatment of children and animals are against our mores.

At the other end of the spectrum of folkways are conventions and etiquette, which have meaning that is not as deep. While convention is a matter of principle, etiquette is a matter of adornment. When one is invited to dinner, it is convention that makes us arrive on time, and it is etiquette that makes us bring a dozen roses for the hostess. In Europe, however, it may be a matter of convention, not etiquette, to bring the roses.

An interwoven pattern of customs, be they folkways or mores, laws, convention, or etiquette, is built around a social function, such as socialization of the young. A social institution is a part of the social structure that is characterized by the distinction of its function(s). This requirement makes it rather difficult to agree with Dumazedier's (1967) and Kaplan's (1960) view that some Western societies are becoming "societies of leisure." Leisure does not have a distinct function or functions. Rather, leisure behavior is diffused among the four basic societal functions forwarded by Parsons (1966): pattern-maintenance, integration, goal-attainment, and adaption. These functions are performed through the five basic social institutions: kinship, religion, government, economics, and technology (see figure 1.1). When one of these dominates a society, the society can be labeled accordingly. For instance, we could have a kinship society, a religious society, or technological society. Is there such a thing as a leisure society? As previously stated, leisure does not have distinct functions. Also, it has come to serve other social institutions, despite the fact that it has its own structures: sports associations, voluntary organizations, and social clubs. But its function(s) is diffused within the family, children's play, the educational system, college sport, the economic system, and tourism.

LEISURE, FAMILY, AND KINSHIP

Kinship refers to human groups whose relationships are based on blood relations and marriage. The basic unit of the human group is the nuclear family: a male, a female, and their offspring. The extended family includes those related directly, or related to the spouses of the nuclear family. The kinship system is an elaborate network of blood relations and marriage relatives that characterizes early human societies.

Leisure and the Family

The nuclear family seems to be either the sole prevailing form of family or the unit from which other complex familial forms are compounded. These are the functions of the nuclear family:

1. **Reproduction.** This is the most important function of the nuclear family where society is concerned. It is necessary for any society to replenish its membership through reproduction.
2. **Sexual satisfaction.** This function is supposed to be limited to the nuclear family. But the percentage of extramarital relationships reported has recently increased dramatically. de Grazia has suggested that with increased leisure love affairs increased (1962:175).
3. **Psychological sustenance.** This function is predicated on the assumption that the family is supposed to mitigate its members' loneliness and psychological isolation, and allow for self-realization. The complication of modern living may have added to this function. In a highly technological society, loneliness may occur faster at work. According to Kaplan (1960:59), play becomes more than a mere diversion in modern societies. It becomes a cause, a clue, and an index of sources of respect, love, interdependence, and knowledge about the other members of the family.
4. **Economic unit.** Some sociologists believe that the family functions as a micro-economic unit, at least in consumption, in this society. This consuming unit is now armed with its single-dwelling home, with a family room perhaps equipped with television, a stereo or a bar, and a recreation room with a ping-pong table, a billiard table, or a card table.

In the backyard there may be a swing set, a barbeque pit, a croquet set, or a swimming pool. The do-it-yourself market floods the family unit with all it can consume, from furniture making to figure carving. It is also estimated that an average American family spends more on its first three days of vacation than the per capita income of half the people in the world.

5. **Socialization.** A manifest function of the nuclear family is the socialization of the young. This is a crucial function, not only for the family but for society in general. According to Kelly (1978a) the family is central to leisure behavior of both young and old. For example, an outing with the family was ranked fifth and playing with children seventh in importance to family welfare.

Aside from members of the nuclear family, other persons, such as grandparents, may be included in what is termed the *extended family.* Although the extended family has weakened in many societies, it is still strong in others. The related people in the extended family are bound together with strong ties of mutual loyalty and helpfulness.

Kinship Societies

In kinship societies, roles are based on familial ties only. Such societies are characterized by conservatism; new ideas are warded off through effective control over the conduct of the members. Taboos, or prohibitive laws, are abundant and are thought to be sanctioned by supernatural power. Such restrictions are needed to survive in the face of the adverse conditions that usually surround these societies.

LEISURE AND RELIGION

The origin of religion in human society is rather obscure. Nonetheless, attempts to uncover it continue. A few theories on the origin of religion include a rationalistic interpretation, which argues that religion started as a result of the cognitive efforts of early humans to interpret their external environment. Another theory says that religion sprang from our affective state in the act of daily living, in reaction to wonder, awe, and fear of natural phenomena. Or did religion rise out of a feeling of dissatisfaction with life, along with mystic emotions? Freud asserted that the primeval sons united, slew their father out of jealousy over his control of women, and in atonement took to worship God, the Father.

It was Durkheim who located the origin of religion in a communal ritual, in support of, and for the unity of, the society. Common social sentiment is crucial to the survival of society (1915). Rituals are symbolic expressions of these sentiments that reaffirm them and maintain their intensity. According to Turner (1982a:85–86), from the early rituals of the early religions to today's life in the post-industrial world the following may have happened:

It would seem that with industrialization, urbanization, spreading literacy, labor migration, specialization, professionalization, bureaucracy, the division of leisure sphere from the work sphere by the firm's clock, the former integrity of the orchestrated religious gestalt *that once constituted ritual has burst open and many specialized performative genres have been born from the death of that mighty* opus deorum hominumque. *These genres of industrial leisure would include theatre, opera, film, the novel, printed poetry, the art exhibition, classical music, rock music, carnivals, processions, folk drama, major sports events, and a dozen more. Disintegration has been accompanied by secularization. Traditional religions, their ritual denuded of much of their symbolic wealth and meaning, hence their transformative capacity, persist in the leisure sphere.*

Such transformation took centuries, and was incrementally taking place all over the globe. Evidence of this will be elaborated on in the later discussion of ancient Greece, Mesoamerica, medieval England, and colonial America.

While Turner's outlook on leisure concentrates on leisure's recreative and amusive aspects, Pieper's outlook is directed to the contemplative aspect of leisure. He prefaces his work with Psalm 46:10: "Have leisure (be still) and know that I am God." Thus the point is to dwell on the reality of creation. Leisure is a mental attitude and condition of the soul. It is a form of silence that is a prerequisite for the apprehension of reality (1964:27). Later Pieper approaches Turner's view by suggesting that celebration is essential, particularly the one of divine worship. Such celebration is the deepest spring by which leisure is fed and continues to be vital.

> *Cut off from the worship of the divine, leisure became laziness. . . . The vacancy left by the absence of worship is filled by mere killing of time and boredom, which is directly related to inability to enjoy leisure; for one can only be bored if the spiritual power to be has been lost (1964:48).*

Certainly there are a number of atheists in this world who do not worship a divine and are not bored to death with free time. Other institutions, besides religion, come into action where leisure is concerned.

LEISURE AND THE POLITICAL STRUCTURE

Many early political philosophers equated the state with social order, and declared that all before was anarchy. Men acted rationally in society and came together to create law and government. Modern anthropologists do not agree with this, nor with the notion that forms of economic inequality are the basis for the development of political structure. In fact, it seems that the early human bands were much more egalitarian than has been commonly believed (Service 1975:267).

Leisure and Early Structure

It was the success of a person in war and/or in peace, coupled with his charisma, that led to the rise of a political leader in early human societies. With the expansion of the band into a clan, then a tribe, some distinction may have taken place, making the society hierarchical. This is demonstrated by status burial places. Chiefdom, which grew out of egalitarian societies, gave the leader a status arrangement with some aristocratic ethos, but bestowed no formal legal apparatus of forceful repression. Consequently, the leader had no more access to greater free time than did any other member of the society. The success of a leader might lead to primogeniture, and to the institutionalization of power on a hereditary basis. Eventually, the governing family might become an aristocracy with certain privileges, including more free time.

Differentiation of political roles from other roles and the autonomy of the political subsystem from kinship roles are both very limited among the primitive bands. These steps began to take shape in intermediate structures.

Leisure and Intermediate Structures

So that they may perform their role, leaders are given or acquire the means of employing force. This is a function of political legitimacy, which is usually derived from three sources: (1) traditional values, norms, and customs; (2) legal prerogative based on agreements; and/or (3) rational expertise and knowledge.

Legitimacy is especially strong if it is based on all three, but such was not the case in intermediate societies. Four basic problems had to be dealt with: state building, nationhood, participation, and distribution of authority. Participation in and distribution of political authority necessitates two types of input: demands and support. Such development came very slowly, and in fact sometimes never came. Perhaps this was because the ruling class, along with its army and bureaucracy were, usually, foreign to the society. For example, the Roman Empire was hardly Roman. The normative order, which was observed by the masses, was always below the ruling class, not above it as it should be ideally. The ruling class became what Veblen (1953) describes as the leisure class, which was an outcome of the accompanying economic structure, as will be seen later.

Leisure and Modern Structures

Modern political structures are specialized infrastructures that include interest groups, political parties, and methods of communicating demands and interests, as well as a paid army and bureaucracy. Moreover, modernity connotes a secularized system with a policy that is aware of the role of government in changing human conditions. Such a structure emerges when a unified legal-behavioral code is observed by all, or almost all, members of society. The modern structure can be divided into two basic categories, according to the level of differentiation among infrastructures and the degree of secularization (fig. 3.1):

I. Premobilized political structures (low differentiation and secularization)
   A. Premobilized authoritarianism (e.g., Iran)
   B. Premobilized democracy (e.g., Egypt)
II. Mobilized political structures (high differentiation and secularization)
   A. Democratic systems (subsystem autonomy with participant culture)
      1. High subsystem autonomy (e.g., U.S.)
      2. Limited subsystem autonomy (e.g., Great Britain)
      3. Low subsystem autonomy (e.g., France)

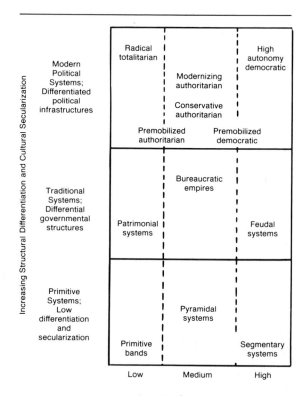

FIGURE 3.1 *Relationship between autonomy of subsystems and degree of structural differentiation and cultural secularization of political subsystem.*

   B. Authoritarian systems (subsystem control with subject culture)
      1. Radical totalitarianism (e.g., Albania)
      2. Conservative authoritarianism (e.g., Saudi Arabia)
      3. Conservative totalitarianism (e.g., USSR)
      4. Modernizing authoritarianism (e.g., Yugoslavia)

According to Kelly, the place of leisure in the social system has often been defined without recognizing that political dimensions are implicit in the analysis. "Leisure is political in the sense of being developed in ways that serve the social system." This may seem limited to societies with subpolitical systems that are low in autonomy, differentiation, and secularization (see fig. 3.1). But there are indications that even in the most democratic systems, with high subsystem autonomy (e.g., U.S.), leisure serves the system first rather than offering the openness necessary for existential freedom and beginning. Kelly believes that real leisure will develop when the conditions of modern life are liberated from subservience to the means of production and from control by the elite with devisive interest (1987a:198–201). Here leisure is looked upon as an ideal, more philosophically than sociologically. It is hard to imagine that Americans are spending $300 billion a year on leisure that is not real.

LEISURE AND ECONOMICS

The economy of a given society rests upon its natural resources, such as topography and climate, technical skills in food gathering/producing, agriculture, and manufacturing, as well as upon its value system.

Leisure and Simple Economic Systems

The simplest societies have a very simple economy, such as gathering food, which is completely controlled by the kinship system. The members perform their simple technological/economic tasks by virtue of their social position in the system, which is based on sex, age, and lineage. Yet these tasks are shared rather equally by the members of the early human bands.

When and if a group within the kinship system attempts to improve its position, it does so by trying to control some of the resources. Among the resources usually acquired are the sacred places, as seen in Mohammed's taking over of Mecca in 632 and establishing Islam as Arabia's religion. Custodianship over the sacred place gives status distinction to the lineage in control. Change takes place eventually; the egalitarianism enjoyed before

is lost, and free time is no longer equally distributed. Such elevation of a single lineage to a privilege rank, and perhaps elevation of its senior member to top authority, might be the basis of a monarchy with both political and religious foundations.

Leisure and Intermediate Economic Systems

Little is known about the changes that take place in a society that lead it to become a nation-state, as in the case of ancient Egypt. It seems that a lineage grew in power as the community increased in number. This increase was not accompanied by any substantial increase in role differentiation among the masses. "The whole society was most basically differentiated between the Kingship Complex and the Common People. It was a kind of archaic socialism" (Parsons 1966:57). In ancient China, the story was somewhat different. There, a gentry lived in a large household, with many servants. While the economic base consisted of ownership of surrounding agricultural land, it was supplemented by artisan workshops and mercantile enterprises, all owned by the gentry. Max Weber contrasted China and colonial America in that Confucian rationalism meant rational adjustments to the world and Puritan rationalism meant rational mastery of the world (1955). Chinese peasants accepted their lot in life; early, white Americans wanted to improve it.

A two-stratum system also existed in India for centuries. The upper stratum was composed of Aryan invaders from the north who eventually became divided into three Varnas: the Brahmans, the priestly class; the Ksatriya, the warrior-nobility; the Vaicyas, the landlords and merchants. These three groups combined made up the twice-born privileged class, in contrast to the tillers, servants, and occupiers of humble functions.

Thorstein Veblen brought attention to what he termed the leisure class in the above societies and others. He believed that in "the cultural evolution the emergence of a leisure class coincides with the beginning of ownership" (1953:33). Veblen defined leisure as nonproductive consumption of time from a sense of the unworthiness of productive work and as an evidence of pecuniary inability to afford a life of idleness. It must be pointed out that Veblen's work was first published in 1899, and his ability to validate what is unworthy or consumptive was hampered by a lack of scientific tools. Nonetheless, the concept of a leisure class is an intriguing one and will be used to analyze the emergence of leisure pursuits in many societies.

Leisure and Modern Economic Systems

How does change take place? Is it possible to transform an underdeveloped area into a developed one by changing everything at once? While change is necessary and can be done, a number of preconditions must be in place before any changes are planned. Basically, in the social order concerned, a complete consensus should exist on the goals of human activities and the meaning of life. Variables such as prevailing values, social organizations, and motives should be considered. Rostow (1960) called these the preconditions of economic take-off. An important variable to consider is the type of production. Production is related to the level of economic advancement based on the bulk of the labor force, as follows:

1. Primary economy, where most of the labor force is engaged in agricultural and extractive processes.
2. Secondary economy, where most of the labor force is engaged in manufacturing.
3. Tertiary economy, where most of the labor force is engaged in services, trade, and communications (including leisure delivery systems).

Rostow extended the stages of economic growth to five categories and advocated that it is possible to identify all societies, in their economic dimensions, as lying within one of these five categories (1960:4).

1. **The Traditional Stage.** Traditional stage societies, because of limitations on productivity, have to devote very high proportions of their resources to agriculture. Family and clan connections play a large role in social organization. The value system is generally geared to what might be called long-run fatalism. The center of gravity of political power lies in the hands of those who own or control the land (Veblen's leisure class?)
2. **Transitional Stage.** A stage of transition occurs between the traditional period and the take-off period that follows, yet certain conditions have to exist. This is characterized by the building of an effective centralized national state, which may accompany a premobilized political period.
3. **The Take-Off Stage.** In the take-off stage, the rate of effective investment and savings may rise from 5% or so to 10% and more. As new industries and new agricultural techniques develop, profits are reinvested into new plants and a class of entrepreneurs is created and expanded. Usually the basic structure of the economy and the social and political life of the society are transformed in such a way that a steady rate of growth can be, thereafter, regularly sustained. A minimum of two decades is needed before results are witnessed.
4. **The Drive to Maturity.** Once 10%–20% of the national income is invested, output can finally outstrip the increase in population. This stage is reached within forty years after the end of take-off.
5. **The Stage of High Mass Consumption.** This occurs when real income per capita rises to a point where a large number of persons gain command over consumption, transcending basic food, shelter, and clothing. Also, the structure of the working force is basically urban-bureaucratic-technician in nature.

This is the stage of technology beyond which a new stage could evolve, which may not be political or economical. A leisure society was advocated by Dumazedier (1967).

Rostow provides us with a timetable on the different stages of economic growth in 14 societies. While Britain was the first country to take off economically in 1800, it took 50 years to reach maturity at the middle of the nineteenth century, and another hundred years to reach the stage of high mass consumption. It was during the period between the first two stages of take-off and maturity that growth was witnessed. The same may be said of Japan now (see fig. 3.2).

Granted, Rostow's work is not recent, but it takes into consideration the historical dimension. "Historical perspective is one of the best safeguards against taking a superficial view of these problems" of the evolution of developmental economics (Meier 1989:67). Moreover, the passage of only three decades does not render Rostow's work invalid.

Recently some scholars have blamed the fading of the classical concept of leisure on the passion-driven economic man who emerged victorious in one or more of the countries listed in figure 3.2 (Dare, Welton, and Coe 1987:199). The classical concept of leisure is easily equated with the concept of real leisure of Kelly (1987a:197). This is an ideal to which many aspire, and which very few achieve, whether now or in the past. It was Aristotle who forwarded the ideal, but he also defended slavery so that the elite of Athens could achieve their ideal, classical, real leisure. The present work, however, looks at a tripartite leisure: contemplative, recreative, and amusive, and at leisure's source and evolution over the millennia—not just the activities of a certain class in a certain society at a certain time in history.

Needless to say, industrialization gave the time and the opportunity for more of us to delve into the leisure sphere. Moreover, technology, an outcome of the era of industrialization, gave us implements that are crucial to many contemporary leisure activities. This is the subject of the next section.

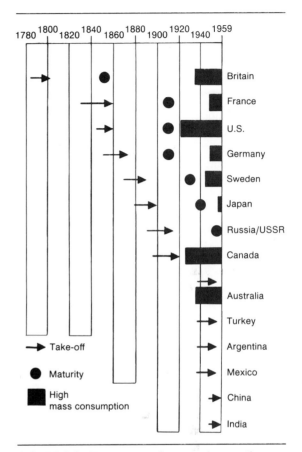

FIGURE 3.2 *Five stages of economic growth.*

LEISURE AND TECHNOLOGY

Many equate technology with tools and machines, but this view is limiting. This author suggests that technology encompasses human adaptation to both the physical and the social environments. Accordingly, there are two types of technology: material and social. These two technologies help our adaptation to collective living and our dealing with the physical environment.

Technology also includes the organization, dissipation, and utilization of human knowledge for the purposes of achieving human goals. Basically, the organization of knowledge falls under the heading of education. Dissemination of knowledge may come under the sphere of the media, be it visual, audio, or both. The utilization of human knowledge may fall within two areas: science and industry.

Leisure and Education

In its sociological connotation, education means the conscious, purposeful, and deliberate process whereby accumulated knowledge (including ideas, standards, and techniques) is transferred to, or imposed upon, the rising generation. One must bear in mind that this process includes not only the rising generation but also the newcomer, and that there is such a thing as unconscious or incidental education. In essence, education is the inculcation of one individual with the knowledge accumulations of others. The first efforts to inculcate others were by parents in the early human societies. As life became more complex, role differentiation occurred and the new custom of induction through ritual began in early societies. This activity helps impress on the child the importance of conformity and the desirability of becoming an accepted adult. The ritual is performed by a specialized person, through intensive instruction during the initiation period.

Since there was no distinction between work and leisure in early society (Thomas 1960:50), there was no leisure education of which to speak. While not labeled as such, the nobility of the early nation-states, Egypt, Mesopotamia, China, and India, must have had different training for their offspring than did parents among the common people. But a separate education was distinctly clear in ancient Athens, where the male offspring of the citizens (only 15% of the population) underwent a *schole*-education, or leisure education. *Schole*, which means being occupied with something desirable for its own sake (the noble music and the exercise of the speculative faculty), was the basis for another ideal, liberal education. This concept survived, despite the practicality of the Romans, and had enormous secular influence on Western thinking. One current passed northward as far as the English schools. The peasants of medieval Europe may have had no ear for noble music nor time for contemplation; nontheless, leisure education and liberal arts survived.

Leisure and Mass Media

From the simple gestures, grimaces, and ritualization that conveyed a message to another, communication has become an elaborate system, the core of which is the symbol. The spoken word became a written word, then a printed word, and now it is the electronic word that has become most effective. New and effective mechanisms to convey the spoken, printed, and electronic word have been added in the last century—namely the press, telegraph, telephone, cinema, radio, and television. The impact of mass communication on mass leisure is very clear in the modern society.

Leisure and Science

Science is looked upon as the means through which knowledge is acquired that is potentially applicable to all phenomena. These phenomena include physical, biological, and psychological phenomena. Scientific advances in these areas have had a direct impact on leisure behavior. Advances in biological research have led to the phenomenal growth and increasing interest in physical fitness and sport. There are two components of athletic performance. The first is the general component, which shows that the performer possesses certain traits such as strength, endurance, agility, and flexibility. The second component shows that the performer has acquired certain skills in throwing, shooting, jumping, and so on. Although the first may be present naturally, the second requires a great number of hours in practice, which is a function of leisure. The term "natural athlete" does not indicate that the person is born with these qualities as much as it indicates the capacity for strength, endurance, agility, and flexibility. The challenge, then, is to identify the components essential for the performance.

Then there is the psychological side of leisure. Health has been understood somatically (i.e., as a function of the body) since it was first used in the lexicon of the Western culture. But today it is viewed holistically. We recognize mind and body as a single unified organism. In a technologically-oriented society, people are accustomed to thinking of health in terms of medicine, surgery, and related physical technologies. In other cultures, magic, faith, ritual and the like are thought to be healers. In the West, as early as 350 B.C.E., Aristotle talked about leisure as a state of mind, and discussed its effect on everything, including health. Since the term *health* is very limiting, the new term *wellness* has been recently adopted.

Wellness begins with one's state of mind. Being angry, frightened, tense, or depressed can initiate physiological changes that may result in disease. Contemplative and amusive leisure play a role in alleviating some of the causes of negative physiological responses. If the mind is relaxed and at peace with itself and the environment, the bodily functions will be more harmonious.

Leisure, either as activity or contemplation, pleases. It is rather ironic that the term *placebo* comes from the Latin term meaning "to please." Today *placebo* refers to substances or treatments that have no medicinal value in and of themselves. In his article on placebo, Norman Cousins argues that placebos can cure almost anything; because the sick person believes that his or her health is improving, the brain and body chemistries change (1977). Might leisure (activity or contemplation) operate on the placebo principle as well?

Leisure and Industry

From simple toolmaking to robotic techniques, manufacturing, the heart of modern industry, has had some impact on leisure. On the one hand, it has provided humans with tools that make life easier; on the other, it has led to an obsession with productivity.

In the area of sport know-how led to the manufacturing of the ball, the racket, and the club in primitive and intermediate societies. Vulcanization of rubber by Charles Goodyear in the 1830s led to the development of elastic and resilient rubber balls for tennis, golf, and all other activities.

In the area of contemplative leisure, which includes reading and writing, the mass production of paper and the invention of the printing press have helped immeasurably.

Technology helped cause a tripling in number of sport fishermen in this country from the early 50s to the late 60s. Fishing rods are now made of fiberglass, which enables the amateur to match the professional (Hammel and Foster 1986). Hunting has also witnessed a boom; there is a pay-and-shoot preserve in each state. The mass production of bows and arrows has helped in this development also.

Advances in technology has allowed ice skating fans to skate in all seasons. The first mechanically refrigerated ice rink was introduced in London in 1876. In 1879, the first artificially frozen rink was installed in the old Madison Square Gardens in New York City (Ibrahim 1975:143).

The introduction of artificial snow-making machines has spread to skiing. Also, the durable aluminum ski has made wooden ones obsolete, and the use of nylon for bindings has added to the safety of skiing. The introduction of artificial alloys has made possible the mass production of this equipment.

With the introduction of the automatic pin setter, the almost dying recreation of bowling was revived. Also, the use of synthetics such as fiberglass and dacron widened the market of the boating industry. A boat with a one-piece hull of fiberglass is not only cheaper but easier to maintain. The Outboard Marine Corporation was the first American manufacturer to use aluminum die casts for engines; now the automobile makers use it as well (Ibrahim 1975:143).

From a technical point of view, Boyle has suggested that nothing made a greater contribution than did the bicycle (1963:31). The bicycle played a key role in the development of the motorcycle and the automobile.

The Eastman Kodak Company developed around 1888, and cameras found a mass market among nature lovers. Outdoor sportsmen were introduced to taking action shots in both nature and sport. Interest in the movement of the horse helped in the evolution of motion pictures. By establishing a battery of cameras, Eadweard Muybridge captured not only the movements of the horse, but also the gallop of the dog, the flight of the bird, and the performance of the athlete. His monumental study, entitled *Animal Locomotion,* demonstrated the "work and play of men, women, and children of all ages; how pitchers throw the baseball, how batters hit it, and how athletes move their bodies in record-breaking contests" (Betts 1953). By 1895, Woodville Latham made a four-minute motion picture of the Griffo-Barnett fight.

The interest in what was called the first flickering commercial motion picture, cited above, led to the photographing of the Fitzsimmons-Corbett fight in 1897 for public distribution. With the introduction of the newsreel, the motion picture industry became interested in supplementing the news with a short subject, which often centered on a sporting event (Betts 1953).

With the invention of electricity, recreational events could be held at night. The first account of such an event was in 1885 in the annual equestrian show at Madison Square Gardens. Another outgrowth of electricity was the streetcar, which opened suburban areas and led to the construction of parks outside the city limits (Ibrahim 1975:143).

LEISURE AND THE ECOSYSTEM

Coppock (1982) asserts that no adequate understanding of leisure behavior will take place until the dimensions of demand and supply of leisure places are carefully investigated. Supply and demand are functions of the ecosystem. The ecosystem, in turn, is formed by the interaction between living things in a particular physical environment. Humans, wildlife, and vegetation constitute living things; topography, land form, climate, and water resources constitute the physical environment. The relationship of the ecosystem to leisure activities will be presented in later chapters dealing with individual societies. The following sections will only make some general points about leisure and components of the ecosystem.

Topography and Land Form

Topography describes the general shape of the earth's surface; land forms are specific surface structures. For example, mountains are land forms characterized by their prominent height above adjacent land and their narrow summits. The summits distinguish mountains from highlands and plateaus. All these provide recreational opportunities to the participants. Mountain resorts are a case in point. According to Chubb and Chubb (1981:307), air temperature drops 2 degrees Celsius for every 300 meters increase in elevation (3.5 degrees per 1,000 feet). They provide comfortable accommodations in summer and skiing opportunities in winter. Camping, hiking, sightseeing, and rock climbing are also provided.

Climate

There are seven climatic regions in the world. Their impact on leisure pursuits is summarized by Chubb and Chubb (1981:300–301) as follows:

1. Tropical wet: No prolonged activity; outdoor swimming year-long.
2. Dry: Outdoor swimming most of the year.
3. Mediterranean: Favorable for recreation; outdoor swimming most of the year.
4. Humid/warm: More indoor activities; outdoor swimming most of the year.
5. Humid/cool: Short swimming season; short winter sport season.
6. Cold: Little opportunity for summer activity.
7. Highlands: skiing; nature study.

Vegetation

An important accompaniment to topography and climate is vegetation, or the lack of it. Forests and woodlands provide for recreational activities that differ from the ones provided in a desert. Hiking, camping, and the nature study are the main activities conducted in forests, woodlands, and deserts. The enjoyment of nature through photography is another pursuit. Forests have been a place for contemplative leisure by many poets and philosophers.

Water Resources

Water is an important source for varied leisure pursuits. Sea and ocean shorelines provide opportunities for multitudes around the world—from swimming to surfing to sun-tanning. Rivers and estuaries provide opportunities for nature study, water-skiing, boating, and fishing. Lakes, fresh or seawater, are another source of enjoyment for lovers of aquatics.

Wildlife

Animals, birds, and fish are parts of the physical environment that have provided for a number of leisure pursuits, such as hunting, fishing, and bird-watching. In fact, animal watching has become a favorite leisure pursuit instead of shooting, as a result of restrictive laws protecting certain endangered species and the advocacy of certain groups aiming to protect animal life.

Wildlife, vegetation, and physical characteristics of the environment, singularly and in combination, provide shelter and food for the human race. Today, as we harness their energy and transform their elements and substances, we also use them for a myriad of leisure pursuits. These elements are finite and exhaustible. With increased participation in leisure pursuits all over the world (as this volume shows), overuse and abuse of these natural resources causes serious problems.

SUMMARY

This chapter expanded a discussion of the cultural and social systems and their relationship to leisure behavior. The meaning of an activity is de-termined by how much value we give to it. Humans use symbols that have certain meanings, which are affirmed in social interaction. Understanding meanings and symbols helps one adjust to one's worlds, including the leisure world, and helps one play one's roles, including leisure roles. Values are attached to these roles; one may be more prestigious than the other (a quarterback over a lineman! a mountain climber over a hiker!). Values are general guides for behavior; norms are specific ones. Norms cluster into custom, folkways, and law. The pep rally is a custom; a potluck dinner is a folkway. An interwoven pattern of custom, folkway, and law revolves around a social function, creating a social institution (e.g., family). A social institution is characterized by the distinctiveness of its functions. It is rather difficult to label leisure as a distinct social institution because it serves many functions that belong to other institutions.

Leisure serves the functions of socializing the young and of providing psychological sustenance to family members. Leisure shares ritualization with religion, and is seen as a form of prestige in many political structures. From an economic viewpoint, recreative and amusive leisure are related to the stage of high mass consumption present in advanced economic systems. Technology has had its impact on leisure through industry, science, mass media, and education. The elements of the ecosystem that could have an impact on leisure behavior include topography and land form, climate, vegetation, water resources, and wildlife.

REVIEW QUESTIONS

1. List the variables that constitute a culture. How are they related to leisure behavior?
2. In what way does leisure affect and is affected by the five basic social institutions?
3. Considering the three levels of society— "primitive," intermediate, and modern—how does each relate to the basic social institutions? What does this mean to leisure?
4. What is an ecosystem? How is it related to leisure?

SUGGESTED READINGS

Chubb, M., and H. R. Chubb. 1981. *One third of our time: An introduction to recreation behavior and resources*. New York: John Wiley.

Dumazedier, J. 1967. *Toward a society of leisure*. New York: The Free Press.

Parker, S. 1976. *Sociology of leisure*. New York: International Publications Service.

Veblen, T. 1953. *The theory of leisure class*. New York: New American Library.

AN OVERVIEW OF PART ONE

Leisure is defined as a state of mind or being that allows a person to choose contemplative, recreative, or amusive activity at the time in which he or she is relatively free from work, civil, or familial obligations. Leisure has gone through an evolutionary process. Leisure is a social fact, but it is practiced by a biological being who also has gone through an evolutionary process. Of interest to us are not only the bodily changes of that biological being, but also changes in its brain. After all, by definition leisure is a state of mind or being.

Along the evolutionary scale, the brain has gone from simple to complex, an important principle in evolution supported by another principle, differentiation. The primitive brain of the reptile serves basic survival needs; the old mammalian brain adds an element of decision making. The neocortex allows for flexibility, and the hemispheric specialization allows for both order and creativity. These new components are additions and not replacements.

The evolution of the brain was accompanied by an evolution in a phenomenon that is still not clearly understood—play. The more complex the brain, the more play is witnessed. Play is manifested clearly among primates, and the fact that it serves many social functions is supported by animal behaviorists. Despite differences in cultural backgrounds, the sequence of play seems to be universal among young humans. Is there a genetic blueprint for play? While research is unable to verify such a possibility, this idea will be accepted at face value because of its importance in understanding leisure behavior.

Another phenomenon that has intrigued social scientists for some time is ritual, which is also biologically based, at least in its rudimentary form. Ritualization is witnessed among animals and to a greater degree among mammals. Among humans it has become an elaborate system that, it is now believed, enhances social order and allows for creativity.

But since leisure is predicated on time freed from work, civic, and familial obligation, understanding time becomes necessary. While its physical nature is important, biological, psychological, and social time play important roles in determining our leisure behavior. For example the freeing of time from the aforementioned obligations is a function of societal value, the source of which could be our religious, political, or economical orientation. It becomes important then to delve into the social system, which is affected by two more systems: the cultural system and the ecosystem. The result of the interaction among these three is human behavior, including leisure behavior.

Since the cultural, social, and even the ecosystem have evolved, one concludes that leisure activities, and subsequently leisure behavior, have also evolved. Keeping the two evolutionary principles in mind—simple to complex, and societal differentiation—Part Two will discuss the evolution of leisure that accompanied the evolution of human societies through their "primitive" and intermediate stages.

PART TWO

EVOLUTION OF LEISURE

Part Two deals with premodern societies that either have disappeared or are fast disappearing today. Understanding their cultural and societal structures will help explain the evolution of leisure behavior. Fortunately, studies of some of these societies took place over a century ago before they went through changes that dramatically altered their structure and thus the members' behavior. Also, some of the intermediate societies of past kept records valuable for our understanding of them. A third group of premodern societies has not been "contaminated" by our modernism and will help us in this process of understanding their social structure, cultural patterns, and members' behavior.

4

"PRIMITIVE" SOCIETY AND RITUALIZED LEISURE

In the dimness of prehistory, man evolved from the *Ramapithecus* of 12 million years ago and came to settle in communities. The oldest community, Jericho, existed ten thousand years ago. These communities were usually the outgrowth of tribal bands that were able to settle around water. The tribal bands themselves may have originated from the cooperative venture of a number of extended family structures. The extended family, in turn, was an extension of a nuclear family—a male, a female(s), and their immediate offspring.

Parsons (1966:33) put forward two formulas as criteria for societal primitiveness: the first is the overwhelming importance in all spheres of action of the religious and/or magical orientation to the world; the other is the prominence of kinship relations. In fact, the kinship structure is so prominent that these societies are often called *kinship societies*. Moreover, the constitutive symbolism, which gives members of the society their self-definition, is always linked in some way to the kinship system. Usually there is a connection, through ancestry, to supernatural beings who are the original founders of the society. The normative order is believed to have been established by their actions and/or decrees.

RITUALIZED LEISURE

At this point it may be important to ask when humans began to develop these notions of an ancestry, a supernatural being, and so on. Or rather, under what circumstances? Clearly, human beings did not spend all their waking hours struggling for survival. They must have had some free time to reflect on their condition. Is this the rudiment of the first form of leisure—contemplative leisure? The other two forms, recreative and amusive leisure, probably started then also.

According to Turner (1982a:31), it was during ritual that some of the human activities that are now considered recreative or amusive started. Turner asserts that the early human community participated, in toto, in the rituals out of obligation, not choice. Sooner or later no one was exempt from ritual duty, just as no one is exempt from economic, political, or legal duty today. The ritual was, and still is, the hallmark of the "works of the gods" as well as sacred human work.

But such work is not work in today's industrial sense of the word. Ritual has both sacred and profane dimensions. An element of novelty was introduced from time to time into ritual. Liminality, the seclusion period, is particularly conducive to such "ludic" innovations. As we will see later, these ludic aspects of ritual are connected to the work of the collectivity, who perform symbolic action and manipulate symbolic objects in order to promote rain and fertility, to cure the ill, to avert disasters, to transform people, and to ensure the hunt. Originally, these activities were means to an end, not an end in themselves. The characteristics of primitive society kept these rudimentary activities from becoming full-fledged "leisure" activities.

THE NATURE OF "PRIMITIVE" SOCIETY

The kinship society is characterized by conservatism, where new ideas are almost automatically rejected. Effective control is exercised through prohibitive laws called taboos that are sanctioned by a supernatural power. This results in social solidarity, which enables the group to survive in the face of adverse conditions, yet renders the society static. The group is emphasized over the individual and land is usually owned by the community and is controlled by the elderly. Members of the society share their food.

There is no educational structure as such and the parents carry out education. Children learn by doing, and values are inculcated through the fear of the supernatural powers. The gradual induction into rituals impresses upon the child the importance of conformity. An initiation ceremony that includes intensive instruction for a number of weeks sets the young into adulthood.

The political unit of the kinship society is usually very small and its structure varies. Some have a little political machinery with designated leaders. Others have a group of elders who wield political powers. Still others have chiefs who rule by the consent and advice of wise men, and some have a standing army.

The religious practices of most of these societies are closely associated with magic and witchcraft. Some kinship societies believe in a single supernatural force. Perhaps the helplessness that develops in the face of inexplicable phenomena caused humans to seek religion. Religion allows for a mysterious force to dominate human affairs.

The technology of kinship societies is limited. The economy is usually at the subsistence level. Family and kin share their labor as a cooperative unit. Surplus food, if any, is used for ceremonial purposes and prestige but not for trade. Competition is not common among individuals, although it may occur among families.

Social control in most of the "primitive" societies is based on the assumption that a deviant act that is considered criminal in our society, such as stealing, would be considered civil among these people. The mere restoration of a stolen object is satisfactory. The most important thing is that the status quo is restored. Usually the culprit's kin share as much civil responsibility as the culprit. The members believe that their laws are backed by their gods, who will bring punishment on the culprit (Ibrahim 1975:78).

According to Veblen, these communities do not have a leisure class per se (1953). He believes that the institution of a leisure class is most clearly seen at the higher stages of the barbarian culture. In feudal Europe and feudal Japan, a leisure class emerged with the beginning of private ownership, which the primordial human communities rarely practiced. de Grazia (1962:13) does not believe that early societies had any leisure. But this probably is a result of his definition of leisure as a state of being rather than a combination of such a state with free time and nonwork activities. Keith Thomas thinks that the most obvious contrast between modern industrial societies and these ancient communities (primitive societies) as far as leisure is concerned is the lack of distinction between work and leisure:

> *Here the distinction between work and leisure is not one which it is possible to draw. Life in such a world follows a predetermined pattern in which work and nonwork are inextricably confused (1960:50).*

Thomas is describing contemporary primordial communities, which provide us with a reliable sample of early primordial communities.

Kraus (1971:32) believes that the playlike activities carried out in primitive cultures were central to the needs of the tribe. These are the following:

1. Religious ritual, often providing a means of supplicating the gods or asking for their favor at times of marriage, birth, death, planting, harvesting, or war.
2. A form of education to prepare children and youth for adult responsibilities.
3. A means of achieving tribal solidarity and morale.
4. A form of therapeutic or healing experience.
5. A means of communication.
6. Aesthetic pleasure, in the sense that even after primitive customs and rituals lose their religious meaning, they continue to be performed as a form of entertainment.
7. Recreation, which was carried out for the purpose of providing relaxation, recovery, and replenishment of one's strength and vitality after toil.

Level of Primitiveness

The evolutionary approach suggested by Parsons (1966) is useful in distinguishing a "primitive" society from an intermediate one, and an intermediate society from a modern one. The assumption is that society, with all its subsystems and social units, evolves just as the physical and biological dimensions of life evolve. There are evolutionary stages in all three dimensions of life on earth, the physical, biological, and social.

The three evolutionary stages of society as suggested by Parsons have been interpreted differently by scholars. For example, Elman Service (1963) believes that there are five levels of "primitive" societies: band, tribe, chiefdom, primitive state, and archaic civilization. I agree with him on the first four, but see the fifth as the ushering in of the intermediate society.

THE HUMAN BAND AND LEISURE

The human band at this level is very small, consisting of between 16 and 25 persons who subsist on hunting, gathering, and foraging. The size is controlled directly by resource availability, yet households are economically independent. Relationships are defined by kinship positions, statuses are largely familial, and leadership is determined by the leader's place in the kinship system. Following are some examples.

Australian Aborigines

The continent of Australia was inhabited by humans as long as 20,000 years ago. The descendants of those original settlers, the Australian aborigines, physically distinct from other peoples of the world, are known as Australoids. Although the environment presented a challenge to human survival, these hunter/gatherers managed to survive. The technology of the Australian aborigine is one of the most basic and least complex, for there is no agriculture, no bow-and-arrow, no pottery, no basketry, no cooking utensils, and no iron tools. Their technology is limited to the boomerang, the spear, and crude stone tools for cutting, scraping, and chopping.

Among the many ritualistic activities of these people are rhythmic movements which have lost their original function but continue to be performed in ceremonies. John Wood (1871:751) wrote that in the frog-dance, the performers paint themselves, beat their *wirris* (sticks) together, then squat down and jump after one another in a circle, imitating the movements of a frog. In the emu-dance, the gestures imitate emu-hunting. The man who enacts the part of the bird imitates its voice. In the canoe-dance, both men and women take part and paint their bodies white and red. Each is furnished with a stick and pretends that it is a paddle. At a given signal they bring the sticks to the front

Early parades. Source: Wood, J. The Uncivilized Races of Man, *1871, p. 733, J. B. Burr.*

and hold them as they do paddles, swaying themselves in unison as if they are paddling. According to Roberts (1962:4), just as children often seem to "play pretend just for fun," so too "primitive" man has engaged in what seems to be purely pleasure play. The canoe dance is a good example of that.

There is a rather curious dance, or movement, with which the aborigines conclude the performance of the evening. They sit cross-legged around their fire, keeping time with spears and *wirris.* Suddenly they all stretch out their arms and point to some distant object, rolling their eyes fearfully. Then, they leap to their feet with a simultaneous yell that echoes for miles (Wood 1871:751).

Many physical activities have been witnessed among Australian aboriginal groups in their ritual gatherings. One was noted by Harney (1952:377):

A disc of soft wood or bark is made, generally about eighteen inches in diameter, and as it is thrown along the ground, the players, generally the old men and youths in groups, throw reed-spears at it from a distance of

fifteen feet. When the disc is struck, it is knocked upright to the accompaniment of the shouts of the players, who generally have a good deal of joyful argument as to the owner of the winning spear.

Roth (1902:17) discovered that wrestling, which he had assumed to be a rare occurrence, was an amusement common to the natives of Australia. It frequently took place in connection with initiation ceremonies:

The combatants were all collected on a cleared circular space, about eight yards in diameter—a disused initiation ground— where I watched them playing one morning for quite a couple of hours. Any individual who happens to pride himself on his skill in the game will open proceedings by challenging another, while the bystanders, egging them both on, and barracking for their respective favorites, will sing away and clap their hands in accompaniment. The wrestling itself takes place somewhat on the fol-

lowing lines. Bending forwards, the challenger will grip his adversary with both hands round the loins where he interlocks his fingers so as to maintain a very firm hold: the latter, with arms raised, remains passive, and in this position is lifted from off the ground on to which he is next thrown. Honors are divided so long as he touches ground with his feet, i.e., not thrown off his balance. The individual who is temporarily gripped may, however, steady himself with his arms on the other's shoulders, and usually prepares himself for a fall on his feet by keeping his lower limbs strongly flexed, thus rendering them springy on whichever side he may be thrown. There is no mutual clutching, or both combatants falling: strictly speaking, it is a throwing, rather than a wrestling match. Only males engage in this sport: as soon as one proves himself victorious, another challenges him, and so on.

According to Service (1963:9), the Arunta, the largest dialect division of Central Australia, despite their undeveloped technology, are one of the most leisured peoples on earth. Blanchard and Cheska agree with this and claim that the Arunta's leisure-rich life characterizes Australian aborigines in general. These level I bands of hunters and foragers have always had ample time for play (1985:137). Service emphasized that *"When times are good, there is little to do in order to acquire sufficient food, and little is done except for visiting and observance of the great seasonal ceremonial occasions"* (1963:9).

Eskimos

Sparsely settled over a huge expanse of the Arctic that stretches from the Bering Strait to Greenland, a small population of Eskimos manifests a surprising degree of cultural, linguistic, and physical uniformity. They survive on hunting and fishing; their economies and technologies are very simple. They have neither agriculture nor domesticated animals other than the dog. Their ability to adapt to their environment, long winters and short summers, is intriguing.

According to Blanchard and Cheska (1985:142), despite the hazards of an Arctic existence Eskimo life is playful; they have a pervasive good humor and elaborate leisure activities. They like singing, storytelling, and games. They know very little of music because they possessed, until very recently, only one musical instrument: the *keeloun*, a tambourine-like instrument formed of thin deer skin or the envelope of whale's liver, stretched over one side of a wooden hoop. A handle is attached to the hoop, and the performer strikes it, and not the skin.

Their dances are remarkable for their simplicity (Wood 1871:1349), as the dancer invents steps according to his or her own taste. In one dance, women stand in a ring, with their hands under the front flaps of their jackets. They sing a song entitled "These are the band." One man enters in the middle of the ring, swings his head and arms from side to side, and occasionally flings one leg as high as he can. Sometimes the men challenge each other to dance. If the challenge is accepted, the challenged performs the ritual of rubbing his nose against his challenger's nose, then together they inhale strongly through the nostrils.

Friends of the Laubins (1977:408), who have lived with the Eskimos, told them that they are the happiest and most carefree people in the world. "It has been reported that Eskimo dances have no religious significance, but they do portray ancient myths and legends, even though they are apparently given only for recreation."

Ceremonial wrestling is a popular physical activity among men and is engaged in celebration of a successful hunt or as an entertainment.

Methods of defeating an opponent apparently varied from region to region. Among the Copper Eskimo a match ended when a wrestler was thrown off his feet; the Ungava Eskimo wrestling match ended when the head of a competitor touched the floor; and the western Arctic Eskimos stated that the match ended when the buttocks of either man made contact with the floor (Glassford 1976:318).

TRIBES AND LEISURE

The term "tribe" refers to collections of level I bands. Here, the population is denser and larger. The tribe uses the same survival techniques, including hunting and foraging. Some familial ties with somewhat enlarged rules exist. Examples of these communities follow.

Navajos

The Navajo, the largest among contemporary Native American tribes, is a clear illustration of the concept of secondary tribalism. Once isolated bands with similar physical, linguistic, and cultural patterns, they are now a unified political entity with their own form of tribal government. The local authority is the headman, who leads by example rather than coercion, exercises limited authority over his own people, and has no voice in the decision of other bands.

Despite their anxiety about the supernatural, their seriousness, and a distrust of outsiders (Kluckhohn and Leighton 1974:303–6), the Navajo seem to have a "keen sense of humor."

> They appreciate ridiculous or incongruous situations, either accidental or prepared, at least as much as do whites. However, their practical jokes are seldom cruel, and individuals are not often satirized in their presence. All types of humor are about equally indulged in and reacted to by all classes of persons. There is much less difference due to age, sex, and social position than there is in white society. A respected older man who is usually quite dignified does not feel that there is anything out of the way in acting the buffoon for a few minutes (Kluckhohn and Leighton 1974:97).

According to Blanchard and Cheska (1985:152), that keen sense of humor is a factor in their recreational life. In addition, the Navajo have ample time for playing. Folk tales told around open campfires and ceremonial occasions, such as the ubiquitous "squaw dance," are settings for other forms of activities.

Erma Ferguson wrote of her observations of the Navajo rituals in 1931. She described what is called the "mountain chant," which include four ceremonies all founded on the same legend of a family that lost a son, who later returned to his people, now grown into a tribe, and told them the tale of his wanderings. Runners were selected and sent out to invite guests to the ceremony held in honor of the family. According to Ferguson (1966:211), in the tale there were many shows performed by the Navajo and invited guests. When the visitors suggested a race, the course was drawn. Bets were laid using strings of coral, shell, turquoise, buckskin garments, and embroidered dresses. The strangers lost and asked for another race, a longer one. They won and were satisfied. Today, the performance has been linked to a great sacred vaudeville show that attracts hordes of Navajo, as well as many visitors (Wyman 1975:15). It takes nine nights to complete and it must be done in the fall, following the season of harvest.

According to the Laubins (1977:424), the Navajo speak of their ceremonies as "sings." A sing is where the people come to be entertained and to gossip. Since there was no tribal center, the sing was the only opportunity for the Navajos to get together.

The ceremonies are held in a sacred hogan, where a new sand painting is made each day. Sometimes as many as twelve medicine men work at one time on a sand painting. The paintings and the songs depict the life of the mythical hero. In the past, eleven or twelve dances were held.

Reagan (1932:69–70) wrote of the Navajo that "wrestling matches took place wherever there was a gathering: at feasts, daytime dances and the like. The spectators surrounded a central place into which two men entered, walked about and sparred for a strategic hold." They tried to seize each other by the hair or by the thighs; but if the holds failed, they seized each other wherever they could; then they wrestled. Those present sang, danced, talked, and shouted. It was all decided by pure strength. The wrestlers performed in the nude; if they kept their clothes on, they would become tattered very quickly. They wrenched and twisted each other till one was thrown on his back. If neither could throw his opponent, they parted by mutual agreement, or were parted by others.

The Dani

In the highlands of western New Guinea, a population of over 50,000 lives in the area called the Grand Valley. The Dani live in a series of small communities that are part of larger alliances. Social life in the Grand Valley is built around a system of clans, whose political organization revolves around the "big man," an individual who by virtue of his charisma, largess, and good nature leads by example, and persuades with reason rather than with force. The Dani have an elaborate ritual life, and their supernatural world is filled with ghosts. The concern for these ghosts is reflected in the lengthy funeral ceremony, which can extend over several years (Blanchard and Cheska 1985:160).

On the other hand, Dani life as a whole contains little competition (Heider 1977:72–80). The society is quite egalitarian. There is little or no overt importance to roles, statuses, or wealth; thus there is an absence of competitive physical activity. According to Heider, the Dani's traditional culture is so strong that as late as 1970 they resisted the introduction of a competitive game and altered it into a more compatible form of play. Heider defines a game as a recreational activity characterized by organized play, competition, two or more sides, criteria for determining the winners, and agreed upon rules.

The Javanese game of flip-the-stick was introduced to Dani schoolchildren and very soon the Javanese game became a Dani game. The Dani children managed to strip the formerly robust Asian game of most of its game attributes. Heider suggests that if games are a culture's way to prepare children for adult life, a competitive game would not be useful in the Dani culture.

Dani children participate in what may be called the basic forms of play, which we "inherited from the animal kingdom." Heider (1977:60–61) describes it as follows:

But what is most interesting about Dani play is that it is quite casual and unorganized. Children run about in groups, sometimes just exploring, sometimes having mock battles with grass stems as spears, sometimes making model houses. If we follow the classic definition of games (see Roberts, Arth, and Bush 1959:597) as organized play with rules, in which there is competition resulting in a winner, then the Dani have no games, for none of Dani play fits these criteria. In fact, the Dani seem to be one of the cultures in the world which do lack games.

Yet intratribal warfare has been going on for years among the Dani. According to Blanchard and Cheska (1985:161), it is more or less a social warfare. It differs from economic warfare in that it is fought for purposes other than taking over territory, capturing resources, or subjecting people. In social war, the objectives of the combatants tend to be more ephemeral and include such goals as prestige, honor, revenge, supernatural reward, and *entertainment* (emphasis added).

CHIEFDOM AND LEISURE

This third level of "primitive" society includes the sedentary, more populated people whose subsistence still depends on hunting and foraging, in addition to horticulture. While social life is still based on familial connections, a new hierarchical relationship begins to emerge. A family branch becomes politically dominant, and political leadership becomes inherited. Examples of chiefdom are the following.

Choctaws

The Choctaws are native North American descendants of Mississippian people, whose culture flourished. The Choctaws grew maize, squash, pumpkins, and beans. They hunted deer and small game. They had a matrilineal system of four clans that served also to regulate marriage. Each of the 100 Choctaw communities was under the jurisdiction of a local head, the Choctaw chief, who had limited powers and led by example.

The most important traditional activity among the Mississippi Choctaws was *ishtaboli,* or *toli,* which Cushman (1899:127–28) describes as follows:

> *Like a herd of stampeded buffalos upon the western plains, they ran against and over each other, or anything else, man or beast, that stood in their way, and thus in wild confusion and crazed excitement they scrambled and tumbled, each player straining every nerve and muscle to its utmost tension, to get the ball or prevent his opponent, who held it firmly grasped between the cups of his trusty kapucha, from making a successful throw . . . a scene of wild confusion was seen—scuffling, pulling, pushing, butting—unsurpassed in any game ever engaged in by man.*

Toli was a fast-moving, physical, and dangerous activity where two teams were pitted against each other, armed with specially constructed rackets (*kapucha*). The rules of the game were minimal: players were not to touch the ball with their hands. The number of players on a team varied, with both sides fielding an equal number of players. As a result of the flexible team size, a team could be composed of as few as ten or as many as several hundred players. *Toli* is known by various names, as is the two-racket game, stickball. (Stickball is the parent game of lacrosse, which has been declared the national sport of Canada.) According to Blanchard and Cheska (1985:170), the formal *toli* game involved entire communities. Preparations were extensive, the ritual practitioners played central roles, and the players went through a strict regimen to prepare themselves for the game. The match was part of a large ceremony

with singing, dancing, socializing, and *ritual* (emphasis added). Everyone participated: men played, the women and children cheered, and the religious functionaries prayed for victory.

Debo, whose work on the Choctaw Indians was first published in 1934, states that they seemed to be deficient in religious conceptions and ceremonials, but on the other hand were the most active of all the tribes of the southeast United States in recreational and social activities (1967:10). She also suggests that their interest in practical matters over mystical ones may be the reason for their advanced economic condition in comparison with their neighbors.

Maori

Another level III primitive society are the original inhabitants of New Zealand. The Maori were farmers, cultivating sweet potatoes and other root crops, which they supplemented by fishing, game hunting, and trapping. The Maori village is composed of huts built around the extended family unit. The Maori have no clan system, but the *hapu* nonexogamous group (*hapu* refers to blood-related household) functioned like a clan. Maori society was stratified into the chiefs, the commoners, and the slaves. Differences were attributed to *mana,* the spiritual power that possessed and was possessed by individuals, groups, and things. It accounted for their effectiveness. Basic to Maori cosmology is the concept of *tapu,* the sacred essence of reality, the focus of Maori magic and religious life. A person or thing thought to have *tapu* is to be approached with caution.

Under certain conditions, a celebration of life, crises, the completion of a meeting house, or the opening of a war campaign attracted *hui,* a gathering where feast, competition, and dancing took place. The *hapu* in charge played hosts.

According to Joan Metge (1976:28), ritual penetrated every aspect of Maori life, even death. Death is surrounded by extremely powerful *tapu,* which Metge defines as being under religious restriction, a state that required respectful treatment and which is dangerous to the transgressor. After ten days of wailing and dirges, speechmaking begins. Then hosts and guests engage in displays of song, dance, and physical activities.

The Maori do not separate words from music or dancing; they all go together. Music is secondary to words. Accordingly, their musical instruments are very simple—a flute made out of the thigh bone of a slain enemy. Even drums were not known to them at the time of John Wood's writing (1871:822).

According to Wood (1871:822), most of Maori "sports" are accompanied with songs that seem to be suited to all phases of their life.

> In paddling canoes, for example, the best songster takes his stand in the head of a vessel and begins a song, the chorus of which is taken up by the crew, who paddle in exact time to the melody.
>
> Respecting the general character of these songs, Dieffenbach writes as follows: "Some songs are lyric, and are sung to a low, plaintive, uniform, but not at all disagreeable tune." E' Waiata is a song of a joyful nature. E' Haka is accompanied by gestures of mimicry. E' Karakia is a prayer or an incantation used on certain occasions. In saying this prayer there is generally no modulation of the voice, but syllables are lengthened and shortened, and it produces the same effect as reading the Talmud in synagogues. Most of these songs live in the memory of all, but with numerous variations. Certain Karakia, or invocations, however, are less generally known, and a stranger obtains them with difficulty, as they are only handed down among the tohunga, or priests, from father to son.

The above description shows the interplay between "sport" and ritual among the Maori. Another example of the connection between ritual and a joyful activity was related by John Wood:

> The mode of salutation at parting and meeting is very curious and to a European, sufficiently ludicrous. When two persons meet who have not seen each other for some time, it is considered a necessary point of etiquette to go through the ceremony called tangi. The "g" by the way, is pronounced hard, as in "begin." They envelop themselves in their mats, covering even their faces except for one eye, squat on the ground opposite each other, and begin to weep copiously. They seem to have tears at command, and they never fail to go through the whole ceremony as often as etiquette demands. Having finished their cry, they approach each other, press their noses together for some time, uttering all the while a series of short grunts! Etiquette is now satisfied and both parties become "very cheerful and lively, chatting and laughing as if there had never been such a thing as a tear in existence. (Wood 1871:823)

According to Wood (1871:845), before a Maori party engaged in war, they performed a dance characterized by discipline and precision. They began by smearing the whole of their clothing and faces. They assembled in a line, three deep, and excited themselves with screaming. Suddenly with a yell, they leapt sideways into the air as if actuated by one spirit. They landed with a stamp that made the earth tremble.

Despite the preparation for war and the need for physical fitness, the Maori, according to Best (1952:137), referred to these activities as nga mahi a te rehia, "the arts of pleasure." Wrestling was one of these pleasures. Before each match, the wrestlers "would recite a charm and spit into their hands and close them for luck." A variety of holds and tricks were used, including "catch-as-catch-can, holding by the arms alone, and holding around the body" (Buck 1949:240). Buck also reports that boxing was done with bare fists and usually in the context of resolving quarrels. Boxing was done with either the opponents hitting each other with the front of a clenched fist or with a blow delivered with the side of the fist.

The Maori raced long-distance runs and were noted for their love of swimming, surf-riding, and jumping into the water from great heights. In addition, they competed in canoes and dart throwing. They also competed at stilt walking, using stilts made from aristolochiaceous. They engaged, while on stilts, in a form of wrestling in which participants attempt to throw their opponents to the ground (Best 1952:143).

Samoans

The people of Samoa live on a group of islands located in southwest Polynesia. They view themselves as belonging to a single political unit, a corporate entity that is administered by an all-Samoan council, the *fono*. They were horticulturalists, growing a variety of plants, such as tara, sweet potatoes, yams, and bananas. They also fished. The basic unit of Samoan social organization was the extended household, which ranged from eight to fifty individuals in size.

According to Mead (1937:302–4) "religion played a very slight role in Samoa; the gods were conceived as having resigned their sacredness to the chiefs." On the other hand, "war in Samoa was part of the ceremonial rivalry between villages and was fought for no gains other than prestige, nor were there any important rewards for individual warriors."

That land of plenty must have had an abundance of free time. In 1899, Churchill described it as follows:

Time is plentiful in the South Seas, and cares are few . . . there are great slices of time for which there are no pressing engagements . . . life has no engagement so important that the islander will not cancel it at once on the plea of sport. (1899:562–63)

But they had the time and surplus for other activities as well. According to Wood (1871:1010):

The Samoans tattoo the whole body from the hips to the knees, covering the skin so completely with the pattern that it looked at a little distance exactly as if the man were

Surfers of Sandwich Islands. Source: Wood, J. The Uncivilized Races of Man, *1871, p. 1093. J. B. Burr.*

wearing a tight pair of ornamental drawers. The production of these elaborate decorations is a work of considerable time, the operation being in the first place, too painful to be continued for a long time and in the second, it is apt to cause so much disturbance in the general system that the result would be fatal if the whole were executed at once.

THE PRIMITIVE STATE AND LEISURE

Primitive state societies differ from chiefdoms in that the state is socially stratified, meaning that it has social classes. The different social classes have different and unequal access to goods, services, and positions. This signals the possible appearance of what Veblen calls the leisure class (1953). The primitive state reserves for itself the right to determine what is legitimate, including the right to use physical force.

Leadership is formal and the result of either achievement or ascription. Primitive state population is usually larger than in bands or tribes. Accordingly, law is defined in terms of territory and not familial relationships or kinship. The primitive state does not have cities or urban centers. It lacks a writing system, a step necessary for the evolvement of an intermediary society, according to Parsons (1966). Examples of primitive states are the Zulu and the Ashanti.

Zulu

The Zulu, a group of over two million Bantu-speaking peoples, were pastoralists who raised cattle, goats, sheep, and chickens. They grew maize, sorghum, pumpkins, and sweet potatoes. They also hunted and gathered.

Under the leadership of a tribal chief called Shaka, the Zulu state conquered and consolidated a large territory with a population of almost half a million people. They maintained their independence until the British conquered them, ending their 70 years of sovereignty.

Their culture was marked by the products of a sophisticated ironworking technology and dwelling structures called *kraals,* beehive-shaped grass huts that were the center of their social life.

At the head of the state was the king, who exercised authority through a system of district chiefs and a standing army. All land was considered his property. Members of the royal family formed a distinct ruling or upper class.

Perhaps the most unique feature of their ritual life is one described over one hundred years ago by John Wood (1871:19).

> *"The natives of South Africa undergo a ceremony of some sort, which marks their transition from childhood to a more mature age."*

Wood goes on to describe what occurs after the ceremony:

> *After the ceremony, which is practiced in secret, and its details concealed with inviolable fidelity, the youth are permitted three months of unlimited indulgence, doing no work and eating, sleeping, singing, and dancing, just as they like.*

This is a very clear example of what Turner (1982a) defines as the "Phase of Liminality." Shaka, the ruler who united the Zulus and ruled them from 1816–20, tried to forbid that ritual, but it gradually came back after his death, as the men of the tribe believed those who had not undergone the rite were weaker than the ones who did.

Among the activities that these youth would engage in was the "public hunt." According to Bryant (1970:682), it was a systematically and scientifically arranged battle with beasts. The district chief sent his messengers out to announce the time and place of a public hunt. The hunters gathered in parties defined by wards, managed by a master hunter. After a series of songs and dances, the hunters went to sleep quietly in the bush, for fear of provoking their prey. In the morning they ate a special breakfast, prayed to the ancestors for protection and good luck, and danced before the spirits. Then they gathered their gear—a small bundle of spears, a hunting shield, and a short stick with a knob at the end to give a heavy blow to the beast, and assembled at the announced location. These were public hunts open to all. The royal hunts, on the other hand, were reserved for the pleasure of the king and his family and were much more elaborate (Blanchard and Cheska 1985:184–85).

In a recent publication on recreation among the Zulu, the modern concept of leisure was found to be poorly related to their traditional life patterns. In fact five terms could not be traced to authentic Zulu equivalents: recreation, leisure, free time, refreshing, restoration. But seven terms had some connections: play, pastime, entertainment, amusement, relaxation, rest, idleness. The author concludes that the African view stresses that engagement in "recreational activity" must include the purpose of achieving pleasure (Magi 1989:3).

Ashanti

A collection of chiefdoms united in response to European intervention in West Africa during the eighteenth century. The Ashanti developed one of the "most complex civilizations ever attained by nonliterate peoples" (Service 1963:366).

Their economy is built around a horticultural system of maize, yams, manioc, sweet potatoes, millet, peanuts, and beans, supplemented with fishing. They are accomplished ironworkers and weavers and use "talking drums" as a means of communication over long distances, which unites the many villages of the Ashanti network.

At the end of the seventeenth century, a priest-leader united the Ashanti, defeated their enemies, and was able to keep the military confederacy on a peacetime basis. The vigorous new state was an elaboration of the earliest primitive hierarchy under a paramount tribe. This form of organization is seen by Service as the normal development of a "primitive" society, clearly paralleling the European feudal experience where the barbarians were able to consolidate themselves hierarchically and territorially (1975:133). The king claimed ownership of all land, along with the chiefs. In essence "a leisure class" was in the making, which followed Veblen's model (1953).

For example, in the case of the Ashanti, there was a troop of professional dancers attached to the Royal Palace who performed for all state occasions. According to Royce (1977:82), when dance is performed as an aesthetic activity, two constraining factors are to be considered: leisure and surplus.

If a society wished to have dance performed as an aesthetic activity, that is, where there is a dividing line between performers and spectators, then it must have a certain amount of leisure time in which to produce and enjoy dance performances. Since dances that are performed only by a selected group of persons are usually more technically demanding, the society must also produce a surplus so that it can afford time from their labor to learn and practice the necessary skills and then to perform (emphasis added).

We see from the above the incipient social institution of amusive leisure, the third form of leisure according to Aristotle. In amusive leisure, some individuals become spectators, or an audience—not participants as in the case of recreative leisure, the second form of leisure.

SUMMARY

Leisure at this level of society is very much connected to the rituals that dominate the lives of members of the human band, the tribe, and chiefdom. In their rituals, certain activities are practiced that have many of the characteristics and elements of leisure. Originally these activities served external ends, appeasing the gods, affirming a social bond, and the like. Eventually they were practiced for their own sake, often in the time freed from social obligation, and sometimes connected to the liminal phase in a rite of passage. Examples from the different societies show that these activities were participatory (recreative leisure) up to the emergence of the "primitive" state. With political power becoming hereditary (monarchial) and community land ownership ending, a leisure class is formed. Some of the participants in a given activity then become performers, while the members of the leisure class become spectators/audience. An incipient form of leisure evolves: amusive leisure, which to Aristotle is the third form (the second form is recreative leisure, and the first is contemplative leisure). The existence of leisure class becomes quite clear when intermediate societies are discussed in chapters 5 and 6.

REVIEW QUESTIONS

1. What are the characteristics of a "primitive" society?
2. In what way does the early human band differ from a tribe? What effect does this have on leisure?
3. Why are chiefdoms so entitled? Does this have any bearing on leisure?
4. Veblen believes that the leisure class possibly appeared in societies that we now call "primitive states." Discuss this notion.

SUGGESTED READINGS

Blanchard, K., and A. Cheska. 1985. *Anthropology of sport: An introduction.* South Hadley, MA: Bergin & Garvey.

Mead, M. 1937. *Cooperation and competition among primitive people.* New York: William Morrow.

Royce, A. P. 1977. *The anthropology of dance.* Bloomington: Indiana University Press.

Wood, J. 1871. *The uncivilized races of man.* Hartford, CT: J. B. Burr.

5

CLASS LEISURE AND INTERMEDIATE SOCIETIES I

In the previous chapter, some of the societies discussed were characterized by stratification, central organization, and relatively secure territorial boundaries. Nonetheless, they lacked the necessary step to be considered intermediate societies: a written language. (Many societies were interpenetrated with written languages not their own, and so continued at the primitive stage.)

According to Parsons, among the first societies to enter the intermediate stage were Egypt and Mesopotamia. Yet the literacy acquired there was esoteric, in that it was limited to priests and so was a craft literacy (1966:52). In these archaic societies, the priesthood administered the cult in a temple, a step that differentiates those societies from even the most advanced of the primitive societies. The temple itself became a focal point because of its social significance and its economic connections, and the cults expanded beyond kinship and the local community. Yet political and re-

ligious leadership continued to be controlled by particular lineage, with significant overlap between the political and religious.

The society itself revolved around three class patterns: the nobility headed by a monarch with a combined religious and political authority; a small middle class responsible for the routine functioning of society; and the mass of tillers of the soil, craftsmen, and merchants.

In most of these societies a cosmological cultural system developed, a system of beliefs concerned with the beginning and composition of the world or universe. In comparison with the previous level, the society was concerned with its own history, and not with that of the whole world. Such a shift in emphasis led to the appearance of a highly specialized priesthood and the hierarchy that governs it. Rituals were also affected by the shift to concentration on the cosmos.

EVOLUTION OF RITUAL

Two theorists of ritual, Gastor (1961, 1962) and Turner (1969, 1977, 1982a, 1982b), agree that there occurred an evolution from primitive ritual to new forms of ritual. Gastor believes primitive ritual could have evolved into literary composition, leaving a deposit of writings that bear marks of their ritual origin. Ritual sometimes shifted from a seasonal basis to a historical-political basis. Also, in the course of time, what was done ritually by a whole group came to be focused on one representative of the whole. This representative became a performer, the rest spectators. There seem to be

three agents for this evolution in the history of rituals: (1) the performers, (2) playfulness of the spectators, and (3) urbanization.

In chapter 4 we saw an example of the appearance of performers of dance among the Ashanti of West Africa. In lieu of total community participation, the royal palace selected a group of women to perform dances. Such a step necessitated two elements: enough leisure to allow for the release of a number of women from social and/or work obligation; and enough surplus to allow for such leisure. This level of societal evolution, the entry into intermediate society, was usually accompanied by the appearance of cities, or urbanization.

This brings us to playfulness of spectators who were, at the previous level of ritual, participants. Not all rituals will evolve from total participation of the community to a dichotomized ritual of performers and spectators. Also, not all ritual will be dominated by the playful element. Turner, the second theorist who devoted his life to the study of ritual, has emphasized that the ludic quality will automatically take over the ritual once the participants give way to one or two representatives.

According to Grimes (1982:150), Turner's theory of liminality, which was discussed earlier, stood the anthropology of ritual on its head. To Turner, ritual is no longer a Durkheimian collective representation that both reflects the society and ensures its solidarity. Ritual possesses the generating force of cultural and social transition. The question then arises: can ritual be a source both of affirmation and of creativity? The answer is yes, since evolution is not necessarily linear and unidirectional; rather, it branches out, with each branch finding its own niche in society. In fact, some branches die out when no niche is found in their social system. Others become differentiated and complex.

Myth, Ritual, and Agon

Language, the most effective method of communication, is associated with ritual. Is it possible that the expressive cries during ritual (naming those who are present, or invoking those who are not present) led to the rise of myth (Burkert 1983:30)? The relationship between myth and ritual is subject to great controversy, in that some scholars believe that myth is often a misunderstood ritual, while others believe that myth is the outspoken part of the ritual. Nonetheless, myth, in comparison to fairy tale or folklore, is connected to ritual. At best, it is more or less a traditional tale.

Burkert believes that ritual dramatizes the order of life while myth clarifies it. Myth adds two dimensions beyond social interaction, which is the realm of ritual, for myth underscores sexuality and

aggression. "The as-if element in the ritual becomes mythical reality; conversely, the ritual confirms the reality of myth. In this way, by mutually affirming each other, myth and ritual become a strong force in forming a cultural tradition" (1983:34).

Since speech (the way of myth) is superior to the act (the way of ritual), myth may supplant ritual. One word could easily replace a ritual dance. Language is powerful and flexible, but it is also fickle. It can be abused or used to deceive, and the community would find it necessary to revert back to ritual.

Burkert implied that a sense of community arises from collective aggression (Lornez 1966), which gives rise to sacrificial ritual. While I agree that a community arises from a need for collectivity, aggression is not necessarily universal; it is a learned behavior (Fromm 1973).

Sacrificial Ritual

The ritual of killing animals and humans served as a mode for collectivity in some early societies but not necessarily in all of them. Ancient India, for example, did not have sacrifices. On the other hand, in the New World societies and the early Mediterranean societies communal festivals and ceremonies included sacrificial rituals. The closer the bond, the more gruesome the ritual (Burkert 1983:36). This was particularly true among Aztecs.

The shock created by killing, even an animal, is rectified through reparation and re-construction. Reparation lies in the custom of collecting bones, skull, and horns, and burying them. Constructing sacrificial edifices above the burial ground is the next step in mitigating the shock. On the anniversary, the community repeats the sacrificial ritual; for in the sacrifice there is renewal of life through the consumption of the sacrificial meat. Altars and statues are set on top of the victims in the course of a ritual. Another form of reconstruction is blowing breath into the bone-flute, and playing the turtle shell lyre or the tympanum covered by the victim's hide. According to Burkert (1983:39), a slain man is easily made a hero, or even a god, because of his horrible end. The ritual would take place at his funeral. Myth would possibly emerge out of the ritual. A significant example is the murder and subsequent deification of Caesar.

As social life becomes more complex, ritual becomes more symbolic. Also, hunting/food gathering societies give way to agricultural societies. In these societies, with their domesticated animals, the importance of hunting declines. Men's roles change drastically as women share the work. Men form their secret societies, whose initiates become the victims. They are to be sacrificed, but a sacrificial animal is substituted at the last minute. The ritual continues to fulfill its function—preservation of the social structure. Once again life arises from the perils of death. There is a resurrection and a rebirth.

According to Burkert (1983:47), "male societies find stability in confronting death, in defying it through a display of readiness to die, and the ecstasy of survival." No wonder, then, that on the grave reliefs of ancient Grecian youth they are depicted as hunters, warriors, or athletes. While the hunter and the warrior face real death, the athlete faces a symbolic death through defeat. In fact, among the Aztecs, the losing captain in the ball game was actually sacrificed.

Funerary Ritual

Grief over a dead person may lead mourner(s) to direct their frustration toward the cause of death. Since the cause is unknown in many instances, the emotion may return upon the mourner in weeping, wailing, tearing one's clothing or hair, scratching the face, beating the breast, smearing one's face, or strewing one's head with dirt or ashes. Seeking a substitute for self-destruction, sacrificial animals or humans were used and still are used in many societies. "Once again death is mastered when the mourner becomes a killer" (Burkert 1983:53).

There seems to be a connection between funerals and competitive contests. Very clear examples of these come to us from the Greek *agon* (see "Ancient Greece," this chap.).

The Macedonians pretended to fight a battle after the dog-sacrifice at the ceremony of purification in Xandika (Burkert 1983:5). In Rome, a ritual battle took place between two groups at the October horse festival. Examples of the relationship between these "new" forms of ritual and leisure will be given in the discussion of the second level of societal evolution—intermediate societies.

Class Leisure

As was shown toward the end of the previous chapter, community ownership of land ends with the rise to power of a family or a clan that dominates the religious, political, and economic life of the society. Among the many privileges that the "new group" would gain is ample free time for its members to participate in activities that are usually unique to them. The troop of dancers attached to the royal palace among the Ashanti is an example. There are no royal palaces at the previous levels of societal development, let alone a troop of royal dancers. As the society moves into the intermediate stage of development, the new leisure class "enjoys" activities that are originally limited to them. Such development does not occur at the expense of the ritualized leisure that was practiced at the earlier level.

Members of the new elite class continue to participate, though much less so, in the ritualized activities of the group. But their own activities begin to take shape and eventually find a niche in the social order. Eventually, the combination of ritualized and class leisure, or aspects of this, will be practiced by the common man. But such development is a long way in the future.

LEISURE AND NEW WORLD SOCIETIES

Some of the early societies of the New World—the Mayans, the Incas, and the Aztecs—are good examples of the early level of intermediate societies, having had written glyphs depicting their spoken languages. The following are descriptions of their social structures, with their ritualized leisure and incipient class leisure.

The Mayans

There is no tangible record of the origin and development of the Mayan society from 2,000 B.C.E. to C.E. 900. It was then that they began their great descent from the highlands into the Yucatan peninsula. There they built cities, erected temples, provided ball courts, raised maize, and sculpted art.

There too, the society became stratified into a nobility who were in full control and the masses who were wedded to the soil. Each family was assigned a piece of land, about four hundred square feet. Monogamy was the rule among the masses. Matchmakers were employed when the son reached the right age. The adobe houses of the common people stood in contrast to the stone houses of nobility.

Mayapan is the only Mayan capital we know of from a written glyph history. It gave its name to the league of city-states around it. Mayapan included temples with ceremonial centers, gateways, ball courts, sweat baths, and raised platforms where drama was presented. The Mayan society had other large cities as well.

The Mayan year was divided into 18 months of 20 days each, leaving an extra five-day lucky period. Each month had its special festivals. *Pop*, the new year, fell in our July, and was the time for renewal. In the last three months of the year, the festivals were of a personal nature. Otherwise, the festivals were religious in nature; much, if not all, that happened then had a magical or religious purpose (Von Hagen 1967:156). Each month had a special festival. The literature shows little distinction between the common people and the rulers in their leisure activities.

Having no string instruments, percussion instruments were important in the group music of the Mayans. Drums, particularly, gave a hypnotic feeling to the group, making them act as one. A deer membrane was stretched across the hollow log of a highly decorated wood, high as the beater's breast, and was struck with the hands. If the wind was right, the sound could be heard two miles away. Another drum rested on the ground, with the drummer sitting on it while it was beaten. A third drum was beaten with sticks tipped with rubber. The dancers themselves held small drums made out of tortoise shell. Conch shells were made into trumpets that carried a dull sound. Other trumpets made of wood or ceramics carried the melody. A human leg bone or a deer femur was made into a six-note flute. Bells of gold, silver, or copper were tied to the legs, waist, or wrists of the dancers.

The dance of the reed, which took the whole day, was performed in a large circle of about 150 performers. At a given signal, two performers leapt into the middle of the circle. One was the hunter, the other the hunted. For the most part, men danced with men and women with women.

Dramatic presentations took place along with the dances. In fact, stages were built for these performances, both indoors and outdoors (Von Hagen 1967:160). The drama included farces and comedies for the pleasure of the public. This represented an increase in amusive leisure at the expense of recreative leisure.

But the passion of the Mayans was the game of *Pok-a-rok,* which was played with a rubber ball on a long, rectangular court in an "][" shape, with tiered seats on both sides for spectators. In the middle and on both sides of the court, often as high as 30 feet, was a stone ring, vertically placed. Using their elbows, knees, and hips, the players try to pass the rubber ball through the stone ring. The team who scores first wins. The game was no longer played by the Mayans at the time of the Spanish conquest, and scholars had to fall back on a description of how the game was played by the Aztecs. But the game had also been described in the Mayan archives.

The Incas

The people over whom the Incas established their rule about 600 years ago were natives to the Andes and surrounding areas of today's Peru. A cultural evolution had been taking place for 3,000 years prior to the Incas' takeover. The political pattern, and in turn the economic patterns as well, became basically pyramidal. For each ten workers there was a straw boss; ten straw bosses had a foreman; ten foremen in turn had a supervisor, the head of the village; and so on to the governor of the province, and to the Inca himself. For every 10,000 people, there were 1,331 officials (Von Hagen 1967:244).

By age 20, a man was expected to get married to someone picked for him, and every married couple was given a plot of land 300 × 150 feet. They lived in an adobe house with no doors or windows. Work began at daybreak in the terraced fields and ended before sunset.

Holidays were public ceremonies in which all people participated, and were bound to the market and to the agricultural year. The Inca year began in December with the "magnificent festival." Coming-of-age rituals coupled with public sport and games were included in the first festival of the year. The festival lasted for a few days, with public dancing that was essential to a good festival (Von Hagen 1967:263).

The dances were sedate, being limited by their musical instruments. Drums made from hollow logs and covered either with llama or tapir hide were beaten by a rubber-knobbed stick. Tambourines were also used, along with bells of copper or silver mounted on clothing, bracelets, or wooden maces. Sometimes anklets of bells, shells, and snail shells were attached to the dancer's legs. Monotonic trumpets made of enormous conch shells added to the stirring of the performers. Flutes made of human and animal bones were also used.

According to Von Hagen (1967:264), all forms of religious expression involved dancing, and dancing was bound to the music. The dance itself included singing, which led to collective hypnosis. The songs were repeated endlessly, monotonously; and the revolution of the dancers, with their rapid movement, gave the spectators the feeling that all their needs had been satisfied.

The dance was also dramatic in that masks and costumes were important parts. Some dancers dressed in mimicry of animals. The farm dance was done with farmers carrying their equipment and tools, and formal dances were led by the Inca royal family.

When the Inca died, the new Inca fasted for three days before he was crowned, a festive occasion for pomp, dancing, and drinking. The Inca's life was governed by elaborate rituals. He travelled around the empire in majesty, seated in rich litters, fed on gold plates, and encountered by his subjects. The society became exploitative in that it demanded goods and services from the masses to support the special nonproducing groups, the leisure class of priests, warriors, and nobles.

The Aztecs

The Aztecs, the native people of Mexico, are one of history's great social climbers, evolving from band, to tribe, to chiefdom, to state in three centuries (Farb 1968:208). After years of wandering, they found two unoccupied islands in the marshes that surrounded today's Mexico City. They believed themselves to be chosen people who, it had been prophesied, would found a mighty city at the place where they saw an eagle sitting upon a cactus, devouring a snake.

The religion of the Aztecs was similar to the religions of ancient Egypt and Mesopotamia in that there was an absence of shamans. Instead, the temple priests, who exercised no supernatural power of their own, performed the sacred rites. The shamans of the previous stages in societal development were impelled by inner religious feelings rather than by special training.

At this level of societal evolution, an increased number of priests participate in, and in fact maintain, a tight grip on ritual. Depending on the societal and cultural orientation, the ritual may be deprived of the play element that was seen earlier and become solemn and serious. In fact, in the case of the Aztecs it became rather grim.

Human sacrifice in the Aztec ritual reached unprecedented proportion in cruelty and in numbers. Farb (1968:228) believes that once their religion initiated human sacrifice to forestall an expected cataclysm, sacrificial victims could not be obtained but through war; but war could be won only by human sacrifice; and a vicious circle grew in the Aztec's lives. This created an enormous problem for the Aztecs: the lingering hatred of the people whom the Aztecs had conquered but failed to incorporate into their own system. Such hatred was exploited by the Spaniard Cortés.

Another problem was that the Aztec society became very highly stratified (Soustelle 1962:37). The hereditary nobility were the policy-makers who lived on their own land, whereas the majority of the population lived in neighborhoods made of smaller kinship units. Each neighborhood had its temple and sometimes a military school. Between the nobility and the masses were the "managers," who were usually the original owners of the conquered land. According to Farb (1968:221), Diaz del Castillo was awed by the luxury in which Moctezuma lived, his palace, and the great number of dancers he kept for amusement. The palace also had a royal zoo and a private show of monstrosities of nature.

Aztec religion was very complex, based on repetition of cyclical rituals. The year was divided into 18 months with 20 days each, with five "dangerous" days. A special ceremony was held each month in which every Aztec was obligated to participate. Moreover, the rituals instituted, called rites of intensification, reinforced recollections of the old ways. In other words, the rites became objects of conservation. These rituals are good examples of liturgy rather than celebration.

In the month of *Tlaxochimaco,* there was a solemn dance that took place at noon, since it was a dance for the god of the sun. Here the warriors was arranged according to rank, with youths from district schools at the end. They held hands with a woman placed between every two men. The most seasoned warriors were allowed to hold the women by the waist. They sang as they danced.

According to Soustelle (1962:144), the dignitaries bore the brunt of the lengthy, complicated, and frequent rites. There was a fresh set of rites and ceremonies for each of the year's 18 months. During the five intercalary days of evil omen, all activities were reduced to a minimum. But the festivities called for great effort and required time and money. For instance, during the first seven days of the month, the emperor had all the population served with food and drink. Every evening at sunset, songs and dances began, and for long hours the warriors and the women held hands, danced, and sang well into the night.

Leisure Class. Those of means among the Aztecs loved to hear poetry as they ate or while taking cocoa after the meal. They loved, too, to hear a song sung to the accompaniment of flutes and drums. Sometimes, the guests danced to the sounds of these instruments. But hunting, for the pleasure of it, was the leisure class's favorite pastime. "In their gardens and their parks, and in the game-filled countryside, they went after birds with their blowpipes" (Soustelle 1962:158).

Among the amusements of the wealthy Aztecs was *tlachtli,* a ball game limited to nobility (Von Hagen 1967:61) and which had religious significance. The court on which it was played represented the world, and the rubber ball a heavenly body. On the side walls of the court were two carved stone rings, and if one of the sides managed to knock the ball through either of them, that side won the game. It was an extremely difficult game since the players were not allowed to touch the ball with their hands or feet; only their knees or their hips.

According to Soustelle (1962:24), the Mexican emperors had grown used to a way of life that the higher dignitaries imitated. The young men would come from the local schools in the evening to their palaces to sing and dance, while skillful singers and musicians were ready in another room with their drums, flutes, bells, and rattles.

In the combination of recital, song, dance, and music, one finds the elements of dramatic art, for in these performances some actors dressed to represent historical or mythical heroes. These performances were at once ballet and tragedy; there was also an exchange between characters and choir. No wonder that Pieper (1964:xix) suggests that "culture depends for its very existence on leisure, and leisure in its turn, is not possible unless it has a durable and consequently living link with the cultus."

LEISURE AND ANCIENT MEDITERRANEAN SOCIETIES

The societies presented in this section had written languages that either disappeared, as in the case of Mesopotamia and Egypt, or are no more in use, as in the case of Greece and Rome. Their cultural systems have had great impact on human thinking, but their social systems are no longer followed. Their influence on leisure, particularly that of Greece and Rome, is tremendous, for they led the world into class leisure.

Mesopotamia

In the land between the two rivers, the Euphrates and the Tigris, relatively autonomous city states arose and began to control the agricultural territory around them. Originally the cities were run in a democratic fashion, as was the case with most early societies. But with the growth of theocracy, there was a tendency toward a separation of power, with the governor and other priests increasing their social distance from the masses.

External threats by outside forces led to the selection of a capable, courageous leader and the adoption of the institution of kingship. Eventually the whole region was consolidated under a single religio-political system, stratifying the society into a three-level complex: a gentry class of notables and priests, a small class of merchant-traders, and a mass of peasants and artisans. As happened in the societies governed by chiefdoms, chiefs and priests in Mesopotamia did not produce foodstuffs but accepted or required gifts (Service 1975:212). In other words, they became a leisure class.

To protect the society from fragmentation, the various kings of Mesopotamia emphasized their religious legitimation. Accordingly, the New Year ceremonies were important to re-establish the king's solidarity with divine forces. That led to what is described by Oppenheim (1964:181) as the royal religion, which was separated from that of the priest and that of the common man. The priest's religion was centered on the service of the images in the temple. The religion of the common people is the unknown element in Mesopotamian religion, for they were not allowed in the temple. They were given the opportunity to admire it only from afar. They became spectators when the images were carried in processions or displayed as a part of the temple's wealth and pomp. The only person who had the right to claim the cultic functions of the temple was the king.

Leisure Class. Three types of cuneiform text were used by Oppenheim to analyze Mesopotamian religion: prayers, ritual, and mythological texts. While prayer was always linked to concomitant ritual of the cults, in their myth is evident not only creativity but a great deal of contemplation. Oppenheim (1964:181) believes that "these literary formulations are the work of Sumerian court poets and of the old Babylonian scribes imitating them." They were not only literary but insightful, as Kramer (1961:95) indicates:

> Intellectually speaking, the Sumero-Akkadian myths reveal a rather mature and sophisticated approach to the gods and their divine activities; behind them can be recognized considerable theological and cosmological reflection (emphasis added).

Such reflection required time freed from work and work-related activities. Other than that, it appears that the war-like atmosphere prevailing in Mesopotamia did not allow for as much leisure as in ancient Egypt. Their real contribution to leisure was the park concept. They established the first known parks, called public gardens. According to Doell and Fitzgerald (1954), their parks included in their confines freely roaming lions and gazelles. Hunts were arranged in these parks. Lion hunting in chariots and on foot with the use of spears was practiced. One of the most famous parks was the

Hanging Gardens of Babylon, where feasts, assemblies, and royal gatherings took place. Other leisure activities were boxing, wrestling, archery, and a variety of table games. The dancing and music that were part of the religious ceremony were also included in the social life of the nobility.

Ancient Egypt

The class structure in ancient Egypt may have been symbolized by the pyramid itself, with the top more sacred than in the previous level of societies and the bottom more profane. To understand the ancient Egyptian society, its religion must be understood. Understanding the Pharaoh is of utmost importance since he was himself God. On the other hand, when it was expedient that one man should die for his people, it was the Pharaoh (Murray 1963:111). A bite from the cobra was used to put him to death. The lungs and heart of the king were removed and buried unmummified in the ploughed land to give breath (life) to the earth (Murray 1963:113).

This may have been the most important ritual in ancient Egypt, but other rituals came down through history as dramatics. *Horus and Setekh* was a drama to celebrate the victory of *Horus,* his coronation over a unified Egypt, dismemberment of his foe, and his justification before the tribunal of gods in the Broad Hall. It was actually a narrative, recited by a reader, with a prologue, three acts divided into scenes, and an epilogue. Other rituals included storytelling and triumph and love songs.

All these were performed in the temples that dotted the Nile up and down the Egyptian countryside. The emphasis was on the solemn and not the playful. It was no accident that Egyptian rituals were more liturgical than they were ceremonial. The chief center seems to have been a mystery play, showing forth the passion, death, burial, and resurrection of Osiris. In Ptolemic times, this became a puppet play, but under the Pharaohs the performers were living actors, and there is little doubt that in early times the men who took the part of Osiris and Setekh were actually sacrificed.

Other occasions were more festive. For instance, the Feast of Opet began when the shrine of the god Amun was carried from the Karnak Temple to his barge by shaven-headed priests, to go up the Nile to the other temple, which is now called the "Luxor" Temple. The entire city of Thebes came to the river bank to see the god's procession. Along the bank paraded all the conglomerated exotica of be-feathered African drummers, bands of lute-playing girls, blind harpists, the priestly singers, naked dancing women, and the wrestlers (Romer 1984:49).

Eight months later, for the Feast of the Valley, Amun crossed the river in his barge to visit the temples of the west. His barge was pulled across the river by a boat that held rows of oarsmen. On the west bank the Pharaoh rested for a few days and was entertained by an army of musicians, dancers, singers, and wrestlers that he brought with him from the east bank.

Leisure Class. The leisure class in ancient Egypt was one of nobility and high officials, who formed a small, closed stratum in society and enjoyed the good life. Among their leisure pursuits was the formal banquet. Remnants of the world's oldest papyrus, from the Seventh Dynasty of 3,000 years B.C.E., were found at Sakkara where the Pharaoh Zoser built his step pyramid. Included in the find was an invitation to a banquet. The menu called for barley porridge, quail, kidneys, pigeon stew, fish, ribs of beef, honey cake, and the cherry-like fruit of the siddar tree. As soon as the guests arrived, they went into a special room to be scrubbed, anointed, scented, and beflowered. They progressed to a reception hall for wine with music, enhancing the welcome. In ancient Egypt, men and women ate together, a custom which soon disappeared in Greece, Rome, and medieval Europe. Dwarf wrestlers and storytellers enlivened the first course. Dancing girls followed, alternating between slow erotic dances and wild acrobatic stunts. The complex choreography included splits, pirouettes, cartwheels, somersaults, and backbends (Ibrahim 1978:53).

According to Romer (1984:52), traditionally, a male harper sang at these feasts to encourage the revellers to enjoy themselves. One song, already 300 years old, was still popular:

Follow your desire,
Allow the heart to forget . . .
Dress yourself in garments of fine linen . . .
Increase your beauty,
And let not your heart languish.

Follow your desire and what is good.
Conduct yourself on earth
After the dictates of your heart . . .
Celebrate.
But tire not yourself with it.
Remember, no man takes his goods with him,
And none have returned after going.

Another popular activity among the elite of ancient Egypt was "sport," if it can be called that. These ancient people had no word for what we mean by *sport* today. They used expressions such as *it sum,* "to occupy oneself with," *sd jhr,* "to enjoy," and *shmh ib,* "to delight the heart with." All these meant to engage in sport. The relationship between "sport" and religion was very strong in ancient Egypt. Praise of Sekhet, goddess of the marshes, was interwoven into descriptions of the joy of the chase. This particular type of activity, fowling and fishing, was enjoyed by the whole family. A stock scene in an Egyptian tomb painting shows the noble throwing sticks at a flock of geese, while his wife clings to his waist, a daughter to his leg (a stylized way of depicting the family group), while another daughter appears in the background, imitating her father's hunting form.

On one of the murals of the Beni Hassan Temple a frieze of wrestlers shows at least 400 positions. What is depicted on the walls of the temple might have been sham matches performed at a religious festival.

The commoners started to imitate the nobility, and a number of festivals took place in the larger rooms of the village houses and on open land around the village. The villagers held their public feasting in open air in garlanded pavilions built especially to shade them from the sun. There was music, dancing, and red wine to drink. Guests sat with flowers in their hands. Drummings, rattlings, the bouncing rasp of stringed percussion, and the liquid sounds of lutes and flutes were heard. Nude dancing girls tattooed with blue patterned dots and small images of the god Bes performed in rhythmic acrobatic display.

Ancient Greece

Unlike in Mesopotamia and Egypt, central control over Greece was impossible. First, the Gulf of Corinth cuts the peninsula into two sections. Secondly, the valleys are separated by large limestone mountains. Thirdly, a series of islands to the east seems to be a continuation of the mainland, ending south with the island of Crete. Mountains and the sea separate the regions from each other. There emerged in these islands city-states, characterized by strong local loyalty. Yet the inhabitants of these city-states spoke some form of the same language, worshipped the same gods, and followed similar customs. Eventually, they saw themselves as one people.

At first, historians discarded the claim that the ancient Greeks were descended from the legendary heroes, until uncovered evidence showed that rich civilizations flourished prior to 1200 B.C.E. For centuries, the Minoans of Crete were a lively, pleasure-loving, and peace-loving sensuous people. They were fond of colors, intricate games, and elegant cloth. On the mainland, the Mycenaeans built their homes with ten-foot thick walls; in their tombs they left death masks made of gold, bronze swords, and silver cups. Clay tablets containing the official records were found, which showed that the Mycenaeans had an efficient bureaucracy headed by a king and assisted by an officialdom. The records showed that they were taxed, had titled land holdings, and owned slaves. The Mycenaeans had close to one hundred occupations, yet reverted to piracy. They attacked the Hittites of today's Ankara, Turkey, and besieged the city of Troy for ten long years. Within a century they succumbed to the Dorian invaders from the north. From 1200 B.C.E. to 750 B.C.E. ancient Greece fell into a Dark Age. For five and a half centuries the ancient Greeks lived on the old glories of Mycenae and Minos.

Some of the Mycenaeans moved north into a small hamlet called Athens. Another settlement by the Dorians became known as Sparta. Centuries later, these two city-states represented opposing philosophies in Greek life: the intellectual and political freedom of Athens versus the stern, military discipline of Sparta.

The population pressure led to emigration, which began around 1100 B.C.E., toward the Aegean Islands and the western coast of Asia Minor. The new settlement was called Ionia. Despite the distance, the Ionians were extremely conscious of their ties with the homeland. The epic songs and stories kept the ties and were passed from generation to generation. The epic stories drew upon several kinds of legends or myths concerning gods and men alike, the climax of which came in the latter part of the eighth century B.C.E., with Homer's two great epic poems, the *Iliad* and the *Odyssey*. He represented the new spirit that flowered in Ionia. Developments in the arts followed in Ionia, and the Greek homeland began to copy and compete with the colonies. Localism aside, the people mingled somewhat freely in the several *poleis* (sing., *polis*), drawn together by communal religious rites and festivals.

The appearance of the Greek alphabet, an adaptation of the alphabet of Phoenicia, led to closer relations still. Now that a written language had been adopted, Greece entered the intermediate stage of societal development, as suggested by Parsons (1966). Now laws could be incised on stone and set up in the public square for all the people to read. Records could be kept, and trade treaties could be made more precise. A Hellenic culture became a reality.

The polis went through a period of revival economically, culturally, and politically from the eighth century B.C.E. on, which eliminated all the

kings or reduced them to figureheads in almost all the poleis. Authority fell into the hands of local aristocracy. Under their leadership, the polis acquired stable government, which led to the rich civic life that distinguished Greece. Within two centuries, Greek art, music, poetry, literature, philosophy, and sport reached great proportions.

Leisure Class. For the first time in history, the question of leisure was taken very seriously. The term used was *schole,* which meant to halt or cease, hence to have quiet or peace. It came to mean having time for oneself, for free time used unwisely is not leisure. Aristotle condemned Sparta for using leisure to prepare for war and Spartan women for their licentiousness.

Schole meant being occupied in something desirable for its own sake: noble music, noble poetry, the company of noble friends, and mainly the exercise of the speculative faculties. The exercise of the speculative faculties was supported by the Greek religion, which encouraged inquiry into the nature of things. Curiosity made the gods' marvelous work known to man. To the aristocratic elite, the pursuit of knowledge gave as much pleasure as the enjoyment of the fine arts (de Grazia 1962:11).

The Athenian aristocrats loved to play. They had time for good talk and, on occasion at the end of the day, a rousing banquet. At the banquet, the guests at first concentrated on the food. Next came the symposium, which was also a drinking session. The symposiarch, chosen for his expertise or by a throw of a die, controlled the amount of water mixed with the wine, and called the entertainers in: dancing girls, acrobats, and magicians. A symposiarch, like Socrates, might pose tough riddles for his audience. Others may have organized games among the guests (Ibrahim 1978).

Dionysius was the god of fertility whose power was applied to the wine. Four festivals were held a year in his honor. They were the festival of Vintage, or Rural Dionysia, in December; the Winepress, or Linaea, in January; the festival of tasting, or Anthestria, in March; and finally, the festival of celebration where Greek drama became dominant. These festivals dominated public life. According to

Burkert (1983:213), Anthestria is one of the earliest of the Greek festivals. It dealt with Dionysius and wine, and attracted attention for three reasons: as a children's festival, as a festival of the dead, and as a festival of fertility. People gathered for the collective celebration of tasting the new wine. Participants were, first, anyone who joined; "later the performers were specialized, just as in the primitive drama elsewhere" (Roberts 1962:23). Tasting was done by mixing wine with water at the sanctuary of Dionysius in the marshes, where the celebration of song and dance grew into a drinking competition.

When a child became three years of age, he was taken to the festival and given a wreath of blossoms, his own table, and a wine pitcher; this initiated him into the Athenian society. It was a festival of death because the drinking of new wine fulfilled the function of a sacrificial meal; the wine represented the blood of a god, Dionysius, torn apart (Burkert 1983:225). The temple was administered by a priestess, who had the most spectacular role to play in the festival: she was given to the god as his bride.

During the Anthestria, so goes the legend, masked spirits or aboriginal inhabitants invaded the city and its homes together with the new wine. They rode on the oxen-pulled carts and pursued with lewd gestures anyone they saw. The Athenians' wine pitchers began to depict grotesque faces that induced terror and aggression.

It is theorized that Greek drama started around Dionysius' temple about 534 B.C.E. All that was required then was an open space for performers, an altar (sacrificial table), and temporary wooden bleachers for the spectators. When the bleachers collapsed, a new site was dedicated to Dionysius, located south of the Acropolis and overlooking the Agora. The temple included an altar and an orchestra (dancing place) (Butler 1972:29).

Theatrical productions in Athens were confined to great yearly festivals. The Greek Dionysia and Lenaea became the focus of comedy. Playwrights submitted their scripts and applied for chorus. Once the script was accepted, the playwright could direct, choreograph the dances, design the set, and also act if need be. The chorus was an effective part of the play. All actors wore masks, which was a carryover from the previous era of the Dionysian Festival. The performers combined dramatic action, poetic dialogue, dancing, and singing with flute music. According to Butler, the audience was volatile and enthusiastic, "more characteristic of present day football and baseball spectators than the quiet, decorous, often passive demeanor exhibited by our theater audiences" (1972:69).

Once again, we see the participants in a leisure activity branching out into performers-spectators, in contrast to the previous practice when most of the people present were participants who wore masks, danced, and sang. Perhaps the reason for their volatility and enthusiasm is that they thought of themselves as actual participants. The chasm between performers and spectators grew wide over the years, leading to the passivity of today's theater audience, who wait to be amused.

Although the audience in the Greek dramatic festivals included a few women, boys, and possibly slaves, it was predominantly composed of adult males, for it was indeed an activity for the leisure class.

The ancient Greeks referred to music in their literature, had copious theoretical writings about it, and esteemed it as the second most important leisure activity after contemplation. Yet their music was entirely lacking in harmony (Small 1977:37).

According to Richard Mandell, the ceremony that included an acrobatic bull leaping among the Minoans of the island of Crete must have been performed for an audience. The 4,000-year-old frescoes show well-dressed, made-up ladies in what seems to be a spectator's box. Also the "cult surroundings suggest that for the upper or priestly classes, the performers were essential aspects of sacred ritual" (Mandell 1984:30).

The Mycenaeans, who lived in the indented peninsula connected to mainland Greece, were a restless and pushy lot. The aspiration of their "upper classes seems to have been dominated by a generalized internalized compulsion to seek personal supremacy, which came to be called *Agon, later*" (Mandell 1984:34). Architectural, literary, and artistic monuments suggest that for recreation the Mycenaeans mostly hunted or practiced war. This led them to pursue with all their powers certain practices that in most cultures are pursued by children or entertainers, such as foot races, wrestling matches, or weight lifting. Victory was thought pleasing to the gods.

Scholars also believe that athletic contests might have been offered at the funerals of fallen heroes to give them pleasure. Sacrifices and festivals were necessary to appease the spirits of these restless heroes. Excavation at the ancient Olympic site shows that it was used for cult observance for at least one thousand years before the first Olympics took place in 776 B.C.E. In one section of the *Iliad*, Achilles organizes some contests as a tribute to his dead friend Patroclus. Two men wrestled, and the match went on until the spectators became bored. One of the wrestlers prayed to the goddess Athena. Homer's epics, the *Iliad* and *Odyssey,* contain several narratives of foot races, long jump, and spear and discus throwing. These epics served partly as catechism for heroic behavior. Homer made it clear that these contests were adjunct to other gatherings and "were *pursuits exclusively of the warrior-aristocrats* who are characters in the Epics" (Mandell 1984:39; emphasis added).

A few years later, almost every polis in ancient Greece staged athletic games in honor of the gods. They were pan-Hellenic, encompassing all Greece. Four of these games were the most heavily attended: the Olympic Games and the Pythian Games, which were held every four years, and the Nemean Games and the Isthmian Games, which were held every two years. The athletes competed as individuals, not as teams, and strictly as amateurs. Their cities gloried in the victories. Wars among the city-states were put aside for the Games.

The Olympic Games were held in honor of Zeus at Olympia, a group of temples and arenas. Those who came to participate or watch lived in tents and slept in the open. Political leaders arranged peace treaties, and business agreements were consummated. It was more than a religious meeting or a sports event; it was more or less a fair. Among the altars and the statues one could find artists and poets entertaining the crowd. At night, there was always time for a feast.

For the first thousand years of the Olympic Games, from 776 B.C.E. to C.E. 249, the schedule of events remained the same: races of horses and chariots, three combat events, boxing, wrestling, four foot races (200 yards, 400 yards, a long distance race, and a race in armor), as well as the pentathlon (javelin and discus throwing, 200-yard foot race, long jump, and wrestling). The pankration was a fight to the finish, with nothing barred save gouging and biting.

Rome

In its attempt to "neutralize" its neighbors, Rome became engaged in wars with some of the Greek colonies and those who came to their aid from mainland Greece. Confidence followed victory and led to a policy of expansion. Carthage, the pride of the western Mediterranean, was engaged and destroyed. Then Rome destroyed the Seleucid of Syria and the Ptolemies of Egypt and annexed Alexander's Macedonia. It grew larger and richer, but the wealth went to the upper class in Rome. The ordinary Roman farmer found it harder and harder to make a living; the political structure became fragmented. There emerged two political factions, the optimates who were mostly of the old patrician class, and the populares who were mostly of the plebeian class. A third group, the equestrians or knights, were courted by the two.

When the monarchy was eliminated in Rome in 509 B.C.E., a unique system of government evolved: the imperium, where two consuls ruled for a year. One could veto the acts of the other, and neither could institute changes in laws without the other's agreement. The government included a senate and two assemblies. The plebeians and patricians were citizens who served in the army and paid taxes. The basic difference was one of religious status. Certain religious rituals could be performed only by patricians. Since these rituals were prerequisite to holding high office, plebeians were automatically barred from advancement in government. This continued until 187 B.C.E., when the plebeians won the right to pass laws in their own assembly without the consent of the Senate.

Before expansion, the Romans had been very much affected by the previous Etruscan civilization. A group of Etruscan dancers were invited to Rome to appease the wrath of the gods and to persuade them to withdraw a pestilence supposedly inflicted by them upon the Romans (Butler 1972:73). The Roman youth were very much attracted to the Etruscan dances and added to them dialogue and gestures. It was probably also during that period that some of the Etruscan games found their way to Rome. Grenier believes that these games came originally from Greece (1926:36).

After the Roman expansion, more activities spread to Rome. Wild beasts were brought from African expeditions to be sacrificed in public ceremonies. Greeks of all professions were hired to serve in Rome. For example, out of southern Italy, where the Greeks had some colonies, mime was introduced into Roman leisure life.

The *Ludi Florales* Games, which started in Rome in 238 B.C.E., featured some mimes. The festival was to celebrate the goddess Flora and forestall any famine. Games were held in her honor, and a temple was dedicated on April 28 of that year (Fowler 1925:92).

Roman Games: From Ritual to Amusement.
In general, the *ludi,* or public games, were absent from the old calendar, for they were "adjuncts to certain festivals out of which they had grown in the course of time" (Fowler 1925:16). From then on, after the introduction of the new calendar between 31 B.C.E. and C.E. 46, a number of *ludi* were observed. The first of these was observed from the 4th to the 10th day of the second month, *Mensis Aprilis.* April 4 was made a festival day to commemorate the Roman's victory over Hannibal. A temple where only the nobles attended was dedicated a few years later on April 10. The *Ludi Megalesia* lasted between April 4 and April 10 and

was limited to the upper class. The commoners had to wait until the 12th to start *Ludi Cereales,* which lasted until April 19. The festivals were held in honor of Ceres since the time of the monarchy. The last games in April were the *Ludi Florales,* mentioned above.

There were no public games in the third and fourth months. The fifth month, *Mensis Quinstilis,* witnessed the *Ludi Apollinares,* which commemorated the war with Hannibal. The games had a Greek character in that they included chariot races. They were an appeal to Apollo to show his favor to Rome, to conquer her foe, and avert pestilence in the summer heat. *Ludi Romani,* which took place from the 4th to 12th day of the seventh month, *Mensis September,* was connected with the cult of Jupiter, and began with a sacrifice. Only the magistrates and the Senate partook of the sacrifice. Fowler theorizes that the whole Roman community took part, symbolically, through these representatives (1925:219).

Mensis November, the ninth month, witnessed the *Ludi Plebeii,* a festival of little importance, during the ceremony of Isis. This indicates that the festival of the commoners, *Plebeii,* was a late addition, after the infiltration of Egyptian influence. The *ludi,* which took place in *Circus Flaminius,* built in 220 B.C.E., were probably completed, at first, on a single day (November 13), and were gradually extended like *Ludi Romani.* Eventually the *Ludi Plebeii* lasted from November 4 to November 17.

The games, which grew out of ritual and religious observances, became a means whereby a wealthy person might purchase popular favor. The games had great drawing power among the masses and were in open competition with the theater, which the Romans called *Ludi Scaenici.* The games took place in highly specialized buildings. The oldest of these, the circus, was built for horse races that included trick-riding, foot races, mock cavalry battles, and chariot racing. The free-standing amphitheaters witnessed gladiatorial combats. The Colosseum grew out of an amphitheater and allowed for more spectators. *Venatione* featured a variety of animals and hunters and was staged in the Colosseum. Another spectacle was the *naumachiae,* a ship battle, which required flooding the floor of the Colosseum. This spectacle was staged there only once. In 46 B.C.E., Caesar had a special structure built in *Campus Martius* for ship battles. But the greatest of all *naumachiae* was staged by Claudius in C.E. 52 in Lake Fucine, outside Rome, where a total of 19,000 men dressed as Rhodesians and Sicilians boarded a fleet of 50 ships and battled each other from 10:00 A.M. on. By 3:00 P.M., 3,000 of them were dead (Butler 1972:143).

According to Butler (1972:143), Roman theater deteriorated rapidly when it started emulating the *ludi* that drew the masses away from it. The "paratheatrical qualities of personating, costuming, staging, miming, along with the pomp *ceremony* and *ritual* gave the Ludi a decided advantage" (emphasis added). The masses wanted more amusive leisure.

In the early days of Rome there were fewer than 50 holidays in the year; by the first century B.C.E., there were 76 holidays. Rome committed itself to a policy of "bread and circuses" to palliate civic abuses, and by the fourth century C.E. the calendar included 175 official holidays, with 101 given over to theatrical entertainments, 64 to chariot races, and 10 to gladiatorial combats (Roberts 1962:57).

SUMMARY

The intermediate societies of the New World and the ancient Mediterranean show that a segment of their populations became powerful enough to become the ruling nobility. With their newly acquired position came the privilege of the leisure class. A small middle class and a mass of tillers, workers, and slaves made up the rest of the population. In the meantime, ritual was evolving from a simple unidimensional concentration on the cosmos to a complex multidimensional cultural system. For instance, sacrificial and funerary rituals started, and through them certain "leisure" activities began to appear: dance, drama, and sport.

Evidence for this comes from the Mayan, Inca, and Aztec societies, as well as from Egypt and Mesopotamia. It was in ancient Greece that leisure came to be considered ennobling. This was also the case in early Rome. Later these activities were used as palliative by the aristocracy. Provision of amusive leisure increased at the expense of recreative and contemplative leisure.

REVIEW QUESTIONS

1. List some of the New World societies. Select one and describe the lifestyle there.
2. What were the contributions of Egypt and Mesopotamia to leisure?
3. Why is Greece, particularly Athens, considered the seat of the Western concept of leisure?
4. What lessons should we learn from Rome's experience with leisure?

SUGGESTED READINGS

Burkert, W. 1983. Homo necans: *The anthropology of ancient greek sacrificial ritual and myth.* Berkeley: University of California Press.

Mandell, R. 1984. *Sport: A cultural history.* New York: Columbia University Press.

Pieper, J. 1964. *Leisure: The basis of culture.* New York: Pantheon Press.

Romer, J. 1984. *Ancient lives: Daily life in Egypt of the pharaohs.* New York: Holt, Rinehart and Winston.

6

CLASS LEISURE AND INTERMEDIATE SOCIETIES II

In this chapter, leisure in medieval societies, both Eastern and Western, will be discussed. Despite vast cultural differences, the social structures were very similar. A small, but powerful upper class dominated the poor lower class, with a very small middle class attempting to emulate the aristocracy. The gap between the rich and the poor was very wide, as if they were from two different worlds, each with its own style and leisure pursuits.

The Eastern societies, in particular, showed little distinction between their ancient and medieval forms. This applies to India, China, Japan, and the Islamic society. In Europe the story was different; a cultural shift based on Christian principles and practices ended the ancient regime, ushering in the medieval period.

LEISURE IN ANCIENT AND MEDIEVAL INDIA

The slow infiltration of an Aryan group from the North into India proper about the second millennium B.C.E. brought a new language and a new religion. The invaders became the upper group and the original inhabitants the lower one. On top was the priestly class, the *Brahmanis;* followed by the warrior-noble, the *Kshatriyas;* and the landlord merchants, the *Vaisyas.* All were twice-born, bearers of culture, and occupiers of privileged positions. The *Sudra* and lower caste worked the land. This system remained until the twentieth century.

The Vedic religion centered around a polytheist pantheon and included a sacrificial cult for which the Brahmans were responsible. Their philosophic speculation about sacrifice led to viewing the world as a timeless entity, made of souls that undergo endless incarnation and reincarnation in the form of all members of the animal kingdom, from the lowliest worms up to man. Standing above was a realm of gods who were also mortal incarnations of souls and lived for thousands of years. Souls were

promoted or demoted according to the individual's actions during his or her lifetime on earth.

The path to salvation was thought to lie in withdrawing from the world and its responsibilities and engaging in mystical contemplation and ascetic exercises. Is this a form of leisure? According to Max Weber (1958), social responsibility was religiously sanctioned but not a prime obligation of life; attaining salvation was. Salvation was articulated through the *dharma* system, which institutionalized otherworldly asceticism and mysticism on an individual basis. Consequently, it creates no collectivity, just as in the Christian Church. In groups focused on the otherworldly, rituals were at a minimum. So the possibility for developing recreative or amusive leisure among the masses was very limited.

From ancient India's religious orientation, there branched out Jainism, Buddhism, and Hinduism. Jainism developed into a sectarian, subterranean cult. Buddhism was completely extruded from India. Hinduism became the basis of the cultural and societal framework of the Indian society. Yet,

Hinduism failed to promote and incorporate societal collectivity and so legitimize the fragmented hierarchical order of society.

It was hardly a unified India. Only one empire gained considerable size and duration in the fourth century C.E. The Brahmans' reaction to an attempt at unification was swift and strong, and India reverted back to smaller principalities and kingdoms. Although this made India subject to foreign rule, most of the invaders, such as Muslims, failed to develop a unifying social system, or to convert the Hindus into another religion.

Leisure Class. The invaders from the North developed a cult that included lengthy consecration and rejuvenation ceremonies. Gambling played a small but significant part in these ceremonies. A gambling hall was attached to the king's palace in the later Vedic period and had some magical or religious significance. The palace had an official who was in charge of royal gambling parties.

Board games were played with dice. By the early centuries of the Common Era, there was a game played on a board of 64 squares, with a king piece and pieces of four other types: an elephant, a horse, a chariot, and four footmen. It was played by four persons, whose moves were controlled by the throw of dice. It was copied by the Persians, who modified it and taught it to the Arabs, who then brought it to Europe as chess.

Initiation rites for boys were confined to the upper group, the Brahmans, the Ksatriyas, and the Vaisyas. The Sudra and lower caste could not undergo it and in fact were not allowed to hear or learn the scripture (Basham 1963:163).

Among the little kingdoms of the early Vedic period, each king attempted to raise himself to the status of a "free monarch." A consecrated horse was set free to roam at will for a year and was followed by a band of warriors. The king on whose land the horse wandered was forced to do homage or fight. Such interaction led to an increase of trade among the different kingdoms. Craft developed in response to the needs of the expanding and now diverse population. For example, the literature of the same period shows that a rudimentary entertainment industry existed to entertain the upper classes. Performers included acrobats, fortune tellers, flute players, and dancers (Basham 1963:43).

The origin of Indian theater is still obscure, but there is evidence that dramatic performances took place in the Vedic period. Passing references in early sources point to drama in festivals of religious legends, usually in dance and mime. There were no regular theaters, and drama was normally performed privately in the palaces or homes of the rich. Eventually, dramatic plays were given public showing in temple courts on the day of the festival.

The chief musical instrument was the *vina*. Loosely translated, it means "lute." Originally, the term was used to describe a bow-harp with ten strings. Conch shells were also used. Percussion instruments were numerous. The smaller ones were played with fingers, and there were cymbals, gongs, and bells as well. Neither music nor dance changed much over the years, and both were very much related to drama. For while drama employed word and gesture, dance employed music and gesture. "As in most other civilizations there is little doubt that in India the drama developed from ritual miming, song, and dance" (Basham 1963:387).

The ancient Indians loved flowers and trees. Beautiful parks surrounded the palaces of the fortunate. There are many references in Sanskrit literature showing that wealthy citizens had gardens attached to their houses, and often larger parks containing pavilions in which they spent much of their leisure (Basham 1963:204). There is a reference to artificial hillocks, with landscaped gardens of the Japanese type.

An expanse of water was an almost essential feature of the garden. The parks of the rich contained ponds and lakes with fountains; steps led down into the lake for bathing. Some palaces had water machines, a revolving spray, for cooling the air in a hot climate. In these "pleasure gardens" (as they were called), there was the indispensable swing in which adults of both sexes took delight.

Among the chief recreations of the well-to-do young Indian were amorous adventures. A treatise on erotica told him to have a pleasant, soft bed in his room, with a pure white coverlet, a decorated canopy, and two pillows—one at the foot and the other at the head of his bed. In the morning he should bathe, clean his teeth, anoint his body with perfume, put collyrium on his eyes, and dye his lips with red lac.

The young member of the leisure class spent most of his time in charming, graceful idleness (Basham 1963:208). Yet he had many intellectual pleasures as well. He was encouraged to be creative: a poet or a patron of the arts. He attended the literary parties in the palace or in homes of the wealthy.

Ritualized Leisure. During ancient and medieval times, India's population was mainly rural, as it is in present-day India. Towns sprang up all over the Indian subcontinent. Each had two foci, the palace and the temple. The temple played an important role in the life of the ordinary Hindu, because from it came the great and splendid religious procession. The idols were placed on massive carts adorned with color calicos, green foliage, and garlands of flowers. The cart was pulled by a hundred men or more, using a thick cable attached to it. A party of dancing girls was seated on the cart by the idol. Drums, trumpets, and conch shells made their sounds ahead of the procession, followed by a group of sham combatants who fenced each other with naked sabres (Dubois 1906:605).

There were 18 Hindu festivals a year. The *Mgadi* was the celebration of the first day of the year. Most of the time was spent in visitations. Another festival was the *Dasara,* which was dedicated to the memory of ancestors as well as to soldiers. In order to increase the solemnity of the feast, the kings gave public entertainment. According to Dubois (1906:570), "These entertainments resemble very much the gladiatorial combats of the Ancient Romans, consisting as they do of contests between animals, or between animals and men, and above all between men." The performers were professionals who belonged to a caste called *Jetti,* and were trained from youth to injure one another in the presence of others. They put on gloves studded with pieces of horn and danced using threatening gestures before beginning to fight. Blood flew freely in the bout, which was stopped only by the umpires. Then two more fighters came in. The spectacle lasted for hours. When it was all over, the king distributed prizes among the champions.

In the festival of *Pongul,* Hindus exchanged visits, then took their cattle outside the town and made them scatter in all directions. In a procession and to the sound of music, the idols were taken from the temple to the place where the cattle had been again collected. The temple dancing girls marched to the large gathering, and from time to time would pause to delight the spectators with their lascivious dances and obscene songs. The festival terminated with the crowd forming a huge circle with a hare loose in the middle. In its efforts to escape, it ran round and round, exciting much laughter among the spectators (Dubois 1906:574).

According to Basham (1963:205), public gardens and parks are often mentioned in old stories. In the vicinity of most cities were groves that became resorts for the city residents. Some of the ancient kings planted these groves for the recreation of men and beast. They probably started as hunting grounds for the leisure class.

LEISURE IN ANCIENT AND MEDIEVAL CHINA

Before 200 B.C.E., China was composed of patrimonial, feudal states, each with a prince who was head of the paramount lineage. He was surrounded by a number of aids who were scholar-officials of the state. These states shared a common culture based on a common language. By 200 B.C.E., China was united politically under the Chin dynasty and later by the Han dynasty.

The Confucian codification became the basis of an educational program that bears significant resemblance to that of the ancient Greeks. The goal was to prepare a broadly cultivated person in both the literary and martial arts. The six subjects, which are referred to as the liberal arts of classical Chinese education, were rituals, music, archery, charioteering, writing, and mathematics. The ideal of education was to develop the harmonious and symmetrical aspects of body and mind. In the latter part of the sixth century B.C.E., despite Confucius' emphasis on liberal education, this ideal eroded with the onslaught of bureaucratic necessities (Levine 1984:237). The institutionalization of the Confucian tradition included an examination system for the holders of imperial public offices, the Mandarins, who became a governing, leisure class.

The establishment of *hsien,* or administrative districts, led to the transition from Chan feudalism to the imperial system. The appointed magistrate lived in the town that was the seat of the *hsein* magistry, which was also the residence of the local gentry. The gentry lived in a large household with many servants. They usually owned the surrounding land, the workshops, and the mercantile enterprises in the town. The household included a parental couple, wives and concubines of the master, his sons and their wives and children, the master's unmarried daughters, and many servants. During the Han dynasty inheritance became equal among the sons, which contrasted with earlier primogeniture, still practiced in Japan and medieval Europe. This broke the power of the feudal lineage and made the gentry into an upper class more like that in western Europe later (Parsons 1966:75).

The masses in China were the peasants who tilled the land. They were not serfs but legally free. Although land could be freely sold or transferred, gentry control made large numbers of peasants tenants. They maintained the same basic household patterns as the gentry, though in a truncated form (Parsons 1966:76).

Before the eleventh century C.E., the ruling class formed a very small elite. But the general structure changed between the eleventh and thirteenth centuries when a small but active class of merchants appeared. They became wealthy, but failed to gain what their counterpart in Europe did—political power and the subsequent recognition of their rights.

Leisure Class. Government administrators gained their position through competitive examinations. Still, they came from a very small number of scholar families who formed a small caste united by common interest. Most of them came from the provinces of southeast China. They enjoyed special legal protection and their careers were fairly secure. The power of a newly rich merchant class surmounted little by little the barriers that once existed between them and that elite group, and both became the leisure class.

The residences of the wealthy consisted of a series of buildings set at right angles, or placed parallel to each other, and separated by a series of courtyards, varying in numbers. Each single building was designed to produce some special picturesque effect. Perhaps one was best for admiring the moonlight, another for music making, another for banquets, yet another, set in the shade of pine and bamboos, for keeping cool in hot weather. The garden had little artificial hills, winding streams with waterfalls, and ponds with silver and goldfish (Gernet 1962:118).

The wealthy kept a retinue of people with special gifts: chess players, painters of chrysanthemums, writers, and setters of riddles. Others were hired to entertain guests at parties: singing girls, musicians, acrobats, and conjurers.

The most talented performers were asked to the mansions of the wealthy, and even the court, at festival times and when banquets were held. A text of 1,230 C.E. lists 55 varieties of performers, including those with extraordinary specialization: tellers of obscure stories, imitators of street cries, imitators of village talk, slight-of-hand experts, flyers of kites, ball players, archers, and crossbowmen.

During the Han dynasty, military victories were celebrated by dances accompanied by music and songs, forming a kind of ballet. Some of these became favorite consort entertainment. Emperor

Ming Huang (C.E. 712–56) became known as the patron of actors and established the first dramatic school for the training of court entertainers, known as the Pear Garden.

With the Mongol conquests, the classical examinations were discontinued, and the scholar-officials were disbanded. They embarked on new forms of amusive leisure as a livelihood. The novels that appeared at that time were based on the tales of the past. Another popular form of literature were plays. They were no longer composed of short scenes like the old court drama but of four acts. The court drama had been acted in a polished language; the new drama was in idiomatic form, and the subjects of plays were also more varied. From the limited court entertainment, the drama swiftly developed into a truly national art. It became, and remains, the chief recreation of the common people of China (Fitzgerald 1933:494).

Despite the scholarly contempt for the novel, the fresh and new form of novel mentioned above flourished. "The storyteller, seated at the street corner with his audience of children and *idlers,* is probably one of the oldest figures in the everyday life of an Eastern country. In China, he has no doubt exercised his calling for millennia" (Fitzgerald 1933:502).

In the Sung dynasty (ca. C.E. 960–1127), the common people, either because they were naturally more frivolous than their ancestors or became more prosperous, had more time to spare for entertainment (Fitzgerald 1933:502). But the decline of highly structured ritual may also have moved them in that direction (Gernet 1962:236).

It seems that the original Chinese rituals went through drastic changes with the coming of nobility. The functions that the rituals fulfilled were now attributed to the Lord. His race became a mighty race whose chiefs shared between them a kind of collegiality with the holy place, the virtue of which confers fitness to govern men and things. They needed to reinvigorate their power through a more direct cult, pertaining more to everyday life

than the periodic festivals of mountains and rivers. Along with residences, they set up their own temples in their own towns.

In addition, the systematic classification carried out by the scholar-officials reduced the festivals to a clutter of rites governed by what Gernet called "the ritual techniques." The primitive rituals gradually disintegrated, giving way to particular ceremonies, sometimes associated with solar dates, sometimes to a kind of mnemotechnic date. The ceremonies were spread throughout the month as so many holidays (1962:237).

From Ritual to Amusement. According to Gernet (1962:225), at festival time, in the thirteenth century of the Common Era, the entire population of the town offered sacrifices at the sacred place, watched ceremonies performed at the altar, and heard imperial amnesties declared, then made merry in the street. The residents of the city spent day and night drinking and wandering about seeking amusement. Among the amusements were boxing matches held between the Left and the Right Armies of the Imperial Guard. The winner was awarded a flag, a silver cup, a length of silk, a brocade robe, and a horse.

Gernet discusses the "pleasure grounds," which were kind of a vast covered market where a gaping crowd collected around an acrobat, watched theatrical presentations, and took lessons in drama, singing, and music. These establishments, according to contemporaries, were places "where no one stood on ceremony," where people of all sorts rubbed shoulders with each other (1962:222).

The pleasure grounds contained instruction centers for music and drama. Each had a director, and the instructors wore costumes that varied according to the group to which they belonged. The musicians played the flute, the Greek drums, the Jann string guitar, or the xylophone. The actors presented short farcical tales, acrobatic turns, and satirical sketches. There were also shadow plays performed with cut-out puppets, and marionette shows featuring puppets pulled by strings.

Gernet relates a Chinese author's description, at the end of the thirteenth century, of what he had seen in the pleasure grounds. There was a man showing performing turtles. In a large bowl in which turtles were swimming, he would beat on a small bronze gong and call up one of the turtles by name. It came up, danced on the surface, and when it was finished dove down. There was a snake charmer, who held the strongest and most deadliest snake in his hand. Then there was a Taoist hermit, who carried on his back a creel full of shellfish, all of them hypnotized (1962:256).

LEISURE IN ANCIENT AND MEDIEVAL JAPAN

Its isolation from the Asian continent gave Japan a security that led to a unified empire and a distinct civilization by the sixth century of the Common Era. Buddhism, which arose in northern India and reached Japan about that time, was absorbed, flourished, and became an important element in a distinctively Japanese civilization. It coexisted with Japan's ancient religion, Shintoism. Confucianism, though it had less influence than Buddhism, had a lasting effect upon the Japanese culture.

Japan maintained an open door policy around the sixth century of the Common Era, which allowed a great number of skilled workers to migrate from Korea, China, and beyond. The most influential of these were the writers and scribes. Japan witnessed at that time a rapid rise in the leisure class. The privileged nobles, monks, priests, and warriors were supported in increasing luxury by a farming population (Sansom 1936:171). Although Japan adopted the concept of examination and education for government officials, it was not taken seriously, since the Japanese universities were virtually closed to all but the sons of courtiers, who were guaranteed a position in government automatically (Mason and Caiger 1972:39).

Japan went through political reform around 701 of the Common Era, and the status of the masses changed from serfdom to free subjects as lease holders from the State. The upper class, however, was not affected. In fact, the elite gained greater control over the two main departments: the Department of Worship, which supervised shrines and rites, and the Department of State with its many ministries, along with the 66 governorships (Mason and Caiger 1972:28). In the meantime, the mass of people continued to be peasants, cultivators of all the land that belonged to the ruler.

Leisure Class. Perhaps there is no better evidence of a leisure class than the tea ceremony, which was started by the members of the warrior aristocracy. It was more than a meeting of friends to quench their thirst. "At its best it is a formal social gathering of connoisseurs, free for a time from the cares of the world to give themselves to appreciation of what is modestly beautiful" (Mason and Caiger 1972:120).

The monks had brought the plant from China because they found it helpful in keeping them awake for their meditation. They created the tea ceremony with its ritual. Ornamental cups, incense burners, and the like were developed to enhance the ritual of the tea ceremony. According to Sansom, "philosophy may be said to have promoted ceramics, for tea drinking came into fashion among Zen adepts as an aid to their meditative vigils" (1936:336). The shogun adopted the tea ceremony and developed the tea room, which is usually nine feet square, set in a garden, with a stove, water basin, and lanterns. An incense burner and a flower arrangement sit below a scroll hanging in an alcove. The idea was to stimulate all the senses.

According to Mason and Caiger (1972:35), some of the musical instruments of China, particularly the five-string lute, found their way to Japan and were used for court entertainment. Archeological finds that go back to the eighth century include dramatic masks that are believed to have been used in the dances performed at public ceremonies. Also found were finely made boards for playing games similar to chess, which had also come from China.

Perhaps the greatest contribution to leisure by the elite ancient and medieval Japanese is the Japanese garden. The idea was probably imported from China as early as the eighth century C.E. Zen priests studied the art of garden-making and gave Buddhistic names to each rock that entered in the design. Other cults further complicated the design. Originally, it was placed on the south side of the noble's mansion; its purpose was to be the center of contemplation. The Japanese garden is characterized by a waterfall, a spring or stream, a pond, and hills. Bridges and stones are important features too. Natural rocks are thought to illustrate certain philosophic principles.

Among the Japanese nobility of ancient and medieval Japan, archery, horseback riding, and hunting with falcons were very popular. The ladies rode as well as the men, either sidesaddle or astride (Dilts 1938:41). Their less active pastimes were gambling games and a sort of checkers. At home they were entertained by musicians, acrobats, jugglers, and dancers.

On the outskirts of the ancient city of Yedo, and later in Kyoto, there developed resorts attended by the merchants and samurai (warrior class). They included bath houses catered by women. The idea was copied in other areas with greater elaboration. The Nightless City contained women for the bath houses, for singing, dancing, and other pleasures. "There was a formal etiquette between a house and its client. There was a strict hierarchy among the courtesans, whose rank and appellations were solemnly observed" (Sansom 1936:473).

The social gatherings of the well-to-do were the site of the beginning and development of Japanese poetry. The normal Japanese poem was 31 syllables and fell into two lines. It became a popular pastime for one poet to supply the first line, to which others try to add a suitable second. Sansom (1936:377) believes that it was about this time that Japanese lyric drama, or *No,* came into existence. It was accompanied by scattered or irregular music, as contrasted with the solemn ritual performance. **Kabuki: Popular Drama.** The origin of *Kabuki,*

or popular drama, is obscure. It took place in open-air performances in Kyoto and Osaka. Song and dance were performed earlier. Farcical pieces were later added, and scattered music used. *No* satisfied the taste of all the audiences. That music, and with the lyrical drama mentioned above, may have been the first ingredients of *Kabuki.* Puppets were added because actresses were forbidden, and wooden dolls were a safer investment for theater managers.

Jujutsu and the Common Man. Only the *samurai,* the warrior class, were allowed to carry swords. The common man had little defense against these warriors, who had little money and much time. They began to accost the commoners on the country roads. It was a crime to fight back against the samurai, but there was no law against being pliant. The method of defense known as *jujutsu* was based on the principle of yielding to an attacker's force to make him lose his balance and throw himself without overpowering him.

Those who mastered this art seldom put their methods on paper, but passed it to their students. Secrecy was maintained, and when the samurai class was abolished, *judo,* incorporating jujutsu, became a uniquely Japanese sport.

LEISURE AND THE ISLAMIC EMPIRE

In the city of Mecca in C.E. 570, Mohammed was born. Little is known about his boyhood and youth, except for the trips he took with his merchant uncle to Damascus and Jerusalem. At age 40, Mohammed managed the affairs of a wealthy widow whom he later married. He used to spend his leisure hours contemplating in a cave outside the city. One night he heard a voice, which he assumed to be the archangel Gabriel, calling on him to recite. Mohammed recited the first chapter, *Sura,* of the Holy Book, *Qur'an* (Koran). He acquired a group of followers who, in the beginning, remained a small sect in polytheistic Mecca. Later, they began to preach rather boldly. This brought about strong opposition from local leaders and guardians of the local sanctuary of Mecca's megalithic idols. Mohammed and his sect were forced to flee, signaling the beginning of the Islamic calendar, some 1,410 lunar years ago.

Mohammed was unable to convert the original residents of the Yathrib to Islam, as they felt that his message was not sufficiently new or original. He was, however, able to convert enough of his own Arab compatriots to form a small army for a holy war, or *jihad,* to regain Mecca. After their victory, the first task was to rid the shrine of Abraham (today's Kaaba) of idols, making it the center of Islam. Now the faithful could face, bow, and kneel toward the Kaaba.

There are four major points to the Islamic faith: **The Message.** The basic message is not simply the existence of Deity; Allah and the whole duty of his subjects is Islam (submission). Thus, they are called Muslim (submissive).

The Book. Qur'an (book) means that which is recited or read. Thus, it contains those utterances Mohammed made when he was under the influence of direct revelation. The Qur'an was supplemented by Mohammed's *Hadith,* his guidelines for Muslims.

The Creed. A real Muslim is one who follows five articles of faith: belief in one God, his angels, his revered books, in his prophet Mohammed, and the Day of Judgment. The faithful should also practice the five pillars of Islam: reciting the profession of faith; performing the five daily prayers, which are preceded by ablutions; paying *zakat,* the obligatory tax collected for the needy; fasting during the month of *Ramadan,* from sunrise to sunset; and visiting Mecca, *Haj,* whenever affordable.

The Nation. Upon Mohammed's death, a successor, *caliph,* was selected by consensus. This process lasted for no more than three caliphs. Disagreement over the value of this consensus process split the nation into two camps. The *Sunni,* the majority in Islam, favored selection by *Ijmma* (consensus), while the *Shiites* advocated succession within Mohammed's family. Islam spread through assimilation, coercion, or invasion; although a totally united nation of Islam was never

really realized. Yet, even in this disjointed state, the Islamic empire was one of the greatest in history. The bulk of the empire consisted of Arabs, who shared the language of the Qur'an. The other Muslims were non-Arabs who lived on the periphery of the Arab world. They were Turks, Africans, Iranians, Pakistanis, Indians, and Indonesians. Yet they recite their prayers in Arabic, the only language of the Qur'an.

As dynasties changed, so did the capitals of the empire. First Damascus, then Baghdad, with an independent state in Spain in C.E. 750. This was followed by another one in Cairo in C.E. 969. The last of the dynasties, when the Ottomans took over around 1500, was a non-Arab one, and lasted until World War I.

Leisure and Muslims

A perusal of Islamic literature in both Arabic and English reveals no comparable term for the Western world's definition and conception of leisure (Ibrahim 1982b). Yet other Islamic words, such as those meaning play, free time, recreation, sport, art, music, drama, and literature, can be equated with Roman concepts, despite the fact that the influence of the ancient Greeks on Arabs and Muslims was much greater than that of the Romans. This influence took place after the death of Mohammed and during the Islamic expansion into Egypt and North Africa. By that time, the Muslims had already learned Mohammed's philosophy of leisure in two of his *hadiths,* or sayings:

> *Recreate your hearts hour after hour for the tired hearts go blind.*

> *Teach your children swimming, shooting, and horseback riding.*

From this it is clear that the nucleus of the Islamic attitude toward leisure and recreation is different from that of Judaism and Christianity, regardless of the dynasty. Recreative leisure, in its truncated form, flourished among newly established lords and their entourages. There, as in aristocratic Athens, autocratic medieval Japan, and cavalier medieval Europe, a leisure class emerged. Its leisure activities were later shared by the populace, shaping a culture.

Leisure Class. The first set of caliphs who ruled from Mecca were quite ascetic. It was not until the Second Dynasty, in which the capital was moved to Damascus, that the revival of a pre-Islamic practice came back under the Ummayyads' patronage.

Mohammed had frowned on many of the leisure activities of polytheistic Mecca, particularly music and poetry. In the annual fair of Ukaz, a sort of a literary congress took place. The winner was awarded handsomely and his place in the community was enhanced dramatically. All that ended with the coming of Islam in C.E. 630. But poetry, as a pastime for the listener, was to come back to Damascus around C.E. 750.

The evenings of the Caliphs were set apart for entertainment and social intercourse. Muawiyah (the first Ummayyad Caliph) was particularly fond of listening to historical narratives and anecdotes, preferably South Arabian, and poetical recitation. To satisfy this desire he imported from Al Yaman a story teller (Hitti 1970:227).

Muawiyah's son, Yazid, was the first confirmed drunkard among the Ummayyad Caliphs of Damascus, (ca. C.E. 661–750). One of his pranks was the training of a pet monkey to participate in his drinking bouts. It is said that another caliph in that dynasty went swimming habitually in a pool of wine, which he would gulp enough to lower the surface appreciably. But other pastimes engaged in by these caliphs and their courtiers were hunting, horse racing, and dicing. The chase was a sport developed earlier in Arabia, in which a Saluki dog (originally from Saluq of Yemen) was used to fetch the game. Later cheetahs were used. One of the caliphs of that dynasty had just completed arrangements for a national competition in horse

racing when he unexpectedly died, and the race did not take place (Hitti 1970: 228).

During the following dynasty of the Abbasids (who built a new capital, Baghdad), the wealthy developed new forms of pastimes. According to Stewart (1967:175), they were able to have near-duplicate of paradise on earth. In the Qur'an, paradise for the faithful is envisioned as a verdant garden where the chosen recline on beautiful carpets, and delight in the aroma of flowers and the ripple of running water. The Abbasid caliphs created lush gardens with pavilions, pools, and fountains. The wealthy spent hours in their gardens, relaxing, entertaining friends, and playing chess.

At night, the entertainment came from the personnel of the palace. Men and women danced until dawn. During the reign of Haroun Al-Rashid, Baghdad became the center of a galaxy of musical stars. Salaried musicians accompanied by slave singers of both sexes furnished the anecdotes immortalized in the pages of the *Arabian Nights*.

It was during this time that the Persians were converted to Islam. A number of pastimes, such as polo, backgammon, and chess, were introduced to the wealthy Muslims. Even then, women were completely segregated from men. But the life-style of the wealthy Muslim women improved somewhat during the Ottoman rule (ca. 1500–1800s). According to Fanny Davis (1986:131), the daily life of the upper-class Ottoman woman was enlivened and enriched by a variety of diversions, many of which took place in the harem.

The most frequent diversion at home was the receiving of visitors, game playing, music and dance, the shadow theater, and the tales of the woman storyteller. Music was a favorite Ottoman pastime, despite its prohibition in early Islam. Dancing was a frequent accompaniment of music. Guests in the party danced in twos to a tambourine, their arms high, clicking spoon-like castanets, advancing and retreating and circling around one another in short, staccato steps. Sometimes, a trained dancer and chorus would entertain the guests. Julia Pardoe, who visited Constantinople in the early 1800s, wrote the following:

> *She twirled the tambourine in the air with the playfulness of a child; and having denoted the measure, returned it to one of the women, who immediately commenced a wild chant, half song and half recitative, which was at times caught up in chorus by the others, and at times wailed out by the dancer only. As she regulated the movements of her willow-like figure to the modulations of the music . . . (Davis 1986:161).*

To the upper-class Ottoman woman, the weekly visit to the public bath, or *hammam,* was her out-of-the-house diversion. The men's bath was at one end, the women's at the other. Although the wealthy mansions had private baths, this weekly trip was considered a group outing. They came equipped with a towel, a purse, and a comb. The bather went through a tepid room, then a warm one. The warm room was usually a large octagonal hall with eight jets of water splashing on the women who wore fine linen. They stood either by the jet or sat in one of the marble basins situated against the wall.

The hammam was the Ottoman woman's beauty parlor, where her hair was dyed, her nails tinted with henna, and her eyebrows tweezed. Then she moved to the lounge to lunch, listen to music, and join in singing.

Such was the case with the wealthy Muslims only. The population throughout the Islamic empires was divided into four classes. The wealthy and powerful—at the beginning the original Arabs of the peninsula and at the end the Ottoman ruler—enjoyed a leisure life-style. But not the free Muslim who did most of the work; nor Ahl-al-dhimmah, the Christians and Jews who could be rich or poor but paid excise tax; nor the slaves. Slavery although prohibited by Sharia (Islamic law) and by

Canon (civil law), was practiced throughout medieval Islam. The leisure life of the masses was different in many respects from that of the wealthy.

The Sabbath. In the Muslim world Friday is the Sabbath day. Time is not treated in Islam as it is in the Judeo-Christian theology. The Bible is more concerned with time than is the Qur'an. In Islam, Friday is much more relaxed than either the Jewish Saturday or the Christian Sunday. The only requirement is a community noon prayer in the mosque, lasting only about an hour. The rest of the day is spent as each individual pleases.

Public Festivals. One of the best accounts of traditional public festivals in Islam came from Edward William Lane. His account of the manners and customs of the modern Egyptians became an early Victorian best seller in 1836. He lived in Cairo for six years and spoke Arabic fluently. According to Lane (1836), the Festival of the Prophet, celebrating Mohammed's birthday, took place where several large tents were erected around Birket al-Ezbekeeyeh, a dry bed of an overflow lake. The tents were to be used by the Darweeshens to perform *zikr.* A *zikr* is a ritual performed at night by the Darweeshens while standing in a circle, an oblong ring, or in two rows facing each other. They exclaim or chant "There is no deity but God" over and over until they become exhausted. They were often accompanied by one or more flute players or a string instrument and a tambourine. In the middle of the dry lake were four masts erected in a line, a few yards apart, with numerous ropes stretching across them for lanterns. The festival lasted 12 days and 11 nights. During the day people were amused by *sha'ers,* or reciters of glory, and sometimes by rope dancers. On the side streets a few swings and whirligigs were erected. Numerous stalls were built for vendors, chiefly of sweetmeats.

Another public festival was the birthday of Hussein, Mohammed's grandson, who is revered more among the Shiite than the Sunni. Yet Sunni Egypt had two evenings of celebration similar to Mohammed's, except that they took place around Hussein's mosque where the streets in the vicinity were thronged with persons lounging about, or listening to musicians, singers, and reciters of romances. Every night a procession of Darweeshens passed through the streets to the mosque preceded by two drummers, men with cymbals, and bearers of torches.

Holy Days. Ramadan is the name of the lunar month when Muslims are required to fast. Islamic fasting requires that the person refrain, totally, from ingesting anything: drink, food, or smoke, from dawn to sundown. The faithful usually have two meals; one immediately before dawn and one immediately after sundown. This created a lifestyle that is uniquely Muslim. The faithful sleep a little longer during the day. They usually take a long nap for two hours in the afternoon. After "breakfast," the first meal at sunset, real leisure sets in. For from 8:00 P.M. on, Muslims are free to pursue any activity of their choice (other than consume alcohol). Coffee houses were jammed, and still are today, and social gatherings were organized. Little children roam the streets of the old city carrying lanterns and singing religious songs.

A three-day feast celebrates the end of Ramadan and the breaking of the fast. It was when young people got their new wardrobe for the year. On the first day, when *caak* (cake) was served, it was customary to visit relatives and friends.

Two months after the first feast, the faithful try to visit Mecca's shrine of Abraham and Medina's grave of Mohammed. Four days of sacrifice are celebrated. The sacrifice here was of Abraham, who showed he would obey Allah's order and sacrifice his son, Ismael. An angel descended from heaven with a substitute sacrifice, a lamb. Allah then ordered Abraham and his followers to sacrifice a lamb in His name on that day as they congregated around Abraham's house in Mecca.

Since only two million of the 700 million Muslims perform the Haj to Mecca each year, the remaining Muslims have their own celebration. They slaughter a lamb in the name of Allah for the four days of this Islamic feast.

Public Entertainment. Despite religious prohibition, public performance by female dancers was witnessed by Lane in the 1800s in the streets of Cairo. The "Ghawazee," named after a district tribe, performed in the court of a house, in the street before the door, and on certain occasions, such as marriage, in the *haramlik,* the section in old mansions reserved for the females of the household. They danced unveiled with little elegance, first slowly, then with a rapid vibrating motion of the hips, from side to side, accompanied by a rapid beating of brass castanets.

Among other street entertainers were the performers of sleight-of-hand tricks, who collected a ring of spectators around them. The performer usually had two boys to assist him. One of his tricks was to draw a great quantity of various silk from his mouth (Lane 1836:385). He would also take a large box, put one of the boy's skull caps in it, blow in his shell, open the box, and pull out a rabbit.

Others were *bahluwans,* or performers of gymnastic exercises, who walked tight ropes and swallowed swords. The rope was sometimes tied to the minaret of a mosque, supported at many points by poles fixed in the ground. The performer used a long balancing pole. Sometimes, a child was suspended to each of the performer's ankles.

The *kureydatee,* or monkeyman, amused the lower order in Cairo in various ways. He would dress the monkey as a bride or veiled woman, put it on a donkey, and parade it around. The monkey also danced and performed various antics. These entertainers used dogs as well.

LEISURE AND MEDIEVAL EUROPE

Between the fall of the Roman Empire and the rise of nationalism, the peoples of Western Europe had similar life-styles despite their ethnic differences. Hand labor, hand tools, and physical exertion were the modes of surviving among the masses. The commoners were not safe from the hostility and harassment of transients and neighbors. For once the central authority was gone, the vacuum took years to fill.

There are a number of reasons why Rome's authority and power collapsed. Internal greed and corruption led the way to external threats by the unlatinized Teutonic tribes, who eventually ransacked Rome. Some of these tribes were enlisted earlier to bolster the Roman legions and were awarded lands. As Rome weakened, they filled the gap. By C.E. 500, the Visigoths, the Vandals, the Huns, the Franks, and the Saxons took over. They introduced their clothing, diets, and languages. The disintegration of Western Europe continued until the tenth century, when several political confederations were organized. Cities began to appear in Europe. Though unattractive and filthy, this is where carpenters, weavers, smiths, and cobblers lived. Outside the cities the poor lived a miserable life in hovels of willow frames, tied with vines, covered with clay, and protected by thatch. Although technically free men, the cottars, as they were called, gave their labor to the vassals. A vassal is a person granted the use of the land in return for homage and fealty. Others were serfs who could marry only a bondwoman of the same manor. Serfs were not slaves, but almost were since they could not leave the service of their lords at will.

According to Le Goff (1980:90), the ideology of the Middle Ages was not favorable to labor, particularly the humble form, the one involved in providing subsistence. A threefold legacy from the past may have led to the unfavorable attitude towards labor: a Greco-Roman attitude shaped by a class that lived on slave labor and prided itself on its *otium;* a barbarian legacy originating in groups that depended on war booty; and a Christianized society that emphasized the contemplative way of life, and waiting for providence to fulfill material needs.

The manorial system grew in this era when the dominant feature of social organization was dependency. The condition of war, poverty, and lack of government made people exchange their freedom for services to those who could protect them. The sheer coercive power of the upper class, who had not only wealth but military force, led them to look with disdain on the serfs' activities—ploughing, sowing, weeding, and mowing.

The manor house was the administrative center of the feudal estate, and was composed, at least in England in the eleventh century, of informal groups of related buildings. The manor was highly fortified and protected by knights and vassals. Nonetheless, life was hard. Privacy was unknown except where the lord slept. The rest of the household slept in mass quarters. Eventually, the wealthy lords had rambling mansions with vaulted chambers, large bedrooms, attractive fireplaces, and other amenities.

It was not until the thirteenth century that craftsmen formed guilds to protect themselves, regulate prices, supervise the quality of work, and standardize weights and measures. Eventually, the guilds became instrumental in bringing about less work, bonuses, days off, and in developing the guild hall for members to eat, drink, and make merry.

In the early days of Roman hegemony, Christianity encouraged asceticism and monastic life. Later, concerns over the ostentatious wealth of the Roman Catholic church, its oppressive power, and the immoral activities of some of its leaders gave rise to critics and reformers. By the fifteenth century, the Protestant movement created an irrevocable schism. John Wycliffe translated the Bible into English so people could study it. He and John Hus, who was declared a heretic, were burned at the stake in Rome. Martin Luther, who taught theology at Wittenberg, served as a catalyst for the needed reformation. John Calvin built upon Luther's foundation in his native Geneva, Switzerland.

To battle defection from Roman Catholicism, the Church made a few cosmetic changes and reverted to a revised form of inquisition such as excommunication and interdiction, as well as imprisonment and even torture. A new zealous, dedicated, and militant religious order, the Society of Jesus (the Jesuits), helped turn the tide. Their tactics were such that in two centuries the Pope of that period was forced to declare the order illegal, as their zeal threatened the Church they were supposed to protect.

Despite the burning of Arabic manuscripts that were left in Spain after seven centuries of Arab rule there, there was a rebirth of interest in the ancient world. The *universitus* came out of the guild that was already functioning in France at that time, a system designed to protect the masters' rights. The student-apprentices selected the rector, or chief administrative officer, who enjoyed more prestige than the cardinal. Education below university level also increased, particularly after the invention of movable printing by Johannes Gutenberg. Things started to change in medieval Europe about that time. This change was labeled the Renaissance, a rebirth, on the assumption that Europe had just emerged from a dark period. The center for change was Italy, where translations were made of the work of early civilizations, Greek, Roman, and Arabic. A new humanistic outlook emerged in the academies and literary societies. Humanism spread into Germany, England, the Netherlands, and other parts of Western Europe by the end of the fifteenth century.

Political recovery from the disintegration of Western Europe was slower. In England, France, and Germany in the ninth and tenth centuries there grew monarchical rulers supported by feudalism. The dukes, counts, and other nobles imitated the kings, and a hierarchy of lords and vassals began to appear. A noble might become a vassal for a duke who, in turn, was a vassal for the king. Manorialism, described earlier, became the way of life in Europe.

A system of Estates-General appeared in the later Middle Ages, in which representatives of the clergy, nobility, and other privileged classes were convened by the king, whose chose the subjects for discussion. Very soon, in most of Europe, the monarchy became absolute, save for England. But real representation did not take place in any country until after the French Revolution.

Leisure Class

Labarge (1965) has described the type of amusements that took place in the baronial house in thirteenth century England. Class distinction, of course, applied here also. The magnates were particularly interested in two outdoor activities: hunting and tournaments. Hunting was more than a pastime; it was a passion. The king's exclusive rights in the forests were enforced. The barons obtained from the king the coveted grants of "vert and venison." The clergy did not think very highly of the sport of hunting, but admitted that "it was suitable for earls, barons, and knights, but only to keep them from idleness which might lead them to worse sins" (Labarge 1965:169). Hunting with hounds was the most popular form of the sport. Hawking and falconry were chief enthusiasms of the medieval upper class as well.

The tournament was a source of amusement for that class also. It was the training ground for the young knight. The Church opposed it originally, but adopted it in 1316 as essential practice for training soldiers. Unruly squires often created wild melees of opposing groups. A new variation of the tournament developed, the Round Table. This was a social occasion, accompanied by various games, one of which was jousting with blunted weapons.

Some of the games sound a little odd to us; they included skipping, casting the stone, wrestling, dart-shooting, and lance casting. All the feasting and special games seem to have served as the medieval equivalent of a major sports meeting, and aroused much the same fanatical enthusiasm (Labarge 1965:174).

Another sport of the early Middle Ages was the game of bowls. It was apparently a team sport played by rolling balls across the green.

Spain, in particular, showed an early interest in chess, possibly adopting it from the Spanish Muslims. To be good at chess came to be considered a mark of kingly, and later knightly, quality. While the current form of chess depends on intelligence and ingenuity, the simpler form played mostly in the Middle Ages was played with dice. It was popular because the upper classes in the Middle Ages had a great deal of free time in which to indulge in long, drawn-out games.

Chess was not limited to men. The lady of the manor and her daughters played it as well. In fact, it was used as a frequent maneuver for lovers. It provided a legitimate excuse for a young man and his lady to spend hours close together over the board. Originally, the clergy did not approve, but finally approved of it if not played before noon on Sunday, since at that time all the world ought to be at church. Other manorial pastimes were backgammon and games of chance played with dice. Cards did not become known until the fourteenth century.

Many of the manors had entertainers, called minstrels, who were in effect musicians, acrobats, jugglers, and storytellers all in one. The ability to play a musical instrument was part of the trade. Among these instruments were the harp, the viol, the zither, the organ, the drum, cymbals, and timbales. Sometimes the minstrels danced. They also led the group they entertained into round dances called caroles, in which the participants held hands and sang.

Symbolic ceremonies accompanied all important events: a coronation of a king, freeing a serf, or accepting a vassalage. Ceremonies usually were followed by social activities. The style and complexity of the ceremonies, and the number and status of invited guests, were determined by the social status of the host or family involved and the type of ceremony that took place.

The royalty built for itself elaborate private grounds characterized by topiary work (trees and shrubbery clipped into unique shapes). Aviaries, fishponds, water displays, hunting grounds, and play areas for tennis, bowling, archery, and racing were included in the nobilities' mansions all over Europe. Famed spots such as the Tuileries, the Luxembourg Gardens, and Versailles are examples of these elaborate recreation areas. Following the Italian examples, the French royalty opened some of these grounds to the public, although in an unsystematic way.

Leisure and the Masses

The common person had very little free time during the early Middle Ages; only Sundays and special church-declared saint's days. Although it courted Church censure, these days habitually were times of dancing, singing, and partying, accompanied by much drinking. The folk songs of the day were ribald, sometimes sacrilegious, and frequently vulgar. The local alehouse was popular, where the men of the village gathered to drink, gamble, and indulge in sing-alongs with a wandering minstrel's profane songs and heroic ballads.

European international fairs were a major stimulus to commerce during the early ninth century. Many of them coincided with local religious festivals and attracted enterprising merchants and local small shopkeepers. After the procession of the relics and the solemn church observations, the people still had ample time and opportunity for diversions and recreation.

One village priest had forbidden dancing in or around the church on saints' days and festivals. The youth donned masks to hide their identities and cavorted up and down church aisles while the faithful were celebrating the Mass (McCollum 1979:85).

Paris was the site of the annual fair of St. Dennis. After the harvest, merchants from Italy and Spain gathered outside city walls for the entire month of October to exchange goods for silver, or barter for produce, handcrafts, food, and amusements. The antics of trained pet monkeys and the booths with sweetmeats shaped like birds, pigs, or cats attracted the children.

Performers such as fire-eaters and sword swallowers, shabby dancing bears, jugglers, and tumblers entertained the public. Some performances were public and free, while others required a special fee and were held inside a tent or building.

The European medieval period had a calendar of secular and religious feast days. Each season had its own days of celebration, including three primary holidays or holy days.

All over Europe the twelve days of Christmas brought the appearance of the mummers, bands of masked pantomimists who paraded the streets and visited houses to dance and dine. In England, plays accompanied the mumming. New Year's, like Christmas, was an occasion for gift giving. 'First gifts' were omens of success for the coming year. . . . Easter, like Christmas, was a day of exchanges between lord and tenant. The following week was a holiday, celebrated with games, including tilting in boats. . . . Mayday celebrations (were) a time for lovemaking, when moral taboos were relaxed. A young lord and lady of May were elected to preside over dances and games (Giels, J. and F. 1974:112).

Early plays that were an offshoot of, and partial replacement for, earlier wandering storytellers and jugglers, frequently dealt with religious and mystery themes. Popular with the crowds, by the fifteenth century they often consisted of low comedy and gross obscenities. In sixteenth-century England, political leaders opposed the performances because of the disturbances and dangers from fires; the Puritans supported closing the performances on the grounds of immorality. The same opposition took place in the New World (see later section on leisure in the United States).

The Elizabethan playhouse was a permanent building outside London, catering to a rough uncultured mob. The early plays dealt with street brawls, witches, and the like. This was in sharp contrast to the craft guild of two centuries earlier, in which elaborate plays were staged at public festivals. Portable stages mounted on wheels moved intact from festival to festival and from village to village.

Toward the end of the thirteenth century, wealthy Italians opened their large estates to the public. This was the forerunner of city parks as we know them today. As European cities lost most of their protective walls to gunpowder and cannons, wide avenues with trees planted on both sides became the vogue. Public squares were envisioned where these avenues intersected (McCollum 1979:105).

The French royalty responded to the demand for open space in crowded Paris by designing the *Place Royale*, linked to a long promenade. In the seventeenth century, Paris was dotted with green lawns along the ramparts of the Seine for croquet in the day and strolling in the evening. The French Revolution put an end to parks that were limited to royalty and opened them to the public.

In eighteenth-century London, the great parks that were once the property of the Crown were completely given over to the use of the people. Other areas continued to be royal hunting preserves. The major English contribution to parks was the garden-park in which designers strove to produce a naturalistic landscape. This became the dominant style in Europe at the time. The French style, on the other hand, was ornate and formal.

Various entertainments were held in London's parks, where aristocrats and merchants alike drove their carriages and strolled. There they watched wrestling, racing, fireworks, and so on. Betting became popular, and the government sponsored lotteries. Promoters organized boxing, bearbaiting, bullbaiting, and cockfighting, despite very strong Puritan disapproval. The English middle class is credited with creating the coffee house. There, businessmen met to discuss topics of mutual interest. Soon they became the places for social diversion. Gradually, some of them were limited to membership and became exclusive social, political, or literary clubs. Some, known as the "ordinaries," served one meal at a fixed price at a common table.

SUMMARY

In the intermediate societies, those characterized by the existence of two distinct social classes, a ruling elite and the poor masses, new forms of leisure activities began to appear. The masses continued to sprinkle their rituals with ludic activities but not to the extent that the rich did. The wealthy in ancient and medieval India gave the world table-games. The wealthy of China gave us fireworks and parades. The wealthy in ancient and medieval Japan gave us tea parties and manicured gardens. And the rich medieval Muslims gave us falconry and *One Thousand and One Nights*. Many of today's leisure activities and recreational places can be traced to medieval Europe. The activities practiced by its nobility included hunting, tournaments, backgammon, and games of chance. Their recreational places included grounds garnished with topiary work, fishponds, and aviaries. The masses in medieval Europe attended the fairs that coincided with religious festivals. There street entertainment grew into full-fledged plays. Despite religious and political opposition, particularly in England, these performances continued. Toward the end of the medieval period, the pleasure grounds of the wealthy were opened to the public.

REVIEW QUESTIONS

1. Compare the life-style in ancient China to that in ancient India. What effect did these two life-styles have on the evolution of leisure there?
2. What is unique about ancient Japan? Relate your findings to contemporary Japanese life-style.
3. To what extent did Islam, as a religion, dictate the life-style of Muslims then and now?
4. What factors led to the Renaissance in medieval Europe? What did this mean to the pursuit of leisure?

SUGGESTED READINGS

Basham, A. L. 1983. *The wonder that was India*. New York: Hawthorn.

Gernet, J. 1962. *Daily life in China*. Stanford, CA: Stanford University Press.

Giels, J. and F. 1974. *Life in a medieval castle*. New York: Thomas Crowell.

Hitti, Ph. 1970. *The history of the Arabs*. New York: MacMillan.

Mason, R. H. P., and J. G. Craiger. 1972. *A history of Japan*. New York: The Free Press.

An Overview of Part Two

The simple human bands of 16–25 persons that subsisted on simple food gathering may have been the basis of today's very complex human society. Some such bands still exist. Tribes are formed from several bands. Both bands and tribes revolve around familial ties. With the coming of horticulture, chiefdoms appear when a family branch becomes politically dominant. Rituals play key roles in keeping social order, but they are also occasions for novel activities. Rhythms, sings, and contests take place where these people gather. These societies lack a written language.

Social stratification is almost nonexistent in bands, tribes, and chiefdoms. All adult members are equally responsible and share work. They also all participate in communal rituals. It is during the next stage of societal evolution that a change may take place. In the primitive state, leadership becomes hereditary and communal ownership is replaced by a royal monopoly. Royalty and nobility form a new class that sets itself apart from others. It becomes a leisure class in the sense that it does not participate equally in work activity. It also sets itself apart from communal ritual. But most importantly it begins to practice activities limited, *de facto* or *de jure,* to themselves.

This evolutionary step was observed, to a small degree, in the African "primitive" states as recently as the beginning of the twentieth century. New World societies and the early Mediterranean societies are good examples of societies where leisure classes developed. Most of these societies were capable of expansion spatially and generationally because they possessed the element that made them become intermediate societies: a written language.

Many of the societies just mentioned have since disappeared. But a number that continued to exist at the intermediate level during the Middle Ages have left their imprint on their contemporary societies. Some of these societies are in fact still at the intermediate stage because of their inability to adopt the important ingredient of modernity: a unified behavioral/legal code that applies to all members of society. Previously one code was applied to the leisure class and another one to the common folks. The adoption of a single code signals the possibility of modernity, which is a prerequisite for the next step in the evolution of leisure: mass leisure, the subject of the next part.

PART THREE

MASS LEISURE AND MODERN SOCIETIES

Part Three deals with leisure in modern societies. They are modern in the sense that their moral-legal systems are almost unitary; codes of behavior are applied to all citizens regardless of their social status. Modernity furnishes the ground for mass leisure. When coupled with advanced technology and mature economy, mass leisure is enjoyed by a large segment of the society. The following five chapters depict varied levels of mass leisure in society. The lowest level is found in Third-World countries, represented here by India, Egypt, China, and Mexico. The highest is found in Western Europe (Great Britain, France, and West Germany) and in North America (the U.S. and Canada), followed by the Eastern bloc nations (the Soviet Union, Poland, Czechoslovakia, and East Germany).

These thirteen nations were selected because they represent different levels of modernity, varied cultural and ideological systems, and four continents: Africa, Asia, Europe, and North America. Availability of data was also, to some extent, a determining factor in selecting these countries.

7

LEISURE IN THE THIRD-WORLD NATIONS

The "Third World" is a term used to describe underdeveloped and/or developing countries, as compared to the industrial nations of the Eastern and Western blocs. Most of the Third-World countries try to stay neutral in the ideological struggle between the two blocs. Even China after the Communist takeover in 1949 kept her distance from Eastern bloc alliances. As recent entrants into modernity, the cultural and social systems of Third-World countries, including the leisure sphere, differ from those of other nations. Modernity as used in this work describes the attempt to adopt a single unified behavioral/legal code that applies to all citizens. Modernity should not be thought of as synonymous with advanced technology. There are some countries today that use the most advanced technology yet are hardly "socially" modern. For example, Saudi Arabia enjoys today's technological advances, yet its behavioral/legal code segregates between men and women and to some extent between the rich and the poor. So it is not modern according to our definition.

Leisure in the Third World will be discussed by looking at four nations: India, Egypt, China, and Mexico. They were selected because they reflect four different ideologies, four cultural systems, and four corners of the world. Also, these preindustrial nations may shed some light on the process of transformation from an intermediate society to a modern one and the role of leisure in such transformation. Feudalism was not long ago a dominant force in India, Egypt, China, and Mexico. Traces of India's maharajas, Egypt's pashas, China's gentry and Mexico's hacienda owners are still present. Moreover, their four populations of 751 million, 49 million, 1,060 million, and 79 million represent about 40% of the world population today. They also seem to be representatives of the poor nations in today's world. A fifth, and an important, factor in their selection is the availability of data in a language known to this author.

LEISURE IN INDIA

India stretches from the Himalayan mountain range southward into the Indo-Gangetic plain with hardly a variation from east to west. The southern peninsula, a fairly high plateau, has a coastal line of 3,535 miles. India's climate is basically monsoon-tropical, except in the north where the Himalayan region becomes very cold in the winter.

Most of India's 751 million citizens live in rural areas. Their lives are shaped to conform to ancient and religious conventions that have not changed in 5,000 years. Urban dwellers, who are better educated and have had more contact with the rest of the world, are still profoundly influenced by the same religious and cultural traditions.

India's caste system, although abolished officially, has not disappeared. Still, education and urbanization seem to be nibbling away at it. The caste system corresponds to the god Brahma's mouth, arms, thighs, and feet. The *Brahmanis* are priests, the *Kshatriyas* are administrators and warriors, the *Vaisyas* are artisans and merchants, and the *Sudras* are farmers and workers. Beneath all these are the Untouchables.

Most Indians live in joint families where grandparents, uncles, aunts, and cousins live under the same roof. It is a miniature commune where property is owned in common and earnings are pooled. Economic security and emotional stability are provided through this system. The young are socialized almost completely through the family. There are hardly any other socializing agents.

Despite the gallant effort to eradicate illiteracy, it is still extremely high. Education is now compulsory in India, and 87% of the six to eleven year olds attend school. The schools, particularly in the villages, are very inadequate, with few recreational facilities. The same applies to high schools and universities. Universities are extremely overcrowded. For example, the University of Calcutta has over 100,000 students and teaches three shifts a day (Brown 1961:134).

India's Festivals and Holidays

There are 24–29 holidays in India. Only five are secular, the rest are Hindu (14), Muslim (8), and Christian (2) holidays.

January 1st (New Years Day)
January 26th (Republic Day)
February (Basant Panchami)*
February (Shiv Ratri)*
March (Holi)*
March (Dulhendi)*
March-April (Good Friday)
April (Durga Ashtmi)*
April (Baisakhi)*
April (Mahavir Jayanti)*
May (Eid Al Fitr—3 days)*
July (Eid Al Adha—4 days)*
July (Muharam)*
August 15 (Independence Day)
August (Jan Mashtami)*

Amusement mini-park in India. Source: Ylla/ Rapho/Photo Researchers. Reprinted with permission.

September (Anant Choudas)*
October (Dusehra)*
October 2 (Gandhi's birthday)
October (Diwali)*
October (Bhaiya Dooj)*
November (Guru Nanak's birthday)*
December (Gobind Sigh)*
December 31 (Bank Holiday)

Movable holiday: based on the lunar calendar

Fairs and markets are tied to these festivals in both urban and rural India. They are often held by a temple, or by a nearby hill or spring. Whole families will travel the distance to attend. They also are social occasions. Lannoy suggests that the

Indian festival, through its play element, was "instrumental in maintaining social fusion precisely in those aspects of Indian life where political institutions have failed to achieve unification" (1971:194). This author would like to suggest that the play element of the Indian festival, which is Hindu-based, was especially attractive to the Muslims of India, whose monotheistic beliefs clashed with Hindu polytheism. Yet the festival resulted in a social fusion between Hindu and Muslims that created an aesthetically Indian culture.

In Sanskrit, a term for the play of children, animals, or adults is *kridate,* which can also mean to hop, skip, or dance (Huizinga 1950:31). *Kridate* came to describe rhythmic, repetitive cultural forms (Lannoy 1971:195), and so the elaborate dances and music of India.

It was in the Hindu temple that Indian dances were conceived and developed. Sometimes the dances were performed in the palaces of India's leisure class. The Hindu god Siva is the king of dancers, and he creates the rhythm of the universe. Indian dances express the sensations of love, devotion, humor, pathos, heroism, fury, terror, disgust, wonderment, and peace. All of which are conveyed through posture and gesture, singing, costume and make-up, and facial expression.

Indian music is based on the theory that what a person sings is far more important than how he or she sings. This came from the concept that "words are the Vedic Yoga: they unite mind and matter" (Lannoy 1971:276). Each singer, then, has his or her own rendering of a particular piece, which means that Indian music is purely melodic; since the music has no exact tones, no keyboard instruments are used.

Yoga, which started as a ritual and is still practiced as a ritual by many in India, has gone through many changes. There are many forms of yoga, the most universal of which is Hatha Yoga, the yoga of force. The aim is to achieve full salvation through an intense development of the will so that the process of the body will become fully under control. There is evidence that some yogis (those who practice yoga) have achieved impressive control over their bodies, and so good health, clarity of mind, and a long life. Yoga has become a universal leisure pursuit.

Festival, Play, and Conflict

Lannoy points out that the festivals of India not only served to consolidate the culture, but acted as conflict-management mechanisms (1971:197). These mechanisms are found in many societies and are characterized by structured everyday practices. In some societies, including India, the festival may provide the occasion for the airing of grievances. It serves as a drama of conflict that does not permit rebellions against authority, yet allows for a temporary release:

> *Aside from the holy festival, each of the other thirteen major festivals of the year seemed to me to express and support the proper structure of patriarchy and gerontocracy in the family, of elaborately stratified relations among the castes and of dominance by landowners in the village generally (Singer 1965:206).*

Leisure Pursuits in City and Village

The day's work of the Indian peasants, either the males in the field or the females at home, leaves them too exhausted for any leisure pursuits. Only the young may find the energy to play, if the parents allow it. If so, then the "parents prefer their children to play in groups rather than alone" (Lannoy 1971:97). Children's games are unstructured, and the sexes do not mix. As for the adult rural populations, their many sources of leisure are social occasions such as birth, marriage, and religious festivals.

The urbanized Indians pass their free time in activities not dissimilar to the activities of urban residents in any other country in the world, such as watching television. Television, however, was a late comer to India, and today there are only 11 transmission stations reaching one-fifth of the country's population. Consequently, India's ratio of television sets per person is extremely low (1 set for each 375.5 persons according to table 7.1).

Perhaps cinema compensates for television's limited reach. The cinema was introduced to India before the turn of the century. Exhibition was much more developed than production, and traveling salesmen gained an audience by taking films from place to place with their tent shows (Armes 1987:106). Production started during World War I with silent movies; the first sound film was produced in 1931. Since India's independence in 1947, its cinema production has reached 763 films (up to 1983) (Armes 1987:117).

The success of India's movie industry may be a result of its high illiteracy (67%), which is reflected in a low reading profile. For instance, there are 1,087 daily newspapers in India, with a ratio in circulation of one paper for each 57.76 persons, the lowest among the thirteen nations cited in this study (see table 7.1). There are 10,649 books published there a year, but there are no available data on India's public libraries or their holdings.

Some of the male city dwellers have their own leisure place, the club, an institution that was introduced by the British. There they can play tennis, squash, badminton, or swim. The club is provided with a bar and a cinema as well.

The British also introduced the "hill stations," mountain retreats in the middle of the Himalayas in the north and Nilgiri in the south. Both are forested cool areas. The idea of a beach resort also began with the British. Both hill stations and beach resorts provided the British with places to escape India's heat. Today these are used mostly by Western tourists.

Tourists in India also visit the wildlife sanctuaries, which at one time were the hunting grounds for India's leisure class, the maharajas (see chap.

6). Today the only remaining home of the Indian lion is in the Gir Forest 250 miles from Ahmedabad. The other sanctuaries protect some wildlife that are peculiar to the Indian subcontinent: the four-horned antelope, the spotted deer (chital), the one-horned rhinoceros, and the Indian tiger.

The hill station, beach resort, wildlife sanctuary, and the Taj Mahal are being used by the Indian government to lure tourists to India. According to Chubb and Chubb (1981:279), tourism is on the increase in India.

LEISURE IN EGYPT

When the Greeks annexed Egypt in 367 B.C.E., their general, Ptolemy, married into the Pharaoh's family and made himself the Pharaoh. His great-granddaughter, Cleopatra, was the last pharaoh to rule before the Roman takeover. The Greco-Roman period in the history of Egypt left some relics, though it is no match, in relics, for the previous pharaonic period. The newly Islamized Arabs conquered Egypt in C.E. 643 and left their mark on the country. Three hundred years of Ottoman rule had little impact on the country in comparison to France's three short years and Britain's 70 years. When Egypt was declared a republic in 1952 the claim, then, was that Gamal Abdel Nasser was the first Egyptian to rule Egypt in 2,319 years.

But the curse was not as much foreign domination as the fact that Egypt's population has to live in a narrow strip of land along the Nile in an area that does not exceed 4% of its total size. When health services improved, the population increased at an alarming rate as a result of declining infant mortality and increasing longevity. Population pressure increased, particularly on Egypt's capital, Cairo, and its main port, Alexandria. The peasants whose life-style remained about the same for thousands of years are now seeking a better life in the city.

Modern Egypt

The French invasion of Egypt in 1798 ushered in a new era in the long history of Egypt. The British anxiously wanted the French out in order to secure

Table 7.1 Data on libraries, books, newspapers, and television sets in 13 countries

	Pop. in millions	Public libraries		Books in libraries		Books published a year	Daily newspapers			TV receivers	
		Number	Ratio Lib:persons	Holdings in 000s	Ratio Book:persons		Number	Circulation in 000s	Ratio Cir:persons	No. in 000s	Ratio TV:persons
U.S.	239	8459	1:28,253	460,285	1.9:1	76,976	1710	62,415	1:3.85	142,000	1:1.68
Canada	25	792	1:31,505	46,498	1.8:1	19,063	120	5,570	1:4.54	11,316	1:2.21
France	56	1028	1:54,474	NA	—	42,186	90	10,332	1:5.4	20,000	1:2.80
Britain	50	163	1:306,748	151,888	3.0:1	48,029	113	25,221	1:1.98	25,500	1:1.96
W. Germany	61	NA	—	76,756	1.3:1	58,592	368	25,103	1:4.11	21,834	1:3.57
USSR	279	26,233	1:10,635	370,727	1.3:1	80,674	722	100,920	1:2.70	83,000	1:3.36
Poland	37	9316	1:3971	96,388	2.6:1	9,814	42	8,433	1:4.35	8,300	1:4.45
Czech.	16	9791	1:1634	68,685	4.2:1	10,519	30	4,041	1:3.47	4,307	1:3.72
E. Germany	17	7273	1:2337	55,560	3.2:1	5,938	39	8,936	1:1.9	5,800	1:2.93
Egypt	49	224	1:218,750	2,329	.04:1	NA	10	3,484	1:14.00	1,850	1:25.73
Mexico	79	487	1:162,217	4,916	.06:1	2,818	374	10,212	1:7.74	8,000	1:4.88
China	1060	NA	—	NA	—	22,920	53	33,654	1:31.45	6,000	1:176.66
India	751	NA	—	NA	—	10,649	1087	13,033	1:57.76	2,096	1:375.50

Source: 1985 Statistical Yearbook, Paris, United Nations, compiled from various sections of the volume.

their own route to India. With the help of an Albanian mercenary, the French were forced to depart in 1801. A few years later, the Albanian Mohammed Ali claimed Egypt to himself and established the last foreign monarchy over Egypt. He sent his sons and proteges to France to learn the modern ways of army, politics, and economy. There, his son, Said, met a diplomat and dreamer by the name of de Lesseps who convinced him to build a canal connecting the White Sea to the Red Sea. The Suez Canal was completed in 1869. For its official opening Egypt went into further debt to get Cairo ready with tree-lined, wide boulevards; a zoological garden; a score of public gardens; and an opera house for the debut of Verdi's opera *Aida*.

On the pretext that Egypt would not be able to pay its debts to a British financial house, Egypt was annexed to the British Crown in 1882. The British built their own "country" club on the north end of a large island in the Nile, west of Cairo; it was a club strictly for British and Europeans. Now and then, an "Egyptian" aristocrat was allowed to join. The educated Cairenes retaliated by opening their own "national" club on the southern end of the same island. In the meantime, the common man in Cairo was spending his free time, limited as it was, in the coffee house, the Muslim's response to Western bars. There, he drank tea and not coffee; conversed with male friends and not women; and played backgammon but did not gamble. His female counterpart visited female friends and relatives in her free time. We assume that the lifestyle in Cairo at that time was very similar to the one described by Edward William Lane in 1836 (see chap. 6). Life in the countryside, among the bulk of Egyptians, remained the same then, and for five more decades. They toiled the leased or rented acres (2–10) from dawn to dusk, six days a week, with tools not at all different from the ones carved on the ancient temples. Islam gave the peasant Friday for his Sabbath and put no restriction on its use, except for a community prayer at noon in the modest neighborhood mosque. Life went on like this, generation after generation.

But things were changing fast in Cairo and Alexandria. The British had introduced organized sport—soccer, tennis, field hockey, and table tennis. The "national" club followed suit and was able to send two athletes to the Stockholm Olympic Games of 1912. Cairo got its YMCA a few years later and was introduced to basketball and volleyball. With the reorganization of the Ministry of Education, a Department of Physical Education was established in 1922, which led to the addition of a curriculum for that purpose in the Teachers Training College. With the establishment of a Ministry of Social Welfare, a department of sport and leisure activities was inaugurated to promote clubs, either public ones with nominal fees, or private ones with limited membership. The idea of a rural club was conceived, but progress on that was slow.

Before World War II, the average number of hours of work per week in business and industry was 52. Labor laws passed in the republican period reduced them to 42 hours in five and a half working days. These laws applied only to industry and business; the hired agricultural worker put in many more hours per week, and so did the small farmer. Both represent the bulk of the labor force in the country today despite the increase in nonagricultural workers in the last few decades, from 18% in 1937 to 38% in 1981 (Ibrahim 1981).

Holidays and Festivals. Government, business, and industry have 14 days off, as follows:

May 1st (Labor Day)
June 18th (Evacuation Day)
July 23rd (Revolution Day)
Eid al Fitr (end of Ramadan Feast—4 days)*
Eid al Adha (end of Haj Feast—5 days)*
Muslim New Year*
Mohammed's Birthday*

Based on lunar calendar; vary from year to year.

In addition, the rural residents may have off a day or two, unofficially, for local holymen. The Copts (the 10% Christians of Egypt) observe, officially, their Christmas on January 7th and also Easter.

Table 7.2 Data on clusters of activities, in minutes, in 13 nations

	Work	Family care	Personal needs	Sleep	Transport.	Praying	Leisure
Belgium	263	191	148	501	56	0	297
Bulgaria	363	162	141	418	89	0	231
Czechoslovakia	304	244	136	468	62	0	239
France	255	241	163	498	58	0	245
W. Germany	232	257	156	510	39	0	261
E. Germany	278	283	125	474	60	0	233
Hungary	333	252	125	473	74	0	200
Peru	214	212	147	497	90	0	309
Poland	297	227	128	467	78	0	262
U.S.	241	219	150	470	78	0	301
USSR	338	205	131	462	88	0	217
Yugoslavia	240	228	137	472	77	0	311
Egypt	292	127	150	450	116	20	298

Source: Ibrahim, H., et. al.,"Leisure Among Contemporary Egyptians," Journal of Leisure Research 13(2) 1981, p. 101. The National Recreation and Park Association. Reprinted with permission.

Although work continues during the month of Ramadan when the devout Muslim abstains from ingesting anything through the mouth, including smoking, from pre-dawn to sunset, activities during the day slow down considerably. But four days of festivities (Eid al Fitr) occur at the end of the month-long fasting (see chap. 6). Another five-day festival occasion is Eid Al Adha, the end of Haj, a few weeks later.

Leisure Pursuits of Urban Dwellers

In 1979 this author conducted a study on the use of time among 380 residents of Cairo. The respondents included 162 males representing professional, clerical, and manual workers, businessmen, and students; and 218 females representing college-educated homemakers, homemakers without college education, married working women, unmarried working women, and students (Ibrahim 1981). The instrument was the one used in studying the time budgets of 13 nationals in Szalai (1972).

The original study included samples from industrial cities of four Western bloc nations (Belgium, France, West Germany, and the United States), seven Eastern bloc nations (Bulgaria, Czechoslovakia, East Germany, Hungary, Poland, the USSR, and Yugoslavia), as well as Peru. The amount of free time and the leisure activities in these nations are listed in table 7.2.

The Egyptians are the only sample among the 13 that spent 20 minutes during a weekday praying. The Muslim prayer requires ablution before each prayer and a number of bodily movements that may take two to three minutes. The five daily prayers of the faithful would average 20 minutes a day. These are individualized prayers that can take place at home, work, or in any public place such as a park or a vacant lot and, of course, in a mosque.

Unexpectedly, the Egyptians had about the same amount of free time as the other nationals of Western and Eastern bloc countries. Egypt is a preindustrial, Third-World, and Muslim nation. Just as surprising was the amount of time spent watching television: an average of 85 minutes a day in comparison to 66, 63, and 92 minutes for France, West Germany, and the U.S. respectively; and 66, 81, 70, and 38 minutes for Czechoslovakia, East Germany, Poland, and the USSR, respectively. This makes television the dominant leisure pursuit in many parts of the world, regardless of ideological and cultural differences and despite variance in the level of societal sophistication.

Judo class, Tawfikieh Club, Giza, Egypt.

The Egyptian sample does not represent the country in toto. For example, table 7.1 shows that there is one television set for ech 25.78 citizens, which applies basically to the countryside. Most households in the large cities, Cairo being the largest, have a television set. It should be pointed out that even in the remote villages where the poorest of Egypt live in adobe huts—with dirt floors and with no running water or electricity—a television set operated by a small generator or battery-operated will be found in the rural club. Here most of the villagers congregate, including the once-secluded women.

Socializing at home and away, including conversing in person or by phone, seems to be the second, sometimes even the first, leisure pursuit among the nations mentioned above. It constituted 55 minutes for the Egyptian sample; 82, 62, and 81 minutes for France, West Germany and the U.S.; and 33, 37, 60, and 21 minutes for Czechoslovakia, East Germany, Poland, and the USSR.

While rural residents of Egypt suffer from a very high rate of illiteracy, the urban residents show great interest in reading. An average of nine minutes for reading per day was indicated by the

sample. Taking into consideration that Egypt has one public library for each 213,750 persons, with holdings of 2,329,000 books, or 0.04 books for each one citizen, most of what is read must be personal books that circulate widely. Further comparisons of public libraries, their holdings, and books published in these 13 nations are presented in chapter 12. Table 7.1 shows that Egypt has ten daily newspapers with a circulation of 3,484,000 or one paper for each 14 persons. While circulation is wider here than in India or China, it is much less than in Western and Eastern Europe.

Data on the amount of park acreage is not available for the 412 parks in Egypt, but there is a paucity of parks in the older parts of Cairo, Alexandria, and the large cities of the Nile delta. The new cities along the Suez Canal seem to have adequate park space. There is a large park of about 400 acres north of Cairo, where the Nile bifurcates into the two branches of the delta. Also, Alexandria has a large fee-park that used to be the grounds of a royal palace. Otherwise there is a serious lack of open space in the urban centers in Egypt. Even the public gardens that were built during the opening of the Suez Canal in the 1870s have succumbed to population pressure.

Perhaps the fact that Egypt has two shorelines totaling over 1,200 miles makes up for the lack of open space in its cities. These shorelines provide summer resorts and campgrounds for the millions who escape to them from the summer heat. Egypt has just established its first national wildlife sanctuary and park to preserve the valuable coral reef and marine life along the Sinai shores.

Inland, Egypt also suffers from lack of recreational fields. For example, there are only 400 soccer fields in the whole country, which is very inadequate. Nonetheless, soccer is the most popular sport, both for participation and for spectatorship. Young players are forced to play in the streets around little parks that are either too small for a field or are fenced off by anxious gardner-keepers.

Tourism in Egypt

Tourists from abroad bring to Egypt over 50% of its foreign currency, which has surpassed its income from the Suez Canal. Accordingly, the government encourages tourism by allowing many international hospitality industries to build and operate in the country, and through controlling prices by limiting increases in accommodations, meals, and services to 10% a year. When a foreign, and also local, tourist thinks of Egypt, the following come to mind:

Sakkara Site. Site of the oldest building in history, the Step Pyramid.
The Giza Pyramids and Sphinx. Across the Nile from Cairo.
The Egyptian Museum. Its 250,000 pieces include King Tut's treasures.
Temple of Karnak. Thebes' matchless Sanctuary of Amon.
Valley of the Kings. The fabulous tombs across from Thebes.
Abu Simbel Temple. The world raised Ramses II's temple 3,200 years after his death.
Mataria Obelisk. Site of ancient Greeks' Heliopolis.
Kom El Dekka Amphitheatre. Built by the Romans in Alexandria and completely intact.
Ben Ezra's Synagog. Jesus slept here.

Coptic Churches. Back to the fourth century.
Coptic Monastaries. Where gold coins were found in 1988 that date back to the fourth century.
Saint Catarina Monastery. Where Greek monks followed Moses' steps in Sinai.
The Islamic Museum. Includes 6,500 relics, representing Islam from 643 to 1800s.
Muslim Mosques. Some date back to the seventh century.
Aswan High Dam. One of the miracles of the twentieth century.

LEISURE IN CHINA

The over one billion residents of the People's Republic of China live in an area that is comparable in size to the whole of the continent of Europe. It is a country of many contrasts—deserts, hills, plains, and arid land. It shares its 13,000-mile border with 12 nations, and its coastline is about 9,400 miles long. The land is dissected by many rivers, the longest of which is the Yangtze River, and is dotted by a number of freshwater lakes. China is divided into 22 provinces and five autonomous regions, and its towns and cities are divided into communes and neighborhoods.

The basic political administrative unit is a neighborhood committee consisting of elected members, usually older. China's towns and cities are built on a north-south axis. In the old days, several generations of the same family would live together under one roof in dwellings set around an inner courtyard, surrounded by a high wall, with a large cooking shed situated in the yard. Now modern apartment buildings are seen in China's cities. In rural areas, all produce and crops are handled by the commune and purchased by the state. This system is beginning to change to a free market economy. Nonetheless, the commune still acts as the executive branch of the Communist State. It provides and administers the neighborhood creche (day nursery), schools, hospitals and dispensaries.

Chinese Festivals

Being essentially a rural society, the Chinese still celebrate a few festivals that are based on the ancient traditions of a lunar calendar. Today these festivals are coupled with secular ones.

Spring Festival. The Spring Festival is the biggest annual festival and takes place during the first three days of the first lunar month. It is a holiday across all China. Family reunions and banquets are held and fireworks are exhibited at night in the streets. Prints decorate the houses in celebration of Chinese New Year. Amusive leisure is seen in the Chinese opera, marionette shows, and dances.

Autumn Festival. The Autumn Festival takes place on the ninth day of the eighth lunar month. Families gather on that day to celebrate autumn and eat mooncakes.

Dragon Festival. The ancient Dragon Festival is held on the fifth day of the fifth lunar month. People celebrate by eating little triangular cakes.

These three festivals, and the Festival of the Dead, are still celebrated by the common Chinese. But they have come under severe criticism from the ruling Communist Party, particularly the Spring Festival. The government is exerting great effort to change religious beliefs and practices and to alter secular elements of popular festivals (Ebrey 1981:378). The following festivals are encouraged:

New Year. The Western New Year is an official holiday in today's Communist China and is celebrated in schools and factories. Nonetheless, it is of less importance to families than the Spring Festival, which includes Chinese New Year.

Labor Day. Another secular festival, May 1, is an official holiday with celebration much less elaborate than it once was, as a result of economic cutbacks.

Children Festival. Sweets and toys are given to the young on June 1, and various entertainments are organized for them.

Youth Festival. The Youth Festival commemorates the students' uprising on May 4, 1919, to protest the giving of Shandong to Japan in the Versailles Treaty.

Women Festival. Celebrates the International Women's Day of March 8. Dramatic shows that emphasize women's issues are provided.

China's National Day. Held on October 1 to commemorate the proclamation of the People's Republic of China by Mao Tse-tung. A great parade is held on this most important national holiday, with public dances in the daytime and fireworks at night.

Socialization of the Young Chinese

Under the current regime, young Chinese go through a uniquely Communist-Chinese socializing process. The first agent is the creche, or daycare nursery center, of the commune and factory. Babies are deposited by their mothers early in the morning. The babies stay in the center all day until they are picked up by their mothers in the evening. The babies are taken care of by trained workers; mothers may come to visit during the day. The babies spend their time in cribs lined up in rows across a large room. For toilet training, once they can sit, the babies are lined up, en masse, on miniature toilets that are placed against the wall in the nursery.

Toddlers are allowed to go outside to play, but they have very few toys with which to play, and the ones provided tend to be functional. Hence, toddlers play at planting seeds and pulling weeds. Sometimes they take turns in pulling each other in little wagons. "At an age when many Western children are still at home, deprived of regular peer companionship, Chinese children are being guided into experiences that teach concern for their fellows. They learn to button not only their own but other's clothing" (Galston and Savage 1973:169). The reader will see later that under Communism, play is the other side of work and is supposed to serve it (chap. 8).

By the time the Chinese child is ready to enter kindergarten, he or she is used to associating with peer groups and spends more time with them than with his or her parents. The school curriculum is geared toward creating a more conforming person

Concrete table tennis tables in China. Photograph from DAILY LIFE IN PEOPLE'S CHINA by Arthur Galston and Jean Savage. Copyright © 1973 by Arthur W. Galston. Reprinted by permission of Harper & Row, Publishers, Inc.

who grows up with a strong sense of social responsibility and duty to country. Both the curriculum and the students' behavior are controlled by central authorities.

Completion of middle school at age 16 marks the end of compulsory education, and 80% of China's young then start working in factories or communes. Whatever adult education they may have later is basically political in nature. During these years of formal education, the young Chinese are instructed in highly formalized forms of art, music, drama, and physical training, in addition to science, math, and vocational arts.

Sport in China

Galston and Savage (1973:119) suggest that the sport program in Chinese schools seems to be the only "entertainment and relaxation provided." They observe that the sport program in the school they visited was very lively, and students participated eagerly in the modern sport of basketball, volleyball, table tennis, and gymnastics. In the school's courtyard there was a row of concrete table

tennis tables. The authors witnessed a basketball game between two classes and reported the following:

Before play started, the teams lined up facing each other and recited a sportsman's credo, which emphasized the importance of clean play and good competition over winning. The players of the opposing team then shook hands and, after the tip off by the two centers, played vigorously and skillfully. Dribbling was a bit erratic, however, because of the uneven surface of the court (Galston and Savage 1973:119).

Sports outside schools are encouraged through a number of organizations (*Ency. of China* 1987:537–62). The All-China Federation of Trade Unions has a sport department that organizes sporting activities for workers. Forty million workers participate on more than 230,000 teams, under the supervision of 10,000 full-time and 190,000 part-time professionals. Sport is also organized among the "peasants," for the aged and the disabled, and in the armed forces. Athletes from

China's schools, factories, farms, and armed forces won 15 gold medals, eight silver medals, and nine bronze medals at the Twenty-Third Olympic Games in Los Angeles.

China is trying to both revive and maintain some of its traditional sport and games. *Wushu*, or martial art, is practiced either freehand or with a weapon. A national association has been established for training classes and coaching. *Taijiquan* is a type of martial art practiced in complete sequence. *Qigong*, breathing exercises that can be traced back three thousand years, aim at controlling the mind, overcoming disease, and strengthening physiological functions. *Weigi* is an ancient table game that is gaining popularity in China and Asia in general.

China's Culture Parks

The culture park in the People's Republic of China combines an amusement park with an athletic center. For instance, Canton's culture park has all sorts of games, amusements, and cultural displays. The charge is minimal since it is a part of the city's services to the people. According to Donze and Sauvageot (1979:110), it is a real socio-cultural phenomenon, clearly an expensive place to run, and represents a significant item in the budget of the city. Since Canton has a warm climate throughout the year, the Cantonese like to stroll about in the evening, and the park is a great leisure center.

Among the most popular attractions in Canton's culture park is the skating rink, which attracts skaters of all ages and both sexes. Despite the "primitive" skates and rough concrete, the participants seem to do well. Other attractions in the park are the three giant television screens that stand side by side in the park. They give nonstop showings of plays, foreign films, news and, of course, official government programs. These public television showings seem to compensate for the very low ratio of television sets to persons in China (one for every 176.66 persons, in comparison to one for every two or three persons in the West, and one for every three or four persons in the Eastern bloc (see table 7.1).

Within the park there are also open-air cinemas, restaurants, and exhibits. Canton Zoo has a score of animals from Africa and Asia, but most important are the small and great pandas, the Himalayan bear, and the huge Chinese tiger.

Museums in China

China's first museum was established in 1905, and there were only 20 museums in the whole country by the 1950s. In recent years a rapid expansion in museums has taken place, and by 1985 there were close to 800 museums, which were visited by over 78 million visitors (*Ency. of China* 1987:614).

Museums of the People's Republic of China are arranged in a pattern designed to illustrate the State's philosophy. They are divided into the following:

1. Primitive Societies
2. Slave-owning Societies
3. Feudal Societies
4. First Democracy (1840–1911)
5. Bourgeois Period (1911–49)
6. Liberation (since 1949)

Beijing's *Zhongguo Lishi Bowuguan*, where there is a mixture of art and history, is arranged according to the above plan. The same is observed in all of China's museums (Donze and Sauvageot 1979:84, 112, 144, 165, 204).

Entertainment in China

China has one of the oldest theatrical traditions in the world.The performance, which is called an opera because it combines music, singing, dialogue, dancing, and acrobatics, dates back to the twelfth century. The Chinese opera utilizes illusion and symbolism. There are three hundred local and regional theatres in China. With the Communist takeover in 1949, the themes changed from the traditional ones of praise of the Emperor and nobility to revolutionary ones. This was particularly true after the Cultural Revolution, 1966–1969. Today there is a return to the traditional themes. Most operas are given in Pekinese (the Chinese dialect of Peking), but there are provincial operas that are given in the local dialect. These operas are performed in theatres such as the 4,500-seat Sun Yat Sen in Canton.

Modern spoken/dramatic plays were introduced in 1906, and developed rather fast, particularly during the first two decades of the Communist rule when a large number of plays were performed depicting the new socialist life. Despite a halt for a whole decade, modern drama has entered a new phase since 1976. The Chinese cinema was born in Shanghai during foreign occupation, and all the feature films were foreign. In the early 1960s, twenty studios for movie production were set up in Beijing, Canton, Shanghai, and Xian. The Cultural Revolution restricted the production of Chinese films. Today film directors are free to make original work, and foreign films are finding their way to China's movie theatres.

Television was introduced in the 1970s, and there are two channels that jointly broadcast 10 hours a day. By 1985 televising hours were close to 21. One of the channels is devoted entirely to educational programs. The other channel broadcasts Chinese political and economic news, short films, and international news. The Ministry of Radio, Film, and Television under the State Council oversees all these three activities. The Ministry is attempting to improve the ratio of television sets to population, which, at 1:176.66, is the second lowest among the 13 nations discussed in this volume (*Ency. of China* 1987:588).

China's City Squares

Since the Communist takeover, China's large cities have added gigantic squares to their city designs. For example, Beijing has the largest one in China and possibly the world. It is a continuation southward of Beijing's Forbidden City, and is the site of the Festival of October 1—China's National Day commemorating Mao Tse-tung's proclamation of the People's Republic of China in 1949.

China's city squares are used for a particular leisure pursuit that is uniquely Chinese. Soon after daybreak, millions of Chinese do their exercises together before going off to work.

The older people, especially the men, generally were executing a series of graceful battle-like movements called tai-chi-chuan *(sometimes incorrectly referred to as Chinese Shadow Boxing), a routine carefully designed to exercise and coordinate every muscle of the body. On its completion, each movement is held in its graceful pose for ten to fifteen seconds before the next is begun. No one seemed the least self-conscious about performing such exercise in public, and watching them in the quiet of a Peking (Beijing) morning was like attending a gigantic pantomine (Galston and Savage 1973:159).*

China's Parks and Gardens

Parks and gardens are plentiful in China, and strolling there is a favorite pastime of families. A number of these parks and gardens were built by the nobility in the past and are now open to the public. For example, Soochow has a number of laid-out gardens that are insulated by high walls and situated some distance from the city. One of them is almost 50 acres and is planted with pines and plum trees; a second, of about the same size, has streams, pools, bridges, and grottos. In Shanghai, the Yu Yuan Garden has 30 kiosks and pavilions linked by stairways and winding paths, which were laid in 1577 and took ten years to finish. One of the stairways leads to a kiosk on top of the highest point in the city. One of the pavilions is decorated with plants symbolizing the seasons of the year: bamboo for spring, orchids for summer, chrysanthemums for autumn, and plum blossom for winter. Donze and Sauvageot describe the Commemorative Park in Canton:

Artificial lakes wind pleasantly amid rocks, trees, and Chinese gardens. Dozens of students go out in rowing boats, girls on one side, boys on the other; there are many collisions and lots of laughter. In the shade of the cypress trees, timid lovers walk hand in hand ever so slowly, almost as if they were part of some religious rite. Amateur painters set up their easels and sketch the flowers. A group of young musicians sit on a terrace, tirelessly banging away on big bass drums whilst masked dancers move frenziedly, to the delight of the crowd (1979:109–10).

As a national policy, the government of the People's Republic of China is exerting great efforts to increase the number of tourists from abroad. In 1978, 810,000 tourists visited mainland China, which equals the total number for the previous 23 years. In 1985, it was reported that China attracted over 17 million foreign visitors, up 14% tourism rose from $260 million in 1978 to $1.25 billion (*Ency. of China* 1987:417).
billion (Editorial Board 1987:417).

A government agency, China International Travel Service, caters to foreign tourists who come to visit any or all of these tourist attractions:

Natural resources. These include China's five sacred mountains, and rivers and lakes.

Cultural resources. These include the Imperial Palace in Beijing, the Temple of Confucius in Qufu, and the Great Wall.

Social resources. These include festivals and tours.

LEISURE IN MEXICO

As was shown in chapter 5, the Aztec, the Mayans, and other tribes inhabited parts of today's Mexico. Their religious rituals became the basis for most of today's Mexican leisure pursuits. Most of these pursuits survived over the years despite the tremendous Spanish pressure to change them. Although liturgical dramas replaced native dances and mimes, and the Virgin Mary and the saints displaced Indian deities, Spanish fiestas are still as ritualistic as the Aztec and Mayan ones and are held on the same days as when the pagan ceremonies were held. They are also accompanied by the same Indian dances and songs (Horn 1979:373–74).

Mexican Holidays and Fiestas

There are 14 national holidays in today's Mexico, 20 national fiestas and celebrations that take place throughout the country, and 35 local festivals that take place in different locations in Mexico's 16 states and territories.

National Holidays

January 1: New Year's Day
January 6: Day of the three kings
February 5: Constitution Day
February 24: Flag Day
March 21: Day of the Indian Child
May 1: Labor Day
May 5: Cinco de Mayo

September 15–16: Independence celebration and ceremonies
October 12: Columbus Day
November 1–2: All Saints' Day
December 12: Day of our Lady of Guadalupe
December 25: Christmas Day

National Fiestas

Day of Saint Anthony (Jan. 17)
Day of Our Lady of Candelaria Candlemas (Feb. 2)
Day of San Jose (March 19)
Day of the Holy Cross (May 3)
Day of St. John the Baptist (June 24)
Day of St. Peter (June 29)

Day of St. James (July 25)
Day of Assumption (Aug. 15)
Day of San Francisco (Oct. 4)
Day of St. Martin (Nov. 11)
Season of *Posada* (Dec. 16–24)
Day of Fools (Dec. 28)

These religious national fiestas and the numerous local ones usually begin at dawn with either *las Mananitas* (a good morning song) or a tune played on a drum and a reed flute. After the early mass, dances that may last the whole day are performed, sometimes in the church itself. Fireworks are set off at night, and there is a show for burning a display of *castillos,* an elaborate framework (Carlson 1971:38).

The Spanish Influence

Many of the leisure pursuits of contemporary Mexicans, including the aforementioned religious fiestas, can be traced back to the Spanish colonial period, C.E. 1519–1821. According to Horn (1979:377), nothing in the Spanish heritage is more spectacular than the bullfight, a ritualized activity that became a form of amusive leisure for the well-to-do in medieval Spain. Eventually the masses were allowed admission. In Mexico, it was at one time limited to the owners of the large *haciendas.* The performance has two aspects: first there is the *corrida,* a ceremony in which the *matadors,* their assistants, the *banderilleros,* and the mounted *picadors* enter *El Plaza de Toros.* They salute the presiding dignitaries and the spectators. Second is the actual bullfighting. Today bullfighting is Mexico's number one spectator sport. In Spain, on the other hand, soccer has become the number one spectator sport; bullfighting is left to peasants and foreigners (Baker 1982:306).

In the latter part of the nineteenth century, Mexico's leisure class adopted a new pursuit. They displayed their wealth by riding in elegant carriages drawn by well-groomed teams. It became a daily ritual known as *paseo,* to be conducted at dusk. In the rural areas, the smaller *rancheros* began their own form of recreational activity in contests that tested their equestrian skills. The *charros* performed at *charreadas,* the forerunners of the rodeos of the American Southwest (Horn 1979:379).

Two large groups in Mexico were deprived of the leisure pursuits listed above, the rural poor and women. The rural poor worked long and hard hours, and were malnourished and in ill health. This is still sometimes the case in today's rural Mexico. Women were highly secluded until the nineteenth century, and were not allowed to leave the house unescorted. Poor women spent long hours preparing food for, typically, a large family; wealthy women stayed home to sew, embroider, and entertain friends.

Twentieth-Century Mexico

Things started to change slowly with attempts at self-government in the early years of the nineteenth century. But it was not until 1910 that social reform began. Building schools in rural areas led to a drop in illiteracy from 90% to today's 25%. In the twentieth century, a uniquely Mexican culture emerged. The blend of Spanish and Indian cultures is reflected in the people's leisure pursuits.

For example, it would be impossible to describe Mexican leisure patterns without reference to Mexican music. An important feature of Mexican leisure life-style is the strolling orchestra, the *mariachis,* who perform at every possible leisure occasion, including on street corners for the evening strollers. The custom is more dominant in smaller villages and outlying areas. In fact, some of these villages have a band kiosk in the village plaza, featuring free concerts twice a week, during which young people circle the plaza and perpetuate a promenade. The recreation center of the small Mexican village is still the village plaza, where leisure pursuits, such as reading or table games, take place on the sidewalk (Horn 1979:384).

For family gatherings on birthdays, weddings, baptisms, confirmations, and fiestas, breaking a *pinata* is a must. A gaily decorated papier-mache figure filled with toys and candy is suspended from above so that the young, who are blindfolded, may break it open or knock it down with sticks and release its contents.

Besides the *flamenco* dance, which is a Spanish residual, popular fiesta performances and dances take place during private leisure occasions and the public ones also. Examples are *el volador,* the spectacular flying-pole performance of the pre-Spanish era in which five performers climb a pole, hook their feet into ropes, and jump off, each spinning around 13 times for a total of 52, in a reference to the 13 months and 52 years of the Mesoamerican religious calendar (see chap. 5). In the *quetzal,* or bird dance, performers wearing a magnificent headdress form a cross and circle. The *jarabas* are variations of Spanish dances, one of which, the *jarake tapatio,* is performed in the *charro* costume and is the national dance of Mexico. There are many other forms of amusive activities in this category.

Another form of amusive leisure that has Mexican flavor is *jai alai,* an old Basque spectator sport similar to handball played with a curved basket strapped to the player's wrist. Pari-mutuel betting on the players or teams is allowed, as in horse and greyhound racing. According to Horn (1979:385), gambling is as old as the Aztecs in Mexico, and the Spaniards built on the tradition.

According to Cortez (1989), the YMCA was introduced to Mexico City in 1926, and through it a number of sports were practiced. Ten years later, once again, the YMCA added to the leisure scene in Mexico when it built the first camp, Camohmilla, in the state of Morales. In the 1960s a vice-minister for sport and recreation was appointed in the National Ministry of Education, but the position was eliminated in 1985. Nonetheless, sport has flourished in Mexico.

As for participatory sports, soccer is in first place, with basketball second. Tennis is participated in by wealthy young people. Squash is on the increase, but golf is not. This is probably because of the cost (Horn 1979:385). Nonetheless, golf courses are provided for the many tourists, particularly Americans, who find Mexico's climate amicable to their leisure pursuits.

Despite the increase in the number of literate persons in Mexico, the ratio of public libraries to its population is very low (1:162,217). As for newspapers, there are 374 dailies in Mexico, with circulation of 10,212,000 copies a day, which means that there is one newspaper for every 7.74 persons in Mexico each day. There is one newspaper for each 1 to 4 persons in both Western and Eastern bloc nations.

There is one television set for each 9.88 persons in Mexico in comparison to one for each 2 to 4 persons in industrialized nations. Egypt has one set for each 25.78; China, one for each 176.666 persons; and India has one for each 375.50 persons. According to Horn (1979:381), *cine,* or movie houses,

are very popular in Mexico. Mexico produces more Spanish-speaking films than any other nation in the Western hemisphere, and its per capita attendance at the movies is one of the highest. This is corroborated by Armes (1987:166–71).

Although Mexican municipal parks, both in acreage and facilities, cannot compare to Canada's or America's, one has been singled out by Chubb and Chubb as an outstanding urban park. Chapultepec Park has three lakes, an amusement park, and a museum, in addition to the regular features of a city park (1981:245).

As a result of the great archaeological discoveries in Mexico, its National Museum of Anthropology and History "offers its users, whether scholars or casual visitors, a museum experience that is unequalled anywhere else in the world" (Chubb and Chubb 1981:601). There are five more national museums in Mexico for art, history, religious arts, popular arts, and cultures.

Tourism in Mexico

Mexico's climate and natural resources have attracted foreign tourists, mainly Americans, for many years. Recognizing the economic impact of a tourist industry, the Mexican government embarked on a national promotional program to encourage tourists, particularly from the United States, to spend their vacations and holidays in Mexico. In 1969, FONATUR (an acronym for a Spanish phrase meaning "national funds for promotion of tourism") was established and became engaged in what has been said to be the largest and most sophisticated governmental system of tourism outside the Iron Curtain (Chubb and Chubb 1981:544). FONATUR buys the land, installs the basic services, and sells to private developers to build hotels, resorts, restaurants, and recreational facilities. According to Chubb and Chubb (1981:279), three million Americans visited Mexico in 1978. Tourism accounts for 50% of Mexico's balance of payments income ($2.8 billion in 1978). The tourist will find the following places and activities in Mexico.

Boat Trips. Yacht tours are excursions with music, cocktails, and a stop for a swim. Meals are served as scheduled, depending on the length of the excursion. On some excursions, the crew prepares lunch from the freshly caught lobster or fish and serves it on deck or at one of the palm-framed beaches. Some of the beaches are strewn with huge pink and orange conch shells free for the taking. A stop is also made at a coral reef, where masks and white water boxes are brought for viewing the fish that come to feed. In some areas, glass-bottomed boats are used.

Camping. There are no public campgrounds in Mexico and many visitors camp on the beach and in the interior. There are a number of private campgrounds that are equipped with full hookups for American recreational vehicles. Some of these campgrounds are Tahitian-like villages, and the RVs are parked under the palms lining the shore. Other campgrounds are well-kept trailer parks with patios, bath houses, and purified tap water. There are campgrounds situated near Indian villages and by monastery-churches. Others are within city limits.

Charros. *Charro* groups are usually found in large cities, and they like to put on a show on Sunday morning. They perform feats of horsemanship, demonstrating such stunts as lassoing the feet of running horses, throwing wild steer by the tail, and riding wild horses.

Dances. An example is the *Ballet Folklorico,* which stages dances typical of native villages. The *flamenco* dance, which is seen in night clubs, represents a person who has renounced tradition in favor of freedom. While dining, the tourist will definitely encounter the *mariachis,* perhaps accompanying a dance group performing one of the many national or local dances.

Dude Ranches. Some of these ranches are actually working cattle ranches that play host to dudes and offer them excellent meals, horseback riding, hiking, hunting, swimming, fishing, and sometimes backpacking trips.

Fiestas. Tourists may want to arrange their vacations to coincide with one or more of the national or local fiestas listed above. Travel agents are provided with dates, locations, and the activities of each of these fiestas.

Fishing. Fishing takes place along Mexico's shorelines and in freshwater lakes and rivers. Deep-sea fishing includes the International Sailfish Rodeo in April. In the bay waters of Mexico, anglers try their luck with smaller species. In other areas, the catch may include tuna, red snapper, sea bass, halibut, jack cevalle, and mackerel. Some of Mexico's villages have become fishing resorts for many sport fishermen.

Golf. Although golf is not a very popular sport among its natives, Mexico has a number of fine golf courses for its foreign tourists. While most of them are 18-hole courses, some are 9-hole practice courses. There are a number of golf resorts across Mexico.

Hunting. Depending on the location and the season, expeditions into the mountainous areas are arranged for the hunting of jaguar, mountain lion, puma, deer, peccary, and ocelot. A variety of small game also can be bagged. Duck, goose, chachalaca, quail, and turkey are also available.

Resorts. Mexico has a number of resorts run on a family basis with a native touch, where a guest can find a restful atmosphere. The resorts are provided with thermal pools; some are individualized, others mineral. Steam rooms and massages are also available. Guests can spend their time playing table games, horseback riding, relaxing, or shopping around quaint Mexican shops.

Sight-Seeing. While the subtropical areas in the north and northwest of Mexico's steppe and chaparral are dominant, its Sonora desert may have the greatest cactus garden in the world. In the south, most of the area is either woodland or grassland, with rain forests along the east coast. The sightseer is greeted now and then by roadside vendors selling their crude, unglazed pottery at road junctions. The pottery is decorated with birds, flowers, and animal forms in earthly colors. The sightseer may want to stop at one of the many sixteenth-century Franciscan monastery-churches that dot the landscape of Mexico.

Water Sports. The warm waters of Mexico are ideal, year-long, for sailing, boating, waterskiing, and diving. Many tourists are excited by parasailing—riding a high-flying parachute that is pulled by a speed boat to a height of 300 feet.

SUMMARY

Traces of a strong ritualized leisure linger on in the four Third-World countries discussed in this chapter: India, Egypt, China, and Mexico. There are more religious holidays in India (18) than secular ones (6); the same is seen in Egypt (9 to 3) and Mexico (20 to 12). The picture has changed somewhat in China, where six secular holidays are observed in comparison to four religious occasions. In the meantime, some recreational places, particularly in India and China, are reminders of the once dominant leisure class.

There is much evidence of an approaching mass leisure in the four countries. But it is clear from empirical data and observers' reports that mass leisure is limited to the large urban centers, which hold a smaller percentage of the population than in both Western and Eastern bloc nations. When these Third-World countries are compared, as a group, to the countries of the two blocs, they fare poorly on the scale of leisure occasions and recreational opportunities. Perhaps with an improved per capita income, their life-style would be enhanced. The four countries are embarked on an income-generating service, tourism, directed toward bringing foreign tourists and their badly needed hard currency.

REVIEW QUESTIONS

1. Trace the development of the pursuit of leisure by the natives of India.
2. What role do the Islamic festivals play in the leisure pursuit of an Egyptian citizen?
3. Describe some of the unique recreational places in China.
4. How do recreational offerings help the economy of Mexico?

SUGGESTED READINGS

Armes, R. 1987. *Third-World film making and the west.* Berkeley: University of California Press.

Carlson, J. 1971. *Mexico: An extraordinary guide.* Chicago: Rand McNally and Company.

Ebrey, P. B. 1981. *Chinese civilization and society: A source book.* New York: The Free Press.

8

LEISURE IN EASTERN BLOC NATIONS

First, this chapter will discuss the Communist view of play and leisure. Although Karl Marx did not grant them a place separate from work in the life of men and women, some of his disciples found it necessary to do so. Today "leisure" pursuits are a matter of fact in the lives of the people who live under Communist regimes. This chapter presents those pursuits among peoples in the four Eastern bloc nations of the Soviet Union, Poland, Czechoslovakia, and East Germany. While a neo-communist view of "leisure" provides the philosophical bases for the provision of certain activities, how these activities are managed gives us an insight into what is supposed to be gained. Through them a socialist personality is to be created. In fact, the socialist personality is found in only one of the four communist countries presented.

THE COMMUNIST VIEW OF LEISURE

At the time of the writing of the *Communist Manifesto,* the new science of anthropology was bringing to the forefront rich material on early human history. But Marx and Engels decided to exempt prehistoric man from their work on historical materialism (Hoberman 1984:24). To them myth, ritual as well as play, represents the nonrational side of man, and it would be pedantic to try to find economic causes of all this "primitive nonsense." In fact, Marx's early interest in literature and aesthetics was subjected to self-censorship because they were part of this "primitive nonsense."

The first historical act, suggested Marx and Engels, was the production of the means to satisfy basic needs for eating, drinking, habitation, clothing, and so on—the production of material life itself. Labor is the basic condition of all human existence. It came first, after which came articulate speech. These two were influential in the change from the brain of an ape to that of a human; and labor was the original mode of expression.

But a later Marxist theorist, Georgi Plekhanov, recognized that Marxist theory must investigate prehistory and try to bring it under control; otherwise it would forfeit a crucial authority. He then refuted the notion that labor among "primitive" people was closer to play in form and content, as had been suggested by the cultural conservatives of the West. To him the development of manufacture did not begin with tattooing the body, piercing its parts, preparing masks, or drawing on bark. These technical skills were needed for survival first, and were elaborated in play. In other words, work activity among human beings preceded play and is the factor that determined its content. Plekhanov agreed with Herbert Spencer that beasts of prey show us that their play consists of sham hunting and sham fighting, which means that the content of their play is determined by activities that support their existence.

Some neo-Marxists did not agree with the view that play is antithetical to labor and suggested that the relationship between them should be seen as dialectical. Others pointed out that Marx had distinguished between a primitive instinctive form of labor and its exclusively human form. This allows for a "creative" element to flourish through imagination and the "free" play of the mental and physical powers of humans. Thus, humans withdraw from the instinctive, repetitive form of labor to turn it, through play, into mimetic representation, illusions, and art forms. Accordingly, play and work are a unity of opposites peculiar to the human species (Hoberman 1984:28). This did represent a slight departure from original Marxism, for Marx had talked about play's recuperative powers, which was not an evil luxury but a humane respite from the inhumane regimen imposed upon the exhausted laborer by oppressive capitalists. Play is not an end in itself. Rather, in the future, once a true Communist state is created, a fusion between play and work will take place.

It was up to the neo-Marxist to explain the play-work dialectic. Francis Hearn, a revisionist, tried to establish the significance of play, which Marxist theory had overlooked. He believed that play should be more manageable and meaningful. Lawrence Hinman suggested that the answer to Marxist attempt to overcome the dichotomy between work and play is found in the utility of play. Play is negated when it is not productive of human life and becomes isolated in the imagination. On the other hand, play is affirmed when it is creative of human life.

Hoberman (1984:34) suggests that while Hearn was attempting to change the Marxist myopic approach to the *ludic*, Hinman was trying to find in Marxism "the foundation of a theory of play and leisure." Hinman asserts that Marx had suggested that the realm of freedom actually begins when work as determined by necessity ceases, beyond which begins the human energy that is an end in itself. This condition comes about with the shortening of the workday, a condition for leisure.

Hinman's notion was not enthusiastically received by some of the leisure experts in the Eastern bloc who were wary of the Western view of leisure as a complete distancing of humans from work, something opposed to work. They insisted that social existence is a seamless whole that cannot be divided into spheres. It is the abolition of the contradiction between labor and leisure that makes possible a rich variety of amusements and relaxations, based upon educational, moral, and aesthetic values, all of which are in the service of a socialist personality (Hoberman 1984:35).

According to Moskoff (1984:xiii), leisure emerges as a residual in Marxist analysis. Marx called it free time and equated it to nonwork time. He lived when most workers in Europe labored 12–14 hours daily and had little time but to eat, sleep, and work. Marx wrote that at the highest stage of Communist society, free time will be a measure of wealth. Marx stated that under capitalism the worker is alienated from the object of production. While work is a means to an end under capitalism, it is an end in itself under socialism (a characteristic that commonly describes play and leisure activity). Yet he and many of his followers refused to think of play and leisure activities as having ends in themselves; rather, they are means to an end. Today the Soviets talk about *prostoe vosproizodstvo* (simple reproduction or nonwork activities) and *rasshirennoe vosproizvodstvo* (free time that is regarded as the time in which one regenerates for the real purpose of life—work).

According to Artiomov, and others (1970), the problems and perspectives of free time in the socialist country stem from the fact that free time's activities are becoming an increasingly important factor in the productivity of public labor. In socialist countries, which are based on public ownership, control over free time must be considerably greater. But this must not be interpreted as a mere rigid regulation of human activity. On the contrary, a more profound and many-sided knowledge of this activity will broaden its latitude.

There are many ways of defining free time. On a purely economic basis, it is the time for large-scale regeneration of the labor force. Or is it the time when no earning activity occurs? Freedom can be viewed differently, ranging from a Marxist understanding to an illusory-Philistine one.

In the Soviet literature, which is translated into the languages of the Eastern bloc nations, free time is associated with all-around development of the personality. For the harmoniously developed personality, free time activity should require intellectual, moral, and physical efforts. Although rest and entertainment are an important part of free time, activities such as studying, self-education, and social, physical, and aesthetic activities must be highly valued.

In the capitalist countries, states Artiomov, rest and entertainment are held most valuable because they are a vehicle of the consumption of goods and services. They take people away from the spheres where a highly developed personality can express itself through politics, art, and technology. In the capitalist society, men (and women) are reduced to consumers in the first place.

Artiomov and others suggest that three groups of factors facilitate or impede the rational use of free time:

1. **Material base.** The indices here are national wealth, per capita income, discretionary income, and development of leisure services. In the socialist country public expenditure on education and culture have a high rate of growth, and evidence a high degree of success in physical culture (sport). Yet the level reached in mass sport, aesthetic activities, entertainment, and open air recreation (outdoor activities) should not be considered satisfactory.

2. **Organizational base.** Associations and institutions provide free time services along with diversity and cooperation and are essential at this point. Over the past few years the rate of services growth has increased considerably due to greater manpower directed there and to technical innovations. Some of the problems faced in this base are those of selection, education, remuneration, and public prestige of the workers in the leisure service sector.

3. **Personal base.** Personal base refers to the educational and cultural level of the participant as well as his or her abilities and skills. *"The Communist upbringing is not in giving complete freedom to a man who is in a state of formation, but in guiding him . . ."* with all that has been achieved by the society. Thus a more perfect, rich, all around *free personality* [emphasis added] (1970:44).

The data show that when free time in the USSR, Poland, Czechoslovakia, and East Germany was compared with the Western bloc countries in the aforementioned cross-cultural study, which was conducted in the early 1970s (table 8.1), the Soviet citizen spent 67 minutes a day in leisure pursuits compared to an average of 116 minutes for all nations and an average of 91 minutes for the Eastern bloc nations. For Poland it was 95 minutes, for Czechoslovakia 86 minutes, and for East Germany 91 minutes.

LEISURE IN THE SOVIET UNION

The Soviet authorities have paid attention to the activities in the nonwork sphere since the very beginning of the Communist takeover. Table 8.2 shows the changing patterns of nonwork activities over a span of 47 years.

These data exclude not only work time but also time for basic necessities such as sleeping and eating. Moskoff (1984:83) has a number of observations on the patterns shown in the above table.

The time devoted to housework and the private plot has been cut in half.
More time was devoted to daily cultural activities, reading, studying, and aesthetics.
There was an increase in participatory physical recreation.

In a study conducted in the early 1960s involving 10,000 subjects, the five most popular leisure activities on a daily basis were reading newspapers, listening to the radio, reading books, reading magazines, and playing with children. Watching television did not rate high, probably because of its absence from certain locations at that time. On a weekly basis, the most popular leisure activities were going to the cinema, visiting relatives and friends, reading magazines, watching television, and participating in voluntary work. Soviet citizens depend on their time at home to sustain their leisure life (Moskoff 1984:86).

Another study in 1975 included three urban centers: Moscow (7 million), Klin (81,000), and Kostovo (49,000). It showed some differential in the leisure patterns of the residents of these three cities. There was more studying in Moscow, and its residents read magazines and newspapers more often than the residents of Klin or Kostovo. Also, the Muscovites attended more plays and sport events than did the residents of the other two cities. All this may be attributed to the fact that Moscow has more schools, newspapers, magazines, concert halls, and stadia.

The Soviet Weekend

Before the Revolution, the average workweek was 58.5 hours. By 1955 it had decreased to 47.8 hours. In the 1960s it was reduced to 41.6 hours. This reduction was accompanied by a major change in the life of a Soviet citizen—the two-day weekend. Today the average citizen puts in 39.4 hours a week. A massive time-budget study conducted in 1967 showed Soviet families traded off-market work for leisure, not housework.

On the weekend, the Soviets seemed to continue doing things they previously did, but spent more time doing them. In other words, they watched more television, read a little more, and went to the cinema more often.

Although the five-day workweek created the opportunity for a weekend away from home, there are not enough accommodations, most of which are controlled by the State. Also, passes to those guest houses are typically offered for 12 days of vacation and not for weekends.

Vacation/Holidays

In 1936, the International Labor Conference recommended one week of vacation for each one year of work. In 1954, two weeks were recommended, and in 1970 three weeks were suggested. In the Soviet Union the legal minimum has been 15 days since 1968. But the actual vacation length today is closer to 21 days.

The Soviet policy toward vacation can be traced back to 1918 when the newly established Soviet government issued a decree stating that all workers are entitled to an annual paid holiday. One had to work at least six months to be eligible for leave. Initially, the worker was entitled to one month a year, which was reduced to two weeks for most workers. During World War II, vacations were eliminated altogether, with extra pay in lieu of time off. Only in the case of illness was the worker allowed a few days off. After the war the previous policy was resumed, with longer vacations granted to workers on the night shift, one day for each month. Later, those who were working under hazardous conditions were added to the list. In 1955, a one-month minimum of vacation was granted to workers aged 16–18. Longer vacations, up to 48 days, went to scientific researchers and educational institutions.

Soviet citizens can spend their vacation holidays either at a state-run facility or at a rented country *dasha*. To do the former, he or she must join an organized group that receives passes to houses of rest, sanitoriums, and pensions. Houses of rest are designed for workers on a leave and persons considered overtired by medical authorities.

Table 8.1 Average time spent in 37 primary activities, in minutes per day

	Belgium	Kazanlik, Bulgaria	Olomouc, Czech.	Six Cities, France	100 Distr., Germany	Osnabruck, Germany	Hoyerswerda, Ger. Dem. R.	Gyor, Hungary	Lima-Callao, Peru	Torun, Poland	44 Cities, U.S.	Jackson, U.S.	Pskov, USSR	Kragujevac, Yugoslavia	Maribor, Yugoslavia
Total N	2077	2096	2192	2805	1500	978	1650	1994	782	2754	1243	788	2891	2125	1995
Total minutes	1440	1440	1440	1440	1440	1440	1440	1440	1440	1440	1440	1440	1440	1440	1440
1. Main job	255	388	297	242	225	210	254	315	200	287	225	225	324	230	254
2. Second job	4	0	1	5	2	4	2	3	10	3	5	5	2	1	11
3. Other work	4	25	6	8	6	4	22	15	4	8	12	11	13	9	17
4. Travel to job	24	41	33	22	18	16	32	41	37	37	25	19	33	27	29
Total work	287	404	337	277	250	234	310	374	251	334	266	259	371	267	311
5. Cooking	46	39	64	45	59	49	65	60	71	59	44	45	55	70	76
6. Home chores	64	36	51	70	71	73	78	55	40	51	58	57	38	49	57
7. Laundry	22	12	31	26	25	20	40	35	45	34	26	24	28	28	41
8. Marketing	13	14	27	20	22	26	23	14	16	16	14	16	10	22	14
Total housework	145	100	172	162	177	167	206	164	172	160	142	141	131	168	188
9. Care to pets	8	23	8	11	31	18	11	33	2	3	3	3	8	6	49
10. Shopping	6	4	6	6	3	4	5	4	9	12	18	17	14	5	5
11. Other housework	15	18	27	22	19	21	16	21	6	19	24	25	17	26	27
Household care	29	45	41	39	53	42	32	58	17	33	45	45	39	37	81
12. Child care	12	9	16	32	16	14	30	12	18	16	22	23	18	14	16
13. Other care	5	8	15	9	11	11	15	17	5	18	10	8	17	9	13
Total child care	17	17	31	40	27	25	45	30	23	34	32	31	35	23	29
14. Personal care	44	55	71	57	54	59	49	53	47	56	69	61	49	58	47
15. Eating	104	86	65	106	102	103	76	73	100	72	81	78	72	79	69
16. Sleep	501	418	468	498	510	503	474	473	497	467	470	480	462	472	477
Personal needs	649	618	604	661	665	665	600	599	643	595	620	619	583	609	592
17. Personal travel	17	24	15	16	4	7	14	15	25	21	31	31	34	24	19
18. Leisure travel	14	18	12	15	13	19	11	14	28	17	19	23	21	24	18
Nonwork travel	30	42	27	31	17	25	26	30	52	38	50	54	55	48	36
19. Study	16	11	16	13	6	12	11	16	36	21	12	9	38	14	20
20. Religion	5	0	1	4	5	6	0	1	4	5	10	11	0	0	1
21. Organizations study	4	7	7	2	2	4	12	3	2	4	6	6	8	5	4
Participation	25	18	24	19	13	22	23	20	42	31	28	26	46	19	24
22. Radio	8	20	11	5	7	4	4	11	8	10	4	3	10	16	6
23. TV (home)	81	14	64	55	61	72	80	39	52	64	91	99	33	34	41
24. TV (away)	3	2	2	3	2	2	1	4	2	6	1	2	5	3	0
25. Newspaper	16	14	13	14	12	13	13	12	10	16	24	25	15	20	19
26. Magazine	5	1	3	4	12	13	2	1	6	3	6	5	5	1	1
27. Books	14	21	20	7	5	6	7	14	2	17	5	4	29	7	8
28. Movies	4	10	4	3	3	3	1	5	6	4	3	2	15	7	6

Table 8.1 Continued

Total mass media	131	79	116	91	98	112	108	85	87	120	134	140	113	87	81
29. Social (home)	15	5	7	12	13	18	10	7	10	25	25	27	4	29	13
30. Social (away)	25	8	15	20	32	32	16	16	19	22	38	39	9	42	20
31. Conversation	15	9	11	17	17	18	11	13	27	13	18	16	8	28	13
32. Active sports	2	2	2	1	5	4	1	2	2	1	6	5	4	0	2
33. Outdoors	10	24	12	11	39	32	18	17	13	10	2	5	14	13	19
34. Entertainment	5	14	2	3	4	3	2	3	4	2	1	1	3	2	2
35. Cultural events	3	1	3	1	1	2	1	1	1	1	1	1	3	1	0
36. Resting	27	41	17	33	17	19	10	15	63	24	9	12	11	31	20
37. Leisure	27	13	18	23	14	20	20	9	14	11	20	18	13	36	10
Total leisure	128	116	86	121	140	147	91	81	152	95	123	126	67	181	99
Total free time	297	231	239	245	264	300	233	200	309	262	301	310	247	311	222
Total travel	56	89	62	58	39	58	60	74	90	78	78	76	88	77	78

Source: Szalai, A. (Editor). The Uses of Time: Daily Activities of Urban and Suburban Population in Twelve Countries, 1972, p. 114. Mouton De Gruyter. Reprinted with permission.

115

Table 8.2 Relative importance of several nonwork—time activities, large cities in European parts of the USSR, various years

	1923–24	1936	1963	1965–68	1967–70
1. Housework and work in the private plot (excluding the care of children)	35.0	24.0	21.2	19.5	18.5
2. Daily cultural life					
(a) leisure, including	6.7	5.5	12.4	16.0	17.3
Reading books and magazines	2.1	1.0	2.3	2.1	3.3
Reading newspapers	2.9	1.8	1.4	1.6	2.5
T.V. and radio	—	1.0	5.1	6.2	7.5
Movies, theatre & other public performances	0.6	0.7	0.9	1.3	1.3
(b) studying	—	1.0	2.6	4.0	2.3
(c) amateur talent activities and other kinds of nonprofessional creative works	1.1	—	0.1	0.8	0.4
3. Physical culture sports, hunting and fishing, going to the country	0.2	0.3	0.7	0.7	1.6
4. Meeting with friends, guests, and dances	6.2	7.6	5.8	5.2	5.8
5. Occupied with children	5.6	4.3	3.0	5.0	3.1
Caring for children	5.0	—	1.9	2.9	1.5
Upbringing of children	0.6	—	1.1	3.0	1.6

Source: Moskoff, Wm. Labour and Leisure in the Soviet Union, *1984, p. 83. St. Martin's Press. Reprinted with permission.*

A sanitorium was formerly a health institution administered by medical staff. A pension is similar to the house of rest, except that there is more freedom. Most of the passes are free, and in many instances the worker's transportation to and from the place of vacation is paid.

The *dasha,* or summer cottage, is an important leisure facility in the Soviet life. Despite their small size, they are rather popular because they allow the family to stay together. Individual enterprises own and operate most of these facilities. There are private *dashas,* but on a very limited basis.

Riordan (1982) suggests that since the early 1960s an increase in prosperity, which led to a market growth in consumption and a reduction of work time, promoted a change in leisure pursuits in the Soviet Union. Nothing was more indicative of the changing patterns than the rapid interest shown in tourism. Table 8.3 shows that in 1949

tourism ranked fourteenth among Soviet leisure pursuits, and that by 1970 it ranked second. The ranking was given by a majority of participants.

Another change that took place in these 30 years was the ascent of basketball from the eleventh sport to the seventh sport, and the descent of gymnastics from fourth place in 1940 to fifteenth in 1970.

Of recent, *glasnost* is expected to lead to a new revolution in the leisure sphere in the USSR (Riordan 1989). For instance, physical recreation remains out of reach for most Soviets. This is a result of the requirement that a person be a member of a sport organization, which is typically attached to a place of work. Moreover, favoritism plays a role in who can use the weekend *dasha.* Independent youth clubs are now a fact in the Soviet Union. In addition, there is an emphasis on sport for all instead of elite sports to produce world-class athletes.

Table 8.3 Sixteen recreational activities by order of number of participants, selected years between 1940–70 in the USSR

Sport	1940	1945	1955	1960	1965	1970
1 Athletics	3	3	1	1	1	1
2 Tourism	14	18	14	11	4	2
3 Volleyball	5	6	2	3	2	3
4 Skiing	2	1	3	2	3	4
5 Pistol shooting	6	7	5	6	5	5
6 Football	7	9	7	8	7	6
7 Basketball	11	12	9	7	8	7
8 Chess	1	2	4	4	6	8
9 Draughts	—	4	6	5	9	9
10 Fishing	—	—	—	—	—	10
11 Table tennis	—	—	12	10	10	11
12 Shooting	—	—	—	—	—	12
13 Swimming	8	8	11	13	11	13
14 Cycling	9	10	10	12	12	14
15 Gymnastics	4	5	8	9	13	15
16 Speed skating	10	11	13	14	14	16

Source: Riordan, J. "Leisure, the State and the Individual in the USSR," Leisure Studies 1(1) 1982, p. 69. E. & F. N. Spon. Reprinted with permission.

Soviet Recreational Planning

The vast territory of the USSR contains a range of natural environments, many of which have recreational use. For example, there are the beaches around the Baltic Sea and Black Sea, the many mountainous regions, the inland water bodies, dense forests, tundra, and deserts. All, however, are subject to the extreme conditions of the country's climate, which deter many types of leisure pursuits (Shaw 1980:197). In addition, most of these potential recreational areas lie in remote areas, far from the major centers of populations. Moreover, half of the Soviet population is concentrated in about 7% of the territory, where there is severe crowding of the nearby facilities. For example, the forests and lakes around Moscow and Leningrad and the beaches of the Baltic Sea and Black Sea are heavily used.

All land and most establishments are owned and run by the State. So one would expect the utilization of a piece of land or the establishment of an agency for recreational purposes to be less complicated, since there is no private ownership there.

But Brine and others (1980:200) found that under the Soviet system there is no category for recreational land. There is agricultural, residential, industrial, state forests, water resources, and reserve land, but no recreational land. Bureaucracy stands in the way of providing recreational facilities. This is because national bodies play a larger role in deciding on the facility than local authorities. Moreover, the Soviet centrally planned economy makes planning itself a difficult task.

The Soviet urban population has increased from 18% of the total population in 1914 to over 60% today. The worst off are the newer cities, which were built without much attention paid to providing open space. The older cities such as Moscow and Leningrad have more public open space per capita, not much less than London (Shaw 1980:203). Some ideas for combating the lack of open space are to build multilevel sport complexes and to surround the cities with green belts.

As for the countryside, there are plans to develop forests and parks in the green belts, with campsites, rest homes, and sports facilities. There is a trend to develop parks in remote areas. And although tourism is on the rise, these areas have not been developed at the same pace, once again for the reasons mentioned on the previous page.

Shaw (1980) concludes that central control of land and means of production will not provide an easy solution to recreational problems nor lead to good planning. According to Riordan (1982:74), the Soviet leaders seem to have opted for the following:

1. *The organization of working people in their leisure time to the maximum possible extent within the framework of a tidy hierarchical and functional structure.*
2. *The cultivation of competitive activities, as in sports (a leisure-time analog of the competition between people at work designed to raise work tempos) with, as at work, material rewards for victors, which more effectively improve people's readiness for work and pre-train soldiers for the Soviet nation state.*
3. *Using leisure, specifically, as a means of obtaining the fit, obedient and disciplined work force needed for achieving economic and military strength and efficiency, in particular, in order to:*
   a. *Raise physical and social health standards, the latter meaning to simply educate people in the virtues of bodily hygiene, regular exercise and sound nutrition, but also combat unhealthy, deviant, anti-social (and therefore anti-Soviet) behavior: drunkenness, delinquency, prostitution, "sexual perversions," even religiosity and intellectual dissidence.*
   b. *Develop general physical dexterity, motor skills and other physical qualities useful for "labor and defense."*
   c. *Socialize the population into the new establishment system of values. Character training, advances (so the Soviet leaders seem to believe) by "rational" leisure activities in such values as loyalty, conformity, team spirit, cooperation, and discipline, may well have encouraged compliance and cooperation in both work and politics, including, of course, the development of an uncynical attitude towards political leaders.*
   d. *Encourage a population in transition from a rural to an urban way of life to identify with wider communities: all-embracing social units such as the workplace, the neighborhood, the town, district, the region, the republic and, ultimately, the whole country. By associating leisure activities or organizations with the workplace, the Party leadership and its agencies have been able, moreover, to better supervise, control, and "rationalize" the leisure time activities of employees.*

Leisure in Poland

In Poland, between the two world wars, the leisure patterns of social classes differed considerably. According to Olszweska (1979), the peasantry had a traditional pattern of leisure. Agriculture, which is subject to natural cycles and climate, regulated the rhythm of their lives. Leisure was conditioned by breaks in work, or it was the crowning achievement, the end of work—for example, harvest time, which saw folk dances, singing, couplets, games, and so on. To the privileged classes, the landed gentry's leisure was a way of life, ensuring wide access to the performing arts, games, and sport. The intelligentsia, a class of society with lower finances, but higher status, had leisure dominated by an intensive privacy, known sociologically as "ghetto of the intelligentsia."

The working-class patterns of leisure were of meager proportions and not very differentiated. The typical activities involved family and neighbors' groups and were based on direct relationships. Cultural institutions and media like radios, books, or magazines were attainable by a few, and vacations, if any, were spent at home.

After World War II, Poland went through fundamental political changes, called the widening process of democratization, which affected leisure as follows:

1. Normalization of working time during the week to ensure the same or similar free time for all.
2. Normalization of annual work to provide the same holiday rights both for manual workers and others.
3. Standardization of retirement for all workers.
4. Generalization and facilitation of opportunities for all classes in relation to the higher standard of culture.
5. Popularization of new patterns of leisure so that the personality of each individual is enhanced and can develop to full potential.
6. Extension of an infrastructure, which serves leisure, as based on noncommercial principles to ensure access to various leisure activities.

Leisure in Poland has been affected by many other factors, the most important of which are the following.

Industrialization. Poland had been a rural country with underdeveloped industry, but industrialization began after World War II. About 4 million people are now employed in various industries. Industrialization has secured better living conditions for the people, but it has also created problems.

Urbanization. About 3.1 million persons have moved to towns from the country. The rise of many new towns has created congestion. Urbanization, visible on all planes of social life, created new patterns of leisure.

Cultural Development. In the 1930s radio came into general use. What broke this habit were television programs, which started in 1956. The number of television sets increased from 1,640,000 in cities and 335,000 in rural areas in 1965, to 4,422,000 for urban regions and 2,050,000 for rural regions in 1975. The number of published newspapers and magazines, as well as their respective circulations, increased dramatically in the same period.

The Development of Automobiles. Mobility came slowly. But events in 1969 hastened production. Automotive output increased rapidly, and at present about 1,500,000 cars are privately owned. The automobile is a means of transportation, but it is also a means for leisure activity.

With the termination of the German occupation, economic and social changes also took place. Industry and trade have been put under State control. Land reform has been carried out. Cultural and educational institutions have become public property. The workers' political party has assumed authority.

The consequence of these changes was legislation that provided the working and peasant classes with access to cultural and educational opportunities. Local authorities, industry, and trade unions were obliged to facilitate new leisure patterns and participation in various activities.

Leisure Pursuits in Poland

Two studies conducted in 1969 and 1976, revealed that an adult inhabitant of Poland had 4 hours, 6 minutes of free time per day. Not everyone, however, had such time. Single women had 4 hours, 38 minutes, while married and family women had only 2 hours, 52 minutes. For men there was a similar situation. Single men had 5 hours, 16 minutes; married men had 4 hours, 14 minutes. Rural people had 3 hours, 33 minutes of free time, considerably less than town inhabitants (Olszweska 1979:402).

There is a strong positive correlation between free time and the level of education. Persons with a university education had 4 hours, 43 minutes, while persons with an elementary education had 3 hours, 55 minutes. Leisure activities were listed as follows:

1.	Watching TV programs	67.2%
2.	Nonactivity, e.g. a nap or doing nothing	33.6%
3.	Reading newspapers and magazines	31.1%
4.	Meetings, visits, playing or parlor games	24.6%
5.	Talking to members of the family	20.1%
6.	Religious practices and other devotions	16.4%
7.	Reading books	12.7%
8.	Going out for walks, watching stunts, and sport events	12.3%
9.	Talking to other persons	12.0%
10.	Other leisure activities	9.1%
11.	Listening to the radio	7.9%
12.	Various personal interests; hobby	3.7%
13.	Carrying on welfare work	2.6%
14.	Visits to cinemas	2.0%
15.	Listening to music from records and tapes; performing music	1.6%
16.	Practicing sport; sport and tourist excursions	1.1%
17.	Visits to theatres, concerts, social evenings	0.5%
18.	An active participation in cultural works	0.2%

For the 12 socio-occupational groups represented in the sample, TV watching placed first, with an average time of 1 hour, 28 minutes. For rural people, the amount of time was much lower. Closer analysis of the findings showed that TV watching was primarily an amusement rather than a medium for information and learning. Films, particularly light adventures and thrillers, were popular. Series were also popular, among them "Colombo," "Kojak," and "Tiger's Brigade." In the past, the most popular series were "The Saint" and "Odyssey."

Inactive leisure in the form of relaxation was popular among workers and pensioners, but not among the intellectuals and students. Participatory sport, excursions, attending plays, concerts, or practicing an art were scarce among all socio-occupational groups except students. Reading newspapers, magazines, and listening to the radio placed high among leisure activities. Listening to the radio as a main activity was rare, but was an adjunct function. Gardening, once associated with the peasantry, became popular. Over 750,000 lots, mainly at second homes, were used for that activity.

The findings also showed that home was the main site of leisure activities. Mass media activities took place there, usually in the company of others. Most of the leisure activities did not require going out (Olszweska 1979:408).

Poland's working hours were reduced in 1974 by introducing five Saturdays off per year. Starting in 1975, 12 additional Saturdays were cut, reducing working time to 44.5 hours per week. It was projected that more free Saturdays would be added.

A poll in 1969 showed that a two-day weekend was so attractive that the respondents agreed to a lengthened workweek. The findings showed that the younger groups and the intellectuals were generally more in favor of a two-day weekend than the manual workers. Also, as the educational level rose, so did favoring the proposal for a free Saturday.

Individuals were asked how they would spend a free Saturday. From the results, it appears that there are two types of interests. Nearly half of the respondents anticipated that they would use Saturday for leisure—63.8% of the men and 31.8% of the women. Most of the respondents considered the Sunday after a free Saturday as the real day of leisure. How have free Saturdays really been used since they have been available? A free Saturday has become "the hard working Saturday": 65.6% of the persons polled did housekeeping; 20.4% did their shopping, 2.8% settled their personal matters, and 4.7% undertook additional paid work.

On a Sunday preceded by a free Saturday, the number of persons occupied with additional paid work was four times less, and the number of persons engaged with housework was three times less. Twenty-five percent more persons enjoyed leisure at home. One-third more persons went to a cinema or theatre; while twice as many persons paid visits to relatives or entertained guests.

The number of persons traveling outside of their permanent residences for recreational purposes was nearly the same on Sunday as on Saturday; but on Sunday 25% more persons went to visit their families or traveled for other purposes.

How do the Poles spend their holidays? A standard inquiry was carried out in the 1970s on 10,806 persons, 57.1% of whom were entitled to a 26-day leave and 7.5% to 14 days. It showed that more than half of these persons used all of their leave at one time. The others used it in stages. About 80% of those with university education used their leaves for leisure traveling. Leisure activity in the permanent residence was universal for all other groups (Olszweska 1979:399). Most Poles had ideas for the kinds and nature of institutions needed for leisure. The suggestions included the following:

1. More parks and green areas in town; also playgrounds and cultural centers.
2. Better transportation services for individual excursions on Sundays.
3. More swimming pools, athletic equipment, and sport fields.
4. More amusement parks and circuses in town.
5. More camping areas in the suburbs and inexpensive rental establishments with a full range of equipment.
6. Facilities with land-grant allotments.
7. More theatres, concert halls, and libraries.
8. More places of amusement, beer saloons, cafes, and wine vaults with gaming tables.

Voluntary Education in Poland

The term "voluntary" is used here to include both formal and informal education for adults. Formal adult education takes place in institutions built for that very purpose. Informal education takes place at home, in the library, and through an excursion. All these activities are predicated on the participant's free time, time away from work, work-related activities, and familial/civic obligation.

According to Pachocinski and Poturzycki (1976), there were 23,674 cultural and educational facilities in Poland in 1971 offering courses and activities to 634,600 participants. These institutions and their programs are managed by the Ministry of Culture and the Arts. The main organization is the Association of General Knowledge (Polish acronym, "TWP"), whose mission is to disseminate knowledge to the general population. The General Universities are run for the same purpose by trade unions. In the houses of culture, 769 of them throughout Poland, courses in music, drama, and dancing are provided.

Other cultural and recreational institutions are the 339 museums, 876 exhibitions, and 292 roving exhibitions, with a total of 16 million visitors a year. The 132 theatres across Poland, with their 60,000-seat capacity, offer 50,000 performances a year to audiences totaling 18,000,000. As shown in table 7.1, Poland has 9,316 public libraries, or one library for each 3,971 citizens, with holdings of 96,388 or 2.6 books for each Pole. These books are read by an estimated 18 million readers a year. Moreover, there are 9,814 books published a year, and 42 daily newspapers with a combined circulation of 8,433,000 or one paper for every 4.35 citizens.

The same table shows that there were 8,300,000 television sets in Poland, or one set for each 4.45 citizens. A total of 6,653 hours of television a year was watched, 4,000 of which was films, and the rest miscellaneous programs. Radio broadcasting amounted to 56,699 hours, most of which were talk shows, with 20,000 hours or so devoted to music (Pachocinski and Poturzycki, 1976:23–24).

Leisure in Torun

In the cross-cultural time-budget study of the early 1970s, the use of free time in Torun, Poland, was compared to Maribor, Yugoslavia, and Jackson, Michigan, United States (Skorzynski 1972:265–89). Torun has 113,000 residents, with one-third of its labor force employed in the local industry, such as sawmills, distilleries, textile factories, and chemical plants. It is located 200 kilometres downstream from Warsaw on the Vistula River (see table 8.1).

Its sample of 2,754 had an average of 4.3 hours of free time per day. Watching television occupied the greatest portion of free time available. While employed men watched television the most, employed women watched it the least. In both of these groups, the amount of time spent watching television diminished with the increase in education and elevation in socioeconomic status. Unskilled workers spent over 2.5 hours in front of the television per day, while white collar workers spent 1.5 hours a day doing the same thing.

The time spent watching television increased considerably on Sunday, as did the time spent on reading newspapers, particularly for the white collar group. On a weekday, reading newspapers averaged between 0.5 and 0.75 hours for both blue and white collar workers. On the weekend it increased to almost 1.25 hours for the white collar workers and remained about the same for blue collar workers. Time spent on reading the newspaper on the weekend did not increase for employed women either.

Although newspaper readership was comparatively less in Torun than in Maribor or Jackson (16, 25, and 20 minutes per workday, respectively), book readership was decidedly higher (17, 5, and 7 daily minutes respectively). The time spent reading books increased with growing skills and improvement in occupational status. Torun residents showed greater interest in books on Sunday, with an average of two hours spent in reading them. Although the habit was fairly equally popular among white and blue collar workers, it was most popular among housewives.

Inhabitants of Torun, Poland, spend less time on Sunday reading than inhabitants of Moribar, Yugoslavia. But the analysis revealed that in the European cities, Sunday was a day of a great deal of reading compared to Jackson, Michigan.

Visiting among the residents of Torun was done on a daily basis by every fifth person (19–15%), mostly housewives. Whether at home or away, the residents of Torun spent an average of 60 minutes on that during a weekday in comparison to 80 minutes in Jackson and 100 minutes in Moribar. Visits to cafes and bars were most popular among white collar workers and least popular for housewives. Nonetheless, cafes served a diverse clientele in Torun. In most European cities, the cafes function as meeting places, and Torun's cafe-centered social life is a good example of the custom.

LEISURE IN CZECHOSLOVAKIA

Prior to its independence in 1918, the legal work time in Czechoslovakia was 11 hours a day for six days a week. In 1920, Czechoslovakia was among the first to ratify the International Labour Organization's recommendation of eight hours a day and 48 hours a week. In 1956, the weekly hours were reduced to 46. A decade later, a five-day week of 42.5 hours was adopted. Since it is a socialist state, this practice is applied in all spheres, industrial, commercial, and agricultural, with the exception of the tiny 5.3% private sector (Linhart and Vitechova 1975).

Substantial change has also been seen in the length of holidays/vacations. Today the legal minimum is an annual vacation of two weeks; after five years of employment it is extended to three weeks, and after 15 years of service to four weeks.

Leisure in a Twenty-Four-Hour Cycle

In the cross-cultural study conducted in 13 countries, both Western and Eastern bloc nations (Szalai 1972), the average free time for all nations was 265 minutes per day. The average for the Czechoslovakian sample was 239 minutes. But when compared to the samples from the Eastern bloc nations (235 minutes), the Czechoslovakians were average in their free time gains. While participation in physical activity was extremely low, involvement in mass media, such as watching television, reading, and going to the movies, was about average.

These findings were corroborated by the study of Helena Janisova (1971), who conducted a detailed investigation of the life of the residents of select communities in Czechoslovakia using a daily time-budget survey. The residents of these communities were divided according to age, sex, and socioeconomic status. No data were provided on the number of subjects nor their backgrounds. The methodology of obtaining the data was not clear either.

Janisova found that leisure in Czechoslovakia, at least in the urban centers, was dominated by what she calls "the houseslipper culture," in that the activities are passive, home-based ones. Most respondents complained that their real free time comes in the late evening hours, after an exhausting workday that is followed by housework. It was surprising to Janisova that the subjects did not seek to renew the strength that was lost during the work process by using "contrasting" activities, activities that are vigorous enough for the 69% who have sedentary occupations. Only 10% devoted any free time to active leisure. Others' activities were definitely nonphysical, such as attending cultural programs and sport events, learning, watching television, and listening to the radio.

How was leisure time used on the weekend, when there is more time to pursue vigorous activity? There was a slight increase in participant sport, which was not significant among the older respondents. When these respondents were asked why they did not participate in physical activities, most of them claimed that there was lack of time for such activities. But were the urban residents in Czechoslovakia so much encumbered by work? The investigator decided to ask them if they took work home. The answer depended on the respondent's educational level. While 70% of university graduates took work home regularly, the rest of the workers (nongraduates) took work home only occasionally.

The relative distance of a park or sport field seemed not to be a factor in the disinclination of urban residents to participate in sports. Most of these facilities were within eight minutes of most subjects in central Prague and within seven minutes in its suburbs. The investigator pointed out that the growth of the city had destroyed many of the natural areas. But this had no bearing on the lack of enthusiasm among the subjects for physical recreation, where 34% of them felt that the lack of recreational facilities closer to their homes denigrated their living environment. Younger people were more critical of that condition than the rest of the respondents.

Among the many facilities mentioned in the study was the Prague-Podolf swimming center. Although the center was intended for competitive aquatics, the investigator was somewhat surprised that only 6% of the respondents were interested in competition; the rest were looking at swimming as recreation.

Weekend travel was becoming increasingly complicated. The directions, purposes, and destinations of people departing from Prague were observed and surveyed. About 16% of those departing were taking a vacation, 12% on tourist trips, 3% on recreational excursions (boating, bicycling, etc.), and 1% on a cultural trip. This form of recreation showed a significant increase and was expected to double by the mid-80s.

She pointed out that the greatest number of those leaving town were owners of cottages and bungalows to which they went regularly on the weekend. Interest in rural cottages was evident not only among residents of large cities but residents of smaller ones as well.

Leisure in Olomouc

Olomouc, the capital of the Moravia Province, population 75,000, was selected as the site for the cross-cultural study (Szalai 1972). A sample of 2,192 subjects was selected, composed of skilled workers (48%), unskilled workers (17%), self-employed (13%), and others (22%). Most of the respondents were adults between the ages of 18 and 55 (81%), with the remaining 19% over age 55.

Olomouc is situated on the Moravia River in the plains that make up the basin of Moravia. The city was founded in C.E. 1050 and was subject to occupation by Swedes, Prussians, Austrians, and Germans. Today Olomouc is known for its university and its industries. Most of the industrial plants there deal with the agricultural products of the fertile plains surrounding the city, processing foodstuffs such as sugar, candy, and beer.

In the cross-cultural study cited above, the Czechoslovakian sample of 2,192 residents of Olomouc spent 5 hours, 37 minutes at work; 2 hours, 52 minutes on housework; 41 minutes on shopping; 31 minutes on child care; 6 hours, 4 minutes on personal needs (eating, sleeping, and personal care); 27 minutes commuting; 24 minutes studying; and had 4 hours of free time. Most of the free time was spent around the mass media. Television watching consumed over an hour, reading books 20 minutes, newspaper reading 13 minutes, and magazines 3 minutes. Socializing at home took 7 minutes, socializing away from home 15 minutes, and mere conversation 11 minutes in the life of the Olomouc residents. This was followed by resting, 17 minutes; and being outdoors, gardening, and the like, 12 minutes.

While the sample's average of daily free time was very close to the average obtained from Eastern bloc nations, it was 51 minutes below the average obtained for the Western bloc nations (see table 8.1).

LEISURE IN EAST GERMANY

In a monograph edited by Lippold (1972), he asserts that the German Democratic Republic attempts to organize leisure activities that are necessary for an all-around development of human personality in a socialist society, and provides for better material conditions for a purposeful use of leisure. He castigates the West for believing that manual workers and working people are incapable of using the increasing amount of leisure in a purposeful way.

The monograph is composed of an annotated bibliography on leisure from East German sources, most of which the editor himself translated. One of the pieces in the bibliography is the definition of leisure in the German *Dictionary of Marxist-Leninist Sociology:*

Leisure is defined as a part of the free time given to the satisfying of certain needs and demands, as are, in Marx' conception, first of all idleness and, in the second place higher activities, e.g., socio-political activities, child education, adult education, enjoyment of works of art, artistic activities, entertainment, recreation, physical culture and sport. In socialist society the contradictions between work and leisure are no longer of antagonist nature. The functions of leisure shaping both individual personality and collective feeling correspond to the interests of the working class and of other working people. The development of the practical, intellectual, moral and aesthetic powers achieved through higher activities is a legitimate event in socialism, determining

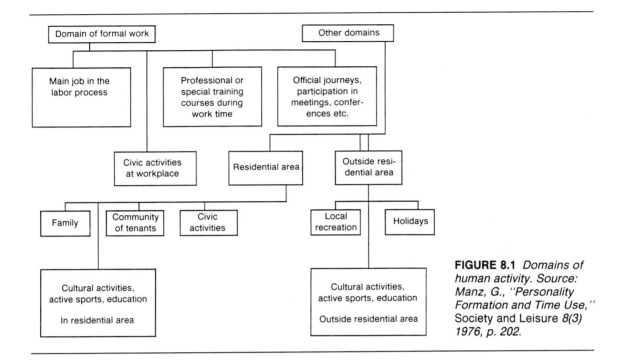

FIGURE 8.1 *Domains of human activity. Source: Manz, G., "Personality Formation and Time Use," Society and Leisure 8(3) 1976, p. 202.*

through changes of consciousness the use of leisure and forming the virtual social wealth, for the very reason that at the same time the productive forces are being developed and with them also the precondition for the increase of this wealth.

The item "Time-budget" is concerned mainly with the methodology of investigation and ascertainment making possible also the determination of the amount and the structure of leisure.

According to Lippold, a comparison of the views of individual scholars reveals a basic agreement about the following:

Leisure is only a part of the time standing at the free disposal of individual working people.

Leisure is the true wealth of human society, not only in the quantitative sense, but also as regards the unity of its qualitative use (Marx).

In socialism, leisure is an essential aspect of the development of personality, its many-sided social determination being realized first of all in an increasing mutual interdependence with the sphere of work.

In another section of the monograph, B. Bittighofer, asserts that in socialism the contradiction between work and leisure is replaced by a unity of creative productive work and purposeful leisure activities. How is this achieved? Gunter Manz (1976:202) provides the answer in figure 8.1, which shows the basic domains of human activity: formal work and other domains. The other domains include participation in leisure activities.

On the function of leisure activities, particularly of sport, in the life of people of socialist societies, G. Roblitz is cited by Lippold (1972:12) as stating that in the modern work atmosphere, the entire organism is subjected to considerable demands. Thus individuals must be allowed to maintain their creative abilities and to pursue them during free time. The leisure of people under so-cialism is by no means time free from work; it is time given to further education, to the reproduc-tion of one's own working capacity, and to cultural and artistic activities.

It is natural then that certain leisure activities would be considered desirable and would be en-couraged by the authorities. A study conducted in 1969 and summarized in the monograph by Lip-pold (1972:93) shows that sport, traveling, and walking were listed as desirable (rated as such, it is assumed, by a highly respected panel), followed by socialization and reading. Actual participation was different. The study showed that among the young workers investigated sport, traveling, and walking ranked seventh instead of first, second, and third as postulated. The share of these three activ-ities together was fifteen minutes a day. Social-izing and television watching ranked first and second, with 76 and 56 daily minutes, respectively.

In a previous study of the importance of sport for leisure and holiday use, the data showed that 15% of 1,850 persons polled by the State Com-mittee of Physical Culture reported that they par-ticipate in sports on a more-or-less regular basis. Also, 43% of the respondents gave lack of time as the reason for not participating in sports. The study concludes the following:

> As highly developed physical culture forms an integral component of the socialist way of life, ways must be found how to guide the majority of people toward regular physical exercise and sporting activities. To achieve this aim due attention must be paid to the motives inducing the people to pursue activ-ities of this kind (Lippold 1972:94).

East Germany began to invest heavily in sport, not only for the reason given above, but also be-cause Walter Ulbricht, the most dominant polit-ical figure from 1945 to 1971, was genuinely interested in sport, both personally and ideologi-cally. As mentioned before, leisure under Marxist-Leninism is not considered autonomous, but rather

is associated with productivity, that is, with the maintenance of life itself. Consequently, in the all-around development of a socialist personality, the inclusion of physical development within the model has become a ritual requirement, more so in the GDR than in any other Eastern bloc nation.

Another Marxist-Leninist idea, *polytechnique* education, fit with the idea of all-around develop-ment of a socialist personality. Polytechnique ed-ucation created a system for sport pedagogy and sport medicine that had never been seen before. One outcome was a team of handball players who were described as follows in the French newspaper *Le Monde* (Hoberman 1984:210):

> Rarely has the comparison of a team to a machine been more appropriate: a steam-roller, the GDR team seems to be composed of tireless human robots who can maintain the same rhythm for an hour, they are cast physically and mentally from the same mold: iron morale, nerves of steel, muscles of brass. It is almost as though one were talking about a team that was metallurgical in nature.

SUMMARY

The early expounders of Communism did not view leisure pursuits as antithetical to work pursuits since the former have recuperative powers that make the latter possible. Attempts to separate the two, philosophically, were not successful, and Communist scholars today assert that the abolition of contradiction between the two make possible the offerings of programs that enhance and serve a so-cialist personality. Accordingly, Soviet authorities have paid attention to nonwork activities since the Communist Revolution. In recent years watching television tends to be the most participated in of leisure pursuits, followed by reading. It seems that the new cities built under communism suffer from a severe shortage of open space in contrast to older cities. In Poland the picture is not dissimilar to that of the Soviet Union in that most leisure pursuits take place at home. In Czechoslovakia, the "house slipper" culture also dominates. The general complaint is that there is lack of nearby facilities and that real free time comes in the late evening hours. The East German takes a somewhat different stand, with an emphasis on physical activities, particularly among youth. In combination with what is termed *polytechnique* education, a system of sport pedagogy was established. The result was the molding of a socialist, "robotic" personality.

REVIEW QUESTIONS

1. What was the Communist view of leisure initially? How and why did it change?
2. What are the salient features of Soviet leisure today?
3. Compare the leisure pursuits of the Poles, the Czechs, and the East Germans.
4. Compare the leisure delivery systems in the Eastern bloc to the Western systems.

SUGGESTED READINGS

Hoberman, J. 1984. *Sport and political ideology.* Austin: University of Texas Press.

Moskoff, Wm. 1984. *Labor and leisure in the Soviet Union.* New York: St. Martins Press.

Riordan, J. 1977. *Sport in Soviet Union.* Cambridge: Cambridge University Press.

Szalai, A., ed. 1972. *The use of time: Daily activities of urban and suburban populations in twelve countries.* The Hague: Mouton.

9

LEISURE IN WESTERN EUROPEAN NATIONS

This chapter discusses the evolution of leisure pursuits in Western Europe. These pursuits are based on modern, Western interpretations of play and leisure. These interpretations led to a new approach to the activities that take place in the time freed from work, civil, and familial obligations. Although the industrial revolution allowed for more free time, the struggle by the masses to gain it was long and arduous. Once achieved, the newly acquired free time was used by the masses who forwarded to us most of the leisure activities of modern society.

THE WESTERN VIEW OF LEISURE

According to de Grazia (1962), the gravitation toward work in Europe began during the Middle Ages. With the demise of the Roman Empire, people lived under frontier conditions, and frontier life demands hard work. The monasteries led the way. The most influential was Saint Benedict's, where idleness was considered the enemy of the soul. Le Goff (1980:80) believes that the monks began to work with their hands and construct machines in order to make themselves available for more important things—the *opus Dei*, or prayer and contemplation. But work was, above all, penitential.

By the tenth century, Western Europe was a tripartite society composed of men of prayer (*oratores*), men of war (*bellatores*), and men of labor (*laboratores*). Most of the latter group were *villiens,* the serfs who served the landlords. They were considered vicious and dangerous, thus the word *villain* (Le Goff 1980:97). Ultimately, a gap grew between the Church and the attitude of masses that continued for centuries. A slight improvement in their life-styles occurred with the urbanization of Western Europe. Yet their attitude toward life did not change. Their designated day of rest, Sunday, and special church-declared holy days were times of dancing, singing, and partying, accompanied by drinking and sexual promiscuity. Their songs were sacrilegious and vulgar, usually a legacy of former pagan times. The local alehouses were popular, as were fairs that coincided with religious festivals.

The manorial system developed under a feudal lordship consisting of the lord's demesne and the lands within which he had certain privileges, including the exacting of fees. Vassals and knights protected the manor, and the serfs performed the menial physical labor in return for protection, food, and lodging. In some cases, a serf might accumulate enough money to purchase his freedom. Yet there were serfs tied to the land in France and Germany into the eighteenth century.

Craftsmen sought influence in trade-formed guilds, which later functioned to protect the rights of the members, settle their quarrels, regulate prices, set standards, and supervise quality. They also served a number of social functions. For example, the guild hall was open to its members for eating, drinking, and merrymaking.

As trade flourished within Western Europe and in regions outside it, a class of merchants appeared and, along with the craftsmen, exerted enough influence to change the attitude towards work. "With the beginning of the Thirteenth century, the working saint was losing ground, giving way to the saintly worker" (Le Goff 1980:155).

According to G. Cross (1986), it was four hundred years later, with industrialization, that workers in the West learned to adapt to factory work discipline, accepted a regular and uniform work schedule, and abandoned traditional leisure patterns. They came to prefer income over leisure and ended the tendency to produce only as much as necessary to maintain the customary standard of living, which included traditional leisure. Workers became, like their employers, "economic men," for whom time is money and leisure is merely time to consume.

In the meantime, changes in knowledge were taking place. To the medieval philosopher, epistemology centered on general ideas, or universals. In the fourteenth century, a new conceptualization was shaping up, which eventually led to the empiricism of Hobbes, Locke, Berkeley, and Hume in the seventeenth and eighteenth centuries. René Descartes' assertion, in the seventeenth century, that knowledge of the world is attained by pure reason, gave birth to empiricism, or verification through senses. One method of empiricism was simple observation.

Among the human activities observed by scholars was play. Those who observed it in man and animal were intrigued by it and tried to explain it. Among them was the Englishman Herbert Spencer (1820–1903), and before him the German Friedrich Schiller (1759–1805). Both suggested that play behavior is the result of a surplus energy that exists because the young are freed from the necessity of self-preservation. This surplus energy finds its release in the aimless pursuit of fun. Another important component of this theory is that man and higher animals are phylogenetically active organisms. Although most of the activity is directed to self-preservation and the preservation of the species, not all energy is needed in that direction. This is especially true in humans, who have the capacity to create a safer environment. Thus

they no longer have to expend all their energy on work. Since humans are active, they channel some of their surplus energy into play.

These two scholars were later criticized by Karl Marx and his followers. Marx accused them of attempting to justify the existence of a social class that exempts itself from work. This is the class that Veblen (1953:21) describes as a leisure class, a vintage of an era gone by.

> *The institution of a leisure class is found in its best development at the higher stages of the barbarian culture, as for instance, in Feudal Europe. . . . In such communities, the distinction between classes is very rigorously observed. . . . the upper classes are, by custom, exempt or excluded from industrial occupations, and are reserved for certain employments to which a degree of honor attaches—chief among the honorable employments in any feudal community is warfare; and priestly service is commonly second to warfare.*

But the *oratores* and the *bellatores* were replaced around C.E. 1750 by capitalists and bourgeoise classes. Those who worked for them put in between 10 and 14 hours a day, six days and sometimes seven days a week. Their quest for free time was not an easy one. Throughout history, capitalists resisted hour reduction more vigorously than wage increases. Cross (1986:70) suggests that this was because hour reduction was a threat to their prerogative in ways that wage increases were not. Shorter work hours disrupt scheduling, raise unit costs, increase the expense of training, limit quick response to market demands, and give more time to workers to contemplate their condition.

But why would workers want shorter work hours that may mean less income? Dumazedier (1967) offers individualism as an explanation for the demand for more free time. Cross (1986) disagrees, saying that Dumazedier's explanation fails to take into account the economic and political contexts in which increased free time was gained. To him, the eight-hour day, five-day week work cycle that started in Western Europe in the 1930s was the fruit of a thirty-year political and ideological struggle that started at the beginning of this century.

In table 8.1 are data representing what some of Western nations, and some Eastern bloc nations, did with the fruit of that struggle. Leisure in three of these Western European nations, Great Britain, France, and West Germany, will be discussed.

LEISURE IN GREAT BRITAIN

Great Britain provides us with a good example of how certain ritualized activities became leisure pursuits, how some remained common among most people, and how others were limited to the privileged class.

Ritualized Leisure

According to Strutt, whose work was originally published in 1801, the leisure of the English nobility emanated, most probably, from traditional "great parades," the ceremonials that were first practiced by the Saxons soon after their establishment in Britain. Their kings rarely appeared in public without being followed by thousands of guards. This example was imitated by nobility and persons of opulence. In the Middle Ages, the practice of show was carried to extravagant lengths.

The Normans introduced tournaments and the jousts into Britain. Originally, the tournament was a made-up martial conflict engaged in by knights to exhibit their strength and dexterity. The joust was limited to knights.

> Tournaments and jousts were usually exhibited at coronations, royal marriages, and other occasions of solemnity, where pomp and pageantry were thought to be requisite. . . . One reason, and perhaps the most cogent of any, why the nobility of the Middle Ages, nay, and even princes and kings, delighted so much in the practice of tilting with each other, is that on such occasions they made their appearance with prodigious

> splendor, and had the opportunity of displaying their accomplishments to the greatest advantage (Strutt 1970:xxii).

Strutt states that the townsmen had many opportunities for amusement as well. In the pre-Reformation days, "their feasts and frolics and plays were usually associated, or at all events, somewhat slightly allied to the observance of religion" (1970:xxxii). The great diversion of the English forefathers was mumming, usually on saints' days. At Leicester, for instance, the images of St. Martin and the Virgin were borne through the streets with music and singing by twelve of the guildsmen, made up as the Apostles.

Not only Christian celebrations and ceremonies but Greco-Roman rituals were involved in the ritualized leisure of the English forefathers. Strutt writes about a popular spectacle exhibited in London at the beginning of the eighteenth century, entitled "The Expedition of Alexander the Great". The expedition opened with Alexander consulting the Oracle at Delphi as the bells rang for the joy of his arrival. In the tent of Darius, Alexander was to fall in love with a piece of waxwork representing the beautiful Statira.

When the leisure pursuits of the commoners and the gentry spilled over onto the Sabbath, many voices opposed such encroachment. In the twenty-second year of the reign of Elizabeth I, the magistrate of London obtained an edict that all "heathenish plays and interludes should be banished upon Sabbath days" (Strutt 1970:lviii).

Leisure Class

Another vice introduced to the British Isles was gambling. According to Strutt, the Saxons, the Danes, and the Normans all had this destructive propensity. It spread down to the commoners and in the Crusade of 1190 of the Common Era, Richard Coeur de Lion prohibited any person beneath the degree of knight from playing for money, which confirmed that gambling was a leisure class activity.

Gambling spread throughout the aristocracy into the reigns of Henry VIII and Elizabeth I. London went from having one gaming club in the sixteenth century to several a few years later. The Church had relaxed its restrictions and, in fact, conducted its own lottery as early as 1596, when 400,000 lots at ten shillings each were drawn at the west door of the Cathedral of Saint Paul. The profits were to go to the repairing of the heavens or ports of the kingdom, that is, the doors.

Some of the activities needed for survival became pastimes of the rich. While hunting rabbit and vermin was allowed for the masses, prizes such as bear and fox were left to the landlords, who were always protective of their lands and resources. The commoners developed their recreation activity despite the limitations imposed upon them by the nobility, who wanted them to practice mainly archery, an activity needed for defense of the nation.

Moreover, the nobility was eventually forced to share its leisure activities with the commoners. Bowling became a pastime of the powerful, although it seems to have originated among Germany's peasantry. In Germany, the poor brought their clubs with them to church and, to dramatize a point, the priests in the fourth century C.E. asked them to stand the clubs at a corner and to roll a large stone at them. The clubs represented evil. To hit them was praised; to fail meant that the peasant must try to lead a better life. The priests became intrigued with the process and took turns at trying. The elite picked it up and some centuries later it was practiced by the English masters. A manuscript in the Royal Library at Windsor contains a drawing representing two players aiming at a small cone. Bowling grew in popularity, but a royal edict in 1541, which was not repealed until 1845, forbade artisans, laborers, apprentices, servants, and the like from bowling at anytime except Christmas, and then only in the master's house and in his presence. Anyone possessing lands of yearly value of 100 pounds might obtain a license to play on his private green. Eventually, in the name of democracy, the green was open to the commoners.

Preindustrial Mass Leisure

A number of historians state that England was demarcated from the rest of European society by the absence of a peasantry and by the presence of a legal system that emphasized civil rights and protected property (Golby and Purdue 1984:20). These characteristics signal the coming of a modern society, according to Parsons (see the introduction). To the eighteenth-century small farmer, leisure was closely associated with work, and both "were engaged in a consciousness of tradition and custom and were surrounded by much ritual" (Golby and Purdue 1984:22). But eventually the religious significance of these festivals was lost: first, because England was trying to get away from the "Popish superstitions," and secondly because of the dwindling importance of kinship as a result of geographical mobility. These two factors may explain the change in the common person's pastime in pre-Reformation England. Pastimes in the English villages became boisterous, bawdy, violent, and even cruel. For example, cock throwing consisted of throwing missiles at a tethered cock until it died. Football, which started as an activity celebrating victory over a foreign enemy, became an intervillage "battle" in which 1,000 players from one village were pitted against 1,000 players from another.

Football, which is known in America as soccer, was played annually on Shrove Tuesday at Chester. Shrove Tuesday, a day of festival, became the day on which all medieval melees eventually took place. Traditionally, the first ball used was the head of a dead Danish brigand, a local way of celebrating victory over one's enemy. As the popularity of these activities increased among the villagers, they were no longer confined to days of festivals, to the dismay of both the nobility and the clergy.

According to Golby and Purdue (1984:42), the attack on the leisure pursuits and the life-styles of the common people gathered impetus in the sixteenth century, particularly when the commoners gave themselves an additional day off during the week, which they called Saint Monday (Baker 1982:104). The Church was concerned about economic efficiency and social order. Both the Reformation and the counter-Reformation (Protestants and Catholics) saw negative aspects to the common people's leisure pursuits.

> *There were more frequent attacks on traditional popular culture and there were more systematic attempts to purge it of both its "paganism" and its "license." This movement has, of course, a good deal to do with the Protestant and Catholic reformations, for the reform of the church, as it was understood at the time, necessarily involved the reform of what we call popular culture (Burke 1978:218).*

During the Industrial Revolution important changes took place in the leisure pursuits of the English common people. First was the eradication of most of the riotous and cruel blood sport of the countryside. Second was the elimination of most of the wakes and traditional holy days from the calendar. By 1834 the Bank of England's 47 weekday closures had fallen to only four (Lowerson and Myerscough 1977:14). But it was during the Victorian era that leisure in Britain was revolutionized.

Leisure in the Victorian Era

Lowerson and Myerscough (1977) believe that leisure pursuits in Great Britain during the nineteenth century went through a virtual revolution. First, there was the acceptance of a clear distinction in everyday life between work and leisure. Second was the rationalization of free time into a weekly and annual timetable of regular holidays and time off work. Finally, there were debates on the "constructive" use of free time.

The two-tier society that characterized eighteenth-century Britain developed a middle stratum. Golby and Purdue (1984:29) estimate that in the nineteenth century some 50% of the population would be classified as laboring poor, 2% made up the landowning upper order, and 18% the landed gentry. This left 30% to the middle class, which received more than 50% of the total national income. That class ranged from small farmers and shopkeepers to doctors and lawyers.

The impact of the middle class on leisure and popular culture was felt in two ways. First, they tried to emulate the upper class, the landed gentry and the aristocracy; and second, they helped in commercializing leisure pursuits into marketable commodities (Golby and Purdue 1984:30, Lowerson and Myerscough 1977:21). Accordingly, the Victorian era saw an acceleration in the cultural transmission of many of the practices of the upper stratum into the middle stratum and eventually into the lower stratum as well. There was a feeling among the well-to-do that they must practice democracy. As a matter of fact, the rest of the population was asking for it. Among its many benefits was the spread of literacy, which became an important factor in the expansion of leisure pursuits that were once limited to the rich.

The high rate of literacy, one of the highest in Europe, coupled with the increasing availability of the printed word, led to a publishing revolution. One of the products of this revolution was the new literary genre of the novel (Golby and Purdue 1984:32). Although looked upon with suspicion by the literary critics, the novel fulfilled the demands of the middle ranks of society, particularly the growing numbers of educated and leisured women.

Reading, as a leisure pursuit, eventually reached the lower levels of society through the chapbooks that contained traditional material of oral popular culture, such as chivalric tales and legends. Reading was perhaps the most important leisure pursuit that took place in the home of the Victorian poor. According to Lowerson and Myerscough (1977:58), the home proved to be second best to another attractive facility on the outside, the corner pub.

Alcoholic consumption went hand in hand with most sport of the eighteenth century. The inn, the beer shop, and the public house were the principle suppliers. The inns included sleeping accommodations. The beer house was the humblest of the three and sold beer exclusively. The public house grew out of the tavern and the alehouse and sold a wider range of drinks. According to Golby and Purdue (1984:119), drinking continued to be a major leisure pursuit for the working poor, and the pub became the center of their social lives. These people generally had no means of excitement or amusement during the week and the pub provided them with warmth, lavatories, and company.

The middle-class publicans were instrumental in the commercialization of leisure activities. They also played an important part in maintaining football and cricket clubs, cockfighting, and ratting, as as well as skittles, quoits, and pitch and toss.

The Victorian pub was not exclusive to males. Drinking in the daytime with a female was popular. Saturday nights were family nights in the pub and also in the "free and easies," the precursors of the music hall. The transition took place in the 1850s, and by 1866 there were 33 large music halls in London. Their financial structure changed, and the publican was replaced by shareholders and theatre managers. The simple platform became a well-lit, curtained stage. Sales of liquor declined sharply for two reasons. A fixed seating system made it difficult to buy drinks, but more importantly, the shareholders were keen to please the respectable Victorians who associated these halls with an unruly audience, gambling, prostitution, and alcohol abuse. The small halls, numbering between 200 and 300, continued to serve the working and lower middle classes (Golby and Purdue 1984:175). It was in one of these music halls that on 5 March 1900 the first film was shown. In the following year, cinema-shows caught on.

In the meantime, the middle class was looking to emulate the upper stratum who traditionally lived in the country. By the end of the eighteenth century, rich gentlemen built second homes in the country, starting what Lowerson and Myerscough call the "Consumer Towns." "This leisured society established both the physical fabric of resorts and the fashionable taste for the sea, which were exploited in the Victorian popularization of seaside

holidays for the middle classes and the development of excursions for the masses" (Lowerson and Myerscough 1977:29).

A train excursion was organized for the first time from London to Brighton on Easter Day of 1844 and created great popular excitement. It raised the question of the conflict between rough and respectable recreations. *Punch* carried verses on the subject (Lowerson and Myerscough 1977:32).

What does he come for?
What does he want?
Why does he wander thus?
Careworn and gaunt?
Up street and down street with him,
Dull vacant stare,
Hither and thither, it
Don't matter where!

What does he mean by it?
Why does he come
Hundreds of miles to prowl
Weary and glum,
Blinking at Kosmos with
Lack-lustre eye?
He doesn't enjoy it, he
Don't even try!

Why don't he stay at home?
Save his train fare,
Soak at his native beer?
Sunday clothes wear?
No one would grudge it

No one would jeer.
Why does he come away?
Why is he here?

Sunny or soaking, it's
All one to him,
Wandering painfully—
Curious whim!
Gazing at chins-shops,
Gaping at sea,
Guzzling at beer-shops, or
Gorging at tea.

The social life of the gentry and aristocracy alternated between country estates and town houses. Both houses had to be large enough to accommodate the many social responsibilities of their owners' new positions. The family mansions became the recreation center of the upper-class families. In imitating the aristocracy, the gentry introduced the concept of a country house that had billiard and smoking rooms in addition to the bedrooms, study, dining room, and reception hall. The country houses served as symbols of wealth, along with the nannies, croquet lawns, and motor cars (Lowerson and Myerscough 1977:53).

Domestic leisure among the middle classes developed quickly in the second half of the nineteenth century as a result of the increase in the size of their housing, some of which were called villas. Elaborate gardens of the large villas were designed to create, within a quarter of an acre, the illusion of a country estate. Others had recreation rooms for billiards and smoking (Lowerson and Myerscough 1977:55).

It was during the Victorian era that interest in sport increased. Although the old version of football (soccer) was still played in Dorking, Surrey, on a Shrove Tuesday in 1888 (Lowerson and Myerscough 1977:119), the sport had been adopted and modified as a method of diverting minds from drink, gambling, and other wasteful activities—an idea promoted by the headmasters of public (private) schools.

The concept was amenable to "muscular Christians" who argued that a healthy mind depended on a fit body. Amongst the ranks of the ex-public school boys and university men were the chairmen and members of national sport organizations (Golby and Purdue 1984:166). Other than football, rugby, and cricket, which spread rapidly toward the end of the century, new sports that emphasized physical fitness and individual efforts—golf, tennis, and cycling—were becoming popular among the middle class.

As the popularity of sport increased, so did traveling to and watching particular games. Along with this interest came gambling, which was catered to by some newspapers with their tipsters on football and horse racing, once again to the chagrin of many Victorians (Golby and Purdue 1984:171). By 1902, sport gambling seemed endemic and the House of Lords Select Committee on Gambling attempted to plug the loopholes by passing the Street Betting Act.

The Victorians were pleased with adult education. The Museum Act of 1845 and the Public Libraries Act of 1850 gave local authorities permission to build museums and libraries out of the public rates. Yet their growth was very slow: only 60 libraries were built by 1875. Nonetheless, reading was popular and working men found in London's 1,500 coffee houses a place to eat, have a cup of coffee, and read periodicals and newspapers, despite the very long hours at work (Golby and Purdue 1984:131).

The Struggle for Free Time

Great Britain was the first nation to enter the era of industrialization (see fig. 3.2). It started with improved spinning and weaving machines, the railroad locomotives, and the factory system. On the social side, industrialization led to the removal of large numbers of men and women from agricultural pursuits to novel ways of working and living. For one, workers could no longer depend on their gardens to provide them with food, and they became entirely dependent on the machine for their subsistence. Not only did they work 13 hours a day for six days a week, specialization forced them to perform the same task again and again, all day long.

The presence of a large pool of workers meant insecurity, for other than the huge influx of workers from rural areas, women and children were also available for work. Shutdowns, depressions, and business failures added to the problem of unemployment. Moreover, the factories in which people worked lacked good sanitation.

All this led some reformers to label the early days of industrialization in Britain as "the bleak age" or "the new barbarism." The famous Sadler report of 1832 exposed the conditions of industrial workers and stimulated the movement for reform (Lowerson and Myerscough 1977:13).

Work hours were reduced gradually, and by the 1880s the average worker put in 10 hours a day. The "Great Depression" in the middle of the decade led to unemployment of about 10%, and organized trades turned to a shortened workday in order to spread work (G. Cross 1986:73). Despite the business upturn that reduced unemployment, the workers liked the shorter workday. Some unions failed, either through strikes or collective bargaining, to get their employers to agree on an eight-hour day. This increased the demand for legislative solutions.

The push for shorter workdays was stimulated by more than just economics. The expansion of leisure opportunities was instrumental in the workers' demand for shorter workdays. Some workers, and some social reformers as well, suggested that a shorter workday would provide additional hours to be spent with families.

Between 1886 and 1891, an unprecedented wave of discussion of the eight-hour day swamped the press (Cross 1986:74). Some stated that it was the inevitable result of an age of democracy. Others saw in the increased free time a means of eliminating structured and cyclical unemployment. Some felt that workers would be able to participate in leisure pursuits, and so enrich their lives. It was thought that families and familial ties would be enhanced by short workdays.

Employers were not in favor of any legislation to shorten the workday, except perhaps for women and children. In their opinion, any hour legislation would violate the tenets of classical liberalism: the free hour contract. Such legislation would weaken, if not destroy, the self-reliance for which the British worker has been famous. Some of those opposed to shortening work hours invoked the old Malthusian formula that increased free time would simply lead to increased population, and so impoverishment. If not, the free time would be spent unwisely in cabarets and the like.

Well-established labor unions and the smaller ones were unable to win reduced hours through collective bargaining and took to the parliamentary approach. This shift set the British Trade Union Congress on a path toward the Labour Party, which emerged in 1906 (Cross 1986:76).

The fear that a reduced workday would make British business uncompetitive in the world market was somewhat alleviated by the fact that most European and American labor movements advocated a simultaneous reduction in hours. This became the *raison d'etre* of the Second International Labor Congress in Paris in 1889.

Bills for an eight-hour day in 1890 and 1891 failed to go beyond parliamentary committees. Cross believes this was the result of an ideological gap between two groups of supporters. The conservatives who called for improvement in family and church life had nothing in common with irreligious male unionists who demanded hour reduction in order to spread work and pursue leisure activities (1986:84). A recession lasting from 1891 to 1896 put an end to the concept, but not for long.

The short hours issue would reappear periodically with strikes, and each time some little gain was made. At the beginning of the century, a new attitude toward leisure was emerging. It was centered around the assumption that leisure stimulates consumption in addition to strengthening family ties.

The major strikes that took place immediately after World War I combined with Prime Minister Lloyd George's concern over war-weary workers obliged the elite to concede a short workday for their sacrifices during the war. Legislation was passed to this effect in April 1919.

The Leisure Explosion

According to Roberts (1978:21), an explosion in leisure pursuits took place in Great Britain, shown by the increase in the sale of recreational goods and in the attendance at art galleries and the ten large

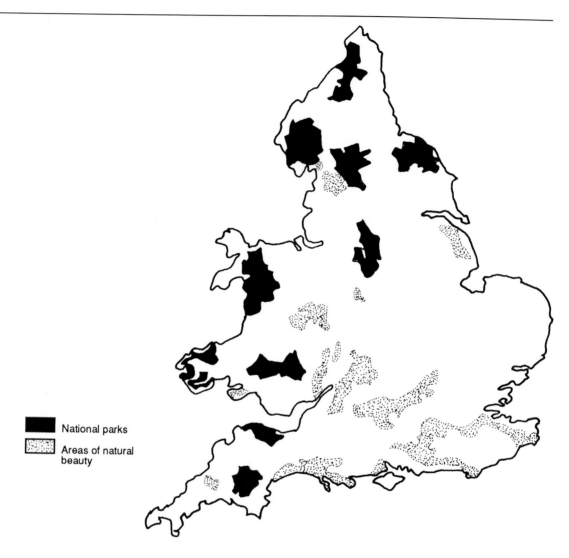

FIGURE 9.1 *National resources in England and Wales. Source: Mr. Lynd Warren, Whittier, CA.*

National parks

Areas of natural beauty

museums in London. Both central and local governments responded with the establishment of Councils for Arts, Sport and Countryside. Catering to leisure pursuits is now accepted as a legitimate function of government, which faces the fact that most of the potential natural resources

are not easily accessible to the public. Chubb and Chubb (1981:527) suggest that the densely settled nations of Europe were unable to establish publicly-owned national parks or forest systems like the ones in Canada and the United States. Britain's first national park was designed in 1950, but its national parks, which constitute one-tenth of

Table 9.1 Participation in broad groups of activity in Great Britain

Quarter*	% Participating in 4 weeks before interview											
	1973				1977				1980			
	1	2	3	4	1	2	3	4	1	2	3	4
Outdoor sports	12†	19†	24†	14†	22	27	39	23	24	27	38	33
Indoor sports	9†	11†	9†	10†	22	22	21	20	23	23	23	23
Watching sport	10	10	10	11	9	11	11	9	8	9	10	10
Open-air outings	12	24	34	14	7	17	29	11	7	10	27	20
Informal recreation—buildings	4	9	16	6	6	13	24	11	7	11	23	17
Entertainment and cultural	17	17	18	19	18	19	22	20	20	20	18	19
Social outings	37†	37†	42†	38†	65	66	71	67	67	67	70	68
Hobbies	—†	—†	—†	—†	79	86	88	85	81	85	89	87
TV and radio	94	92	92	96	99	100	99	99	100	99	99	99
Social activity	—†	—†	—†	—†	92	91	91	92	92	93	93	91
	Activity days: days participation per 1000 population											
Outdoor sports	2120†	4140†	6500†	2960†	4990	6500	10920	5690	5870	6650	10920	8570
Indoor sports	1850†	1960†	1560†	1930†	5330	5630	4620	4640	5620	4910	4620	5500
Watching sport	970	920	970	960	840	1000	1050	890	770	780	1050	1100
Open-air outings	1710	3850	6390	2100	720	2140	4600	1340	940	2470	4610	1440
Informal recreation—buildings	250	580	1360	380	380	860	2370	870	550	1200	2370	1020
Entertainment and cultural	1150	1160	1300	1230	950	890	1120	1020	1090	1100	1290	1040

* Quarter 1: January–March; Quarter 2: April–June; Quarter 3: July–September; Quarter 4: October–December.
† Indicates 1973 data not available and/or not comparable with later surveys.
Source: Veal, A. J. "Leisure in England and Wales: A Research Note," Leisure Studies 3(2) 1984, p. 223. E. & F. N. Spon. Reprinted with permission.

England and Wales, are still predominantly privately owned. Most of these lands are pastures with some remnants of the original hard wood forests. Some areas within these parks were designated state forests and were developed to provide pleasure driving, walking, picnicking, fishing, camping, and orienteering (see fig. 9.1).

Leisure Pursuits of the British

Three surveys conducted in 1973, 1977, and 1980 by the government's office of Population Census and Surveys included questions on leisure. The General Household Survey (GHS), as it is known, is a nationwide survey of over 20,000 persons aged 16 and over. Since a year is a long time over which to ask a person to remember his activities with any accuracy, the respondents were asked to report their leisure activities during the four weeks before the interview. The results are shown in table 9.1 and table 9.2.

Veal concludes that the figures present a fairly usual pattern in which home-based activity and socializing are more popular than participatory activities such as sport or vicarious ones such as cultural events. The data also show that walking for pleasure is dominant in outdoor activities, while darts and snooker/billiards, the usual English pub pastimes, are dominant among the indoor activities. While soccer is the most watched sport on television, visits to historical sites are the most popular informal leisure pursuit. Dancing, theater, and movies are dominant amusive leisure pursuits; and voluntary work seems to be a most-liked social activity among the British.

Reading also seems to be a popular leisure pursuit in Great Britain. Although the number of public libraries, 163, may seem too small, their holdings of over 151 million books create a ratio of 3.0 books to each citizen—one of the best in the world. Also, Great Britain has a high number of books published a year, also one of the best in the

Table 9.2 Individual activities, 1980, in Great Britain

Activity	Most popular quarter	% Participating in 4 weeks before interview most popular quarter	Frequency of participation per week most popular quarter	Activity days per 1,000 population	
				Most popular quarter	Annual total
Outdoor					
Walking	3	21.8	2.0	5,790	18,820
Swimming in sea	3	6.1	1.5	1,200	1,730
Golf	3	3.1	1.1	425	1,240
Fishing	3	3.1	1.0	375	740
Soccer	2	2.9	1.1	410	1,620
Tennis	3	2.8	1.0	380	790
Camping	3	2.7	1.9	680	930
Cycling	3	1.6	2.3	570	1,680
Bowls	3	1.6	1.3	250	500
Cricket	3	1.4	1.2	225	365
Athletics/running	2	1.2	2.4	350	1,190
Indoor					
Darts	1	7.9	1.7	1,750	5,730
Swimming	3	7.9	0.7	780	2,380
Snooker/billiards	2	7.2	1.8	1,710	5,820
Squash	2	2.7	1.1	390	1,380
Badminton	1	2.5	1.0	330	1,110
Table tennis	3	2.4	0.9	370	1,060
Keep fit/yoga etc.	1	2.2	1.3	360	1,110
Ten-pin bowls etc.	3	1.3	0.8	190	580
Watching sport (live, not on TV)					
Soccer	4	5.0	0.7	430	1,390
Cricket	3	1.5	0.6	110	200
Motor sports	2	1.3	0.7	110	250
Horse events	3	1.3	0.6	70	160
Informal					
Urban parks	3	5.8	1.0	780	1,915
Seaside	3	15.5	0.9	1,915	2,935
Countryside	3	6.7	1.0	880	2,055
Other car outings	3	2.5	2.3	775	2,145
Boat trips	3	1.0	0.4	45	90
Other trips	3	2.3	0.4	125	250
Historic buildings	3	17.0	0.9	2,065	3,875
Museums/galleries	3	5.2	0.5	350	830
Exhibitions	3	3.5	0.4	170	495
Zoos	3	3.1	0.3	105	225
Wildlife parks	3	1.0	0.3	45	80
Arts and entertainment					
Cinema	1	10.8	0.4	620	2,135
Theatre	4	5.2	0.3	220	900
Music concerts	4	1.2	0.4	65	195
Other entertainment	3	3.4	0.5	240	1,070
Dancing	1	15.1	0.8	1,680	6,030
Fun fairs	3	3.8	0.6	320	680
Local events	3	2.8	0.3	130	310
Amateur music/drama	1	3.8	3.0	1,530	4,895
Drinking/eating out	3	68.2	na	na	na
Bingo	2/3	8.3	1.2	1,470	5,350

Table 9.2 Continued

Activity	Most popular quarter	% Participating in 4 weeks before interview most popular quarter	Frequency of participation per week most popular quarter	Activity days per 1,000 population	
				Most popular quarter	Annual total
Home-based					
Gardening	3	59.1	na	na	na
Hobbies	4	7.1	na	na	na
Do-it-yourself	3	39.9	na	na	na
Knitting/sewing	4	30.2	na	na	na
Cooking/brewing	4	1.6	1.6	345	925
TV	4	98.1	na	na	na
Radio	4	89.4	na	na	na
Records	1	66.5	na	na	na
Books	4	57.4	na	na	na
Social etc.					
Social clubs	4	15.1	1.1	2,285	7,940
Social/voluntary work	4	8.7	1.4	1,570	6,135
Friends/relatives	3	92.1	na	na	na
Church	4	1.9	1.1	290	1,055
Evening classes	4	2.7	0.9	325	780

Source: Veal, A. J. "Leisure in England and Wales: A Research Note," Leisure Studies 3(2) 1984, pp. 224–25. E. & F. N. Spon. Reprinted with permission.

world. There are 113 daily newspapers published in the United Kingdom, with a combined circulation of over 25 million—a ratio of one paper to every 1.98 citizens, possibly the best in the world (see table 7.1).

Among the leisure pursuits of contemporary Britons is tourism. The country has provided through its long history many attractive sites. Also, historical buildings that are no longer used are maintained by nonprofit organizations or governmental agencies and open to the public. The 900-year old Tower of London is a good example. In addition, the traveler interested in museums can choose from many small and large ones.

The pub continues to be a focus of leisure pursuits among British men, more so than among its women. In some of these establishments special rooms are provided for local musicians to play. In others, "Americana" has appeared: jukeboxes, disco music, and electronic games (Chubb and Chubb 1981:374).

Modern sport had its inception in Great Britain. It is still participated in by the enthusiasts and watched by the aficionados. But it has suffered since the early seventies of what is now called "football hooliganism," a working class youth problem, according to K. Roberts (1983a:29), since other sports do not suffer from the same kind of vandalism. The assimilation of alcohol into teenage leisure life-style added to the problem. Attempts to alleviate this condition have not been very successful. More will be said on the global problem of violence and sport later.

LEISURE IN FRANCE

By the end of the tenth century, there were attempts to unite France under one king. It took almost three centuries to do so. By 1328 the king's *domini*, or rule, was accepted all over France, with a few exceptions. The monarchy was supported by the clergy, who derived from it help and protection. A school established in the early years of the twelfth century later became the University of Paris, the largest center of theological studies in Christendom. Eventually, secular thought and literature developed. Yet France continued to be an agrarian society largely dependent on the efforts of the masses who toiled the land.

Life began to change gradually as trade along the Mediterranean shore and contact with Italian principalities increased. Trade centers and fairs disrupted the manorial economy as the *metiers* (guilds) began to organize themselves in the growing towns. Despite the dynastic change that took place in 1328, life for the rich and for the poor remained the same.

The Heritage

According to de Grazia (1962:112), in the *ancien regime* (the political and social system before the Revolution of 1789) the Church had granted the worker 52 Sundays, 90 rest days, and 38 holidays a year. Whatever leisure pursuits the workers practiced then had a religious flavor. For in France, as in all human societies, festivals at one point or another had magico-religious significance and were eventually divorced from the ordinary life of monotony and misery. These ceremonies took on the character of a total collective freeing of body and soul. In France, the bishops themselves, up to the end of the sixteenth century, allowed the annual orgies of the Feast of Fools between Christmas and Epiphany. These feasts were diluted into daily life and thereby lost their explosive character. Some, in fact, vanished completely. But many remained (Dumazedier 1967:55).

The life-style of the rich was different, in that hunting was recreational and conducted with great flare. The kings of France hunted in the woods of Versailles, where King Louis XIII had a cottage built. Additional buildings elaborately oriented toward recreational participation took place over the years. Around the huge terrace of the main structure, which was adorned with ornamental basins, statues, and vases, the Versailles garden included a grand canal 200 feet wide and one mile long, with gondolas provided for the king and his guests. An artificial lake filled with water fowl adorned the garden, along with numerous groves, one of which had a waterfall. A botanical garden supplemented the grounds, which were basically designed with treillage and parterres. One of the chateaux included a museum of old carriages and harnesses.

Jean Jacque Rousseau proposed the idea of "natural man" living in harmony with the land, which gave rise to the attachment to nature. Yet the French aristocracy continued to erect highly manicured gardens such as Versailles, the Luxembourg, and the Tuilleries, which they limited to themselves. Eventually, the aristocracy succumbed to pressures of the public and opened these facilities to the commoners, a practice that had been followed in Italy since the thirteenth century. They also responded to the demands for open space in crowded Paris by constructing Green Lawn along the ramparts of the Seine and the Place Royale, a large plaza with a long promenade (McCollum 1979:105).

During Robespierre's period of the French Revolution, the Republic adopted a ten-day week, cutting the annual Sabbaths to 36. The new regime also stripped the holiness of many Catholic saints, reducing the number of holy days. The workers of France lost some of the free time they had enjoyed under the monarchy. Nonetheless, holiday celebrations continued on, even later under the industrialization that led to an increase in work hours (de Grazia 1962:112).

The following period in the history of France, from the Empire to the Second Republic of 1848, was a period of both political repression and accumulation of capital. The social structure of the working class was not conducive to its advancement, including its demand for free time (Samuel 1986:50).

La Belle Epoque

July 14, 1880, was a very memorable day in France, not only as a celebration of 91 years since the Bastille was stormed, but also as the first day of *La Belle Epoque* (Rearick 1985:3). France was coming out of an economic slump and its army had just recovered from its defeat by the Germans a decade earlier. The promises of the Republic of Liberty and Fraternity raised hopes. In the manner of traditional religious holidays, the celebration combined ritual and merrymaking. The state had taken over from the Roman Catholic Church the role of creating and organizing festivals, to a point. On that day was dedicated a neoclassical statue of a woman, to be nicknamed Marianne, who came to symbolize the Republic.

All over Paris and the other cities, the young and energetic scrambled up a greased pole to snatch a prize, competed in swimming, foot, and donkey races, and danced in the decorated squares (Rearick 1985:11). In the country, peasants returned to the game of *tir de l'oie:* blindfolded, they threw sticks at a suspended goose to see who could knock its head off first.

France was turning away from German pessimism and English prudish mannerisms to its Gallic inheritance, with an unsurpassed capacity to enjoy this world's delights (Rearick 1985:36). By 1900, Paris had an all-time high number of cafes, cabarets, and wine shops—11.25 for every thousand residents. Cafe concerts appeared around the turn of the century and became the "democratized theater," the Folies-Bergères being the most famous of all. The years from 1880 to 1914 saw unprecedented growth in sport, both in participation and spectating. One of the most popular sports was horse racing. France also developed world-class athletes, particularly in warrior arts such as fencing and shooting.

On a cold night in December 1895, Louis Lumiere gave his commercial show in the basement of Grand Cafe, and word spread quickly by the 35 customers that cinema was born.

Current Practices

In the 1880s, the workday in France was longer than in Britain (Cross 1986:73). Most workers put in 12 hours a day, six days a week. In fact, Sunday work was common in construction, seasonal trades, and in commerce. The immediate objective of the French laborer before the turn of the century was to win a ten-hour day (Samuel 1986). A bill proposing a ten-hour limit was defeated in the Chamber of Deputies under the Third Republic in 1878, 1885, and 1886. It was finally adopted in 1912 (Attias-Donfut and Dumazedier 1975:48).

By that time, the eight-hour day was becoming an objective and was granted to mailmen in 1901. When Sunday became an official Sabbath in 1906, the concept of *semaine anglaise,* the English week of six eight-hour days, was introduced (Cross 1986:73).

Another aspect of free time is vacation, which, until the turn of the century, was practiced only by gentlemen. In 1900, employees of the rapid transit system of Paris (Metropolitan) were granted ten days of paid vacation a year. But the bill introduced in the Chamber of Deputies in 1913 to apply the same to all French companies was rejected. The arguments presented in the French Chamber of Deputies opposing a shortened workday and paid vacation were similar to those presented in the British Parliament.

Although there were a few labor strikes in France demanding shorter work hours after World War I, the Clemenceau government was "sufficiently threatened by the prospect of Bolshevization of workers and veterans that it called for hours legislation" (Cross 1986:85). Shunning employers' concern over a possible collapse of the French economy, the Chamber hurriedly passed an eight-hour-day bill in April of 1919 after eight days of deliberation.

The idea for the reduction of the workweek from 48 hours to 40 hours was first introduced by the World Labor Organization. In 1936 a bill for 40-hour workweeks and 12-day annual vacations was introduced, but only the paid vacation passed. The paid vacation was increased to 18 days in 1956. Although a 40-hour workweek is still not law in France, most French workers put in about that many hours a week (Attias-Donfut and Dumazedier 1975:51). An ordinance was passed in 1982 limiting the workweek to 39 hours for salaried workers (Samuel 1986:53). A 35-hour workweek is expected to be achieved in France in the 1990s.

The idea of compulsory retirement gained ground in 1890 and was passed as a law in 1910, but it failed to materialize until after World War II. At that time, a French national at age 60 with 30 years of work could retire with an entitlement to 20% of his salary; at age 65 it increased to 40%; at age 70 he was entitled to 60%. All this changed on 1 April 1983: a French citizen is now entitled to full benefits, which increases the possibility for more free time (Samuel 1986:54).

In 1936 all salaried employees were entitled to 12 paid working days annual vacation. It was increased to 18 in 1956 and to 24 in 1969 (Samuel 1986:53). This was in addition to 10 holidays a year celebrated in typically French fashion.

Dumazedier (1967:56) suggests that holiday celebrations are still practiced in contemporary society not only because they help social cohesion but because they respond to authority either sacred or secular. On this last point, he is in essential agreement with Grimes (1982:42), in that in ceremonies one has to surrender to the offices or causes of the ceremony (see discussion on ceremony in chap. 1). When, over the years, an office or authority loses its grip and the cause forgotten, the ceremony becomes a celebration, characterized by spontaneity. Such was the case in France and most modern societies. For example, Christmas in France claims to have the greatest number of celebrants, followed in January by the Epiphany, or "La fête des rois" (King's Day). Candelmas Day in February is no longer the feast of the Purification of the Virgin Mary. Easter is still celebrated, and April Fool's Day still holds on. The Pentecost has expanded into three days that are used today for traveling and camping. Saint John's Day is the traditional feast of midsummer. All Saint's Day and Virgin Mary Day are now occasions for family members to get together and are still very much alive as celebrations.

There are, on the other hand, secular holidays, among which is July 14, the most vital in parades and festivities. It has, to a great extent, taken the place of Saint Jean's Day as the greatest traditional feast of midsummer. Victory Day (May 8) and Armistice Day (November 11) are not celebrated as much.

Leisure à la francaise

With the introduction of the eight-hour day in 1919 and the mandatory paid vacation in 1936, as well as the practice of five-day workweeks, leisure pursuits in France changed. Among the activities stimulated by the new free time was tourism. Tourism became an urban activity, particularly among the 18% of the French population who reside in Paris and who account for 51% of expenditure on vacations. Seventy-two percent of the capital's residents took a vacation compared to 37% in Lille. In 1951, 45% of vacationers chose the countryside for their vacation, 25% the sea, 15% the mountains, and the rest stayed home because of lack of means. Most of the tourists took the train in the 1950s, but the proportion using cars has increased dramatically (Dumazedier 1967:129).

But the French were already enamored of one of the technological achievements of the twentieth century, the cinema. By 1950, 75% of residents of French cities attended the movies at least once a month; the remaining 25% went to the movies more than once a month. According to Dumazedier, the reasons given were, generally speaking, to seek release, break monotony, and shed the daily routine. Many of the moviegoers looked at it as a way to pass the time. Dumazedier concludes that interpretations of movies vary significantly among the French audience (1967:141).

In France, most people watched television for two hours a day in 1957. The amount of time may have been higher when television was introduced a few years earlier. In fact, television watching dropped to almost one hour per day in the 1970s (see table 8.1). The slogan of French television, which is controlled by the state through Radio

Television Francaise, is "To entertain, to inform, to educate." French audiences like variety shows, game shows, and sports programs. Films are not enthusiastically accepted because they are usually old (Dumazedier 1967:159), yet theatrical presentations are liked. News coverage and social themes are much more appreciated by the public. Scientific programs are well received, as is literary education such as the program "Reading for Everyone."

When it comes to book production, which is, of course, related to leisure reading, France was in seventh place in the world in the 1950s, following the Soviet Union, the United Kingdom, India, Japan, West Germany, and the United States (Dumazedier 1967:177). The figures used in the above comparison must be considered carefully. Some countries used a very broad definition of "book," others a narrower definition. According to the United Nations Publication, France still holds a very good place in book production, 42,186 books a year (see table 7.1).

France also has a good number of public libraries (1,028, or one library for each 54,474 citizens). All libraries are run by the Central Library Administration. Historically speaking, during the French Revolution, an enormous number of books were taken from the reading rooms of the privileged leisure class and were placed in public libraries, which proved to be too limited in both space and maintenance. It was not until World War II that municipal libraries were modernized. In addition, every educational institution in France has its own library, making a total of over 5,000 libraries. Also, large enterprises such as the French National Railway Company (SNCF) developed their own libraries.

A study cited by Dumazedier shows that French nationals are interested in voluntary education; in fact, "the subjects which the greatest amount of time and importance are devoted to in school are not those that have the greatest interest of adults" (1967:213). Workers are more interested in practical and technical subjects, as well as in mathematics. Executives and managers, on the other hand, show interest in art and literature. When asked if a paid sabbatical of 12 days would be useful to further their education, 61% of executives and 31% of workers indicated interest.

The only cross-cultural time-budget study available (Szalai 1972), although two decades old, is used here to give an idea of the patterns of time use. It shows that the French sample had 245 minutes of free time, 121 of which were spent on leisure pursuits, such as socializing (50 minutes), being outdoors (11 minutes), and resting (33 minutes). In addition, the French sample spent 58 minutes a day watching television and 27 minutes in the movies (table 8.1).

LEISURE IN WEST GERMANY

Germany bequeathed few relics of the glacier age, among which was the Steinheim man, possibly a precursor of the Neanderthal man of 25,000 years ago. There, on the plains and in the forests, humans settled. Their descendants we know as the Teutonic, Gothic, and Vandal tribes. They became Roman subjects, and Christians. Traces of these civilizations are seen in Germany today.

In 962, Emperor Otto began the Holy Roman Empire, but the relationship with the Catholic popes was never smooth. On 31 October 1517, a Catholic priest named Martin Luther nailed on the door of his Wittenberg church his theses protesting the actions of the Catholic Church. A religious cleavage resulted between the Protestant German north and the Catholic south.

At the end of the seventeenth century, the idea of a German state, possibly a Germanic Holy Roman Empire, persisted. The core would be the Kingdom of Prussia, the Sparta of modern Europe, with its disciplined people whose loyalty to their landlords was unshakable. The dominance of Prussia ended with its defeat by Napoleon. Yet the idea of a German state continued and was realized under the leadership of Prince Otto von Bismark, a Prussian aristocrat. One of his successors, Kaiser Wilhelm II, though the grandson of Queen Victoria of Great Britain, transformed World War I into a world conflict. The Versailles Treaty following World War I deprived Germany of its colonies and power. Nonetheless, less than twenty years later, Germany started another devastating war that resulted in the creation of two Germanies: East Germany and West Germany.

West Germany is composed of eleven states, including Berlin, which form the Federal Republic of Germany. The President appoints a chancellor (Prime Minister) upon the request of the Bundestag (Parliament). Despite its phenomenal economic recovery, West Germany has had to deal with a number of problems, mainly concerning its identity and place in the world community.

After almost two decades of political stability, West Germany experienced student unrest in the 1960s. H. V. Schierwater (1971:69) believes that the authoritarian stance of German parents coupled with an undemocratic educational system may have led to the problem. For instance, one-third of persons born in any one year in the 1960s did not finish elementary school (8th or 9th grade). After ten years of education, some German youth take the Intermediate Certificate, which enables them to become a middle echelon civil servant. Others go to the *Gymnasium* for nine years after four years of basic schooling. After these 13 years of school, they are entitled to enter the university. University education is long and protracted; the average age at graduation is 27 years. Despite all that vigor and discipline, at home and school, the average German pursues his *freizeit* (leisure) intensely. This is in spite of the fact that a hundred years ago the term *freizeit* was not yet coined (Hintereder 1988:34).

According to Hintereder, the first attempt at regulating working hours was undertaken in Prussia in 1839 when those under the age of 16 were limited to ten hours of work a day. But it was not until 1910 that the ten-hour workday became the norm in German industry. In 1919 the German workers were entitled to a three-day annual holiday. After World War II, with West Germany's rapid economic development, a five-day workweek was adopted. Today the typical German worker puts in forty hours of work a week and is entitled to five to six weeks paid leave in addition to holidays.

West German Holidays and Festivals

West Germans have 10 holidays: New Year's Day, Good Friday, Easter Monday, Labor Day, Ascension, Whitmonday, Day of German Unity, Repentance Day, Christmas, and Boxing Day. It seems that pagan festivals of nature became associated with the major feasts of the Christian Church. In the pagan era, winter solstice was celebrated; thus Christmas became a great feast. Yule was the feast of newly rising light; Christianity transformed it to the feast of heavenly light, the birth of Jesus. There was slaughtering of animals then, which was retained in Christmas feasting. The burning of incense at pagan time was replaced by lighting candles at Christmas.

All through the Rhineland, a large area that includes the famous Black Forest and many Roman ruins, a great festival takes place on the eleventh hour of the eleventh day of the eleventh month and reaches its peak the week before Ash Wednesday. There is dancing and music and parades. Bavaria, in the south, celebrates *Fasching,* which is an exuberant festival held just before Lent. Its Oktoberfest, sixteen days of beer-sodden revelry, has become a trademark for Germany, as well as a worldwide festival.

Leisure Pursuits

According to Robert Larson (1971:88), "it was in Berlin that the world's first regular television broadcasting began on March 22, 1935." In 1961, the Federal Republic had one television channel broadcasting five hours a day. In ten years, a second channel was added, and a year later educational television was installed. The first color television in Europe began in Berlin on August 25, 1967. Today, 89% of West German households own a colored television and 21% own more than one set (Hintereder 1988). Some 80% of West Germany's population watch television for 61–72 minutes a day (see table 8.1). Table 7.1 shows that there is one television set for each 3.57 citizens. Interest in movies and television seems to have no effect on reading as a leisure pursuit among West Germans. Books are being published at a high rate for mass consumption. New pocket book series are being launched all the time. Table 7.1 shows that 58,592 books of all sorts are published in West Germany every year, with a ratio that is comparable to that of Great Britain and one of the best among all the nations discussed in this volume. While the number of public libraries is not available, their holdings amount to 76,767,000 volumes, or 1.3 books for each West German citizen. West Germany has 368 daily newspapers with a circulation of 25,103,000, or one newspaper per each 4.12 citizens. Yet the West German sample in the cross-cultural time-budget study (Szalai 1972) did not indicate that Germans spend more time reading newspapers, magazines, or books than the rest of the national samples. They only surpassed the French sample (table 8.1).

Theater-going is also quite high in West Germany. Hamburg has the most theatergoers, followed by Berlin, then Munich (Brodda 1971:93). According to Jochen Truby (1987:20), the German stage is subsidized such that admission cost does not exceed that of a cinema seat. There is no shortage of playhouses either. The diversity of the German theater is historically rooted. The kings, dukes, and princes of the past insisted on their own theaters at any cost. This has led to both the variety and universality of the German stage today. At the end of World War II, West Germany began to rebuild; 25 public theaters with seating capacities ranging from 200 to 1,300 were built, and 76 private theaters were built with government subsidies. These were multipurpose theaters for opera, ballet, and music performances. Today, the German stage produces, in addition to German plays, English, French, and Italian plays, translated for the German public. Ballets, operas, and concerts are just as popular.

German music, particularly, has gone through many transformations. Originally, it was influenced by French trouvères who, in the Middle Ages, travelled from town to town singing and composing (see chap. 6). In addition, a form of choral music from the Byzantine tradition was practiced. During the Renaissance, German music was influenced by the Italians from the south with their love of pleasure, and by the Dutch with their gloom and brooding. Extreme human feeling showed up in German music, expressing the composers' inner conflicts. Music and drama were combined in the many operas produced. All these are called early music (Ely 1987:30). Jazz, which became popular in the 1920s, was banned under Hitler, but came back after 1945. In 1968, rock music became the symbol of youth protests and remains so today.

Films have been produced in Germany since the birth of the medium in 1895. It was used as a propaganda tool in the Nazi era. After World War II, movie production did not pick up until state support became available through the Film Promotion Institute (FFA), the Young German Film curatorium, and through national film prizes.

There are over 2,000 museums in the Federal Republic of Germany. At least 57 million citizens, or 93.4% of West Germans, visited at least one museum within a twelve-month period (Seib and Hintereder 1986:18). German museums do not make a clear division between natural and human history. In many museums, one will find rare examples of relics from early cultures and human remains as well. An example is the limestone bust of Queen Nefertiti of ancient Egypt (ca. 1335 B.C.E.) and the lower jawbone of Beijing Man, which goes back 300,000 years, both housed in the Berlin Museum. There are also small, unique museums, such as the Butchers' Museum in Boblinger, the Bakers' Museum in Ulm, and the Pharmacists' Museum in Heidelberg.

But the healthiest of pastimes in West Germany is Sport for Everyone. According to Neumann (1985:18–30), in the early postwar years, sport suffered from a stigma left over from the National Socialism era when sport was used as a vehicle for propaganda and paramilitary training. In an attempt to combat a sedentary way of life, a grass-root movement of Sport for Everyone came into being, which Neumann likens to the great *turn-verein* movement in the early 1800s under the leadership of Friedrich Ludwig Jahn, in which politics and education merged. The gymnastics festivals were banned until the end of the nineteenth century. Today, its triumphant return was seen in the Gymnastics Festival of 1983, held in Frankfurt, which boasted performances by 65,000 young athletes.

But Sport for Everyone is more than gymnastics. Under an umbrella organization, the German Sport Federation (DSB), specialized and state sport associations promote not only competitive sport but the mobilization of the total public. Over 18 million West Germans, or one in every three persons, belong to one of the country's 60,000 gymnastics and sport clubs. Ten million more are encouraged by DSB to take up some kind of sport activity. Neumann writes (1985:18–19):

> *Sport exists at every possible level: in kindergartens, schools, and universities, in clubs and associations, in factories, in holiday resorts and old peoples' homes, for the talented and the disabled, to promote the integration of foreigners and the rehabilitation of juvenile delinquency, to combat stress-related illnesses, smoking, obesity, and the lack of exercise—in other words, to contribute to a healthier life-style.*

Today's sport clubs are different from the early ones. In the 1920s and 1930s, there were separate clubs for Catholics, Jews, and Protestants; and for the upper class, middle class, and working class—a diversity that was not healthy for Germany. This changed after 1945.

Among the very successful and popular leisure sports is jogging, in which an estimated 3.3 million people take part on a regular basis. It all started around 1970 when the DSB contracted an advertising agency for the Keep Fit campaign. Today, there are literally thousands of meeting places where joggers congregate two or three times a week for their run through the woods and parks.

Soccer remains the favorite participatory and spectator sport. Over 4.6 million citizens, both young and old, belong to the soccer association, which is composed of 20,493 clubs with 129,166 teams. More than half are junior squads. Women have 3,400 teams. West Germans enthusiastically follow their national soccer team, which was twice victorious in the coveted World Cup.

In 1987, West Germany produced the highest ratio of tourists in the world. According to Hintereder (1988:37), West Germany spent over 40 billion marks (about $23 billion) on 25.8 million holiday occasions—almost a sixth of the world's total tourism. Almost two-thirds of the population (64.6%) satisfied their wanderlust for five or more days, which they spent within or outside Germany.

The impact of *freizeit* on the West German economy can be measured by what the average West German family spends on it, 5,500 marks ($3,200) a year. This gives employment to 4 million fellow Germans, making the leisure industry of 220 billion marks ($123 billion) one of the most beneficial achievements of postindustrial Germany.

SUMMARY

It seems that emphasis on work in Western civilization began with the demise of the Roman Empire. A manorial system developed, with a landlord guarded by knights and served by the serfs. Most of the leisure pursuits were enjoyed by the feudal lords. Yet the serfs enjoyed their own pursuits as well.

In Great Britain, there was no serf class to speak of. As the principles of democracy took hold, the gentry were forced to share their leisure activities with the commoners. The presence of a legal system that emphasized civil rights for all signalled the advent of a modern society. Two groups were opposed to leisure pursuits for the masses, the "Victorians" and the clergy. Nonetheless, a leisure explosion took place there whose effects are still seen today.

In France, the aristocracy created manicured gardens that they were eventually forced to share with commoners. But it was after the French Revolution that a belle epoque was witnessed in France. From that point on, Frenchmen gained more free time, which they spend in television watching and travelling. Yet their gains are not as far-reaching as the Germans. The Germans enjoy a 5–6 week annual vacation, making the leisure industry one of the success stories of modern Germany.

REVIEW QUESTIONS

1. What is the Western view of leisure?
2. What are the British contributions to today's pursuit of leisure?
3. Describe the French struggle to obtain more free time from work.
4. What are the current leisure pursuits in West Germany?

SUGGESTED READINGS

de Grazia, S. 1962. *Of time, work and leisure.* New York: Anchor Books. New York.

Dumazedier, J. 1967. *Toward a society of leisure.* New York: Free Press.

Golby, J. M., and A. W. Purdue. 1984. *The civilization of the crowd: Popular culture in England 1850–1900.* New York: Schocken Books.

Hintereder, P. 1988. Leisure: Boon or bane? *Scala.* (November/December): 28–38.

10

LEISURE IN CANADA

The physical characteristics of the land as well as the native populations have contributed to the development of leisure pursuits claimed to be uniquely Canadian. Canada's northern climate with its harsh winters, combined with its diverse topographic features, add to a Canadian uniqueness. The eastern section of the country is punctuated by the ocean and is densely forested. Going westward, one finds a fertile lowland, an industrialized region, the Canadian shield, the prairies, and the western region. Above all these are the Arctic regions, where most of the Eskimos live. The Native Americans live across the southern tier.

The French entered the Gulf of St. Lawrence, then ascended the river to found a colony they called Quebec. By 1600, their fur trade with the natives, who desired metal knives and hatchets, extended as far inland as the Great Lakes. English colonists and traders began to menace New France. But it was not until the end of the Seven-Year War in Europe in the 1750s that most of Canada was ceded to Great Britain. Quebec was promised a government like that of other British colonies, but retained a French civil law to protect the position of the Roman Catholic Church. The Dominion of Canada came into being on 1 July 1867.

In the meantime, two minority groups were living in Canada: the Eskimos and the Native Americans. Their contributions to leisure pursuits in today's Canada are well-documented.

LEISURE AND NATIVE POPULATIONS

As shown in chapter 4, the Eskimos survived by hunting and fishing; they had simple technology, with no agriculture or domesticated animals. Blanchard and Cheska (1985:142) show that despite the hazards of life in the Arctic region, the Eskimos' life is characterized by playfulness. They love to sing, tell stories, and play games. Among their games is *agraoruk,* in which the contestant tries to kick a sealskin dangling from a pole. *Nalukatook* finds them bouncing on a walrus hide held by others, and the object of *ipirautaqurnia* is to flip a whip precisely.

R. Johnson laments that their culture is neglected in Canada and is threatened by that neglect. He quotes Peter Pitseolak, an Eskimo artist who describes the situation:

> *This is how we played the game—we threw a ball underhand and we tried to catch it in a sealskin racket. The racket was called an "autak." We made the ball from caribou skin and stuffed it with something. We used to play this game a lot, even in winter. It was a good game, but they do not play it now; they are following the world (1979:338).*

The Eskimos' activities disappeared as the white race's activities were adopted. But some of the Native American activities were adopted by the

Baggataway as played by Native Americans (a pre-lacrosse sport). Source: Wood, J. The Uncivilized Races of Man, *1871, p. 1451. J. B. Burr.*

early settlers. These activities had lost their original religious significance, but continued to be practiced by the natives. They provide good examples of what Grimes (1982:37) called ceremonies or celebrations. An example is lacrosse, which is Canada's official national sport today.

Baggataway was one of the names given to the game practiced by the Algonquians and Iroquois in Canada and the northeastern United States, the Dakotas in the upper Midwest of the United States, the Chinooks and Salishs of the American northwest, and the Muskhogeans in the southern states. Each tribe had its own term and rules for the game. The name *lacrosse* was coined by the French settlers of Canada because the implement used, the curved netted stick, resembled a bishop's crozier. Lacrosse was a "little war," a meek military scrimmage surrounded with religious ceremony, designed to obtain the blessings of the gods who would bestow health and fertility on the victorious.

According to Baker (1982:71), the early Europeans were baffled by the seriousness and ritualistic nature of the game; they attributed such traits to the primitiveness of an uncivilized people (Wood 1871). The Europeans did not realize then that many of their own leisure pursuits had been as ritualistic and as serious as the New World games they observed in the seventeenth and eighteenth centuries.

The Europeans adopted some of these activities and modified them to suit their level of societal sophistication. They also adopted other activities and implements of the Indians, such as the canoe as a means of transportation. But once they imported more powerful and faster vessels, the canoe became an implement in their leisure pursuits. Today close to 14% of Canadians use canoes for recreation (Johnson 1979:337). The societies created by the Europeans were initially at the first level of adaptation to the physical environment. But they soon entered the second level of adaptation to collectivity, and their leisure pursuits were modified accordingly (see chap. 1).

ENGLISH CANADA

The English settlers left lacrosse to the Native Americans initially, but in 1842 members of the Athletic Club of Montreal began to compete against nearby native teams. Very soon, with the Western efficiency that gained momentum from the Industrial Revolution, they drew up a set of rules and standards for fields and equipment. They departed from the native pattern of year-round play and limited participation to amateurs, thus keeping the natives, who played for a prize, from joining the now highly organized sport (Baker 1982:159).

No one knows the precise time and place of the beginning of ice hockey in Canada. Some claim that it was first played by English troops in the winter of 1855 in Kingston, Ontario, but this claim cannot be substantiated (Baker 1982:160). As for curling, it was introduced by Scottish immigrants as early as 1807. Scottish villagers gathered annually for festive events called "bonspiels," featuring the sliding of a round, slightly flattened granite stone toward a designated spot on the frozen lake. The Royal Caledonian Curling Club was established in 1842 in Scotland and became known as the mother club. It has affiliates in the United States and Canada. Yet curling did not flourish in Canada until the turn of the century. Today there are so many teams, both men's and women's, in all the provinces that one might surmise that curling is Canada's national winter sport. There are over 1,600 clubs in the country.

Johnson (1979:339) describes a form of ritualistic activity that evolved among the English residents of Canada. This was the bee. It was a cooperative communal effort to complete a harvest or to raise a barn. The host was to provide the food and drink (usually whiskey). The bee became studded with nonwork activities that soon made the accomplishment of the task difficult, and the bee died out. It failed to fulfill its original goal and was not adopted as a leisure activity. First, modern techniques could accomplish the work faster and more efficiently, and second, leisure pursuits were achieved through other channels.

Inns and taverns, in a manner very similar to the English pub, served the recreational needs of both the traveler and resident in Canada. The same kind of activities that the British client liked to see in the pub were provided to the Canadian client in the inn and tavern. Blood sport, such as cockfighting and dog fighting, bear and bull baiting, as well as musicals, were provided in these establishments.

In the meantime, the upper class, which represented a small segment of the population virtually closed to others, enjoyed leisure pursuits not dissimilar to those enjoyed by the English gentry, whom they anxiously tried to emulate. According to Guillet, they

> were fond of horse racing, and field sports, fishing and sailing, football and cricket in summer, and skating and carrioling in winter, while at all seasons dancing, chess, whist, wine, and conversation served to while away the time (1933:323).

FRENCH CANADA

According to Johnson (1979:343), the leisure pursuits of the early French Canadians were determined by the person's position in the social system. Basically, three distinct groups were identified: the affluent who lived in the large settlements in a grand European life-style; the typical French Canadian who depended on kinships and neighborhoods; and the *coureur de bois,* the lover of nature, who followed the ways of the Native Americans.

The first group lived in a fashion similar, but not identical, to the French aristocracy, in lavish ceremonials, banquets, and the like. According to Douville and Casanova (1967:193), on those occasions one could easily imagine oneself breathing the atmosphere of Versailles rather than the air of Quebec.

Life along the St. Lawrence was different. The Catholic Church's influence was stronger and restricted the leisure pursuits of its followers. The Church condemned gambling and dancing. In addition, the settlers had to contend with long, harsh winters and had to concentrate on survival skills. Yet there were more leisure pursuits in the winter than in the summer, mostly socializing and a few competitive activities. The summer required a great deal of work for a livelihood that was not easily extracted from the soil. Eventually, life became less difficult and services were provided through federal and provincial authorities.

ROLE OF GOVERNMENT

The federal and provincial governments' role in recreation prior to 1900 was limited to the provision of open space for the purpose of development of the country. Now and then, a city council would provide a park space, such as the Toronto city council did in 1859. The council regarded parks as "breathing space where citizens might stroll, drive, or sit to enjoy the open air" (McFarland 1970:14).

According to Johnson (1979:346), it was not until the National Council of Women of Canada had its third annual meeting in 1896 that the value of leisure pursuits were brought to national attention. This, in turn, led to greater governmental roles.

As in the United States, today the three levels of governments—federal, provincial, and local—are involved in leisure through legislation, providing recreational facilities and programs and enforcing laws pertaining to leisure pursuits.

Role of the Federal Government

In Canada, the formal authority rests with the Governor General, who is the head of state but does not hold executive powers. He or she acts on the advice of the Prime Minister. The actual executive authority rests with the Cabinet, which is selected by the Prime Minister from among his or her party members who serve in the House of Commons. The Prime Minister is normally the leader of the political party that is holding the majority of seats in Parliament. The federal legislation is bicameral: the Senate has 102 appointed lifetime members, and the House has 265 members elected by the people for five-year terms.

The Prime Minister is the head of the Cabinet whose members serve as ministers, or heads of agencies of national concern. Some of these federal entities have direct influence on leisure services and pursuits among Canadians. Others have indirect influence, and some have nothing to do with leisure services at all.

For example, the Economic Council of Canada, through its interest in the economic situation, affects the commercial aspects of leisure and tourism. The National Research Council aids some industries that affect the production of recreational equipment such as boats and recreational vehicles. The Federal Department of Agriculture seeks to improve farming viability in Canada. Loans are given through the Farm Credit Corporation to develop secondary nonfarming enterprises on farm land, such as summer cottages, campgrounds, and hunting facilities.

The Department of Communication issues licenses to amateur radio operators. The Canadian Radio-Television Commission licenses and regulates commercial, cable, and educational broadcasting and televising, and hence has an important role in the leisure pursuits of Canadians.

The Department of Transport provides and supervises land, rail, air, and sea transportation and their direct impact on leisure pursuits. For example, the creation of the Rocky Mountain Park (Banff) in 1885 was primarily due to the suggestion of the Canadian Pacific Railroad, which viewed the creation of the park as a means of stimulating tourism. During the first half of this century, the dual objectives of nature protection and tourism/recreational use led to the establishment of Canadian National Parks (Statistics Canada 1986a:157). Within two years of setting the Banff area aside as parkland, the Banff Springs Hotel opened its doors.

The Federal Department of the Environment works on the provision and protection of Canada's natural resources, such as fish and wildlife. Its Canadian Wildlife Service has entered into agreements with the provinces for land designated as national wildlife areas. Today, 29 such areas consist of close to 100,000 acres varying in size from a few acres to 14,000 acres. These areas are designed for interpretive, nonconsumptive use only. The Outdoor Recreation—Open Space Division of the Department of the Environment undertakes planning, research, and information projects related to leisure.

The Department of Consumer and Corporate Affairs protects the recreationist and sees to his or her safety through enforcement of laws banning certain equipment. For example, certain children's toys and hockey helmets were proved unsafe by its research branch and were banned. The Standard Branch enforces the Hazardous Products Act, which bans or regulates the sale of particular items that are not under the control of specific legislation. The Bureau of Consumer Affairs receives all complaints and attempts to resolve them, including the ones pertaining to leisure.

The Department of State for Urban Affairs was established to develop policy concerning urban Canada. But it is the Central Mortgage and Housing Corporation that assists in providing leisure opportunities as part of urban life. Through its Neighborhood Improvement Program, it provides up to 50% of land acquisition and improvement costs of social and recreational facilities. The municipalities can borrow 75% of their share of the costs. Other programs are available for residential rehabilitation, new communities, housing for Native Americans, and children's environment.

The National Capital Commission is charged, among other things, with the improvement of the quality of life, including leisure provisions, in the National Capital region. The Commission provides public access to outdoor recreation possibilities on its 125,000 acres. In addition, it controls 88,000 acres of wilderness parks and 60 miles of hiking and skiing trails around the Capital. A network of walking paths and bikeways are constructed around the Rideau Canal and the Ottawa River, with a boat concession along the canal.

But the major contributions from the federal government come through three agencies: the Ministry of Indian and Northern Affairs, the Ministry of National Health and Welfare, and the Secretary of State. The Ministry of Indian and Northern Affairs offers a program that has direct impact on leisure in Canada: Parks Canada, now called Environment Canada-Parks.

Environment Canada-Parks is an agency of three branches: the National Parks Branch, the National Historic Parks and Sites Branch, and the Policy and Research Branch. The Canadian national parks system consists of 28 parks covering 50,000 square miles or 32 million acres, making this system one of the largest in the world. The philosophy behind the national parks is to preserve them for their significant scenic, geological, geographical, and biological resources and for the enjoyment of present and future generations. There are five very large national parks: Wood Buffalo, Kluane, Jasper, Glacier, and Banff. These total 26.1 million acres, which constitute 82% of the whole national park system in Canada. The rest are smaller units (see fig. 10.1).

The National Historic Parks and Sites Branch of Environment Canada-Parks controls 75 units that are operated like parks. There are 600 lesser historic sites under that branch's control. Of the 20 million recreation occasions that take place in the Canadian national parks, one-fifth occur at historic units (Chubb and Chubb 1981:526).

The second federal agency that has direct bearing on leisure pursuits among Canadians is the Department of National Health and Welfare. Within the National Advisory Council on Fitness and Amateur Sport is a division called Fitness and Amateur Sports. Under the Fitness and Amateur Sports Act, the Council of Thirty appoints members representing all provinces, who advise the Minister on national policy regarding fitness

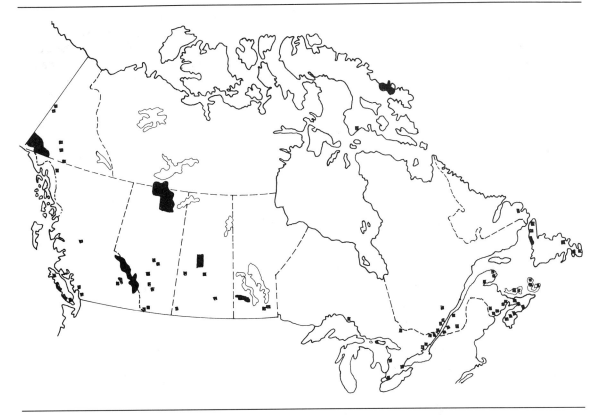

FIGURE 10.1 *National parks of Canada. Source: Mr. Lynd Warren, Whittier, CA.*

(Burton and Kyllo 1974:77). The Fitness and Amateur Sports Branch espouses the following objectives:

To promote fitness, physical recreation and amateur sport.
To increase participation in physical activity.
To increase the level of performance in international and national amateur sport.
To develop means to allow participants to freely choose activities.

The branch is divided into Sport Canada, which is responsible for national and international levels of competitive sport; and Recreation Canada, which is responsible for the development of leisure pursuits of the general population. Recreation Canada is decentralized. The Central Office provides funds and offers assistance to organizations in the provinces to provide physical recreation. Grants are given in areas where disparities in recreational opportunities exist. Demonstration projects are carried out wherever they are needed. Special populations, such as the handicapped and minorities, are given special attention. Recreation Canada encourages industries and businesses to provide recreational programs for their employees (Burton and Kyllo 1974:73).

The Canada Fitness Award attracts many schoolchildren to become involved in fitness programs. In Canada, fitness is defined as an ability to function at a physical and mental optimum. Schoolchildren are encouraged to strive for higher levels of fitness.

The Developmental Programs Branch in the Federal Department of National Health and Welfare offers a program, New Horizon, designed to enable groups of retired citizens to participate in projects initiated by the group. Direct cash grants are provided for projects that utilize the knowledge and experience of retired persons in a manner beneficial to themselves or the community. Funds are to be used only for accommodations, rentals, travel, publicity, and consultations. No salary or profits are allowed. According to Burton and Kyllo (1974:76), virtually all projects are recreational in nature.

The third federal department in Canada that is involved in leisure services and pursuits is the one headed by the Secretary of State. Its primary responsibilities include encouragement of literary, visual, and performing arts; and learning through libraries, galleries, historical resources, theatres, films, and broadcasting. According to Burton and Kyllo (1974:94), there was a realization that strong foreign influences were distorting Canadian identity and heritage. This led to a period of self-examination during the 1960s, which ended in the adoption of a policy, beginning in 1967, that made the Canadian Federal Government a major patron of genuine Canadian art and culture. The task of making the means of cultural expression available to artists and consumers fell to the Department of the Secretary of State.

Five components relating to Canadian art and culture were adopted:

1. **Cultural pluralism.** The recognition that Canada is a multicultural society and that all cultural values are to be promoted.

2. **Cultural democratization.** Attempts would be made to reduce inequalities and privileges at all levels.

3. **Decentralization of services.** Services are to be diffused throughout the diverse regions of the country.

4. **Federal-provincial-municipal cooperation.** Services are to be effective and meet the highest standards of excellence.

5. **International relations.** A two-way recognition of cultural dimension is to take place through exchange, assistance, and education.

The following agencies and programs affiliated with the Department of the State are involved in providing leisure services and activities on the national level in Canada.

Canada Council. The Canada Council is charged with promoting the arts, humanities, and social sciences. The arts program, more so than humanities and social science, has direct bearing on leisure pursuits. Although the Council assists professionals in the fields of music, opera, drama, dance, visual arts, and writing, their audience benefits from their products. There is an explorations program that provides a once-only grant to an aspiring amateur. The Council's Bank is a collection of visual artworks that is displayed in public areas. The Council Touring Office promotes tours of Canadian performing arts: drama, music, and dance. According to Burton and Kyllo, there has been a rise in interest in the arts of up to 10% in Canada since the establishment of the program (1974:102).

Canadian Broadcasting Corporation. Since its primary responsibility is to provide radio and television coverage to as many Canadians as possible in both English and French, the Canadian Broadcasting Corporation plays a very important role in the leisure pursuits of Canadians. It strives to provide coverage to all communities of over 500 persons. Through its two television networks (English and French), two AM radio networks (English and French), a number of multicultural FM stations, and short- and medium-wave radio systems that reach the Eskimo population, CBC promotes Canadian identity, augmented by cultural and regional differences.

Canadian Film Development Corporation. The Canadian Film Development Corporation strives to promote and encourage the production of Canadian feature films. It can invest in a film or make loans or grants. The program for feature films provides the needed funds for, and priority is given to, films that can be shown on Canadian television. A Canadian feature film is defined as one with significant Canadian artistic, creative, and technical know-how and is owned by Canadians. A low-budget program is designed to encourage new talent.

National Film Board. The National Film Board was established to promote the production and distribution of films of national interest. The films are produced in English or French to depict the features and cultures of Canada. Travel and tourism films are available for all interested groups. Distribution is provided for communities, schools, and interested groups through the NFB Film Library.

National Museums of Canada. The major objective of the program is to provide maximum access to all Canadians to exhibits and collections that have special reference to Canada. This is accomplished in concert with certain museums that have both regional capability and professional competency to be designated Associate Museums. A network has been established to combat regional disparity in museum resources. The National Museums of Canada have four permanent collections in Ottawa: The National Gallery, the Museum of Man, The Museum of Science and Technology, and The Museum of Natural Science.

National Library. The National Library is the depository for all books published in Canada, as well as all government documents. It provides special assistance to the handicapped and has initiated an ethnic program. It has a center for distribution of works in languages other than English and French, to be disseminated to provinces and municipalities.

Company of Young Canadians. The Company of Young Canadians is a program designed to help young Canadians, particularly disadvantaged ones, gain access to leisure opportunities and improve the quality of their lives. The program has to be initiated by the local communities, but CYC facilitates its realization through support, training, information, and some funds. The youth become involved in the recreational programs in rural areas and native settlements.

National Arts Centre Corporation. The National Arts Centre Corporation is the home for three performance facilities, which host Canadian and foreign attractions such as ballet, opera, and folk music and dances. It is charged with encouraging performing arts in the National Capital Region and is the home for Canada's National Orchestra.

Role of Provincial Government

Ninety percent of the 25 million Canadians live in a belt 200 miles wide along the United States border. There are ten Canadian provinces. Ten percent of the population lives in the four Atlantic provinces: Newfoundland, Nova Scotia, New Brunswick, and Prince Edward Island. Ontario is the most populous province, with almost 30% of the Canadian population. Quebec is one of Canada's most important commercial and industrial centers, with almost one-quarter of the population. The prairie provinces have a wedge of population that broadens westward. In Manitoba, farm settlements are mainly in the southern quarter. They expand to almost half of Saskatchewan and continue on to Alberta and British Columbia. Figure 10.1 shows that most of Canada's national parks are in the least populated areas.

According to Chubb and Chubb (1981:490), most Canadian provinces are less dependent on the national government for aid than are the states in the United States. Moreover, most of the open space and unsettled public land is under provincial control (Crown Lands), unlike in the United States where the federal government owns and controls all 600+ million acres of open land. Also, the population concentration and agricultural land are in the southern tier of Canada, leaving a large area of land on the northern tier of the country uninhabited and not suitable for agriculture. Consequently, all the large provinces found it comparatively easy, politically and financially, to set aside huge provincial parks and forests.

Ontario. In 1885, the Ontario Legislature allocated 20% of its budget ($435,000) to purchase property adjacent to Niagara Falls. Today, Queen Victoria Park, as it has been called, is part of the 2,800-acre Niagara Parks system, extending for 32 miles between Lake Erie and Lake Ontario. Overlooking the world famous Niagara Falls, the parkland's facilities include playing fields, picnic areas, and amphitheaters. In addition, a horticulture display attracts people by day, while the lighted falls attracts them by night.

The Provincial Parks Act of 1954 made Ontario's system the largest in Canada in terms of number of units and amount of use. The total acreage is 10 million and the annual attendance exceeds 11 million visits a year, one-fourth of which are for overnight camping.

The Ministry of Natural Resources of Ontario is in charge of the provincial parks and uses a five-class system:

1. **Primitive parks.** large undeveloped areas.
2. **Nature reserves.** distinctive land forms or ecosystems.
3. **Natural environment parks.** outstanding recreational landscapes.
4. **Recreation parks.** a wide range of activities.
5. **Wild rivers.** undeveloped rivers.

Ontario is also well endowed with forests, many of which are designated Provincial Forests to be used by its 8 million residents and others who come from the adjacent provinces and states for fishing, hunting, canoeing, camping, and hiking. Chubb and Chubb estimate that at least 75 million recreation occasions occur in Ontario's forests each year (1981:501). As a result of the increased demand for the recreational use of these forests, the Ministry of National Resources, which administers Ontario's Provincial Forests, is currently reviewing the role of recreation in relation to timber, mineral, and water-power production.

According to Chubb and Chubb (1981:502), most of the 75 million recreation occasions that take place annually in Ontario's Provincial Forests take place in and around vacation cottages (33%). Camping is the second most important leisure pursuit (21%). The remaining activities are fishing (15%), swimming (8%), boating (6%), hiking (6%), snowmobiling (5%), hunting (4%), and canoeing (2%).

Ontario's Department of Education started a community programs branch after World War II for adult education, sport, and fitness. By 1970, the responsibility shifted to the Youth and Recreation Branch within the Ministry of Education and the Sport and Recreation Bureau of the Ministry of Community and Social Services. But in the mid-1970s a Ministry of Culture and Recreation was established to assume these responsibilities. These programs have expanded despite the termination of the earlier federal assistance (Kraus 1984:129).

British Columbia. The first provincial park in British Columbia was Strathcona on Vancouver Island in 1911. The system has now grown to over 340 units. The British Columbia Park Act classifies parks into six groups:

Class A: Preserves offering outstanding features.
Class B: Parks providing public outdoor recreation opportunities.
Class C: Locally controlled parks.
Class D: Parks providing public recreation.
Class E: Wilderness conservancy.
Class F: Nature conservancy.

According to Chubb and Chubb, Class A are the most numerous, composing two-thirds of the system's units. Class B are fewer, but are larger in size. Class C parks are smaller (1981:493).

Saskatchewan. According to Kraus (1984:130), the Department of Culture and Youth in Saskatchewan is responsible for promoting participation in the province's cultural, recreational, and sport activities. It has a number of administrative units, each charged with a program area. Some of these areas are directly related to leisure pursuits such as amateur sport, recreation and fitness programs, museum and gallery programs, performing visual and literary arts, and heritage and historical conservation and interpretation. The Department has been active in encouraging ethnic art festivals and historical study. It has also provided for grants of up to 50% of the cost to help municipalities develop recreational facilities such as community centers, field houses, skating and curling rinks, and swimming pools.

Role of Municipalities

Kraus (1984:126) states that despite the early hegemony of the first four provinces (New Brunswick, Nova Scotia, Quebec, and Ontario), and the slow development of local self-government in Canada, a number of major municipal parks were established there, even before such a trend began in the United States. It was not until the mid-1800s that large Canadian communities received their charters for self-government. Yet the extensive Halifax Commons was granted to the city in 1763, public squares were used in Montreal in 1821, and Gore Park was built in Hamilton in 1852. In the 1860s Montreal established Mount Royal Park, and in the 1880s Vancouver built Stanley Park, London-Victoria Park, and Saint John-Rockwood Park. During that period the provinces passed enabling laws empowering the municipalities to establish parks and set procedures for acquisitions and standards for management.

The concerns that motivated social reformers in the United States were also voiced in Canada: that recreational opportunities must be provided in urban slums for the benefit of poor families. Private citizens also urged the development of playgrounds and vacation schools. The National Council of Women passed a resolution in May of 1901 to the same effect (McFarland 1970:37). While progress was slow, pressure from women's groups led to the formation of playground associations by 1914. Eventually, municipal park boards were established in the large cities of the eastern provinces. In the prairie and western provinces, community leagues promoted playgrounds, parks, community centers, and swimming pools. The community league is a merger of civic organizations concerned with local development (Kraus 1984:127).

LEISURE PURSUITS OF CANADIANS

In 1981, a time-budget study was conducted on a nonrandom sample of urban and rural Canadians. Fourteen sites were selected and 2,500 respondents from 11 urban and 3 rural areas were interviewed by phone. The data show that the average adult Canadian has 5 hours and 24 minutes of free time a day (Department of Communications 1987:14). The data also show that watching television at home took 113 minutes a day, followed by entertainment away from home (74 minutes, most of which was 37 minutes for visiting friends). Hobbies, arts, and crafts took 31 minutes, socializing at home 29 minutes, active sport 20 minutes, reading books 15 minutes, and newspaper and magazine reading 11 minutes and 4 minutes, respectively.

While it is rather difficult to compare Canadians' leisure pursuits in the above study to the nationals in Szalai's study (table 8.1), it is interesting to note that they were closer to the American sample from Jackson, Michigan, in television watching (99 vs. 113 minutes). The difference of 14 minutes could be a result of the fact that the American sample was polled in the early 1970s while the Canadian sample was polled in the early 1980s. Moreover, the number of minutes allocated for watching television in America increased by the mid-1970s (Robinson 1981). Other studies concentrated on the outdoor leisure pursuits of Canadians.

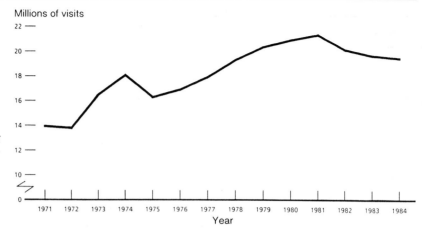

FIGURE 10.2 *National park attendance, Canada, 1971–84. Source: Park Use Statistics, Parks Canada, 1985, p. 2.* Statistics Canada. *Reprinted with permission.*

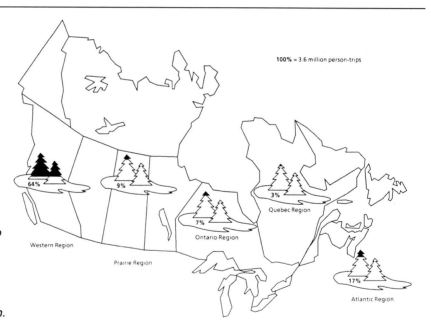

FIGURE 10.3 *Visitation to national parks by Parks Canada regions, 1984. Source: Canada Travel Survey, 1985, p. 3.* Statistics Canada. *Reprinted with permission.*

Outdoor Leisure Pursuits

With an abundance of natural resources, the Canadians are a real outdoor people. But they are also very involved in cultural pursuits and physical activities. A substantial increase in park attendance took place in 1973–74, possibly a consequence of the establishment of a number of new parks. The decline since 1981 could be attributed to the fact that no new parks opened near population centers. There has also been a decline in domestic tourism in general (Statistics Canada 1987:1). Figure 10.2 reflects these trends. Figure 10.3 shows that visits to Canadian national parks were predominantly to parks in the western region.

Table 10.1 **Percentage of Canadians 18 years and over participating in selected recreation activities**

Activity	1967	1969	1972	1976
Tent camping	13	12	19	19
Trailer camping	6	6	10	12
Camping with a truck	—	2	4	9
Swimming	—	—	—	42
Canoeing	5	8	10	14
Bicycling	—	13	19	28
Walking and hiking	13	37	38	54
Wilderness tripping	—	—	—	17
Cross-country skiing	—	—	2	10
Driving for pleasure	—	67	63	66
Sightseeing from car	—	—	37	49
Picnicking	40	54	52	57
Canal use				
Commercial use	—	—	2	5
Private boat	—	—	6	9
Nonboating	—	—	8	12
Visiting historical sites	16	37	35	43
Visiting national parks (past 12 months)	13	—	22	29

Source: Johnson, R. ''Leisure in Canada,'' in H. Ibrahim and J. Shivers (Editors), Leisure: Emergence and Expansion, *1979, p. 350.* Hwong Publishing. Reprinted with permission.

Table 10.2 **Percentage of Canadians who participated in cultural events, 1975**

Nonattendance activities	%	Attendance activities	%
Television	97	Art galleries	18
Radio	84	Science/technical	11
Records	63	Museums	17
Newspapers	75	Historic sites	24
Magazines	58	Zoos	27
Books	55	Libraries	27
Music	13	Commercial movies	54
Arts	13	Classical music	8
Crafts	17	Other dance	6
Hobbies	34		
Instruction	23		

Source: Johnson, R. ''Leisure in Canada,'' in H. Ibrahim and J. Shivers (Editors) Leisure: Emergence and Expansion, *1979, p. 352.* Hwong Publishing. Reprinted with permission.

Johnson accumulated the percentage of Canadians 18 years and older who participated in selected activities over a nine-year period (1967–76). This is the period in which there was an increase in park attendance. The data show that driving for pleasure was the most participated-in outdoor pursuit, followed by picnicking and hiking. The greatest increase was in walking/hiking, from 13% in 1967 to 54% in 1976. Although visiting historic sites was the fourth most participated-in activity, it has experienced a more than 400% increase in the nine-year period (table 10.1).

Leisure and the Media

Participation in cultural pursuits was also on the increase in the period studied by Johnson. Table 10.2 shows the percentage of Canadians who participated in these activities. The United Nation's

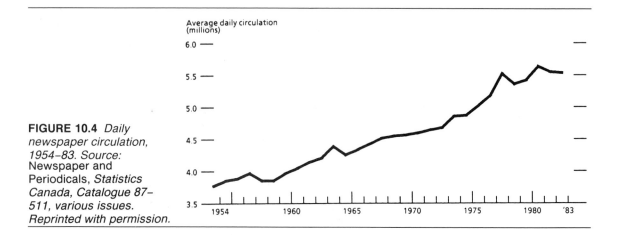

FIGURE 10.4 *Daily newspaper circulation, 1954–83. Source:* Newspaper and Periodicals, *Statistics Canada, Catalogue 87–511, various issues. Reprinted with permission.*

sources (table 7.1) corroborated the findings in table 10.2: that 97% of Canadians watch television, making it the most pursued leisure activity. The data in table 7.1 show that there is one television set for each 2.2 Canadians, the third highest ratio among the 13 nations cited in this work, after the United States and Great Britain.

Reading newspapers is a leisure pursuit for 75% of Canadians, who read them for 11 minutes a day; 58% read magazines for 4 minutes a day; and 55% read books for 15 minutes a day. Canada has 792 public libraries, or one library for each 31,565 citizens, with holdings of over 46 million books or 1.8 books for each citizen. There are about 19,000 books published a year in Canada (table 7.1). In 1985, the government announced a new policy designed to encourage Canadian presence in an increasingly foreign-owned publishing industry (Statistics Canada 1988:1–14).

Table 7.1 shows that there are 120 daily newspapers in Canada with a circulation of 5,570,000, or a ratio of one paper per 4.54 persons. This is comparable to the ratio in the United States and Europe. The daily circulation has increased in the last two decades (fig. 10.4).

Fitness and Sport

Two program areas, Fitness Canada and Sport Canada, provide, for one, financial assistance to national and local agencies dealing with fitness and sport.

Fitness Canada tries to reach youth, workers, and seniors. They organized the first Federal-Provincial Ministers Conference on Fitness. According to Statistics Canada (1988:15–17), in 1986 more than 6 million Canadians took part in over 12,000 events across Canada, organized by more than 200,000 volunteers in the annual National Physical Activity Week (now called Canada Fitweek).

Sport Canada assists amateur sport in a different way. Through the Athlete Assistance Program, it pays $5 million a year to Canada's top amateur athletes to meet expenses incurred through intensive training programs and competition schedules. The Women's Program tries to improve women's status through courses in sport administration and high-level coaching. The Program for the Disabled intends to increase the quality and quantity of their participation in sport.

Performing Arts

Professional performing arts companies performed to audiences totalling 9.7 million in 1982, an increase of almost 50% since 1976 (Statistics Canada 1983:30). Live theater accounted for 65% of the total attendance, having presented by far the greatest number of performances. Symphonies and orchestras drew the largest audiences, about 1,000 per concert. Theaters drew the smallest audiences,

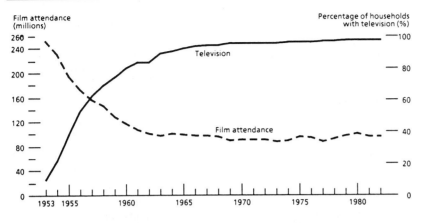

Film attendance (millions)

260
240
200
160
120
80
40
0

Television

Film attendance

1953 1955   1960   1965   1970   1975   1980

Percentage of households with television (%)

100
80
60
40
20
0

FIGURE 10.5 *Film attendance and percentage of households with television, 1953–82. Source:* Motion picture theatre and film distributors, *Statistics Canada, Catalogue 63–207, various issues;* Household facilities and equipment, *Statistics Canada, Catalogue 64–202, various issues. Reproduced with the permission of the Minister of Supply and Services Canada, 1990.*

of 300 each; while dance and opera companies attracted audiences of about 700. There has been a gradual increase in attendance in recent years in the four areas of performing arts. On the other hand, movie attendance peaked at 256 million in 1952 and declined rapidly over the next decade as television viewing took over (fig. 10.5). In 1982, Canada's 983 regular movie theaters sold 87.6 million tickets and the drive-ins sold 9.7 million. That represented more than four visits per person aged five and older to the movies that year.

Tourism

The year 1986 saw the highest number of international trips between Canada and other countries recorded (86 million) since the statistics began being kept in 1972 (Statistics Canada 1986a:vii). The main components of this figure were the 40.4 million trips by Canadians abroad and 40.5 million trips of Americans and others to Canada. The balance comprises trips of resident and foreign crews, immigrants, diplomats, and military personnel and their dependents.

Trips of 24 hours or more, which conforms to the international definition of tourists, increased by 18% over 1985. This can be attributed mostly to Americans whose trips to Canada have been on the increase since 1983. Visits to Canada by nationals other than Americans were also on the increase. Tourist trips abroad by Canadians rose only

4% over 1985, which helped reduce the deficit in travel accounts, showing a balance with the United States of $77 million, the first such plus since 1974 (Statistics Canada 1986b:viii).

Canada accounts for the second largest share of the United States travel abroad, 18% in 1986 in comparison to Mexico's 22%, with Great Britain coming in third at 8%.

Other Leisure Pursuits

Table 10.3 shows that eating out is a very desirable leisure pursuit among Canadians. Seventy-six percent report that they eat at family restaurants at least once a year, 68% at fast-food restaurants, and 56% dine at private club restaurants. Seventy percent of Canadians stated they go to the movies at least once a year, 49% to dance places, 39% to live music concerts, 38% to watch ice hockey games, and 32% to the theater.

According to Langlois (1984), leisure expenditures in Quebec households represent 10.7% of total expenditure. This is a higher percentage than the one reported for the United States, which ranges from 6.6% to 6.9% (table 11.1). The Canadian percentage of 10.7 increases by one-third in two income households and is cut by half in monoparental and low income households. Langlois suggests that spending on leisure increases with increased income and with a wife's employment.

Table 10.3 Use of facilities and attendance at cultural and sporting events, 1980 and 1981

At least once during last 12 months	Percentage of people 18 years and older
Has personally rented a car	
For business	5
For pleasure	7
Has used following eating facilities	
Private club	9
High quality restaurant	56
Family restaurant	76
Fast-food restaurant	68
Take-out	59
Cafeteria	27
Has attended following event	
Movies	70
Theatre	32
Ballet/opera	10
Live music	39
Dance or disco	49
Auto racing	13
Baseball	29
Basketball	8
Football	19
Horse racing	14
Hockey	38
Soccer	10
Tennis	9
Track and field	9
Wrestling	8

Source: Travel, Tourism and Outdoor Recreation: A Statistical Digest, *1980–1981, Statistics Canada, Catalogue 87–401 Biennial.*

SUMMARY

Leisure pursuits of Canadians were shaped initially by the interaction between the original inhabitants (mainly Native Americans) and the European newcomers. Lacrosse and canoeing came from the first group, and the bee and curling developed through the second. Eventually the three levels of government—local, provincial, and federal—played important roles in the Canadian scene. In comparison to the United States, the local government in Canada was slower in formation, yet local parks were established earlier. Also, the Canadian federal government plays a larger role in facilitating and providing recreational opportunities than does the United States government. A number of Federal Ministries are directly involved in recreational programs, which is a result of a national policy adopted in the 1960s to create a genuine Canadian "culture." In the meantime, unlike in the United States where the federal government "owns" most of the open space, provincial governments in Canada are the owners, allowing for greater service. Today Canada boasts the largest national park system in the world. Also, at 10.7% of total expenditure, Canada's expenditure on leisure pursuit is the highest among the 13 nations in this study. The citizens there are engaged in outdoor pursuits, sport and fitness, tourism, and the arts.

REVIEW QUESTIONS

1. Who are the natives of Canada? What are their contributions to today's leisure pursuits?
2. What roles do the three levels of governments in Canada play in the provision of recreational outlets?
3. What are the dominant leisure pursuits among Canadians?
4. Compare the Canadian and the European life-style, with emphasis on leisure.

SUGGESTED READINGS

Baker, Wm. 1982. *Sports in the western world.* Totowa, NJ: Rowan and Littlefield.

Douville, R., and J. Casanova. 1967. *Daily life in early Canada.* New York: Macmillan.

Kraus, R. 1984. *Recreation and leisure in modern society.* Glenview, IL: Scott, Foresman.

McFarland, E. 1970. *The development of public recreation in Canada.* Ottawa: Canadian Parks/ Recreation Association.

11

LEISURE IN THE UNITED STATES

The United States had to be built before people could live in it, let alone pursue happiness in it. Gradually a life-style emerged that is enjoyed today by most of the 240 million Americans—thanks to a political system (see fig. 3.1) and an economic system (see fig. 3.2) that are unique to this world. It was not an easy struggle for Americans. Their early thinkers suggested that building the country was a priority and that other activities would have to be postponed. This attitude was enhanced by a dominant Puritan work ethic. Eventually the rules were relaxed against what was once labeled extravagance and dissipation.

As the might of the country was being developed by the many early entrepreneurs, egalitarianism was being lost. The offspring of these entrepreneurs were becoming a classic leisure class. In the meantime, the country's rising middle class was seeking reduced work hours, and their gains there allowed for the rise of commercial recreation. Yet the poor who lived in the slums of American industrial cities were in need of many services. A social movement known as "organized recreation" was initiated by concerned private citizens. Eventually the three levels of government—local, state, and federal—became involved in providing recreational programs and facilities. Today Americans, on the whole, enjoy the rich leisure life-style that is depicted in this chapter. Moreover, the United States is the only country that has kept track of what its citizens do with leisure, and how much they spend on it.

THE COLONIAL PERIOD

The first settlers had little time for play. The Virginia Assembly declared in 1619 that any person found idle would be bound over to work. It rigidly enforced the Sabbath observance, prohibited gambling, and regulated drinking. Massachusetts and Connecticut banned dice, cards, quoits, bowls, or any other unlawful game in house, yard, garden, or backside (Dulles 1965:5–6). According to de Grazia, of the immigrants landing in New England between 1630 and 1645, 140 had received a higher education in Great Britain and 90 of them were churchmen steeped in Augustine's pessimism about human nature, which was enhanced by John Calvin who considered play a sin. Puritanism won the day, but only the day (1962:240).

The original settlers had to take up their land in townships. No one was to settle a land without a grant, and it was the policy to award such grants only to groups of seven or more people who desired to live and worship together (Ibrahim et al. 1987:3). Each town had its own meeting house and its tavern. It was in the tavern that the English love of games and sport was rekindled. Later it was in the bees, or working groups, that American forms of recreative and amusive leisure emerged from the ritual of the get-together.

According to Dulles (1965:24), it was perhaps the wealth of game that drew out the townsmen and the farmers of New England and Virginia. Deer, moose, turkey, and pigeon were so abundant that it made hunting more than just a way of getting food; it was easy and pleasurable. Moreover,

163

there were no landlords to restrict the common people from hunting as they pleased. In fact, in George Alsops' seventeenth-century account of life in Maryland, he states that every servant had a gun, powder, and shot that allowed him to enjoy sport on all holidays and leisure times.

In Boston, upwards of a thousand men would gather to attend training days, to drill, practice marksmanship, and then celebrate the day by descending upon the local tavern. Another day to celebrate was college commencement. Quite soon, fete days were expanded and shooting matches became commonplace in taverns. Taverns served as headquarters for cockfighting, animal baiting, and country dances. Some of the taverns provided entertainment with a small orchestra of flutes, viols, and spinets. Others provided popular exhibitions of strange creatures.

But real leisure was found among the landed aristocracy. Prosperity induced a more liberal attitude, and the barriers that had blocked all worldly pleasures were being let down. They were soon to be imitated by the rising mercantile class whose wealth depended on trade with the West Indies. "Their recreational life did not include commercial amusements, nor did it extend to active sports. In some respects it was typified by those impressive dinners" (Dulles 1965:49).

The Puritans in Boston and the Quakers in Philadelphia might have known about these private leisure pursuits and either tolerated them or ignored them all together. But when it came to pursuing undesirable activities in public, they stood rather firm. In 1750 the Puritans were able to obtain a court order keeping some English actors from putting on a play. The court reaffirmed the traditional ban in the colony of Massachusetts on "public stage plays, interludes and theatrical amusements, which not only occasioned great and necessary expenses, and discouraged industry and frugality, but likewise tend generally to increase immorality, impiety and a contempt for religion" (Dulles 1965:49).

Public readings and moral lectures were accepted, and periodically some amateur musical performances were also tolerated. Eventually, plays were accepted in Boston and Philadelphia. But it was New York that led the way. New York City had its own theatre, and its then wealthy mercantile class engaged in diversions in winter and summer. In winter they rode their sleighs about three miles out of town to the Bowry, a house of entertainment. In summer they were ferried to Long Island, to the horse races held there since 1665. Balls, assemblies, card parties, and evening frolics were fashionable. They also attended plays in New York's first permanent theater on John Street, which opened in 1767 and housed the American Company of Comedians (Dulles 1965: 55–57).

But the most festive occasions anywhere in America took place in Williamsburg, Annapolis, and Charleston. Wealthy Southern gentry in blue coats and scarlet waistcoats seized on any opportunity for diversion and did not care if their amusements were inspired by God or the Devil. But many among them were more or less contemplative in their leisure and spent their free time reflecting on more serious matters.

Ben Franklin conceded that agriculture and the mechanical arts were more immediately needed and that cultivating the mind by the finer arts and sciences should be postponed until times of more wealth and leisure (de Grazia 1962:237). In 1749 he thought that these times had come.

Among those who were more concerned about the growing laxity of the New England aristocracy was John Adams, destined to become the second President of the nascent United States. In his youth he wrote in his diary in 1759,

Let no trifling diversion or amusement; no girl, no gun, no flute, no violins, no dress, no tobacco, no laziness, decoy you from your books (1856:59).

Adams as well as Thomas Jefferson, who became the third President of the United States, were men of contemplative leisure, the highest form according to Aristotle (Barnes 1984). They were the *otiosis* according to Cicero (Petersson 1920)—those who, at the third stage of Ibn Khaldun's hierarchy, helped create the State (Ibrahim 1988).

Perhaps others were concerned too, for on the eve of the American Revolution, one of the articles of the Association in the 1774 Continental Congress proposed that the colonies discontinue and discourage "every Species of Extravagance and Dissipation, especially all Horse Racing and all Kinds of Gaming, Cockfighting, Exhibitions of Shows, Plays, and other expensive Diversions and Entertainments" (Dulles 1965:65).

THE FORMATIVE YEARS

During the American Revolution many commercial recreation enterprises were closed. Theatres, music halls, and horse tracks were not to be opened until after the war (McCollum 1979:109). After all, the pursuit of happiness was one of the revolutionary aims. Every American learned then, and learns today, that statement prepared by Thomas Jefferson:

We hold these truths to be self evident, that all men are created equal, that they are endowed by their Creator with certain inalienable rights, that among these are life, liberty, and the pursuit of happiness.

According to de Grazia, it was George Mason who brought the concept of the pursuit of happiness into the Virginia Declaration of Rights, ten years earlier. In it, the natural rights of men "include the enjoyment of life and liberty, and obtaining happiness and safety" (1962:263). George Mason was a Virginian classics scholar who spent his time in retirement, content with the blessing of a private station and a modest income—an *otiosi* par excellence.

France came to the rescue in the Revolutionary War, and the United States fell into a period of Gallomania, which dissipated with the reign of terror that gripped France after its own revolution. America was coming of age.

In the meantime, with the western expansion, new leisure pursuits were being formed. The settlers were no longer transplanted Englishmen, but rather people born on American soil, imbued with American ideals. The frontiers offered a lonely and hard life, for there were fewer opportunities for people to get together. The abundance of game in the new frontier made shooting matches even more popular here than in the original colonies. Physical prowess was needed for survival in the frontier and was tested in wrestling matches, jumping contests, footraces, tomahawk hurling, and rail flinging. It is recorded that both Andrew Jackson and Abraham Lincoln participated in these tests of physical skill (Dulles 1965:73).

Bees became an important part of frontier life and provided opportunities for dancing and horse racing. Logrolling was a major purpose of bees in the western frontier. Clearing the land was hard work for the settlers. After felling the trees to clear the land for planting, the settler needed help to roll the logs into place for burning. Neighbors came from miles away, and logrolling was made into a holiday spree where dinners were feasts, followed by dancing, drinking, and contests.

A CHANGING SOCIETY

An industrial giant was in the making, once the War of Independence was over. John Adams had predicted that Americans would have to devote their time to economic and political problems before they would have time for poetry, music, and fine arts (Morrison 1965:282), and they did. Americans had to find new markets now that the markets of Great Britain and its colonies were closed to them. America was exporting primarily raw materials. Industries producing finished goods had to be developed. Both trade and manufacturing required good communication and transportation systems, which the country lacked.

The United States' economic growth was unparalleled in history. As shown in figure 3.2, which is developed by Rostow (1960:xxii, 5), its economic take-off stage started about 1850, seventy years after Great Britain's. It reached economic maturity at the first decade of this century, and reached the final stage of high mass consumption only ten years later. This achievement may be attributed to the wealth of natural resources, but also to a political system that is unique to the world.

Figure 3.1 shows that the American political system has a highly differentiated and autonomic infrastructure, which provided the original base for its fast economic growth. This was helped by material factors such as transportation, manufacturing, capital investment, a growing labor force, and a lack of internal trade barriers. According to Welton (1979:123), all these alone would not have produced such results if America had not developed the appropriate life-style: an industrial life-style. That life-style was supported by a social philosophy that recommended practical activity and commitment as the way to self-betterment. It was tempered by Social Darwinism with its notion that survival of the fittest requires minimum government interference, and by utilitarianism with its notion that social ills, such as poverty and disease, could be eliminated through a stable economy.

On the one hand, the Puritan work ethic and Puritan moralism were on the rise again, and applied to America's poor in the urban slums. On the other hand, the theory that wealth would not remain in the same families ceased to be true. The American capitalistic system created a new leisure class, which became the subject of Veblen's ([1899]1953) book at the end of the nineteenth century.

In the introduction to one edition of Veblen's book, sociologist C. Wright Mills states that Veblen's theory is not "the theory of the leisure class"; it is a theory of a particular element of the upper class in one period of the history of one nation. Veblen points to three practices by this new American leisure class.

Pecuniary Emulation. Emulation lies at the root of private ownership, and ownership, in the sequence of cultural revolution, signals the emergence of the leisure class. Among its members, the tendency to make the current pecuniary standard the point of departure for a fresh increase in wealth gives rise to a new classification of wealth.

Conspicuous Leisure. The wealthy will go to any length to show that they are free from all tasks by having more helpers and more servants. Leisure is the most conclusive evidence of pecuniary strength, and so is a superior force. It is a nonproductive consumption of time, evidence that one can afford a life of idleness.

Conspicuous Consumption. Both the volume of consumption and the value of what is consumed are important. The greater the consumption of what is expensive, the greater the feeling of being a leisure class member. Here the consumption is for the extreme comfort of the consumers themselves because it is the mark of the master.

Meanwhile American workers were continuing their struggle for reduced work hours.

THE SEARCH FOR FREE TIME

Soon after its independence, the notion of more free time was surfacing in the United States. The notion became a slogan: "Whether you work by the price or by the day, decreasing the hours increases the pay." According to Viau (1939:25), as early as 1806, Ira Steward, a Boston machinist, formed the Grand Eight-Hour League of Massachusetts to advocate the following:

If men were given more leisure, by shortening the workday, they would increase their power of consumption and therefore raise their standard of living. This would tend to force wages up—the employer would be required to pay higher wages because the Laborer would refuse to lower his standards.

In time, wages would absorb all profits and as an inevitable result, private property would no longer be possible.

According to Bosserman (1975:90), the earliest labor organization to ask for reduced hours was the International Brotherhood, which included in its preamble the wish for "the reduction of hours of labor to eight hours a day, so that the laborers may have more time for social enjoyment and intellectual improvement, and be enabled to reap the advantages conferred by labor saving machinery which brains have created."

The American Federation of Labor (AFL), the most powerful labor union during the last decade of the nineteenth century, demanded a fair share of the economic pie, calling for better pay, shorter hours, and improved working conditions. The AFL insisted on getting their benefits through collective bargaining and not through legislation. This attitude fit with the era of social Darwinism, where in a natural conflict, the fittest wins. Yet the reduction of hours took place much later, in the mid-1920s, as a partial solution to combating unemployment. The reduction of work hours without reduction in wages was seen as a way of increasing consumption—a theme that has appeared, now and then, in all the Western nations.

Dramatic changes in the American economy in the 1920s had lasting effects on leisure. For one, mechanization caused a shift from blue-collar workers to white-collar workers. Easy access to additional capital, coupled with the fact that wages were costlier than machinery, led to the shift. This in turn caused increased unemployment among unskilled and semiskilled workers. While national income was rising as a result of the sharp rise in share dividends, wage earners did not enjoy any increase. Industries were reveling in a large supply of labor, available capital, and efficient white-collar management.

Labor pleaded, to no avail, for shorter hours without a reduction of wages as the answer to unemployment. Henry Ford made his dramatic decision to start the five-day week in 1928. *The Monthly Labor Review* (Dec. 1926:1162) published this statement:

This country is ready for the 5-day week. It is bound to come through all industries. The short week is bound to come, because without it the country will not be able to absorb its production and stay prosperous.

We think that, given the chance, people will become more and more expert in the effective use of leisure. And we are given the chance.

But it is the influence of leisure on consumption which makes the short day and the short week so necessary. The people who can consume the bulk of goods are the people who make them. That is a fact we must never forget—that is the secret of our prosperity. People who have more leisure must have more clothes. They must have a greater variety of food. They must have transportation facilities. They naturally must have more services of various kinds.

But it was not until after the Great Depression and the Second World War that Americans began to fulfill the *Review's* prophecy of consumptive mass leisure.

LEISURE PURSUITS FOR SALE

Entertainment for everyone was asserted to be the theater's primary function in the mid-nineteenth-century United States. In spite of the strong religious disapproval, prohibitive laws had been steadily repealed in the early years of the century. The early classic plays introduced by English actors gave way to the farce and variety. The increase in city population "produced patrons whose habits and associations offered no opportunity for the cultivation of the arts" (Dulles 1965:100). A craze for lectures drew away the theater's sophisticated patrons and the theater began to appeal to the masses.

Massive theaters were built. The Park Theater had 2,500 seats and the Broadway had 4,000. Southern cities were also receptive to theaters.

The legitimate theater and popular entertainment were divorced by the midcentury. There was a franker appeal to the blood and thunder taste of the lower classes by producers whose sole goal was to chalk up large box office receipts. Heroic spectacles were introduced, with horses clattering noisily on and off stage. "Even Shakespeare was put on horseback with a neat blend of classic drama and circus" (Dulles 1965:116).

Other forms of amusive leisure came into being. By 1850 almost every city had a museum with a collection of oddities, and a music hall or two. They were soon joined by the traveling circus, which became America's greatest source of amusive leisure for decades. But in order to be accepted, circuses introduced menageries as educational features, historical pageants, or Biblical events.

The United States was becoming more of an urban society. In the process, recreational spaces were not provided, which prevented the games and contests of the earlier settlements. Vicarious participation took the place of actual participation in horse, regatta, and footraces. These were soon followed by prizefighting. Dulles believes that these spectator events helped to make possible the rise of modern organized sport in the second half of the nineteenth century (1965:146).

In the meantime, the rich, particularly the Southern rich, found their Mecca. A virtual *hegira* took place every summer to the Northern spas at Saratoga and Newport. They lived in elegant hotels, woke up early to drink mineral water from the fountain, then took their breakfast. The day usually moved rather slowly while they awaited their evening hops or balls.

Upon their return to the South they led a life of romantic glamour, with music and dancing, charades and cards, riding and driving. Their slaves served them, and on some occasions went out with them on moonlight opossum and raccoon hunts, to cockfights and to horse races on festive occasions.

The slaves were given time off to enjoy their music, dances, and contests in clogging, cakewalks, and Charlestons.

Unable to get together as they did in the ritual of the bee, the urban dwellers found a new communal ritual appealing: the parade. According to Abrahams (1982:175), the parade was a dramatic technique for announcing the beginning of a celebration such as Christmas, the New Year, or the Fourth of July. But it was easily subjected to business needs, reflecting the adage that "what is good for business is good for the country."

SOCIAL RESPONSE: ORGANIZED RECREATION

America's middle class was looking for the good life and the pursuit of happiness. Its poor and huddled masses lived in the slums of the industrial cities. Politicians, social reformers, and educators sought solutions and succeeded, in a relatively short time, in providing highly organized programs to be conducted on elaborately built facilities. Three distinct responses occurred in the second half of the nineteenth century.

Voluntary Education

The Lyceum movement, to bring public speakers to town, started in 1826. The American Lyceum Association was formed in 1831, and by 1840 there were 900 local lyceums. The topics of the lectures varied very widely. According to Dulles (1965:92), reading was the only recreation in Lowell, Massachusetts, at that time. People felt that when not at work, they should become well informed in civic matters, whether through attending a lecture or reading a book. Welton (1979:139) suggests that industrialization brought about boredom caused by lack of intellectual stimulation. The worker performed his task over and over again. He quotes Amass Walker, a noted economist in the 1860s, who said that the division of labor then did not allow for the expansion of all the powers of the mind that normal development requires, and that the solution was in the education of the worker. The most famous lyceum was Chautauqua, which started in 1874 and included guided reading courses.

Another trend that swept the nation between 1865 and 1880 was the formation of voluntary associations dealing with leisure. According to Schlesinger (1944:18), many people were confronted with an increasing amount of idle time because of shorter work hours and other favoring conditions. Most people met the situation by banding together with others and having their use of leisure more or less arranged for them.

It is estimated that 78 societies were founded between 1865 and 1880, 124 between 1880 and 1890, and 366 between 1890 and 1891, with about 5 million names listed. These figures did not include members of college fraternities or sororities (Palisi and Ibrahim 1979:297).

Voluntary education also took place in the libraries and the museums (more on that later).

Organized Sport

Interest in organized sport began after the Civil War, though there were faint stirrings of it just before the war. The nation was becoming so urbanized that the country and frontier festivals were waning. Observers of the national scene were concerned with the rise of spectatorship and the vicarious trends it brought about. Thomas Wentworth Higginson (1858) raised these concerns in the first issue of *Atlantic Monthly:*

> *Even the mechanic confines himself to one set of muscles; the blacksmith acquires strength in his right arm, and the dancing teacher in his left leg. But the professional or businessman, what muscles has he at all?*

The rich had their sport, baseball, which was organized by Alexander Cartwright in 1845 (Baker 1982:140). In 1858, 22 of the 50 teams that played regularly in New York City met and formed the National Association of Baseball Players, which ended the brief period of gentlemanly dominance. Baseball was on the way to becoming America's

national sport. The Civil War had slowed its growth, but it was pitted, after the war, against cricket, the sport of the English, who despite their claim of neutrality, loaned money to and built ships for the Confederacy. Baseball naturally won. Patriotism was also behind the up-and-coming sport of American football.

Rugby was originally chosen as the first intercollegiate contest in 1869 between Princeton and Rutgers. Harvard, Yale, Princeton, and Columbia adopted rugby's rules a few years later. But they began to change them gradually, and by 1881 nothing of rugby was left in American football. It was proved to be America's collegiate sport when more than 40,000 people attended the Yale-Princeton game in 1878 (Dulles 1965:198).

The Young Men's Christian Association was becoming increasingly involved in sport. By 1890, it had some 261 gymnasiums in cities throughout the country (Dulles 1965:206). Americans were playing football in the fall and baseball in the spring. The Springfield YMCA physical director, James Naismith, developed a sport for the winter by experimenting with peach baskets and soccer balls. He offered the world its second most popular sport today, basketball. Wm. Morgan, Holyoke's YMCA physical director, provided us with today's popular sport of volleyball.

After the turn of the century, Luther Gulick, director of physical training of New York City, suggested a mechanism for after-school sport. This was the New York Public School Athletic League, an autonomous entity controlled by an athletic board that included businessmen and politicians (Ibrahim 1975:130).

The Playground Movement

New York City was the first to respond in the playground movement by allocating land for Central Park in 1855. The original idea was to provide rest and aesthetics. But in 1876 the meadow area in Chicago's Washington Park was opened for team sport. Dr. Maria Zakresewska promoted the idea of a sand garden in her native Boston, and a large sandpile was placed in the yard of the Children's

Mission in 1885. As a result of its success, a playground was opened in New York City in 1889, and in 1892 a model playground was opened in the Hull House of Chicago.

As more playgrounds opened around the country, a small group of dedicated individuals, Jane Addams, Henry Curtis, Luther Gulick, and others met in the White House in 1906 and organized the Playground Association of America, with a magazine, *Playground,* to voice its concerns. The name was changed to Playground and Recreation Association of America in 1911; to National Recreation Association in 1926; and finally to National Recreation and Park Association in 1965. The first issue of *Parks and Recreation* magazine was published in 1917 by the American Institute of Park Executives.

Rainwater (1922:192) suggests that nine transitions took place in the playground movements since its inception in 1880 until the end of World War I:

1. The limited provisions of activities to little children expanded to all ages.
2. The summer-only programs expanded to year-long programs.
3. The offerings expanded to include indoor activities, instead of outdoor activities only.
4. The program expanded to rural areas, rather than merely in congested urban centers.
5. The support shifted from philanthropical groups to total community support.
6. Play became organized instead of being free, with schedules provided for activities.
7. The projects became rather complex and varied.
8. The philosophy shifted to include use of leisure, and not just the provision of facilities.
9. Community and group activities were set above individual interests.

Rainwater believes that these nine transitions are reflected in seven stages through which the playground movement passed (1922:60).

1. The Sand Garden: 1885–95
2. The Model Playground: 1895–1900
3. The Small Park: 1900–1905
4. The Recreation Center: 1905–12
5. Civic Art and Welfare: 1912–15
6. Neighborhood Organization: 1915–18
7. Community Service: 1918–present

Hjelte suggests that the playground movement that started in 1885 went through five important additional transitions from 1920 to 1940 (1940:16):

1. The play movement became a recreation movement.
2. The movement became more than just municipal; it became a state and national movement.
3. The program became integrated with public education curriculum and systems.
4. The organization expanded into rural as well as urban areas.
5. The organization eventually came under the public sector in place of the previously subsidized quasi-public control.

Three levels of government—municipal, state and federal—began to play crucial roles in the leisure pursuits of Americans.

ROLE OF GOVERNMENT

Another movement was afoot after the Civil War. The conservation movement was intended, at least initially, to preserve the national heritage of America at the time of increased industrialization. It was not intended to affect the leisure pursuits of Americans to the degree it did in the ensuing years. Yet there had to be an element of pleasure in preserving Yosemite Valley and the Mariposa Grove of the Big Trees of California, as enacted by the United States Congress in 1864. This was subsequent to a similar movement, on a smaller scale, to have a park in New York City. The involvement of the three levels of government is described in the following sections.

Municipal and County Government

Americans were involved in their local affairs from the very beginning. No one was allowed to settle a land without a grant, and grants were given to groups who agreed to participate in the community affairs that were handled in the town meetings. As towns grew in size, a committee was selected to run its affairs. Neither leisure pursuits nor recreational facilities were part of these affairs. Perhaps because the Puritans influence excluded leisure pursuits, there was no need for the provision of recreational areas. In Europe, the ancestral land of most Americans, there were areas that were designated for recreation. But Europe had an aristocracy that provided itself with these huge estates for hunting and other pleasures. Some of them were eventually opened to the public. The American public did not inherit areas for that purpose; they had to be developed.

The first such attempt at developing a public park was in New York City in the 1850s. Manhattan Island was being depleted of open space and public pressure to develop a park mounted. The legislature passed a bill in 1856 to establish a park on a 843-acre site. According to Fazio, in designing the park, Frederick Law Olmsted adapted the English natural style to the rectangular restrictions of American parks and established the basis for city parks throughout the United States (1979:210).

Frederick Law Olmsted was engaged to design a great number of municipal parks: Prospect Park in Brooklyn, Fairmount Park in Philadelphia, Mount Royal Park in Montreal, Belle Isle Park in Detroit, and South Park in Chicago. In the closing years of the nineteenth century, Charles Eliot, an associate of Olmsted, convinced the Massachusetts Legislature that a Metropolitan Park Commission was needed to cross city and town lines with a park system. Within a few years, New Jersey passed its first regional park act, enabling Essex county to develop the first county park system in the United States in 1895.

Initially, these areas were used, in the words of Aristotle, for contemplative leisure. Soon after, a movement arose to offer, as President Calvin Coolidge put it, play for the child, sport for the youth, and recreation for adults (G. Butler 1940:48). The debate over whether a park is a place of contemplative leisure or recreative leisure is still with us today.

According to Butler (1940:417), the establishment of children's playgrounds in the larger metropolitan areas was the first step in the development of the municipal recreation movement in the United States. Initially, the authority of the municipal recreation movement was established, not on enabling legislation, but on either the general welfare or police powers in state constitutions and local charters; and on broad interpretations of existing park and school legislation. Many local authorities were reluctant to provide any programs on these bases and sought broader park and/or school legislation. The broadening of park legislation, as in Kansas and Minnesota, allowed local authorities to offer wide programs. Indiana passed legislation authorizing community use of public schools as early as 1859. California and Texas provided, through their constitutions, the basis for many local recreation systems.

Local legislation became necessary. City charters were amended to allow for the appointment of recreation commissions. Local ordinances were also issued for the creation of recreation commissions according to the state's enabling law. In 1940 Butler gave seven reasons for municipal recreation (1940:49–53):

1. Municipal recreation affords a large percentage of people their only opportunity for forms of wholesome recreation.
2. It is only through government that adequate lands can be acquired.
3. Municipal recreation is democratic and inclusive.
4. Municipal recreation is comparatively inexpensive.

5. The municipal government gives permanency to recreation.
6. The job is too large for any private agency.
7. The municipality cannot afford not to provide recreation.

Yet Butler conceded that the municipality does not aim to meet and can never hope to serve all the recreation needs of all the people. He suggested that semipublic agencies continue their efforts to serve the leisure time needs of individuals who desire to "engage in forms of recreation with others of a similar religious, social, economic, or racial background" (1940:55). He also suggested that private agencies that afford recreation for their members will assist municipal efforts, as will commercial agencies. Butler emphasized that state and federal agencies should attempt to complement local offerings.

State Involvement

The motivation behind granting the Yosemite Valley and the Mariposa Grove to California was to protect and preserve them for future generations. Yosemite was taken back by the federal government and became the second national park after Yellowstone in Wyoming. Mackinac Island Park started under the auspices of the federal government in 1875 but became a state park in 1895. In the interim, it had become a rich man's resort.

Frederick Law Olmsted was again instrumental in the attempts to develop a state preserve around Niagara Falls. The Canadian government took similar steps across the river. That same year, 1885, saw the creation of New York's Adirondack wilderness area. Although fear of water shortages had prompted the move, the New York Forest Commission saw another value, and suggested changing it to a park, "a place where rest, recuperation, and vigor may be gained by our highly nervous and overworked people" (Fazio 1979:215).

Although many states followed New York's example and provided state parks and forests, very few of them provided recreation programs before World War II. But by 1972 the states managed almost 42 million acres of land for outdoor recreation purposes in parks, forests, and nature preserves. After World War II, nearly every state acquired land for recreational use and became involved in recreation programs. They also became responsible for allocation of state and federal funds to localities. Kraus (1984:151–55) lists seven functions of state government where recreative leisure is concerned.

1. **Legislation.** Specific legal authority is needed by local authorities to provide areas and programs.
2. **Resources and programs.** Many states not only provide resources for leisure pursuits but organize programs.
3. **Conservation and open space.** Most states promote the concept of conservation and work on providing open spaces.
4. **Assistance to local government.** Consultation and direct aid are provided to local governments.
5. **Development and enforcement of standards.** Some states develop standards related to health in camps and conduct periodic inspections.
6. **Promotion of recreation.** Since tourism and travel are economically beneficial to the state, many states now try to attract tourists and travelers.
7. **Specific offerings.** In many of the specialized institutions such as mental hospitals and prisons, the state provides for leisure pursuits.

Federal Government

A group of Montana businessmen visited the Yellowstone backcountry to see the reported natural wonders of the area. The intention was to assess its potential for commercial enterprises. After seeing it, they agreed that it should become a permanent national preserve. After two federal parties explored the area, a bill was introduced and was passed in the U.S. Congress in 1872 to establish a

1.6-million-acre reserve as a public park or pleasuring ground for the benefit and enjoyment of the people. This event signalled a change in public policy from allowing private exploitation of America's natural resources to setting aside large areas of public lands for protection and public enjoyment.

In 1890, a bill was passed in the U.S. Congress creating Yosemite National Park. The abuse and misuse of the park led naturalist John Muir to form the Sierra Club two years later, the purpose of which was to encourage appreciation and protection of mountain environments. Despite attempts to stop predation, it continued until the passage of the Antiquities Act in 1906. Once again, it was conservation and protection that President Theodore Roosevelt invoked to preserve many historic and scientific areas for future generations. Fourteen other parks and 22 national monuments were established before President Woodrow Wilson signed the act establishing the National Park Service. The initial concept of setting aside a large primitive piece of land was uniquely American. As expressed by Native American George Catlin, the park's character would be such that nature could roam free (Knudson 1984:225). Most of the land administered by the National Park Service in the early years was west of the Mississippi and away from urban centers. However, in recent years it has added areas in the East and closer to urban centers. The total is about 32 million acres spread across 49 states, consisting of 333 separate areas.

Although multiple use of national forests was envisioned from the very beginning of the establishment of the United States Forest Service, the potential for recreational value was evident. Today these forests, totalling 188 million acres, receive millions of visitors each year. This is true also of the areas managed by the Bureau of Land Management, which started as the General Land Office in 1792. Now it has jurisdiction over one-fifth of the United States land. These vast areas are visited by sightseers, fishermen, off-road vehicle enthusiasts, campers, and hunters. Data on visitation to federal areas, 1970–85, are presented in tables 11.7 to 11.11.

But the involvement of the federal government in the leisure pursuits of Americans goes beyond the mere provision of areas and facilities. MacLean and others (1985:116) list the following:

1. Ownership and management of land, water, and wildlife in the public interest. The federal government maintains, in the name of the people, about one-third, or 740 million acres, of the land in the United States. It also protects wildlife on these lands.
2. Grants to state and local governments. Direct financial assistance for land acquisition, planning, and programs for special populations such as the aged and the handicapped is provided.
3. Regulation of hunting, fishing, boating, as well as telecasting and broadcasting that affects the leisure pursuits of Americans.
4. Program offerings in national parks and forests provide many leisure activities to visitors.
5. Research of the use and demands for leisure, including travel, are conducted by federal agencies or through federal grants. The information is then disseminated directly or through institutions of higher education.
6. Assistance and advisory services are provided through low interest loans to recreational enterprises and through technical assistance to local and state agencies.
7. Coordination among various agencies is done to avoid duplication of services and programs.
8. International agreements on water quality; migrating birds, fish, and mammals; and on international waters.

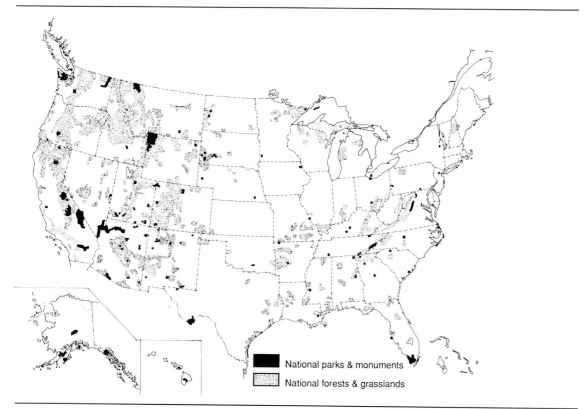

FIGURE 11.1 *National resources in the United States. Source: Mr. Lynd Warren, Whittier, CA.*

IN PURSUIT OF HAPPINESS

The Depression prompted the federal government to attempt a 34-hour workweek to relieve the massive unemployment at that time, but by World War II the whole plan changed. Overtime became a necessity for the war efforts.

A 1938 act remained the basis for federal legislation, and was updated in 1947, 1948, 1950, and in 1966. Although the standard has become a 40-hour workweek, there is no federal or state legislation dealing with annual vacation time. Yet there is a federal act dealing with national legal holidays, making some of them fall on the day before or after the weekend to give the worker a longer weekend. These are New Year's Day, Martin Luther King's birthday, Washington and Lincoln's

birthdays, Good Friday, Memorial Day, Independence Day, Labor Day, Veteran's Day, Thanksgiving, and Christmas.

Bosserman (1975:101) showed that within a period of 100 years, from 1870 to 1970, productivity continued to increase and work hours continued to decrease (see fig. 11.2). Income rose in a similar fashion until 1920, when hours started dropping; then they rose again during World War II. After the war, hours dropped modestly while income increased steadily. In 1950, the median family income averaged $11,361; in 1980 it averaged $21,023. At 2% annual growth, the median income is expected to be over $26,000 in 1990. Disposable personal income per capita is used to estimate consumer purchasing power. It is calculated by subtracting tax and nontax payments from

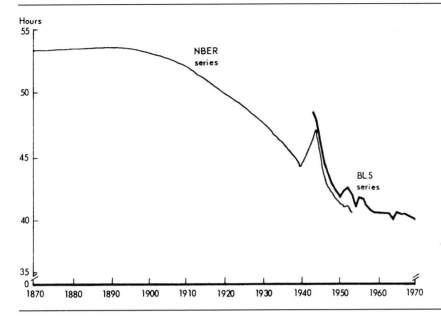

FIGURE 11.2 *Average weekly hours per worker, U.S., 1869–1970. Source: Bosserman, P., "The Evolution of and Trends in Work and Non-work Time in the United States Society (1920–1970)."* Society and Leisure *7(1), p. 94.*

personal income. There has been a steady gain in these figures from 1950 until today. As income increased, so did the personal spending on recreative leisure. Table 11.1 shows these personal expenditures from 1970 to 1985. While the percentage of the expenditures remains about the same, ranging from 6.6% to 6.9%, the total amount has increased substantially—more than four times, from $42 billion to $176 billion. These figures do not include expenditures met by governmental agencies, commercial recreation, and cultural enterprises. These expenditures have reached $130 billion, bringing total leisure expenditures to over $300 billion this year, which makes leisure a leading industry in the United States. *U.S. News and World Report,* which reported on leisure expenditures since 1965, estimated them at $58 billion then, $100 billion in 1970, and $150 billion in 1975. In a little over a decade it has doubled to over $300 billion. The fact is, the leisure industry is a great success (see table 11.2). Many nations—West Germany, for example—are attempting to follow this example.

Income alone is not responsible for the unprecedented explosion in leisure pursuits. Advances in medicine that have increased longevity and changes

in retirement policies that allow for early retirement are important factors in this explosion, along with factors to be discussed in chapter 12. These pursuits vary significantly, but in general they are depicted in studies such as the cross-cultural one of Szalai (1972).

United Media Enterprises conducted a study on leisure choices among 1,024 persons from the general public, 101 newspaper editors, 105 cable television directors, and 116 network television news directors (1983). The study revealed that the free time available for leisure is about 32 hours a week for all respondents, which averages 4 hours and 40 minutes a day (see fig. 11.3).

When it comes to leisure pursuits, the United Media study concludes that most pursuits take place at home, such as watching television, reading, and socializing. The daily participation in these and other activities is shown in table 11.3. The most home-focused are the senior citizens, followed by parents with grown children, and then traditional parents. The least home-focused are teenagers, singles, and married couples with no children.

Table 11.1 **Personal consumption expenditures for recreation, U.S.: 1970–85 (in millions of dollars)**

Type of product or service	1970	1975	1980	1981	1982	1983	1984	1985
Total recreation expenditures	42,718	70,233	114,972	128,625	138,321	152,052	165,291	176,289
Percent of total personal consumption	6.7	6.9	6.6	6.7	6.7	6.8	6.8	6.8
Books and maps	2,922	3,570	5,595	6,174	6,551	7,185	7,823	7,972
Magazines, newspapers, sheet music	4,097	6,356	10,438	11,012	11,445	11,967	12,695	13,196
Nondurable toys and sport supplies	5,498	8,954	14,633	16,005	16,826	18,004	19,796	20,350
Wheel goods, durable toys, sports eqpt.	5,191	10,514	17,185	18,727	19,336	20,419	23,243	26,727
TVs, radios, records, music instruments	8,540	13,489	19,888	22,020	24,515	28,182	31,280	35,119
Radio and TV repair	1,383	2,229	2,555	2,659	2,774	2,834	2,837	3,100
Flowers, seeds, and potted plants	1,798	2,659	4,047	4,413	4,495	4,806	5,217	5,459
Admission to spectator amusements	3,296	4,317	6,490	6,929	7,799	8,601	9,403	9,661
Motion picture theaters	1,829	2,197	2,671	2,853	3,326	3,583	3,938	3,678
Operas and nonprofit institutions	531	787	1,786	2,049	2,141	2,389	2,678	2,991
Spectator sports	1,136	1,333	2,033	2,027	2,332	2,629	2,787	2,994
Clubs and fraternal organizations	1,465	1,921	3,020	3,430	3,842	4,154	4,430	4,752
Commercial participant amusements	2,367	4,858	9,666	11,677	12,471	13,606	14,132	14,554
Parimutuel net receipts	1,096	1,662	2,095	2,229	2,240	2,269	2,462	2,605
Other	5,065	9,704	19,360	23,350	26,027	30,025	31,973	32,802

Source: U.S. Bureau of the Census, Statistical Abstracts of the United States: 1987 (107th Edition) Washington, DC, 1986, p. 211.

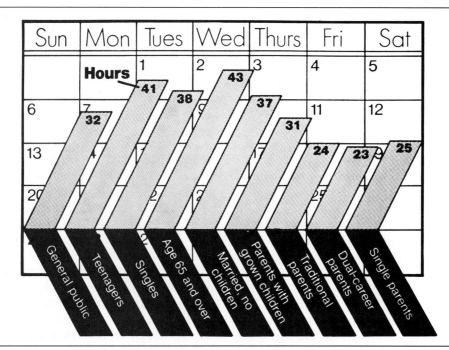

FIGURE 11.3 *Hours available for leisure per week. Source: The United Media Enterprises Report on Leisure in America. © 1983 United Media. Used by permission.*

Table 11.2 Sporting goods sales, by product category: 1980–86, U.S. (in millions of dollars)

Selected product category	1980	1981	1982	1983	1984	1985	1986 (proj.)
Sales, all products	16,691	18,725	18,684	23,111	26,401	27,446	29,119
Percent of retail sales	1.7	1.8	1.7	2.0	2.0	2.0	na
Athletic sport clothing*	3,127	3,201	3,014	3,226	3,432	3,376	3,503
Athletic sport footwear	1,731	1,785	1,900	2,189	2,381	2,610	2,791
Gym shoes	465	616	659	639	669	656	675
Running shoes	397	372	421	557	591	572	572
Tennis shoes	359	284	287	340	371	470	507
Aerobic shoes	na	na	10	29	54	178	266
Basketball shoes	86	80	81	119	159	185	198
Golf shoes	68	78	99	115	110	109	116
Baseball shoes	56	58	48	66	87	103	108
Athletic equipment	6,487	6,762	7,114	7,925	8,317	8,922	9,311
Firearms and hunting	1,351	1,454	1,567	1,666	1,620	1,699	1,716
Fishing tackle	539	689	586	606	616	681	715
Camping	646	663	735	790	699	724	775
Golf	386	413	493	633	630	730	767
Snow skiing	379	307	332	386	502	593	650
Optics	na	na	na	na	294	309	327
Tennis	237	254	277	293	315	273	287
Archery	149	169	168	179	212	212	212
Baseball and softball	158	157	154	173	153	176	187
Water skis	123	123	106	133	146	125	131
Billiards	173	146	124	199	100	117	125
Bowling accessories	107	107	103	106	108	106	106
Recreational transport	5,345	6,977	6,656	9,771	12,271	12,539	13,514
Bicycles and supplies	1,233	1,299	1,148	1,638	1,840	2,109	2,109
Pleasure boats	2,718	3,656	3,684	4,612	6,209	6,753	7,428
Recreational vehicles	1,178	1,820	1,701	3,368	4,082	3,515	3,807
Snowmobiles	216	202	123	153	140	162	170

na = not available

*Category does not cover all sales

Source: U.S. Bureau of the Census, Statistical Abstracts of the United States: 1987 (107th Edition) Washington, DC, 1986, p. 213.

Mass Media

When compared in 1972 to the Eastern European samples, television played a considerably greater role in the life of the Americans sampled (Skorzynski 1972:270). This was corroborated by a study conducted a decade later. John Robinson (1981), who participated in the study of Szalai and Skorzynski above, conducted a time-budget study of a national probability sample of 1,519 respondents. They reported all their activities for a 24-hour period in the fall of 1975, across all days of the week. He concluded that an increase in time spent watching television took place in that decade, and that the increase came at the expense of other free-time activities, especially newspaper reading and visiting, as well as from a decline in obligatory time activities such as work and housework. The sample reported an average of 2 hours and 24 minutes of television watching a day.

The data from the United Media study (1983) also shows that watching television is the most popular leisure pursuit among Americans (table 11.3). Seventy-four percent of the sample in that study stated they watch television for an average of 2 hours and 51 minutes a day. Reading the newspaper comes next, with 67% of the sample stating that they do so daily; followed by listening

Table 11.3 Daily participation in leisure pursuits in U.S.

Group (N)	Leisure Weekly HR/M	Leisure Daily HR/M	Watching TV Hours HR/M	Watching TV %	Exercise %	Newspaper %	Reading Books %	Magazine %	Listen to music %	Fix things %	Hobbies %	Gardening %	Talking On phone	Talking With friends
Teenagers (74)	41:00	5:51	3:47	89	54	49	20	34	78	17	39	11	62	34
Singles (208)	33:00	5:27	2:53	67	48	62	18	21	76	7	29	6	50	32
Age 65+ (153)	43:00	6:11	3:30	81	34	87	35	20	20	12	39	30	47	30
Married/no children (61)	37:00	5:13	2:25	70	24	63	30	14	56	25	17	19	42	33
Parents/grown children (172)	31:00	4:27	2:47	73	28	76	28	21	31	23	20	29	44	26
Traditional parents (142)	24:00	3:25	2:31	74	35	65	17	14	42	24	14	34	48	32
Dual-career parents (169)	22:00	3:15	2:14	72	30	68	27	14	46	22	19	24	40	29
Single parents (45)	25:00	3:38	2:41	62	39	66	25	12	50	14	13	9	65	37
Average	33:37	4:40	2:51	74	37	67	25	19	50	18	24	20	47	32

Source: © 1983 NEA, Inc. Reprinted by permission of United Media.

to music (50%); talking on the phone (47%); talking with friends (32%); reading books (25%); hobbies (24%); and reading magazines (19%).

It seems that television watching has increased rather sharply in the last two decades in the United States. John Robinson (1981) reports an increase from 1 hour and 30 minutes in 1965 to 2 hours and 24 minutes in 1975. The United Media (1983) reported 2 hours and 51 minutes of television watching a day in 1983. All this is supported by the United Nations figures (table 7.1), in that the United States has the highest ratio of television sets to persons in the world (1:1.68). Great Britain is second (1:1.96), with Canada third (1:2.21). Also, the United States has the most hours of transmission and the widest variety in programming. In fact, A. C. Nielson, the watchdog over transmission, states that televisions are left on for 7 hours, 49 minutes a day in the typical American home (Gertner 1986:14a). More on that in chapter 14.

Despite the increase in the time allotted for watching television (Robinson 1981), supposedly at the expense of other leisure pursuits, reading is still a favored leisure activity of many Americans. It seems that newspaper reading is the most favored: 67% of the United Media's sample cite newspaper reading, followed by reading books (25%), and magazines (19%). In a cross-cultural study almost two decades ago, the sample from 44 American cities spent, on the average, 24 minutes a day reading newspapers, 5 minutes on books, and 6 minutes on magazines. In that study, the American sample spent more time reading the newspaper than did all other samples. There are 1,710 daily newspapers in the country with a circulation of 62,415,000, for a ratio of one newspaper for every 3.85 Americans, one of the highest ratios in the world (table 7.1).

There are 8,459 public libraries in the United States, or one library for every 28,253 citizens. There are holdings of over 460 million books, or 1.9 books for each person in the country, making the United States second to the USSR with its 1.3 books for each citizen. In the ratio of books published a year to population, the United States is ahead of most Eastern bloc nations, but lags behind Great Britain, West Germany, France, and Canada (see table 7.1).

Movies and the Performing Arts

In 1984, there were 9,254 movie theaters in America, 7,125 of which were walk-in theaters and 2,129 drive-in theaters. These figures represent an increase of about 51% since 1975. These theaters grossed over 3.5 billion dollars, which is estimated to be an increase of about 39% for the same period (table 11.4). While the studio's share of the box office continued to climb, from $1,216 billion in 1981 to $1,750 billion in 1987 (Ciepley 1988), the movie theaters' share was not only leveling off but declining.

Table 11.1 shows that receipts in millions of dollars declined from 3,938 in 1984 to 3,676 in 1985. Nonetheless, more movie theaters were planned for, and by the end of 1987 there were an additional 1,500 new movie theaters in the United States (Farley 1986). The movie industry is trying to combat both television and video cassette recorder watching by changing movie theaters from "the cramped multiplexes" that are dominant now to spacious theaters not dissimilar to those of the 1930s and 1940s.

An increase in leisure pursuits among Americans is seen in the performing arts, particularly in opera and concerts, but not in Broadway shows (table 11.5). While the number of shows on Broadway declined from 62 in 1970 to 31 in 1985, possibly because each show was scheduled for a longer period, gross box office receipts quadrupled in the same period. The number of tickets sold climbed from 1978 to 1982, then declined again.

Table 11.4 Amusement and recreation services—summary 1982 (represents establishments with payroll or firms subject to federal income tax)

Kind of business	Number of establishments	Receipts				Annual payroll (mil. dol.)	Paid employees
		Total (mil. dol.)	Percent change 1977–82	Per establishment ($1,000)	Per employee (dol.)		
Amusement and recreation services, incl. motion pictures	67,215	33,115	67.6	493	41,199	8,805	803,776
Motion picture production, distribution, and services	7,905	10,117	90.4	1,280	79,531	2,451	127,209
Motion picture theaters	9,344	3,576	39.1	383	34,561	567	103,461
Theaters, excl. drive-ins	7,215	3,224	51.4	447	34,969	497	92,203
Drive-in theaters	2,129	351	-20.2	165	31,222	70	11,258
Producers, orchestras, and entertainers	6,712	3,301	86.7	492	58,084	971	56,833
Bowling alleys, billiards, pool	7,379	2,264	33.0	307	20,788	648	108,909
Billiards and pool	896	80	-7.9	89	22,816	19	3,503
Bowling alleys	6,483	2,184	35.2	337	20,720	629	105,406
Commercial sports	2,360	3,418	37.4	1,449	54,742	1,170	62,447
Pro sports clubs	498	1,128	20.4	2,266	58,077	684	19,430
Baseball clubs	117	321	28.4	2,748	69,073	252	4,654
Football clubs	37	177	-28.7	4,779	55,488	203	3,187
Racing, incl. track oper.	1,862	2,290	47.6	1,230	53,236	486	43,017
Auto racetrack oper.	386	163	20.7	423	55,530	25	2,941
Horse racetrack oper.	104	1,533	49.9	14,743	59,059	322	25,961
Dog racetrack oper.	48	292	52.8	6,093	43,581	64	6,711
Public golf courses	2,289	588	43.4	257	35,996	164	16,336
Coin operated amusements	5,434	1,423	192.2	262	52,917	285	26,886
Amusement parks	466	1,824	55.6	3,914	39,250	603	46,464
Membership sports and recreation clubs	7,544	2,488	116.7	330	25,795	792	96,572
Concession, operators of amusement devices, rides	905	180	10.2	199	46,267	37	3,889
Carnivals and circuses	298	196	26.3	659	50,966	33	3,851
Fairs	82	25	-34.3	307	89,821	5	280
Museums, botanical and zoological gardens	220	65	(na)	297	32,791	19	1,992
Other	12,852	3,447	58.8	268	25,949	995	132,835

Source: U.S. Bureau of the Census, Statistical Abstracts of the United States: 1987 (107th Edition) Washington, DC, 1986, p. 220.

Table 11.5 Performing arts—selected data: 1970–85 (receipts and expenditures in millions of dollars)

Item	1970	1975	1977	1978	1979	1980	1981	1982	1983	1984	1985
Legitimate theater:											
Broadway shows											
New productions	62	59	63	54	47	67	76	53	50	36	31
Playing weeks	1,047	1,101	1,348	1,360	1,472	1,541	1,545	1,461	1,259	1,119	1,062
Number of tickets sold	(na)	(na)	6,815	8,621	9,115	9,380	10,882	10,694	8,102	7,898	7,156
Gross box office receipts	53.3	57.4	93.4	103.8	128.1	143.4	194.5	221.2	263.1	226.5	208.0
Road shows											
Playing weeks	1,024	799	987	1,025	1,192	1,351	1,343	1,317	990	1,057	993
Gross box office receipts	48.0	50.9	82.8	106.0	148.9	181.2	218.9	249.5	184.3	206.2	225.9
Opera companies	648	807	914	956	966	986	1,019	993	1,031	1,051	1,123
Major	35	54	68	78	95	109	127	133	144	154	168
Expenditures	36.5	(na)	79.7	96.3	111.5	133.6	161.6	191.1	212.4	236.7	256.5
Other companies	266	335	424	458	456	458	456	416	488	491	576
Workshops	347	418	422	420	415	419	436	444	399	406	379
Opera performances	4,779	6,428	7,389	7,806	8,554	9,391	9,683	9,510	10,693	10,421	10,642
Operas performed	341	387	427	448	489	497	559	571	590	576	578
Musical performances	(na)	(na)	(na)	906	1,430	1,397	2,251	2,333	2,749	2,787	4,983
Musicals performed	(na)	(na)	(na)	43	72	104	118	122	120	129	242
World premiers	17	16	33	42	64	79	88	94	96	101	121
Attendance (mil.)	4.6	8.0	9.2	9.8	9.9	10.7	11.1	10.1	12.7	13.0	14.1
Symphony orchestras	1,441	1,463	1,453	1,470	1,540	1,572	1,572	1,572	1,572	1,572	1,572
College	298	300	358	278	379	385	385	385	386	380	371
Community	1,019	1,003	888	950	909	926	926	919	920	937	946
Urban	24	41	69	76	79	85	85	94	101	89	89
Metropolitan	72	90	86	106	113	115	115	110	98	96	96
Regional	(na)	(na)	23	29	29	29	30	34	30	40	40
Major	28	29	31	31	31	32	31	30	30	30	30
Concerts	6,599	14,171	17,421	18,027	22,096	22,229	19,327	19,204	19,167	19,086	19,969
Attendance	12.7	18.3	21.0	21.4	22.4	22.6	22.8	22.0	22.0	23.2	23.7
Gross income	73.3	124.5	154.1	178.1	216.8	246.9	288.9	325.5	348.9	379.0	435.4
Earned income	43.1	70.9	89.0	102.5	122.6	141.2	163.3	187.6	201.8	220.2	250.7
Contributed income	30.2	53.6	65.1	75.6	94.2	105.1	125.6	137.9	147.1	158.8	184.7
Gross expenses	76.4	129.5	106.9	183.1	221.0	252.1	289.3	315.3	352.2	289.8	441.8

Source: U.S. Bureau of the Census, Statistical Abstracts of the United States: 1987 (107th Edition) Washington, DC, 1986, p. 221.

Table 11.6 Participation rates for various arts performances and leisure activities by selected characteristics: 1982 (represents percent of respondents 18 yrs. and over)

Characteristic	Attended at least once				
	Jazz perform.	Classical music perform.	Opera perform.	Musical plays	Ballet perform.
Total	10	13	3	19	4
Male	11	11	3	17	3
Female	9	15	3	20	6
White	9	14	3	20	5
Black	15	7	1	10	2
Other race	9	10	3	13	4
18–24 yrs.	18	11	3	17	4
25–34 yrs.	15	13	4	20	5
35–44 yrs.	8	16	4	23	6
45–54 yrs.	7	15	5	21	4
55–64 yrs.	5	13	4	19	4
65–74 yrs.	2	12	7	14	3
75 yrs. and over	1	7	3	9	2
Northeast	9	14	4	23	6
Midwest	10	14	4	18	4
South	9	11	3	16	4
West	12	13	3	18	4
Household income:					
Under $10,000	8	9	1	10	3
$10,000–$14,999	7	8	3	9	2
$15,000–$19,999	8	10	3	13	4
$20,000–$29,999	9	11	3	17	4
$30,000–$49,999	9	18	5	28	6
$50,000 and over	13	30	11	44	11

Source: *U.S. Bureau of the Census*, Statistical Abstracts of the United States: 1987 *(107th Edition) Washington, DC, 1986, p. 221.*

For the period 1970–85, the number of operas performed in the United States climbed from 341 to 578, with attendance going from 4.6 million to 14.1 million persons. Expenditures increased by 700%, from $36.5 million to $256.5 million. The same growth occurred in symphony orchestras, where attendance rose from 12.7 million in 1970 to 23.7 million in 1985, with earned incomes of $43.1 million in 1970 and $250.7 million in 1985. Contributed income also increased from $30.2 million to $184.7 million in the same period.

This is in spite of the fact that relatively few Americans attended performing arts. In a survey conducted by the Bureau of Census in 1982 56% of the respondents indicated that they read novels, short stories, poetry, or plays, and 22% indicated

that they visited art museums or galleries. But as for the performing arts, only 19% of Americans attend musical plays, 13% classical music performances, 10% jazz performances, 4% ballet performances, and only 3% opera performances. It seems that neither age, race, nor religion are differentiating factors for attending performing arts. But income is—the higher the income, the greater the attendance (table 11.6).

The Sport Scene

In December of 1985, the Gallup Organization conducted a national survey of 1,500 households and concluded that swimming is the most popular sport activity in America, with 72 million Americans or about 41% of the population preferring

Table 11.7 **Adult* participation in leisure time activities, by selected type: 1985**

Type of activity	Number (mil.)	Percent
Flower gardening	77	44
Swimming	72	41
Fishing	60	34
Bicycling	58	33
Bowling	44	25
Jogging	40	23
Softball	39	22
Camping	37	21
Weight training	33	19
Billiards	33	19
Aerobics	32	18
Motor boating	28	16
Volleyball	28	16
Calisthenics	26	15
Basketball	26	15
Hunting	25	14
Golf	23	14
Baseball	23	13
Tennis	23	13
Table tennis	21	12
Canoeing	16	9
Rollerskating	16	9
Horseback riding	16	9
Target shooting	16	9
Skiing	14	8
Racquetball	14	8
Waterskiing	12	7
Touch football	11	6
Sailing	9	5

Source: U.S. Bureau of the Census, Statistical Abstracts of the United States: 1987 *(107th Edition) Washington, DC, 1986, p. 215.*

swimming as their physical leisure pursuit. Fishing came in second with 60 million participants or 34%, followed by bicycling with 58 million or 33%, bowling with 44 million or 25%, and jogging with 40 million or 23%. Table 11.7 lists additional data on softball, camping, weight training, billiards, and aerobics.

The United Media study (1983) shows that different groups vary in their pursuits of participant sport. Fifty-four percent of teenagers indicated that they partake in physical activity, in comparison to 48% of singles, 39% of single parents with grown children, and 24% of persons married with no children (table 11.3).

American participation in sport is not limited to the ten listed above. Walking for pleasure, which may be considered more a sightseeing activity than a rigorous physical activity, appeals to as many Americans as the number one sport, swimming. In addition, there are participants in every conceivable sport, as shown in tables 11.7, 11.8, and 11.9, proof of a leisure explosion in this country.

Table 11.4 shows the number of bowling lanes (6,483) and billiard/pool halls (896) in 1982. This is an increase of 35.2% for the former and a decrease of 7.9% for the latter since 1977. Also, the number of public golf courses increased 43.4% in the same period, to 2,289.

Spectator sport attendance increased by 26.5% over a period of ten years, from 176,381,000 in 1975 to 223,157,000 in 1985. The figures in table 11.10 show that horse racing has been and still is the most attended spectator sport in America, attracting over 73 million in 1985. It was followed by professional baseball with over 47 million, college football with 36 million, college basketball (men's) with 32 million, greyhound racing with 23 million, professional football with 14 million, professional hockey with 11 million, professional basketball with 11 million, college basketball (women's) with 5 million, and jai alai with 4 million.

Spectator sport in America saw growth and decline in attendance from the 1970s to the 1980s. The largest increase took place in professional baseball: attendance of 30 million in 1975 increased 57% by 1985. Greyhound racing came in second with an increase of 36%, and professional basketball was third with 25%. Soccer, although the number one participant and spectator sport in almost every other country in the world, met with difficulties in the United States. Attendance at professional games totalled 1,825,000 in 1975 and climbed to 6,194,000 in 1980, an increase of about 240%. Then it declined sharply to 1,158,000 by 1984. The North American Soccer League is now dissolved.

Table 11.8 Selected recreational activities: 1970–85

Activity	Unit	1970	1975	1979	1980	1981	1982	1983	1984	1985
Softball, amateur										
Total participants	Million	16	26	30	30	30	30	30	35	35
Youth participants	1,000	255	450	600	630	685	690	700	700	710
Adult teams	1,000	29	66	102	110	117	133	146	146	152
Youth teams	1,000	2	9	15	18	20	22	27	29	31
Golfers	1,000	11,245	13,036	14,612	15,112	15,566	16,003	16,514	17,009	17,520
Golf rounds played	1,000	266,169	308,562	345,866	357,701	368,791	378,791	390,886	402,603	414,777
Golf facilities	number	10,188	11,370	11,966	12,005	12,035	12,140	12,197	12,278	12,346
Class:										
Private	number	4,619	4,770	4,848	4,839	4,789	4,798	4,809	4,831	4,861
Daily fee	number	4,248	5,014	5,340	5,372	5,428	5,494	5,528	5,566	5,573
Municipal	number	1,321	1,586	1,778	1,794	1,818	1,848	1,860	1,881	1,812
Tennis										
Players	1,000	10,665	29,201	32,271	na	na	25,450	na	19,456	18,951
Indoor	1,000	na	4,072	5,760	na	na	4,015	na	na	na
Courts	1,000	na	130	160	na	180	185	200	220	220
Indoor	1,000	na	8	12	na	11	11	13	14	14
Ten-pin bowling										
Participants	million	51.8	62.5	na	72.0	na	68.9	na	67.0	67.0
Male	million	24.8	29.9	na	34.0	na	32.2	na	32.0	32.0
Female	million	27.0	32.6	na	38.0	na	36.7	na	35.0	35.0
Establishments	number	9,140	8,577	8,699	8,591	8,528	8,481	8,404	8,351	8,275
Lanes	1,000	141	141	154	154	154	154	154	155	154
Membership	1,000	7,733	8,751	9,649	9,595	9,621	9,550	9,268	8,401	8,062
Amer. Bowl. Cong.	1,000	4,210	4,300	4,662	4,688	4,645	4,685	4,556	3,791	3,656
Women's Bowl. Cong.	1,000	2,988	3,692	4,163	4,118	4,049	4,065	3,947	3,886	3,713
Young Amer. Bowl. Alliance	1,000	535	759	824	789	927	800	765	744	693
Motion picture theaters	1,000	14	15	17	18	18	18	19	20	21
Four-wall	1,000	10	11	13	14	15	15	16	17	18
Drive-in	1,000	4	4	4	4	3	3	3	3	3
Receipts, box office	mil. dol	1,225	2,115	2,821	2,749	2,966	3,453	3,766	4,031	3,749
Admission, avg.	dollars	1.55	2.05	2.52	2.69	2.78	2.94	3.15	3.36	3.55
Attendance	million	921	1,033	1,121	1,022	1,067	1,175	1,197	1,199	1,056
Bicycles										
Domestic shipments	million	5.0	5.6	8.7	7.0	6.8	5.1	6.3	5.9	5.8
Imports	million	1.9	1.7	1.8	2.0	2.1	1.6	2.7	4.2	5.6

Table 11.8 Continued

Boating										
Rec. boats owned	million	8.8	9.7	11.6	11.8	12.8	12.9	13.0	13.5	13.9
Outboard	million	5.2	5.7	6.7	6.8	7.0	7.1	7.2	7.3	7.5
Inboard	million	.6	.8	1.3	1.2	1.2	1.3	1.3	1.4	1.5
Sailboats	million	.6	.8	.9	1.0	1.0	1.1	1.1	1.1	1.2
Canoes	million			1.2	1.3	1.4	1.5	1.6	1.7	1.8
Rowboats, other	million	2.4	2.4	1.5	1.5	1.9	1.9	1.8	1.8	1.9
Expenditures, total	bil. dol	3.4	4.8	7.5	7.4	8.3	8.1	9.4	12.3	13.3
Outboards in use	1,000	7,215	7,649	7,958	8,241	8,527	8,776	9,051	9,400	9,733
Motors sold	1,000	430	436	376	316	318	203	337	411	392
Value, retail	mil. dol	281	411	597	554	698	759	964	1,294	1,319
Outboards sold	1,000	276	328	322	290	281	236	273	317	305
Value, retail	mil. dol	177	263	469	408	431	409	502	706	759
Inboards sold	1,000	43	70	89	56	51	55	79	106	115
Value, retail	mil. dol	182	420	827	616	653	686	975	1,442	1,663
All terrain vehicles										
Tot. in use	1,000	na	na	na	na	na	na	1,100	1,600	2,000
Imports	1,000	na	na	na	na	na	275	430	635	683
Snowmobiles										
Factory sales	1,000	172	144	84	62	40	29	27	32	35
Apparent consumption	1,000	405	145	136	96	57	55	53	68	67

Source: U.S. Bureau of the Census, Statistical Abstracts of the United States: 1987 (107th Edition) Washington, DC, 1986, p. 217.

Table 11.9 Participation in outdoor recreation activities, by selected characteristics: 1983
(in percentage of people interviewed)

Activity	All persons	Sex Male	Sex Female	Education Less than high school	Education High school	Education 4 yr. college	Income Under 5,000	Income 5,000–14,999	Income 15,000–24,999	Income 25,000–49,000	Income Over 50k	Race White	Race Black	Age 12–24	Age 25–39	Age 40–59	Age 60 & over
Walking for pleasure	53	45	61	35	56	67	45	46	54	61	62	54	49	57	58	53	42
Swimming	53	56	51	19	52	66	34	39	57	68	72	56	32	79	65	41	16
Visiting zoos etc.	50	50	51	26	51	61	32	40	55	62	62	51	40	65	62	41	26
Picnics	48	45	51	29	51	61	36	41	53	56	58	49	42	52	59	46	29
Driving (pleasure)	48	47	49	31	54	59	29	43	53	55	60	50	35	48	59	46	35
Sightseeing	46	45	46	27	50	63	27	38	48	57	67	47	36	46	54	47	31
Sports events	40	44	36	15	39	51	24	30	43	51	61	41	33	55	44	36	16
Fishing	34	47	23	26	35	30	24	30	38	38	35	35	27	43	40	31	17
Bicycling	32	33	32	11	28	37	23	24	35	41	42	33	29	55	37	22	7
Boating	28	32	24	11	28	41	16	20	27	39	43	31	6	38	35	25	9
Canoeing	8	10	7	1	7	13	6	5	8	12	10	9	1	14	9	6	1
Sailing	6	7	5	1	4	14	4	3	5	9	14	7	1	9	7	5	2
Motorboating	19	22	16	8	19	25	10	13	18	27	32	21	3	25	23	17	7
Jogging	26	30	23	6	20	34	21	20	27	33	37	26	30	51	31	13	2
Concerts, plays	25	25	26	10	24	40	17	21	24	32	38	26	21	34	29	22	12
Camping	24	28	22	10	25	27	15	19	29	31	25	27	6	36	30	19	6
Backpacking	5	6	3	z	4	7	3	3	5	7	5	5	1	9	5	2	z
Outdoor sports	24	30	18	7	19	23	22	20	25	29	28	24	27	50	26	11	2
Tennis	17	18	16	2	13	31	12	11	16	22	37	17	13	32	20	10	1
Hiking	14	15	13	3	13	25	10	10	13	18	25	15	3	19	17	12	5
Golfing	13	20	7	4	12	24	6	6	13	20	27	14	3	16	13	13	7
Birdwatching	12	11	12	6	13	17	9	10	12	14	19	13	5	10	12	12	13
Hunting	12	22	3	10	13	7	8	12	14	14	8	12	7	15	13	13	5
Off-roading	11	14	8	3	10	10	9	8	10	15	13	12	3	20	11	6	2
Sledding	10	12	9	1	7	11	9	6	12	13	15	12	2	22	11	5	z
Waterskiing	9	11	7	2	8	12	6	5	10	13	14	11	z	17	12	4	z
Snow skiing	9	10	7	1	6	18	5	5	7	13	21	10	1	15	11	5	z
Horseback riding	9	8	10	2	8	9	7	6	9	11	15	10	4	18	10	5	1
Ice skating	6	6	6	1	4	8	5	3	7	10	10	7	1	15	6	3	z
Other activities	4	4	3	2	4	5	4	4	4	4	9	4	1	3	6	4	3
No participation	11	8	14	29	9	5	28	18	16	13	3	10	18	3	5	13	30

Source: U.S. Bureau of the Census, Statistical Abstracts of the United States: 1987 (107th Edition) Washington, DC, 1986, p. 218.
(z = less than 0.5 percent)

Table 11.10 Selected spectator sports: 1970–85*

Sport	Unit	1970	1975	1979	1980	1981	1982	1983	1984	1985
Baseball, major leagues										
Attendance	1,000	29,191	30,373	44,262	43,746	27,285	45,415	46,269	45,262	47,742
Regular season	1,000	28,747	29,789	43,550	43,014	26,544	44,587	45,540	44,742	46,824
National League	1,000	16,662	16,600	21,178	21,124	12,478	21,507	21,549	20,781	22,292
American League	1,000	12,085	13,189	22,372	21,890	14,066	23,080	23,991	23,961	24,532
Playoffs	1,000	191	276	344	407	403	443	425	248	581
World Series	1,000	253	308	368	325	338	385	304	272	327
Basketball										
Men's college										
Teams	number	na	na	1,240	1,258	1,275	1,264	1,266	1,260	1,266
Attendance	1,000	na	na	30,025	30,692	30,935	31,106	31,471	31,684	32,057
Women's college										
Teams	number	na	na	na	na	na	1,095	1,114	1,147	1,166
Attendance	1,000	na	na	na	na	na	4,203	4,269	4,812	5,440
Pro										
Teams	number	14	18	22	22	23	23	23	23	23
Attendance, total	1,000	4,912	7,591	10,697	10,697	10,235	10,732	10,262	11,110	11,491
Regular season	1,000	4,341	6,892	9,761	9,938	9,449	9,989	9,638	10,015	10,506
Avg. per game	number	7,563	9,339	10,822	11,017	10,021	10,593	10,220	10,620	11,141
Playoffs	1,000	556	685	904	740	765	727	606	1,096	985
Football										
College										
Teams	number	617	634	643	642	648	649	651	654	661
Attendance	1,000	29,466	31,688	35,020	35,541	35,807	36,539	36,302	36,652	36,312
Nat. Football League										
Attendance, total	1,000	10,071	10,769	13,916	14,092	14,326	8,504	13,953	14,053	14,056
Regular season	1,000	9,533	10,213	13,182	13,392	13,607	7,367	13,277	13,398	13,345
Avg. per game	number	52,381	56,116	58,848	59,787	60,745	58,472	59,273	59,813	59,576
Postseason games	1,000	538	556	734	700	719	1,137	676	655	711
U.S. Football League attend.	1,000	x	x	x	x	x	x	2,681	4,394	3,295

Table 11.10 Continued

Sport	Unit	1970	1975	1979	1980	1981	1982	1983	1984	1985
North American Soccer League										
Teams	number	6	20	24	24	21	14	12	9	na
Attendance	1,000	na	1,825	5,800	6,194	5,429	3,251	2,669	1,158	na
National Hockey League										
Regular season attend.	1,000	5,992	9,522	8,333	10,534	10,726	10,710	11,021	11,359	11,633
Playoff attend.	1,000	462	784	694	977	966	1,058	1,008	1,107	1,109
Horse racing										
Racing days	number	9,962	13,110	13,160	13,133	13,464	13,523	13,545	13,683	13,745
Attend.	1,000	69,704	78,662	72,783	74,690	75,463	76,858	75,693	74,076	73,346
Parimutuel turnover	mil. dol	5,977	7,862	10,728	11,218	11,677	11,888	11,733	12,032	12,226
Revenue to govt.	mil. dol	486	582	681	713	680	653	639	650	625
Greyhound										
Total performances	number	3,023	3,960	6,110	5,855	6,379	6,499	8,257	8,661	9,590
Attend.	1,000	12,660	17,458	21,127	20,874	21,424	21,375	22,140	22,076	23,853
Parimutuel turnover	mil. dol	730	1,261	1,985	2,064	2,173	2,179	2,306	2,421	2,702
Revenue to govt.	mil. dol	53	91	145	152	152	160	170	177	201
Jai alai										
Teams	number	6	9	10	9	12	12	12	12	12
Attendance	1,000	2,247	4,229	4,607	3,939	5,453	4,948	4,829	4,878	4,722

*Source: U.S. Bureau of the Census, Statistical Abstracts of the United States: 1987 (107th Edition) Washington, DC, 1986, p. 216.

na = not available

x = not applicable

Table 11.11 Visitation to federal recreation areas, by administrating federal agency, 1978–85

Administrating federal agency	1978	1979	1980	1981
All areas	7,093.9	6,718.0	6,366.9	6,522.1
Fish and Wildlife Serv.	84.1	25.4	17.4	23.1
Forest Serv.	2,621.9	2,642.0	2,818.8	2,828.5
Army Corps of Enginrs.	2,071.2	1,960.6	1,926.3	1,487.5
Nat. Park Serv.	1,154.3	1,066.4	1,041.7	1,198.3
Bureau of Land Managemt.	634.0	524.9	68.3	443.8
Bureau of Reclamation	431.4	410.8	407.2	460.7
Tenn. Valley Authority	97.0	87.8	87.2	80.1

Source: *U.S. Bureau of the Census,* Statistical Abstracts of the United States: 1987 *(107th Edition) Washington, DC, 1986, p. 208.*

America was the first country to televise sport events and does so on a very large scale (Baker 1982:311–29). Professional prizefights were the first prominent televised sport in the post–World War II era. The "Friday Night Fights" of the 1940s were the precursor to baseball's "Game of the Week" in the 1950s, "Wide World of Sports" in the 1960s, and "Monday Night Football" in the 1970s. Today, ESPN is a channel devoted completely to sport.

Travel and Tourism

Americans travel to the vast lands that are set aside for their leisure pursuits. They travel to national parks, national forests, and national recreation areas, as well as state areas, for a myriad of outdoor activities. Table 11.7, on adult participation in leisure activities, shows that swimming, fishing, camping, motorboating, and hunting are among the favorite outdoor activities of Americans.

Another five outdoor activities that may not require too much traveling are listed among the top outdoor activities in the United States: walking for pleasure; visiting zoos, fairs, and amusement parks; picnics; driving for pleasure; and sightseeing. Table 11.9 shows some of the demographic characteristics of the participants. While males and females share the same interests almost equally, white Americans show greater interest in outdoor activities than do black Americans. Also, the more years

of education and the higher the income, the more involvement in these activities. It also seems that walking for pleasure, visiting zoos, fairs, and amusement parks, picnics, driving for pleasure, and sightseeing are enjoyed more by those between the ages of 25 and 50 years. Further discussion of leisure and demographic traits appears in chapter 12.

Equipment-use on these occasions shows definite trends. Sales of fishing tackle, for example, went from $539 million in 1980 to $715 million in 1985, an increase of 32% and greater than the compound increase in the cost of living for that same period. Camping equipment sales increased a modest 20% in the same period, but pleasure boat sales increased a whopping 173% from $2 billion to over $7 billion in these five years. Firearms and hunting equipment sales climbed from over 1.3 billion dollars to 1.7 billion, an increase of over 27% between 1980 and 1985 (see table 11.2).

These pursuits take place in areas administered by federal agencies discussed earlier in the chapter, as well as on state, local, and private land. Federal agencies keep track of the visitation in millions-of-visiting-hours. These data are shown in table 11.11 for the years 1978–85. The data do not lend themselves to comparisons easily, but visitations to federal recreation areas may not only be tapering off, but possibly declining. Fish and wildlife land, U.S. forests, Corps of Engineers areas, national parks and monuments, recreation areas, Bureau of Land

Table 11.12 U.S. travel to foreign countries—travelers and expenditures: 1970–85 (travelers in thousands; expenditures in millions of dollars, except as indicated)

Item and area	1970	1975	1978	1979	1980	1981	1982	1983	1984	1985
Total overseas travelers	5,260	6,354	7,790	7,835	8,163	8,040	8,510	9,628	11,252	12,316
Region of destination:										
Europe and Med.	2,898	3,185	4,150	4,086	3,934	3,931	4,144	4,780	5,760	6,482
Avg. length of stay	27	24	20	20	21	na	na	19	17	18
Caribbean and C. Amer.	1,663	2,065	2,365	2,533	2,624	2,453	2,637	2,989	3,313	3,497
South America	249	447	515	434	594	567	529	535	557	554
Other	450	657	805	800	1,011	1,089	1,200	1,324	1,622	1,783
Expenditures abroad	3,980	6,417	8,475	9,413	10,397	11,479	12,394	13,556	15,449	16,502
Canada	1,018	1,306	1,407	1,599	1,817	2,070	1,936	2,160	2,416	2,694
Mexico	778	1,637	2,121	2,460	2,564	2,862	3,324	3,618	3,599	3,552
Total overseas areas	2,184	3,474	4,947	5,354	6,016	6,547	7,134	7,778	9,434	10,256
Europe and Med.	1,425	1,918	2,942	3,185	3,412	3,587	3,787	4,201	5,171	5,877
Avg. per trip (dollars)	490	602	717	783	867	912	914	882	897	907
Avg. per day (dollars)	18.15	25.19	35.85	39.15	41.28	na	na	46.42	52.76	50.39
Caribbean and C. Amer.	390	787	888	1,019	1,134	1,277	1,349	1,428	1,786	1,831
South America	90	242	306	288	392	383	380	408	357	366
Japan	97	131	155	142	185	214	272	276	400	454
Other	182	396	656	720	893	1,086	1,346	1,465	1,720	1,728
Foreign flag carriers	1,215	2,263	2,896	3,184	3,607	4,487	4,772	5,485	6,502	7,322
U.S. flag carriers	985	1,463	1,784	1,978	2,504	na	na	na	na	na

na = not available
Source: U.S. Bureau of the Census, Statistical Abstracts of the United States: 1987 (107th Edition) Washington, DC, 1986, p. 224.

Reclamation areas, Bureau of Land Management land, and the Tennessee Valley Authority had fewer visiting hours in the mid-1980s than in the late 1980s.

Yet the number of participants in outdoor activities is increasing, which may mean that the users are paying more visits to state and local outdoor recreation areas and to private commercial enterprises. Also, Americans are becoming more interested in tourism these days than in outdoor recreation, as corroborated by recent statistics. Table 11.12 shows that for the same period of 1978–85, the number of Americans who traveled abroad increased from 7,790,000 to 12,316,000, an increase of over 63%, and higher than the increase in population. Table 11.13 shows that Americans in 1985 traveled by air mostly to Great Britain, then to Mexico, Jamaica, Germany, and the Bahamas. Discussions of tourism in Great Britain, West Germany, Canada, Mexico, Egypt, China, and India was presented. According to Jafari, tourism has become an important international industry, bringing in about $700 billion or 6% of the total world's gross national product (1983:3).

Researchers are finding out that leisure pursuits are at the core of tourism (Epperson 1983:31). Contrary to previous assumptions, people go on vacation to do and see things, not just to a destination or place. In a survey of 11,000 persons, the following were the reasons for taking a vacation (Rubenstein 1980):

Rest and relaxation	63%
Escape routine	52%
Visit friends and relatives	45%
Recharge and get renewed	45%
Explore new places	35%

According to Epperson (1983:32), traveling for pleasure is increasing in the United States where over 70% of households travel over 100 miles for some sort of vacation.

Volunteerism in America

Since its inception, America welcomed volunteerism as a means of enhancing the quality of life in the Colonies. Volunteerism was reflected in the bee, a social work-gathering for accomplishing a task such as raising a barn. It included festivities such as games, contests, and merrymaking. Volunteerism has gone through many changes. During the Industrial Revolution, secular and religious organizations were formed to assist the needy, those who were the victims of the Revolution. The organized recreation movement, previously discussed, came into existence as the result of these very conditions (Ibrahim et al. 1987:7).

Up until the Great Depression, these organizations did not seek government assistance. But as the dollars donated by industry and business declined, the volunteer movement in the United States turned to the government for financial help. Government policy included citizens' involvement in its plans for improving the quality of life of indigent and affluent alike. The inclusion of citizens/ commissioners in the local, state, and national affairs increased, particularly in the 1960s. The board members of the voluntary organizations brings the number of people who use their free time in such activities to close to 40 million (MacLean et al. 1985:267).

Volunteerism has not traditionally been associated with leisure pursuits, for it was considered more lofty than the frivolity usually attached to leisure. Henderson attributes this to a constricted view of leisure (1984:58). She cites a study in which 75% of volunteers indicated that volunteering was a creative use of their free time. The United Media study (1983) shows that parents with grown children, parents with dual careers, and single parents volunteer more than the other groups (table 11.14). Also, those between the ages of 35 and 49, followed by those between 50 and 64, volunteer their time and efforts more often than any other age

Table 11.13   Air travel between the United States and foreign countries: 1980–85 (in thousands)

Flag of carrier and country	Arrivals					Departures				
	1980	1982	1983	1984	1985	1980	1982	1983	1984	1985
Total passengers	20,262	20,216	20,840	23,212	24,154	19,256	19,322	19,724	21,608	22,487
Flag of carrier										
United States	10,031	10,163	10,698	11,623	11,797	9,369	9,485	9,888	10,531	10,696
Foreign	10,231	10,054	10,142	11,588	12,357	9,886	9,837	9,837	11,076	11,791
Country of embarkation or debarkation:										
Australia	227	254	242	277	277	245	252	201	223	232
Bahamas	1,123	1,153	1,344	1,373	1,503	1,006	1,009	1,075	1,063	1,151
Barbados	135	115	167	211	216	126	113	168	212	204
Belgium	242	299	250	242	281	231	283	226	216	249
Bermuda	497	441	439	441	434	467	413	394	395	389
Brazil	300	308	308	321	352	291	303	303	304	322
China: Taiwan	113	148	154	187	206	90	123	128	167	187
Colombia	315	314	309	285	279	299	300	302	290	294
Denmark	267	243	230	239	241	254	235	219	235	254
Dominican Rep.	468	501	532	575	606	443	464	490	479	528
France	689	695	705	795	955	635	647	656	748	894
Germany	1,175	1,174	1,223	1,404	1,582	1,178	1,164	1,220	1,419	1,539
Grand Cayman	121	132	144	170	173	112	116	135	160	161
Greece	208	198	234	265	187	190	197	222	234	210
Haiti	133	146	159	175	192	124	131	144	156	169
Hong Kong	228	197	217	295	270	152	144	184	263	238
Ireland	220	250	222	256	274	212	234	196	212	233
Israel	189	189	233	255	294	186	211	228	278	255
Italy	537	529	572	649	662	495	500	561	647	660
Jamaica	429	587	682	712	707	382	526	601	616	607
Japan	1,624	1,819	1,896	2,267	2,435	1,602	1,779	1,854	2,127	2,255
Korea	234	245	249	290	390	186	212	212	244	333
Mexico	2,886	2,456	2,691	2,901	2,719	2,886	2,516	2,670	2,808	2,674
Netherlands	427	482	467	558	583	409	477	458	513	562
Neth. Antilles	327	332	370	426	407	282	297	321	346	395
Panama	150	146	146	169	180	142	136	164	194	209
Philippines	194	212	158	165	145	160	175	133	166	165
Spain	312	337	376	418	419	273	321	350	378	397
Switzerland	312	332	314	427	452	306	330	327	409	434
United Kingdom	2,973	2,694	2,812	3,222	3,460	2,840	2,607	2,687	3,103	3,322
Venezuela	533	581	312	255	248	518	571	321	257	245
Other	2,674	2,707	2,683	2,987	3,025	2,534	2,536	2,574	2,746	2,720

Source: *U.S. Bureau of the Census,* Statistical Abstracts of the United States: 1987 *(107th Edition) Washington, DC, 1986, p. 224.*

group. Those with a college education, either graduates or not, with household incomes above $40,000 volunteer more frequently than others. Volunteers accomplish the following (MacLean et al. 1985:267):

1. **Fund raising.** Aid in promoting community drives through articles, mass media interviews, or personal contacts; ticket selling for special attractions or duty at the concession stands.

Table 11.14 Percentage of participation in volunteer activities, U.S.

Level (N)	%	Age (N)	%	Education (N)	%	Income (N)	%
Teenagers (74)	51	14–17 (75)	52	8th grade or less (171)	41	Less than $10,000 (185)	36
Singles (207)	40	18–24 (186)	38	Some high school (216)	45	$10–14,999 (122)	52
Age 65+ (151)	38	25–34 (222)	40	High school grad (367)	43	$15–19,999 (138)	42
Married/no children (60)	42	35–49 (217)	59	Some college (166)	53	$20–24,999 (157)	52
Parents/grown children (171)	59	50–64 (198)	55	College grad (13)	61	$25–29,999 (102)	45
Traditional parent (142)	42	65+ (151)	38			$30–39,999 (95)	54
Dual-career parents (169)	59					$40,000/over (103)	56
Single parents (44)	59						

Source: United Media Enterprises, Where Does the Time Go? 1983, p. 28. Newspaper Enterprise Association. Reprinted by permission.

2. **Leadership roles.** Leadership in scout troops or sponsoring a church dance are some of the service opportunities in many communities.
3. **Professional services.** Representatives of most professions give their talents and energies to community concerns. Guiding the planning and layout of facilities, conducting physical examinations for youngsters, directing discussions, lecturing, writing or drawing promotional materials, and instructing special classes.
4. **Transportation and communication.** Service to chauffeur the young, the elderly, the disabled, or others who are without transportation. The home-bound, who are unable to participate in other activities, find a real opportunity to help community organizations by providing telephone contacting services for special events. Such contacts make the disabled less isolated.
5. **Visiting the ill and disabled.** Individuals and groups find visiting the home-bound or institutionalized, in person or by letter, a rewarding service. The Forgotten Patient program in mental hospitals gives patients and visitors satisfactions and lasting rewards.
6. **Officiating at athletic events.** Whether the sport activity is a seasonal, special, or weekly affair, good officiating is necessary. Extra services are always needed for official timing, scoring, refereeing, and umpiring, if the event is to be beneficial for teams in community leagues.
7. **One-time specials.** Special events give wide opportunity for service activities. The garden club holds a planting day to give the playground or park a needed look. Another group would prepare a meal for the drama club, and a third would judge costumes in the local parade.
8. **Service clubs.** The programs conducted by the many civic and service clubs such as the Lions, the Kiwanis, and Rotary are initiated and developed with a service motive.

The United States government provides an agency to administer volunteer service programs, known as ACTION. Its purpose is to mobilize Americans for voluntary service throughout this country and developing countries. Its activities include the following:

1. **The Foster Grandparents Program.** Part-time volunteers are sought from the aged population to render supportive services in health, education, and welfare.
2. **Retired Senior Volunteer Program.** Volunteers are sought from the aged population to provide assistance to those who need it in the local community.
3. **Volunteers in Service to America.** This program supplements local efforts to eliminate poverty and related problems. Volunteers of all ages and walks of life are recruited.
4. **National Student Volunteer Program.** This program is designed to provide technical assistance, materials, on-site consultation, and training for students who are serving as part-time volunteers.
5. **The Senior Companion Program.** This program provides part-time services to low-income senior citizens, 60 years of age and over, who have special or exceptional needs.
6. **Mini-Grant Program.** This program provides a small amount of money to be used by local nonprofit organizations to mobilize local volunteers to work on human, social, and environmental needs.
7. **The National Center for Service Learning.** This program provides support for independent student learning programs at the secondary and post-secondary levels.
8. **The Urban Crime Prevention Program.** This program utilizes volunteers to develop crime prevention projects for low and moderate income neighborhoods.
9. **Peace Corps.** The Congress declared that its mission was to promote world peace and friendship through the use of volunteers to help the peoples of other countries.

SUMMARY

America's founders gave the building of the country first priority. Many were guided by a system of belief, known as Puritanism, that frowned on the lighter side of life. But not all early Americans adhered to those beliefs. Particularly in the South the prosperous gentry adopted a liberal attitude towards leisure. Their slaves provided them with the necessary free time to pursue their leisure activities.

A new, mercantile middle class formed on the Eastern seaboard whose ambition was to emulate the wealthy class. With the advent of the Industrial Revolution a new leisure class was appearing, a group that was bent on conspicuous consumption. But the Industrial Revolution also created a poor class that lived in the slums of the now industrial cities of the East. To alleviate their conditions, certain welfare programs were proposed and in fact implemented by social reformers who recognized the necessity of organized recreation.

The conservation movement was also taking shape toward the end of the nineteenth century. Its advocates proposed national parks and open space. All these forces came together around the turn of the century, producing a life-style for mass leisure. A very unique political structure combined with an advanced economic system has created favorable conditions for the leisure in the United States.

Americans have ample opportunities for recreational activities at home and away from home. Americans surpass other nations in almost every recreational activity. Perhaps what is most unique about leisure in America is that citizens spend a great amount of their free time as volunteers.

REVIEW QUESTIONS

1. To what would you attribute the leisure explosion in American society?
2. What role do the three levels of government play in providing leisure pursuits in this country?
3. What type of leisure activities are pursued by the typical American citizen?
4. When compared to other Western nations in chapter 9, what is unique about the leisure pursuits of Americans?

SUGGESTED READINGS

Dulles, F. R. 1965. *A history of recreation.* New York: Appleton-Century Crofts.

Knudson, D. 1984. *Outdoor recreation.* New York: Macmillan.

MacLean, J., J. Peterson, and D. Martin. 1985. *Recreation and leisure: The changing scene.* New York: Macmillan.

Rainwater, C. E. 1922. *The play movement in the United States.* Chicago: University of Chicago Press.

AN OVERVIEW OF PART THREE

A unified legal/behavioral code applied to all members of society, a characteristic of modernity, is becoming universal. It does vary in degree. For instance, the adoption of a five-day workweek or a 40-hour week may not apply to all workers in some countries. Some Third-World countries (for example, Egypt) that adopted the principle of reduced work hours find it applicable to workers in their tiny industrial and expansive service sectors but not to their agricultural workers. This means that there is more free time, at least from work, among city dwellers than among villagers. An element of modernity, similar time freed from work for all, is not attainable. The unequal distribution of leisure is a hindrance to real mass leisure. But the data clearly show how much ritualized leisure is dominant in three of the four Third-World countries presented here.

Eastern bloc countries are also recent entrants to modernity, except that they entered it after World War I, not after World War II as did most of the Third World. Take-off in the leisure scene did not really occur until World War II when the democratization of sport, provision of facilities, and the training of professionals took place (Horna 1988). Yet equal leisure opportunities, as shown in the data, are still lacking. For instance there are shortages of accommodations, which could be a result of an inadequate economy. But attitudinal-organizational factors may also enter the picture. For example, weekend *dashas* in the Soviet Union are given to a privileged few.

The new policy of *glasnost,* however, may bring changes to the leisure sphere in both the USSR and other Eastern bloc nations. Riordan (1989) suggests that until recently the providers of leisure pursuits had an "I know what is best for you" syndrome. The sudden opening up has stirred acrimonious debate about leisure and recreation and may soon lead to fresh and innovative approaches to providing these activities on an equitable basis, and in a democratic manner.

Three Western European countries were presented in this part. The data show that their quest for free time began earlier than those of the Eastern bloc nations and at about the same time as in the United States. Yet they are behind the United States in their leisure scene. Parker believes that this may be due to Americans approaching leisure in "a workmanlike, instrumental spirit," which was not the case in Britain where free time was a celebration of idleness (1980:271).

Although Canada's quest for free time started at the same time as Western Europe and the United States, the provision of programs and facilities came faster than in Europe but somewhat slower than in the United States. A distinguishing feature of the Canadian scene is the larger role of the three levels of government in offering programs and providing facilities in recreation. Also, half of the national surveys of the level of attendance in various activities were undertaken by academic institutions, a practice not seen at this magnitude elsewhere. One-third of the surveys were conducted by government, a usual practice in other countries, and the rest by consulting firms and voluntary organizations (Burton 1979).

Workers in the United States followed their Western European counterparts closely in acquiring reduced work hours after World War I. Yet the leisure scene in the United States had taken a gigantic step forward. One might attribute this to the usual factors of industrialization, urbanization, education, and the like. But above and beyond these are the attitudinal, organizational, and educational factors that helped to increase the quality and quantity of leisure offerings in the United States.

Within a decade after Henry Ford's historic decision for a five-day workweek in 1928, Americans were "skillfully and very gradually taught that leisure and play were not sinful if they could be classed under the head of recreation. . . . The corollary was plain—one must play more in order to work better" (Pack 1934:16). Also, as a nation of joiners, Americans engaged in the business of recreation began to form professional organizations which, along with voluntary associations dealing with leisure, sought to control the field by providing informal training for "professionals" who eventually were formally trained.

Modernity alone, as here defined, would not allow for mass leisure at the level found in the United States. It, along with the factors listed above, has led to a leisure scene that others are trying to emulate. Such is a macro view. But a micro view of how leisure shapes human behavior is needed to understand this complex phenomenon. This is presented in Part Four.

PART FOUR

THE SHAPING OF LEISURE BEHAVIOR

12 THE SOCIAL CONTEXT OF LEISURE
13 THE PHYSICAL CONTEXT OF LEISURE
14 CONCERNS AND CONSTRAINTS

Ultimately, the cultural system with its dominant values will manifest itself in what people do when they have time freed from work and from civic-familial obligations. In general, such behavior is shaped by two interacting sets of variables. The first set revolves around social variables, that is, human grouping and demographic factors. The second set revolves around the physical setting of the society—its topography, wildlife, and vegetation. For instance, Egypt has a long beach shoreline and weather ideal for swimming. But these factors have not immediately led to an increase in swimming as a leisure pursuit once mass leisure prevailed. Socially this activity is not valued among males and is highly discouraged among females. This devaluing is a function of socialization through the institutions of family and religion.

On the other hand, an activity that is socially acceptable and develops a niche in the physical setting of a given society may become dysfunctional, creating problems not anticipated originally. An example is the hunting of the buffalo in the American West, which rendered it almost extinct.

This part will elaborate on the shaping of leisure behavior in both the social and physical context, and discuss some of the concerns recently expressed in the literature in regard to a number of leisure pursuits. Also, some of the constraints and barriers of leisure behavior will be discussed.

12

THE SOCIAL CONTEXT OF LEISURE

What has been presented so far are macro-factors that may affect leisure pursuits in general. Above and beyond these are micro-factors that have a direct relationship to leisure behavior. Among these factors are membership in a particular family and attendance of a particular school. Family members and schoolmates represent what are termed in sociology *primary groups*. There are also secondary groups that affect one's leisure choices. Demographic factors such as age, gender, and occupation are other important determinants of leisure choices. Also, personal traits such as physique and temperament affect our choice of leisure pursuits. Finally, life-style and subculture play important roles in these choices.

PRIMARY GROUPS

Primary groups are the social groups in which the individual has primary face-to-face relationships on a daily basis. Among these are the family, school, and the neighborhood.

The Family

The family is the most important socializing unit, yet little attention has been given to its role in leisure behavior. As reported by Glyptis and Chambers (1982), most free time is spent at home, but it is difficult to know precisely how much time is spent in different activities and social settings. They suggest that the home is both a physical source for leisure in that it provides equipment and space for certain activities and a social source in that it provides the group or groups for leisure pursuits.

In one of the earlier writings on family and leisure, the Neumeyers (1949:350–355) state that "various studies of recreation interests and habits have shown that the family exerts the strongest influence on children's thinking and activities." Yet they did not cite the studies.

On the other hand, Bradshaw and Jackson (1979:93–117) conducted a study to determine the ages at which high school students were introduced to three major leisure activities and to determine the relationship between age of introduction and other demographic variables. The study strongly showed that high school students are introduced to the majority of their leisure pursuits before they reach age 13. This finding was consistent with previous empirical research by Hendee (1969) and Yoesting and Burkhead (1973). Both of these studies were conducted on adult populations. Hendee found that 70% of his adult sample of wilderness campers had taken their first camping trip before the age of 15. Yoesting and Burkhead concluded that individuals active in outdoor recreational activities as children continued to be active as adults and that inactive children continue to be inactive adults.

Kelly (1974) conducted a study of 78 subjects using the interview technique. He asked a number of questions related to age of socialization into leisure pursuits. Of the 744 activities reported, 49% began in childhood and 51% in the adult years; 63% began with the family and 37% with peers at school or work. While recreational activities such as sport and outdoor activities began with the family, cultural activities such as reading began outside the family.

Kenneth Roberts (1970:41) states that "despite the growth that has taken place in large-scale organizations catering specifically for leisure interest, the family has remained the most popular group in which people choose to spend their free time." While the choice is great for the adult parents, the young's choices are very limited. Hence they are exposed to leisure activities they have not really selected.

John Kelly (1983a:59) calls the period in which the young attends school, which is the basis for later productivity in society, the *preparation period*. This period is characterized by role-taking, in which the growing child learns what role to play and why. The term *role model* provides an heuristic tool for understanding how the young, and sometimes the not-very-young, assume certain roles in life, including leisure roles. The family plays a crucial part in this process.

Does this mean that the family that plays together is happier or stronger? There is no conclusive empirical evidence on that. On the one hand, Young (1964:95) shows circumstances under which family recreation produced stress. On the other, Stone (1963) found that teenagers who join family recreation feel that their parents are more understanding. Orthner and Mancini (1978) examined the relationship between perceived sociability in the parental family and present marital patterns. They concluded that among middle class husbands and wives the degree of marital interaction during leisure is not significantly influenced by childhood sociability experiences. This means that marital sociability may be more dependent on a constellation of factors operating in the marriage than on a previous parental model.

On the other hand, the Family Services Association of America reported that 33% of the couples observed by its counselors reported time and leisure problems as a major source of marital difficulties (Beck and Jones 1973). Straus and others (1980) list leisure and recreation problems as the third most frequent source of marital conflict. Orthner (1985) suggests that the following factors, among others, may lead to leisure conflict:

1. **Inadequate free time.** Obligatory time devoted to work, sleep, and personal grooming impinges on discretionary time. Orthner (1980) states that this was the cause of marital conflict for 32% of men and 25% of women at a U.S. Air Force base. Carlson (1976) states that 75% of both husbands and wives in his sample felt that family recreation was inadequate.

2. **Differential leisure preference.** Seventy-five percent of couples in Carlson's study (1976) reported that they disagree on what to do in their free time, which results in feelings of neglect. The compatibility that exists early in the marriage seems to dissipate, particularly when the children reach adolescence (Orthner and Mancini 1978).

3. **Inappropriate choice of activities.** Men, particularly, were found to be out of sync with the activity selected for the couple. Vacations, particularly using a motor vehicle, were found to be a strain on families (Orthner 1985:136).

4. **Interruption in leisure patterns.** The abrupt change in a routinized leisure activity leads to conflict. An example is when one or more members of a family ask to change the favorite TV program to watch another channel.

5. **Circadian rhythms.** Circadian rhythm is discussed in detail in chapter 2. The concept of morning—night people has been investigated by Adams and Cromwell (1978), who conclude that these preferences tend to be associated with characteristics that affect the interactional quality of any relationship between spouses, siblings, children, and parents.

School

Leisure (*schole*) to the ancient Greeks meant being occupied in something desirable for its own sake. That was the idea behind their school, which was open only to the fortunate who did not have to toil the land, do manual work, and learn trade by doing. To learn how to live gracefully was an ideal that survived despite the pragmatism of the Romans, and the fact that the peasants of Medieval Europe had no ear for noble music or moving poetry. When schooling of the young came back, it was practical and was intended to train people rather than educate them. The Church, then the aristocracy, influenced the curriculum to be composed of academic activities with hardly any expressive ones.

The situation has changed rather drastically. Today's school includes many expressive activities either through the curriculum or through extracurricular activities. Many critics, however, still think it a waste to allow art, drama, music, and sport to be part of school life.

Perhaps the study conducted by Hendry (1978) in England may be convincing. He found that academically successful pupils often fuse school life with leisure; while educational failures, overwhelmingly working class, compartmentalize these two spheres. In the United States, Rehberg and Schafer (1968) showed that high school students who participate in athletics were more likely to aspire to attend college than nonathletic peers of equal academic ability. In fact, Roberts (1983a:111) concluded that when young people are taught to equate school with failure, they tend to base their leisure interests and relationships on out-of-school activities.

White (1975) found that interest and involvement in leisure pursuits such as the arts and other cultural activities were closely related to level of education. Bammel and Bammel (1982:244) state that educated persons express a greater affinity for leisure and a greater desire for vacations even though they identify more with work. This confirms what John Dewey suggested over seventy years ago.

Education has no more serious responsibility than making adequate provision of enjoyment of recreative leisure, *not only for the sake of the immediate health, but still more if possible for the sake of its lasting effect upon habits of mind (Dewey 1966:110).*

The Cardinal Principles of Secondary Education in 1918 contain a discussion on the need for leisure education. The need was expressed a few years later in Canada and also in Great Britain (Canadian Youth Commission 1946, and Ragnathan 1954).

In 1976 the Ontario Ministry of Culture and Recreation started a leisure education program, the main goal of which is to enhance the quality of life through leisure opportunities (Mundy and Odum 1979:25). A study conducted in the United States (Odum and Lancaster 1976) showed that only one state considers "leisure education" a learning objective. Others alluded to it, and some viewed it as being outside the realm of schools.

According to Yoesting and Christensen (1978), the number of activities in which one participates during childhood is directly related to the number of similar activities in adulthood. They suggest that as a matter of policy, emphasis should be placed on lifelong activities in elementary, secondary, and college education. Also, the socialization model used in carry-over studies should be expanded to include "significant others."

Continuing or adult education has been presented too often as producing extrinsic and teleologic effects. Jary (1973:263) states that, contrary to this ideology, his survey of his students attending evening courses indicates they do so because they are primarily leisure-centered activities. He concludes that such facts should not be hidden or apologized for. People attend many evening courses, or go to lectures, art galleries, and museums for reasons quite different from their reasons for enrolling in a typical college course, having more to do with their personal relevance and for the immediate pleasure of the activity.

This finding corroborates Thorndike's three laws of learning: law of readiness, law of effect (plea-effect (pleasurable experience), and law of repetition (1905:202). Those who voluntarily attend a lecture are ready for it, and there is pleasure in it by the nature of free choice. Hence, two of his laws are attained in what is now called "leisure education," a recent movement in the leisure services delivery system.

SECONDARY GROUPS

Although secondary groups provide face-to-face relationships, the relationships are usually of shorter duration and less frequent than family and school groups.

Youth Organizations and Clubs

Youth organizations have undergone many changes since their inception in modern societies. The earlier forms were associated with churches. Neumeyer and Neumeyer (1949:327) wrote of Junglingsverein, a club of unmarried men in Bremen, Germany, in 1709. At the time George Williams started his London YMCA, ten of these societies were in existence. The first YMCA in the United States was founded in Boston in 1866, three years after London's. The first YWCA was established in 1858. A club of boys was established in Hartford, Connecticut, as early as 1861, and the name Boy's Club was used by a youth organization in New York in 1876. But the Boy's Club Incorporated was not established until 1906 (Palisi and Ibrahim 1979:324).

It seems that these organizations came into being as part of a general trend at that time in the industrializing nations, particularly Great Britain and the United States. Most writing on these organizations had to do with their role in character building. Most of the concern, then, was with organizational problems and program building, two themes that are closely related to social group work. After World War I, the center of interest shifted from program building to personality development and adjustment. Neumeyer and Neumeyer pointed out that the earlier approach was thought of as a "process whereby the individuals became so socialized and are made an integral part of a dynamic ongoing life, (thus) involves much more than a program of leisure-time activities" (1949:328). The new approach accommodated individual interests.

Both the Young Men's and Young Women's Christian Associations have gone through changes as a result of the shift in emphasis on the individual. For instance, originally the members had to travel to the location of the Y. After World War I, the Y leaders began to go into the community and organize clubs in schools and playgrounds. Also, preconceived programs were not used, and the leaders endeavored to build programs around the interests of the participants. Yet the Y movement continued to have a strong Christian orientation up to today.

A second organization, The Boy Scouts, was built around the ideal of character development and good citizenship. It was initiated by General Baden-Powell in London in 1907 because of the initial British defeats in the Boer War in South Africa. The concept was to utilize the outdoors to develop physical fitness, courage, self-reliance, and patriotism. The American Organization of Boy Scouts was founded in 1910 and the Girl Scouts in 1912.

Scouting was to be open to youth of all religions and races, provided that each member takes the Scout Oath to do his or her duty to God and Country, to keep Scout Law, to help others, and to try to be physically strong, mentally alert, and morally straight. The program for boys operates through three divisions: Cub Scouts (ages 8–10), Boy Scouts (ages 11–17), and Explorers (ages 14–20). The program for girls operates through four stages: Brownies (ages 6–8), Juniors (ages 9–11), Cadettes (ages 12–14), and Seniors (ages 14–17). In an attempt to stop declining membership, two younger divisions were added in the 1980s: Tiger Cubs for the boys and Daisies for the girls (see table 12.1).

Table 12.1 Boy Scouts and Girl Scouts—membership and units: 1960-85 (in thousands)

Item	1960	1965	1970	1975	1978	1979	1980	1981	1982	1983	1984	1985
Boy Scouts												
Membership	5,165	5,733	6,287	5,318	4,493	4,285	4,318	4,355	4,542	4,689	4,755	4,845
Boys	3,783	4,231	4,683	3,933	3,303	3,176	3,207	3,244	3,244	3,245	3,567	3,657
Tiger Cubs	x	x	x	x	x	x	x	x	84	124	145	169
Cub Scouts	1,865	2,064	2,438	1,997	1,788	1,716	1,696	1,643	1,609	1,569	1,493	1,499
Boy Scouts	1,647	1,850	1,916	1,503	1,123	1,058	1,046	1,101	1,126	1,116	1,078	1,063
Explorers	271	317	329	434	392	402	477	499	606	758	941	1,024
Adults	1,382	1,502	1,604	1,385	1,190	1,109	1,110	1,111	1,117	1,122	1,098	1,090
Total units (packs, troops)	130	145	157	150	134	129	129	130	132	134	135	134
Girl Scouts												
Membership	3,419	3,647	3,922	3,234	3,084	2,961	2,784	2,829	2,819	2,888	2,871	2,802
Girls	2,646	3,030	3,248	2,723	2,511	2,389	2,250	2,276	2,247	2,281	2,247	2,172
Daisies	x	x	x	x	x	x	x	x	x	x	x	61
Brownies	x	1,072	1,259	1,160	1,245	1,206	1,115	1,110	1,120	1,163	1,172	1,128
Juniors	x	1,416	1,509	1,188	977	926	894	916	874	847	801	735
Cadettes	x	443	395	301	218	193	172	170	169	176	170	151
Seniors	x	99	85	74	57	52	46	45	41	40	40	40
Adults	773	617	674	511	573	572	534	553	572	607	624	630
Total units (troops)	164	153	164	159	159	157	154	157	160	165	166	166

x = not applicable

Source: U.S. Bureau of the Census, Statistical Abstracts of the United States: 1987 (107th Edition) Washington, DC, 1986, p. 220.

Campfire Girls was formed in 1910 in the United States with a strong American motif, Indian lore. Ernest Thompson Seton was an early pioneer in woodcraft, and the Woodcraft League of America was established in 1902. Its members, the Woodcraft Rangers, used recreational skills rather than competition or military features in their program. The Campfire Girls was founded along the same lines by Dr. and Mrs. Luther H. Gulick in 1910 (Neumeyer and Neumeyer 1949:335).

McLean and others (1985:194) suggest that the Boy's Club movement originated in response to the plight of boys in the crowded and crime-ridden slums of New England where they played in the streets. The Neumeyers (1949:336) state that only some of these clubs have been set up especially for certain classes of boys, an example being the Burroughs Newsboys' Club in Boston.

The Smith-Lever Act of 1914 provided for cooperative extension work in agriculture and home economics. By 1920 the 4H Clubs were organized around a national pledge that read as follows:

> I pledge
> My Head to clear thinking
> My Heart to greater loyalty
> My Hands to larger services, and
> My Health to better living,
> You my club, my community, and my
> country.

The Future Farmers of America was an accompaniment to the same movement and was to promote vocational agricultural education in public high schools.

In Great Britain the welfare of the entire 14–20 age group was made a Local Education Authority's (LEA) responsibility beginning in 1921 (Roberts 1983a:11). But public spending was under restraint between the two world wars and there were no adequate programs. After World War II, the New Youth Service, composed of voluntary organizations recognized and assisted by local authorities, proved successful in reaching three-quarters of school-age youth. But after they left school, young people relinquished their membership. Also, these youth organizations failed to bridge the gap between the leisure habits of boys and girls, and the difference between social classes. By the 1950s the commercialized youth subculture took over (to be discussed later).

According to Kraus (1984:113), during the Depression a unique phenomenon emerged in America's large cities: cellar clubs that catered to youth in low-income neighborhoods. In New York alone there were over six thousand such clubs by 1940. The youth met in vacant stores, lofts, or cellars free from adult supervision. This may have prompted the national study by Lindeman (1939), which voiced the concern that United States' social policy should cater to the vast reservoir of leisure. Lindeman warned that leisure should not be organized for the purpose of propaganda and illiciting loyalty to the State or for keeping youth busy, as was the case in Nazi Germany. Neither should leisure be allowed to become idleness and waste. Lindeman predicted that this country would need at least one hundred thousand trained recreation professionals by 1965.

Place of Worship

Churches, mosques, and temples play important roles in deciding for both young and old what is and is not acceptable as a leisure pursuit. Values acquired in the place of worship are inculcated and exert influence on leisure behavior. That which was prohibited in early human society was called taboo. Women were prohibited from certain male "recreational" activities. Younger boys were not allowed certain activities until they were initiated into adult life.

In "advanced" religions, the Christian Church prohibits certain activities on the Sabbath and often prohibits them altogether. Mixed dancing is not allowed in certain churches nor among certain Orthodox Jews. In others, churches conduct dances, sport tournaments, and recreational trips. Mosques are solemn places of worship in Islam, while Hindu temples provide dances as part of their service. The influence of religion is also seen in

Table 12.2 **Percentage of population with voluntary association affiliation (average 1959–68)**

Nation	Total	Males	Females	ES*	SS*	SC*
Canada	51	51	51	42	60	79
U.S.	50	55	46	36	48	79
Great Britain	33	41	27	26	43	70
Germany	34	47	22	29	61	53
Italy	25	36	17	22	31	46
Mexico	15	21	12	12	19	67

*ES = Elementary School; SS = Secondary School; SC = Some College
Source: Curtis, J. "Voluntary Association Joining: A Cross National Comparative," American Sociological Review 36, 1971, p. 874. American Sociological Association. Reprinted with permission.

amusive leisure, where certain films, television programs, and artistic performances are censored by the religious hierarchy. In countries where there is a separation of State and Church, the role of Church is not felt as much as in the countries where such separation does not exist. A case in point is today's Iran, with its theocracy and the extreme prohibitions imposed on recreative and amusive leisure.

Nonetheless, the trend has been to provide youth organizations that administer recreational activities under the sponsorship of a place of worship. Today there are not only Young Men's Christian Associations and Young Women's Christian Associations, but Hebrew Youth Clubs, Young Men's Muslim Associations, and Young Women's Muslim Associations.

Voluntary Associations

Voluntary associations are the private, nonprofit organizations that an adult joins by choice, not strictly for economic or legal reasons. Some of these associations are instrumental in that they are means to an end and are allied to one's work or profession. Many, however, are expressive in that they involve leisure pursuits. George Lundburg and others (1934) suggested that these organizations are ends in themselves and should be treated as important shapers of leisure behavior. The data in table 12.2,

from a cross-national study by Curtis (1971), reveal that Canadians are more oriented toward expressive associations, followed by Americans—men more than women, and more the better educated.

DEMOGRAPHIC FACTORS

Demographic factors include age, sex, occupation, and residence. These factors usually work in combinations. According to Kelly (1983b), factors such as age, sex, and status do not support a neat or clearly differentiated set of activity groupings. In other words, a set of leisure activities does not appear systematically in any of the aforementioned factors. For example, occupation is usually a function of the level of education attained by the individual, providing him or her with the opportunity to live in a particular section or area of town. Nonetheless, these factors should be looked upon separately.

Age

Play is observable in the very young human being and has an important impact on adult leisure behavior. Play with simple toys begins in the first year of life. Simple peek-a-boos occur at the same time. Later comes the pattern suggested by Parten in her classic study of play (1932). She observed 42 nursery school children between 2 and 4½ years of age while they were playing and delineated six distinct kinds of behaviors in play situations:

1. **Solitary play.** The infant plays alone and shows no interest in the activities of others.
2. **Onlooker play.** The infant shows interest as he or she watches others play, but does not join.
3. **Parallel play.** By the middle of the second year the child will play in the presence of other children, but not with them.
4. **Associative play.** Preschoolers will engage in play activities with one another, but not for long.
5. **Cooperative play.** Cooperative play begins at age 4 but continues on into childhood. It is marked by playing specific roles.
6. **Dramatic play.** Here the growing child can take on the roles of others.

At this point preschoolers become more socially oriented, but prefer to play with familiar peers (Rubin et al. 1983:693). They are no longer limited to one-on-one play, for group play is not uncommon as the child enters the first grade. Also they are ready to run, climb, gallop, and hop. The ability to balance is good; skipping is mastered, as are throwing, catching, and kicking. For the following six years of elementary education, the child's physical skills are refined and modified (De Oreo and Keogh 1980).

Leisure education at this early stage of life is extremely important. This is the time when habits that last a lifetime are formed. According to O'Leary and others (1986), programs designed to convey values and norms of a particular leisure activity will have to target early age groups if the programs intend to make a lasting imprint. Using hunting as an example, these authors proved their point in a 1983 National Recreation Survey.

Those favoring the return to basics now advocated in American educational circles should be aware of an experiment in France. The children of Vanves, a suburb of Paris, were spending long hours in their seats, as were all of France's elementary school pupils. The town embarked on a new program in which the time allotted for academics was reduced (to the apprehension of their middle class parents) and sports, art, music, and drama were introduced. To everyone's surprise, the children's academic performance actually improved. Now all France follows this program (Baily 1975).

As for leisure during adolescence, Csikszentmihalyi and Larson conducted an in-depth study and found that among the 75 adolescents they observed in depth in Chicago, the largest single activity is socializing. It takes one-sixth of an adolescent's waking time. It is followed by watching television, which takes a little over an hour a day. An additional hour is spent on other media such as radio, newspapers, magazines, and movies. The authors report that adolescents in both the USSR and Japan spend about the same amount of time on the media. Another hour and one-half a day are spent on recreative leisure such as sport, art, and hobbies (1984:67–68).

Csikszentmihalyi and Larson state that "The transition between structured time and free time is often enacted with drastic rites of liberation, particularly on Friday afternoon" (1984:77). The experience of the adolescent seems to be divided into two phases, structured time and unstructured time, which are superimposed on a broader yearly cycle of summer vacation, holidays, parties, and so on.

The United Media study (1983) shows that the hours available for leisure per week by age were 42 for the age group 14–17, dropped to 34 in the 18–24 age group, to 32 in the 25–34 age group, to 24 in the 35–40 age group, climbed to 30 in the 50–64 age group, and to 43 in the 65 and over age group.

The fluctuation in hours available for leisure is a function of the life cycle. According to Kelly (1982:140), high school and college students become engaged in identity formations because they go through transitions in a relatively short time. Among these is sexual identity. Dating and courtship take place during hours available for leisure. de Grazia has suggested that the natural occupation of the leisured is love. Without leisure,

Table 12.3 Life-cycle changes in relation to sports, socializing, and culture

Age	Sports	Socializing	Culture
Teens	Active participation in vigorous forms of recreational activity, both indoor and out.	Dancing and teen meeting places; socializing can be a central life interest, highly involving.	Movies; rock music; "cultural heros."
Twenties	Active participants, especially in outdoor activities. Wilderness backpacking, canoeing, and so on.	Dinners out; bars, nightclubs, socializing with peer group of great importance.	Popular entertainments will be patronized; after marriage, TV becomes major entertainment.
Thirties	Less active and less frequent participation in outdoor recreation. Camping replaces backpacking.	Dinners at home, family parties, some travel to other cities to meet relatives and other friends.	Theater, art, museums, books. If the fine arts ever are to be cultivated, now will be the time.
Forties	Less active participation, more spectating; car and van camping replaces sleeping bags.	Family oriented	Travel; as children leave home, Europe, New York, and other major cultural centers and activities may become attractive.
Fifties	Greater emphasis on spectating for the great majority; renewed attempt at physical conditioning; bowling.	Family; grandchildren; visiting old friends.	Television may become central cultural source if traveling diminishes.
Sixties	Spectating and decrease in physical character of activities; gardening.	Family-centered; children and grandchildren; old friends.	Television; possible increase in involvement with civic affairs, but retreat is more characteristic.
Seventies	Some new sport activities may begin with retirement; golf, swimming, shuffleboard, and so on.	New retired friends, especially if a move is made to new surroundings. Card playing and social activities.	Reading, some popular cultural events; books and magazines may assume a new importance, and so do church activities.

Source: Bammel, G., and L. L. Bammel, Leisure and Human Behavior, 1982, p. 232. Wm. C. Brown Publishers. Reprinted with permission.

love could be only a primitive orgy or the fulfillment of a conjugal duty (1962:175). Work and career identity formation also take place in early adult life; this too consumes time available for leisure.

Even after marriage and establishment of career, the time available for leisure is limited, particularly for the wife with young children. Horna and Lupri studied a cross section of couples from Calgary, Alberta. Extensive interviews of both members of the couples, with children 16 years of age or younger, showed that men found their role less taxing and time consuming, affording them more freedom and discretion (1987).

Does the situation change with grown children? Table 11.3, on the daily participation in leisure pursuits, shows that while more parents with grown children read newspapers, books, and magazines than traditional parents, more of the latter group exercised, listened to music, gardened, and socialized than the former. This finding does not support the claim that "shorter working hours, smaller families, increased income, and greater educational opportunities available to middle aged individuals today provides for fruitful conditions for meaningful leisure participation" (Osgood 1987:3). The only "leisure" activity that parents with grown children seem to go into, at a higher rate than that of parents with young children, is volunteering (table 11.14).

Although the mature adult experiences a decline in physical strength and sexuality (among men), and an unwanted increase in weight, he or she may achieve true selfhood. Young and Crandell (1984) found that wilderness experiences provide affirmation of self in midlife. Moreover, role crystallization gives the middle aged an added confidence around family, neighborhood, and community.

Aging takes place gradually, as the number of cells declines and the connective tissue loses elasticity. All the bodily systems grow less efficient. The chances of heart problems, cancer and diabetes, and possible mental malfunctioning increase (Burdman 1986). But the chance of these occurring at the typical age of retirement between ages 60 and 70 (depending on the country) has been reduced drastically in contemporary technological society. After retirement, most senior citizens have up to 20 years for pleasurable leisure. Yet the data do not totally support this possibility. Table 11.9 on participation in outdoor activities in 1983 shows a decline in walking for pleasure at age 60 and over. A very high ratio of no participation is also shown by these data. As for indoor activities, the United Media study (1983) shows that more persons 65 years and older watch television than any other group except teenagers. More of them read newspapers and books than all other groups. Only teenagers read magazines more than do senior citizens. More senior citizens have hobbies than all other groups. Volunteering is not high among senior citizens: only 38% of the respondents age 65 and over indicated that they do so, the least among the eight groups in the United Media study (table 11.14). In Great Britain, persons 61 years and above spend more time on gardening, visiting, and walking in the park

(Harris and Parker 1973:174). In the United States, walking for pleasure declines among senior citizens (table 11.9).

A few American senior citizens have begun to establish new forms of communities that are adapted to their contemporary needs. Using unstructured interviews, questionnaires, and observations of 517 residents of a retirement community, Jobes (1984) refuted the disengagement theory of Cummings and Henry (1961) in which they asserted that aging is a process of quietly receding from view and/or withdrawing from active participation in society. Jobes may have refuted the disengagement theory for that particular group of American senior citizens; but there are others, both in the United States and elsewhere, who are indeed disengaged. For instance, Harris and Parker point out that many elderly people in Great Britain have to stop going out to places of entertainment or other events because they cannot afford it (1973:174). The same must be true in many parts of the world.

In the meantime, a number of American senior citizens are negating the patterns assigned to retired people—passive roles, with emphasis on bingo games and card playing. Ginsberg's study of 143 retired male executives in two Atlantic states reveals that 30% of them had returned to work part-time. He points out that they were brought up during the Depression years, and that work ethics were deeply inculcated in them (1983:366).

Tinsley and others (1987) studied the psychological benefit that older persons may accrue from participation in leisure activities. They confirmed previous assumptions that leisure is central to the mental health and morale of the elderly. When 27 psychological benefits were correlated to personal characteristics, older women of lower socioeconomic status and low morale were more likely to participate in leisure activities that provide companionship. On the other hand, women between 55 and 65 years of age were more likely to participate in leisure activities that provide recognition. Persons of both sexes who are over 65 years of age, with higher socioeconomic backgrounds, were most likely to participate in leisure activities that provide power, such as volunteer professional activities. The authors conclude that an orientation toward home-based passive activities increases with age.

McGuire (1984) developed a list of 30 constraints, based on previous research, and asked 125 persons ranging in age from 45 to 93 to rate the importance of these constraints. A factor analysis of responses yielded five constraint factors: external factors, time, approval, ability, and physical well-being. He suggested that leisure delivery systems assess the extent to which a senior citizen is inhibited from leisure involvement, identify the factor, and plan some form of intervention to help the senior citizen become involved.

Kelly and others (1987) surveyed 400 senior citizens by phone and asked a sequence of questions:

1. Do frequency and breadth of participation in leisure activities contribute to later life satisfaction?
2. Do some activities contribute more than others?
3. Does the type of activity that contributes most to subjective well-being differ with age?

The authors conclude that social activities and travel are associated with higher levels of life satisfaction for those aged 65–74, while family and home-based activities are so associated for those age 75 and over. Leisure in later life provides a context for interaction with significant others and for self-investment.

Gender

Although it was assumed, until very recently, that girl's play is predetermined to be different from boy's play, Sutton-Smith and Rosenberg (1971:33) found that such an attitude has changed in this century. Possibly it has not changed at all in the countries where sex roles are still clearly distinguished. Scientific research shows that sex differences in play exist. As was mentioned in chapter 1, observations of primate play reveal that males are more aggressive. The same has been shown to exist among humans. Di Pierto (1981) introduced three young girls age 4½ years into a room with a few toys. He observed that they organized themselves and played together. When three boys were ushered into the room, they played in a rougher fashion, often wrestling. In three repetitions of the experiment, the same scenario was observed. The boys did not seem to be angry, nor did they attempt to hurt one another; they simply played differently. Do human societies expect boys to act aggressively, and socialize them to act accordingly? Or is there a biological predisposition to act aggressively?

Gender differences are also observed at an older age, in elementary school, as boys show greater ability in running speed and throwing, while girls excel in tasks requiring agility, rhythm, and flexibility. As they grow older, the differences increase. The adolescent male continues to improve in his tasks, while his female counterpart levels off in hers. Corbin suggests that this may be due to a lack of motivation, fear of injury to female internal organs, or fear of appearing too masculine in contradiction to prevailing societal values (1980:100).

Csikszentmihalyi and Larson found in their study of 75 adolescents in Chicago that the basic difference between the sexes, where leisure pursuits are concerned, is that boys spend over six hours a week on sport while the girls spend half that time. In the meantime, girls spend 31% of their waking time on the arts, while the boys spend only half that much time. Also, girls spend much more time talking to adults (1984:80).

McElroy states that despite great increases in opportunities for American young women to participate in organized sport, traditional gender differences in attitudes toward sport persist (1983:997). A study from Israel shows that gender differences in sport are more closely related to deep-rooted socialization effects than to structural constraints (Shamir and Ruskin 1983:253). The same was found in a study in Norway, where the fact that women felt less free to participate in sport was explained to be a function of differential socialization and of a different pattern of motivation (Fasting and Sisjord 1985:345).

Susan Shaw studied 60 married couples in Canada to determine if accessibility to leisure was equally distributed between the sexes. She concluded that while gender differences are small during the week, men have significantly more leisure than females on the weekends (1985:266).

On the other hand, Egyptian women in urbanized Cairo who have not joined the work force seem to have much more free time than their working male counterparts (Ibrahim et al. 1981:98). It has been suggested that once women in the Third World join the labor force on a full-time basis, their free time will be curtailed.

In studying leisure patterns among American women, Bialeschki and Henderson found that despite women's emancipation and entry into the work world, the care of family and home is still expected to be their priority. The authors found that the home was the primary site for leisure for American women who share a "common world" of experience and expectations in their leisure (1986:299).

Moskoff (1984) found Soviet men to have more free time than Soviet women. Yet leisure patterns do not seem to differ a lot between them. While men were more likely to read newspapers and books, attend sport events, have hobbies, women were inclined to watch more television, visit more with friends, and spend more time at home. Soviet women clearly enjoy an increase in free time in comparison to half a century ago. They are also engaged in more activities than ever before.

In a study conducted in Kazan, the most important activities after work, for unmarried persons, are going to the cinema or a play or watching television. These are also the most important activities for married couples without children, followed by walking and gardening. But for those with children, housework dominates their after-work hours. As the number of children increases, the amount of free time decreases. It seems that Soviet women, like Egyptian women, receive little help from their husbands. Free time is greatly curtailed for women with very young children.

Education

Education refers both to the level attained and to the type received. The United Media study (1983) shows that the hours available for leisure per week by education decreased from 37 hours for a person with eight years of education or less, to 36 hours for a person with some high school education, to 30 and 31 hours for high school and college graduates respectively. As to the leisure pursuits in these hours, C. White (1955) conducted one of the early studies in the United States that showed the relationship between the level of education and the use of free time (leisure pursuit). His findings (table 12.4) show that the lower class go to parks more often than the other classes, and that visiting libraries is greater among the lower middle class, while attending lectures is higher for the working class. In Great Britain, Roberts showed that the more education a person attains the lower the proportion of his or her time that is spent watching television and the greater the proportion devoted to socializing with friends away from home (1978:113).

Moskoff (1984:87–97) cites the results of studies conducted by the Soviets over the years. Those with higher education read more fiction, go more to the cinema, and are involved in physical recreation. The less educated tend to attend dances and visit friends. For them radio and television are the primary means of entertainment. The educational process takes place in formal settings known as educational institutions, and in informal settings such as libraries, museums and the media. In both settings, enjoyment of and/or preparation for leisure pursuits take place. As Jary (1973:263) has astutely pointed out, some of the activities that take place in these formal and informal settings are presented to the world as producing extrinsic, teleologic effects, rather than as leisure yielding immediate gratification.

Table 12.4 Rates of uses of leisure per 100 persons of all ages, by social class

	Upper middle	Lower middle	Working class	Lower class
Parks	1.75	6.85	9.50	19.70
Social services	8.75	11.95	10.10	15.45
Church	51.50	71.10	73.65	79.45
Libraries	19.30	22.85	16.40	11.90
Lectures	14.50	6.15	2.90	4.70

Source: White, C., "Social Class Differences in the Uses of Leisure," American Journal of Sociology 61, 1955, p. 147. University of Chicago Press. Reprinted with permission.

Data in Table 7.1 show the degree to which the 13 societies discussed in the present work have provided for their citizens' informal setting in education. While it is rather difficult to pinpoint the exact impact of education on leisure, the study by Brine and others could be helpful. They studied reading in the Soviet Union and suggest that reading is a very popular leisure pursuit there, as shown by the crowded bookstores, the clusters of people around bookstalls, and the preoccupation with books and newspapers in the underground. As a leisure pursuit, reading is affected by one's education, for upon reviewing Soviet literature on reading as leisure, Brine concluded that four-fifths of Soviets who have only four years of formal education cannot be considered book readers. They prefer to watch television or visit with friends.

To Brine, the relationship between reading and educational level is not linear but passes through a series of thresholds. A breakthrough takes place after seven years of education, in that 55%–60% of people with this many years of schooling become readers. Higher education provides a further encouragement. Also, graduates of general secondary education read more extensively than those from a specialized (technical) school (1980:247–48).

Occupation

A few studies have been conducted on the relationship between occupation, free time, and leisure pursuits. Among the first was Lundberg's (1934) study of American suburbia, which indicated that male white-collar workers had an average of 438

minutes of free time a day, while the top executive had about 401 minutes a day, including mealtime. If the 81 minutes designated for eating in the United States sample in the cross-cultural study of Szalai (1972) were deducted, then the white-collar worker and the executive of the 1930s had 357 and 320 minutes of free time daily, respectively. When compared to the 1972 United States average of 301 minutes, it appears that there was more free time. Or do these data indicate that these two groups have more free time than the average American as a result of their higher occupational level?

A study from Great Britain seems to corroborate the second position—that persons in higher occupational roles have free time and are more active in their leisure pursuits (British Travel Association/University of Keele 1967). Later studies confirmed these findings: 54% of professionals participate in outdoor sport in comparison to 14% of unskilled workers. Among manual labor groups, betting, pool, and bingo are popular (Parker 1983:38).

Despite claims to the contrary, in the Soviet Union blue-collar workers have a leisure life-style that differs from that of the managers or that of the "intellectuals." While engineers enjoy 4.4 hours of free time on a workday and 9.1 hours on a day off, blue-collar workers have 3.6 and 8.9 hours, respectively. Accordingly, participation in leisure activities varies, with the "managers" spending more time watching television, going to the cinema, plays, and museums, visiting with friends, and gardening (Moskoff 1984).

To a great extent, one's occupation determines income, social circles, and location of residence. The combination of these has direct bearing on leisure pursuits. Among the early studies conducted in the United States was Clarke's (1956). He established five levels of occupational groupings: professional, managerial, clerical, skilled, and unskilled workers. He showed that at the top of occupational levels leisure pursuits include attendance at theaters, concerts, lectures, and art galleries, together with reading, studying, and bridge playing. The most frequent attendance of spectator sport and commercial recreation such as movies and night clubs occurs among middle occupational levels. Going to bars and watching television seem dominant among those in lower occupational levels. Burdge used the same classification of occupations and, looking at 82 specific forms of leisure activities, concluded that persons at the higher occupational levels seem to participate in the greatest variety of leisure pursuits (1969).

In the study by Brine and others on reading as leisure in the Soviet Union, reading among the technical intelligentsia is particularly striking (1980:248). Surprisingly, skilled manual workers, especially women, seem to read much less than the unskilled workers. But this may be due to the fact that the sample observed was composed of young mothers and busy housewives.

Occupation is a feature of both social class and the status system because it determines income as well as the position in the system. Occupation has a strong influence on leisure. Roberts (1970:28–29) suggested seven reasons why and how:

1. Manual occupations demand a great deal of time and energy, leaving such people unable to cultivate active leisure pursuits.
2. Manual occupations are physically arduous and therefore may result in a need to spend leisure simply relaxing or recuperating.
3. Less financially well-off persons do not have substantial incomes to invest in leisure interest outside the home and do not have discretionary money to spare for club subscriptions, trips to the theater, sport equipment, and so on.
4. White-collar families have a greater opportunity to travel abroad and this exposure may stimulate another leisure interest. Certain leisure activities appear to trigger others.
5. Education awakens white-collar people to leisure interests outside the sphere of the manual worker.
6. A white-collar worker's job may create more opportunities to acquire skills that can be exploited during leisure time.
7. Leisure habits emerge as status attitudes, which are generated at work and spill over into and influence people's leisure lives.

Income

Even in the Soviet Union, money buys leisure. In 1953, households with a per capita income of 50 rubles or less had 116 hours of free time a month according to a Krasnoiark study, while those with more income had 188 hours. In four of the five categories of leisure listed in the study, the consumption of leisure goods rose with income. The poorest of the Soviet households spent their free time doing "nothing" (Moskoff 1984).

Income is reflected in reading as a leisure pursuit in the United States. Data from the United Media study (1983) show that households with incomes of $40,000 or more have 70% book readers, 29% other material readers, and only 1% nonreaders. This compares to 35% of book readers, 54% of other material readers, and 11% nonreaders in households with incomes of $15,000 or less. Gender, ethnicity, age, and educational attainment are also important factors in readership as a leisure pursuit. But income is a greater cause of variation than the factors of gender, ethnicity, and age. The only greater cause of variation in book reading than income is college education.

City Size

In the Soviet Union, Moskoff (1984) found that there are more leisure activities offered in larger cities. It has already been established that residents of Moscow have greater opportunities in this respect than the residents of smaller cities. The same can be said about the residents of midsize cities.

In small towns, free time, particularly on the weekend, revolves around the Palace of Culture. These are community centers of a sort where dances are held and groups can meet. Also social get-togethers with relatives and friends take place more frequently in smaller cities. Participation in sporting events, as well as attendance of these events, tends to be extremely low in small cities, perhaps due to the lack of facilities. Even walking as a leisure activity, which occurs in midsize and large cities, is lacking in small cities. This may be because small city residents walk all the time for lack of mass transit system and do not feel the urge to take a leisurely walk around town.

Wolfe (1978) reported that 13.5% of the inhabitants of Czech cities having 100,000 persons or more own a vacation home, while only 5.5% in cities of 20,000–100,000 persons own such a home. Most, if not all, are apartment dwellers and have a notable propensity to seek open space. Such is the case in most large European cities. But in Canada, Wolfe found that citizens in the eastern provinces have a much higher propensity to own a vacation home than those in the west. Also those living on the frontier with the United States are less likely to own vacation homes. Why those residing on the Precambrian shield, the most valued recreational landscape, wish to own a vacation home remains, says Wolfe, a mystery.

Residence

The region and territory in which one lives have a great impact on one's leisure pursuits. For example, living in warm areas close to water provides opportunities to swim. Nonetheless, proximity and climate are not the only factors determining leisure behavior; values enter the picture. Saudi Arabian men and women who live by the Red Sea, a warm sea, do not swim recreationally. The rich among them build swimming pools with 12-foot walls to protect the family swimmers from the eyes of strangers. In contrast, southern California's single-dwelling homes and apartment complexes have pools surrounded by low fences to protect the young from being tempted. Strangers can look in any time.

An urban-rural dichotomy in leisure pursuits has been found by many researchers. Knopp found significant differences between urban residents and rural residents (1972). For instance, the urban male is more inclined toward exercise and solitude than is his rural-nonfarm counterpart, as shown in table 12.5.

Bammel and Bammel (1982) found that urban residents in West Virginia watch television, swim, and go to movies more frequently than rural dwellers; the rural residents, on the other hand, tend to enjoy nature and hunting (table 12.6).

Allen and others (1987:33) surveyed a random sample of households in 18 rural Colorado communities about their satisfaction with and the importance of community life and services. The residents were neutral about their satisfaction with leisure services and opportunities. The authors suggest that the rural resident may be seeking more than just resource-based recreation opportunities.

Moskoff (1984:7) suggests that in the Soviet Union several factors differentiate the leisure of the rural population from the urban's. Not only is the rural population's income low and their free time limited, leisure offerings and facilities in the rural area are inadequate. Nonetheless, most of the small villages have clubs that are equipped to show films, provide dances, and organize lectures. Yet there are many complaints about the inadequacy of these facilities.

At home, the villagers spend a good part of their free time with the mass media (radio, television, and newspapers). The radio is of greater significance in the farmers' lives than television, since the

Table 12.5 Average scores given to statements representing reasons or motivations for participating in outdoor recreation by respondents, Winona County, 1968

Name of statement	Urban average	Rural nonfarm average	Rural farm average
Exercise	5.91	5.05	4.31
Rest	7.21	6.60	6.75
Solitude	6.67	5.85	3.67
Social	5.60	5.60	6.44
Natural	4.84	5.55	5.10
Freedom	6.78	6.15	5.10
Property	5.60	4.95	4.12
Past	4.66	5.55	4.75
Prestige	6.22	5.30	4.65
Clean	6.90	7.15	6.54

Source: Knopp, T., "Environmental Determinants of Recreation Behavior," Journal of Leisure Research 4(2) 1972, p. 133. The National Recreation and Park Association. Reprinted with permission.

Table 12.6 Activity frequency of rural and urban West Virginians

Rank	Rural activity	Percent	Rank	Urban activity	Percent
1	Watched TV	61.47	1	Watched TV	75.39
2	Listened to music	56.19	2	Listened to music	65.57
3	Gardened for fun	49.54	3	Read for pleasure	55.93
4	Read for pleasure	44.86	4	Gardened for fun	46.78
5	Had friends over	38.32	5	Had friends over	41.83
6	Walked for fun	33.34	6	Craft projects	31.67
7	Watched birds	27.10	7	Walked for fun	26.87
8	Craft projects	25.96	8	Swimming	26.23
9	Hunted	23.53	9	Games at home	23.33
10	Games at home	21.91	10	Watched birds	19.05
11	Nature walks	20.19	11	Hiked	13.33
12	Hiked	17.92	12	Went to movies	11.48
13	Fished	16.35	13	Fished	8.20
14	Boated	6.73	14	Nature walks	7.94
15	Camped	4.80	15	Boated	6.67
16	Swimming	3.96	16	Bicycled	5.08
17	Bicycled	3.88	17	Hunted	4.59
18	Backpacked	3.84	18	Camped	1.34
19	Went to movies	2.94	19	Backpacked	0.00

Source: Bammel, G., and L. L. Bammel, Leisure and Human Behavior, 1982, p. 247. Wm. C. Brown Publishers. Reprinted by permission.

latter is rather expensive for most of them. Newspapers are also intensely read in the villages, the most popular being usually the local newspaper. Although most villages have libraries, they are not as well stocked with books as urban libraries. In addition, distances between rural libraries and the severity of the winters make their use rather difficult. Yet the number of books checked out per person annually had risen from 1.1 in 1937 to 15 in 1963.

Brine found that reading as a leisure activity in the Soviet Union is deeply affected by changes in work patterns throughout the agricultural year in the rural areas. It is also affected by the fact that these rural areas include more older and less-educated people than urban centers. For instance, a study cited by Brine, conducted in the mid-1960s, shows that 32% of residents (41% women and 17% men) of five villages never read books. Another study in the mid-1970s reveals that 47% of the residents of small towns read books often and 30% read them rarely.

Foret (1985) investigated the relationship between life satisfaction, leisure satisfaction, and leisure participation among young-old and old-old adults with rural and urban residences in southern Louisiana. Data from her subjects show that there are significant relationships between the three variables, which she interpreted to mean than an individual who is satisfied in life is also satisfied with leisure pursuits, and that increased leisure participation can enhance one's life satisfaction. The study shows that age and residence cause no significant difference in leisure satisfaction. Residence, however, causes a significant variation in leisure participation, in that urban dwellers participate in more leisure activities than rural individuals.

PERSONAL TRAITS

Personal traits are looked upon as dispositions that determine behavior. Yet trait theorists disagree about what constitutes the basic traits of a personality. Moreover, the concept of personality itself has come under criticism because most of the tests used on it have low predictive validity (Ingham 1986). Some researchers have suggested the notion of person/situation interactions as a more appropriate approach. A few maintain the tradition of ascribing scores on the basis of completed questionnaires. This school of thought adheres to the notion that differences in overt behavior are based on physiological differences arising from genetic variation. Despite the criticism leveled at this approach, it has produced a great deal of data, some dealing with leisure pursuits.

Physique and Temperament Traits

William Sheldon suggested a tripartite approach to human physique, with traits as follows (1954):

PHYSIQUE

Endomorphic (soft and round, over-developed digestive viscera)

Mesomorphic (muscular, rectangular, strong)

Ectomorphic (long, fragile, fearful, large brain, sensitive nervous system)

TEMPERAMENT

Viscerotonic (relaxed, loves to eat, sociable)

Somatotonic (energetic, assertive, courageous)

Cerebrotonic (restrained, introvertive, artistic)

Willgoose tried to relate Sheldon's body typology to physical fitness and sport. In table 12.7 these types and possible sport activities are illustrated. Willgoose admits that there are certain overlapping areas, but asserts that these classes may be useful in considering athletic performance (1956).

Temperamental Traits and Leisure

Temperament is dependent on constitutional makeup and is reflected in mood and speed of response. In one study, the Guilford-Zimmerman temperament scale was used to study 10 traits on 108 male and 116 female subjects divided into 12 leisure groups (Ibrahim 1970:145–54). The findings follow:

1. Male artists tend to be slow in action, impulsive, shy, more interested in overt activity and romance. They are average in their leadership tendencies, objectivity, and friendliness, although they are critical of others.
2. Male athletes tend to be average in their general activity, emotional stability, objectivity, and masculinity. They tend to be self-defensive and to seek the limelight.

Table 12.7 Body types and physical fitness

Mesomorphic endomorphs	Endomorphic mesomorphs	Extreme mesomorphs	Ectomorphic mesomorphs	Mesomorphic ectomorphs
Table tennis	Baseball	Sprints	Lightweight	Bicycling
Floating (swimming)	Football (lineman)	Basketball	wrestling	Cross-country
Croquet	Heavyweight boxing	Middleweight	Long-distance	Table tennis
Fly and baitcasting	Heavyweight	wrestling	running	Basketball center
Bowling	wrestling	Middleweight	Tennis	(short periods)
	Swimming	boxing	Gymnastics	Archery
	Soccer (backs)	Quarterbacks	Weight lifting	(also many athletic
	Ice hockey (backs)	Football (backs)	Javelin	games except
	Weight tossing	Divers	Pole vault	those requiring
		Tumbling	High jump	weight and sheer
		Lacrosse	Fencing	strength)
		Soccer (forwards)	Badminton	
		Handball	Skiing	
		Ice Hockey	Jockey	

Source: Willgoose, G. E., "Body Type and Physical Fitness," Journal of Health, Physical Education and Recreation 27, 1956, p. 77. The American Alliance for Health, Physical Education, Recreation and Dance. Reprinted by permission.

3. Male bridge players are average in their inclination toward activity, in objectivity, friendliness, and sociability. The male bridge player is not as meditative as might be expected, less than average in masculinity and is critical of institutions.

4. The drama-oriented male tends to be average in his inclination toward leadership and overt activity. While he is meditative, he is hypercritical of others, fluctuates in mood, lacks objectivity, and avoids social contacts.

5. The fisherman is more masculine, serious-minded, self-defensive, sociable, optimistic, objective, and tolerant than the average person. Yet he is below average in reflectiveness.

6. The male surfers are more impulsive, submissive, shy, gloomy, hypersensitive, and resentful than the rest of the men studied. The surfer would tend to be disconcerted easily.

7. The female artist is conspicuous (natural), cheerful, objective, agreeable, and more hard-boiled than the rest of the women.

8. The female athlete tends to be average in her inclination toward activity and is tolerant of people, yet she is endowed with leadership qualities. She tends to love excitement, is moody, belligerent, and as romantically inclined as the average female.

9. The female bridge player is average in her tendencies toward activity, restraint, sociability, emotional stability, friendliness, and feminine interest. On the other hand, she is above average in her ascendance, thoughtfulness, and in her personal relationships.

10. Drama-oriented women are average in their inclination toward physical activity and in their feminine tendencies. They are impulsive toward physical activity and in their feminine tendencies. They are impulsive, pessimistic, self-centered, hostile and resentful, and self-pitying. They are conspicuous and are able to persuade others.

11. Women whose leisure interest is oriented toward sewing have an above-average tendency to physical activity, and are average in their leadership habits, sociability, friendliness, emotional stability, and tolerance of people. They tend to be carefree, suspicious, and easily disconcerted.

12. Females who belong to sororities are not inclined to physical activity, lack leadership habits, and are moody and pessimistic. They are average in their sociability, have a strong faith in social institutions, and are much interested in clothes, styles, and feminine activities in general.

Personality Traits and Leisure

Mannell (1984) suggests that most studies of personality as a predictor of leisure behavior have used general personality inventories to measure individual differences. He laments the lack of a theoretical approach that could identify leisure-specific personality differences that may help in understanding leisure behavior. Also little research has examined personality from the interactionist perspective. He suggests expanding on "time competence" and "playfulness" in understanding leisure behavior. Elements of these two notions are contained in his S-A-E (Self-As-Entertainment)—a construct that describes one's capacity to fill one's free or discretionary time with activity. The usefulness of such tool remains to be seen.

SUBCULTURES AND LIFE-STYLES

In most human societies there are more or less homogenous groups whose members tend to identify with one another on the basis of a human type, religion, or cultural identity. The term *human type* is now used in lieu of race, since race has some cultural connotation and is not based on physical traits. The term *ethnicity* is sometimes used interchangeably with subculture; the problem with the term *ethnicity* is that it is linguistically culturally specific. Black Americans and Chicanos are two ethnic groups in America. The Hippies, however, were not ethnically different from the bulk of members in this society, yet developed a subculture that had tremendous impact on their leisure behavior.

Only two of the modern societies included in this work have produced studies dealing with leisure and subcultures: Great Britain and the United States. In Great Britain it seems that the blacks and Asians who constitute less than 5% of the population are the majority in high unemployment of inner city areas—a situation similar to the one of the blacks in the United States. Most of blacks and Asians in Britain settled there around 1950. At first they sought submersion and anglicization, according to Roberts (1983a:140). Such is not the case anymore.

In a manner not dissimilar to what has happened across the Atlantic in the United States, British blacks are beginning to star in international track and field and in football (soccer). Roberts predicts that just as black Americans became the gladiators of white America in the twentieth century, that black British will be its gladiators in the twenty-first century (1983a:153).

While some British theorists try to explain the black superiority in sport in light of some biological endowment, others suggest that sport provides the social and economic ascent for youth otherwise destined for menial tasks. Others believe that these youths are channeled into sport so that they may find self-esteem by excelling in it (Roberts 1983a:155).

The black American's superiority in sport has also been studied (Ibrahim 1975:171–73). A 1968 study of the leisure patterns of black Americans showed that although they were involved in team sport, boxing, and track and field, they stayed away from tennis, golf, and archery. They were active in music, drama, and dance and made extensive use of picnicking, fishing and boating facilities (Bammel and Bammel 1982:248).

Cheek and Burch (1976:105) try to explain black Americans' leisure behavior as follows:

1. Their low income keeps them at the lower end of the social class scale.
2. Their membership there leads to a low level of education.
3. A lower level of education leads to a low status of occupation.
4. Accordingly, they are restricted to certain residential areas.

5. There develops a historical, cultural heritage that leads to different leisure patterns.

Such a theory does not apply well to the Mexican-Americans. McMillen found that leisure behavior among Mexican-Americans may occur in locales isolated from the Anglo culture, yet the social organization of the behavior is similar to that of Anglos. Also there was no evidence to indicate more extensive leisure participation among Mexican-Americans. There was some evidence of a relationship between participation in leisure activities and personal community, particularly kinship networks. Subjects in his sample who reported having relatives close by participated less in organized recreation (1983:164–73).

Edwards (1981) found that black Americans living in predominantly white residential areas favor leisure activities that are similar to the ones favored by their white neighbors. The whites, in general, favor skill classes and organized outdoor activities. The blacks are more inclined toward physical conditioning and dance instruction. Although ethnicity is a significant variable in explaining leisure behavior, other variables cannot be ignored.

Kaplan describes the Jewish-American subculture as encompassing a unique synthesis of flesh and spirit. For example, the Sabbath is a happy day. It is Judaic, not Puritanical—singing and dancing are encouraged and indoor games are played. It is a day of feast. There are, on the other hand, lots of prohibitions: no gambling and no licentiousness. Social clubs and informal discussion of poetry and drama take place. Drama, music and folk dances are also practiced. (1960:101–11).

The hippie movement of the 1960s created an important subculture in recent social history. Although it has for the most part fizzled away, it has affected leisure in the United States as follows (Kando 1975:257–64):

1. The rejection of the dominant society's two major economic principles: work and consumption. The shortening of the working day is a fundamental premise on which the true reality of freedom is founded.

2. The rejection of the middle class deferred gratification principle. The time scale of experience is the now and not the future.
3. The rejection of conventional leisure, which included passive recreation, consumption, spectatorship, and above all star-worship.
4. The use of music as a type of participatory leisure. This is coupled with the heightening of the senses through an electronic psychedelic emphasis.
5. The advocation that sex is not merely biological but a form of leisure—a distinguishing feature of the *Homo sapiens*.
6. The use of mild drugs for mind expansion and for collective consciousness.

The concept of life-style has been introduced in social science lately. As Bradshaw points out, it refers to "the generalized ways people act and consume, that is somewhat more fine grained than subcultures, e.g., ethnic and youth subcultures, but more general than specific groups or experiences" (1978:2). There are many life-styles in modern society, and the concept is now being used in social research to describe quality of life in general. Life-style is the outcome of all the variables used in this chapter: age, schooling, occupation, residence, and national background.

For example, Bensman and Vidich (1971:139) describe the upper-middle class life-style in America as follows:

The style of the Country Gentlemen includes the image of the serious-minded sportsman or the nautical devotee, or some combination of these. During the leisure hours the advocate of this style retreats into his chosen pleasure and invests substantial portions of his earnings to maintain it. The country gentleman emphasizes the estate-like quality of his residence with elaborate gardens, swimming pools and other yard facilities.

Kahler developed five "ideal" types of social class in the United States (1957), associating each type with its value emphasis.

Upper Class: Graceful Living
Upper Middle Class: Career
Lower Middle Class: Respectability
Working Class: Get By
Lower Class: Apathy

The term *social class* is not used as much any-more, and is being replaced by term *life-style.*

Gattas and others (1986) suggest that leisure and life-style revolve around three points: time, social relations, and consumption. They believe that leisure theory will be better served if it focuses on the type of individuals, groups, and societies rather than types of activities. Leisure research should aim for depth, not breadth, collecting a lot of infor-mation about selected groups rather than opting for a finer spread of data from larger samples. A longitudinal approach would be beneficial; life-style should be presented in a dynamic, not static, pic-ture.

Mitchell (1983) uses the concept of life-style and ties it to values in the United States. Values and life-style (VALS) typology, which is forwarded in his national study, incorporates the above con-cepts. A survey asking over 800 questions was used on a national probability sample of 1,600 persons over the age of 18, living in the 48 contiguous states. Four comprehensive groups, subdivided into nine life-styles, emerged as follows:

A. Need-Driven Groups
    1. Survivor Life-style. Terrible poverty marks these 6 million survivors, of whom only 22% made over $5,000 in 1979. Their daily activities are heavily influenced by their high age, low education, and limited resources. They are absent from pursuits requiring a high level of physical energy such as active, and even spectator, sport. They score high on TV watching and cigarette smoking.
    2. Sustainer Life-style. Angry and combative, Sustainers have not given up hope. Living on the edge of poverty with an income of about $11,000 in 1979, the 11 million Sustainers are heavily tied to machine, manual, and service occupations. Sustainers attend horse racing more than any other group, watch nature on TV, like to go fishing, read tabloids, and see a lot of X-rated movies.

B. Outer-Directed Groups
    3. Belonger Life-style. Generally regarded as middle-class America for whom soap opera and romance magazines were created to fill emotional needs, Belongers watch their spending and are not given to faddish activities. These 57 million have a deep-seated desire to fit in rather than stand out. They prefer home and family activities and such pursuits as gardening, baking and watching television.
    4. Emulator Life-style. The Emulators are intensely striving people seeking to be like the Achievers (#5). Despite their young age, a median of 27 years, they had an average income of over $18,000 in 1979. Their activities show they are second in conformity to Belongers and tied with Achievers. The 16 million Emulators like bowling and pool, visit night clubs and arcades, and eat at fast-food establishments.
    5. Achiever Life-style. These are the driving and the driven people of the American "system." Most of the 37 million persons here are professionals such as teachers, lawyers, and physicians. They score high in activities such as playing golf, attending cultural events, drinking cocktails, traveling for pleasure, and reading magazines and newspapers.

C. Inner-Directed Groups
    6. I-am-me Life-style. A shift from outer to inner dimension brings a discovery of new interests and new interior rewards that redirect life goals. Here active sport, artistic work, and readership of

specialized magazines is distinctive. I-am-me's, 8 million, have the highest rate of ownership of recreational gear such as backpacking, exercising, and bicycling equipment.

7. Experiential Life-style. The experientials (11 million) seek direct and vivid experiences. He and she are well educated with good earnings (over $25,000 in 1979). They love swimming, racquet sport, and snow skiing. They engage in yoga and go for health foods. They attend lots of movies and like to entertain. They drive European cars and own racing bicycles and backpacking equipment.

8. Societally-Conscious Life-style. Feeling that they have attained positions of affluence, hence no longer feel the need for self-display, members of this group of 14 million engage in healthful outdoor sports such as bicycling, jogging, swimming, and sailing as well as chess. They, like the Achievers, watch many sport programs on television.

D. Combined Inner and Outer-Directed Groups

9. Integrated Life-style. The author estimates that 3.2 million have reached maturity, balance, and a sense of what is fitting, the prime characteristics here. Since only 2% of the sample was identified as belonging to this group, the author declined to generalize. Another reason is that the Integrateds are highly diverse, subtle in their response, and complex in their outlook. All these make generalizations difficult.

Mitchell extends his analysis into two other Western nations, Great Britain and France. Comparisons of the leisure pursuits of the United States, Great Britain, and France, when divided into the nine aforementioned life-styles, are presented in table 12.8.

A recent article by Nancy Gibbs (1989) makes it clear that the outer-directed achievers of the United States are having difficulties with their leisure. "In fact, for the callow yuppies of Wall Street, with their abundant salaries and meager freedom, leisure time is the one thing they find hard to buy." It is clear from the article that it is not only the paucity of discretionary time but their perception of free time and the way it is managed. "Even leisure is done on schedule." Moreover, "all the promises of limitless leisure relied on America's retaining its blinding lead in the World's Market and unfolding prosperity at home." It is rather ironic that the Japanese Ministry of Labor has released a documentary on how to enjoy leisure. This took place after the adoption of a five-day workweek in Japan.

This does not necessarily mean that the more opportunities for leisure, the happier the person. Bernard (1987) found that leisure-rich respondents were experiencing underlying tension and dissatisfactions, while leisure-poor respondents were managing to achieve a successful balance between leisure and other aspects of life. The data were drawn from lengthy questionnaire/interviews administered to 100 couples, but conducted separately. Although this study was conducted on English couples, it points to the highly complex, dynamic, and holistic nature of real life and to the need to investigate leisure in the context of life-styles.

Now that Japan has adopted a five-day workweek, will Western nations, who went to the five-day workweek four decades ago, adopt a four-day workweek? According to Conner and Bultena (1979), if this were to occur, the significant difference will be in the number of activities pursued and not in an increased number of hours pursuing leisure activities. They used a sample of 226 four- and five-day workers to examine three types of change in leisure participation. They found that four- and five-day workers devote approximately equal amounts of time to leisure participation—only the

Table 12.8 Comparison of European and U.S. life-style types and their pursuits

Bases	United States	France	United Kingdom	Leisure Pursuits
Need-Driven: SURVIVORS Life-styles motivated primarily by the desire merely to survive.	Old; intensely poor; fearful; depressed; despairing; far removed from the cultural mainstream; misfits. Number: 6 million Age: most over 65 Sex: 77% female Income: 100% under $7,500 Education: median, 8th–9th grade	Negligible number, but attributes as in the United States; some older Belongers and Sustainers share characteristics. Number: 1 million	Two groups similar to those in Sweden; older group is very similar to that in the U.S. The younger, unemployed are more aggressive. Number: 3.9 million	Active sports: none Spectator sports: none Outdoor rec: none The arts: none Cultural events: none Youth entertainment: none Table games: none Pleasure traveling: none TV: all programs Movies: once a year Reading: newspaper Other: gardening, baking
SUSTAINERS	Living on the edge of poverty, angry & resentful; streetwise; involved in the underground economy. Number: 11 million Age: 58% under 35 Sex: 55% female Income: median, $11,000 Education: median, 11th grade	Old peasant women & retireds; poor; little education; fearful; live by habit; unable to cope with change. Number: 6.7 million	Working-class values; concerned about economic security; family centered; afraid of government & big business; mainly women; the youngest group is 35 years and over. Number: 6 million	Active sports: basketball, baseball, bowling & football Spectator sports: horse racing Outdoor rec: none The arts: none Cultural events: none Youth entertainment: night clubs, amusement parks, listen to music Table games: cards Pleasure traveling: none TV: all programs Movies: X-rated Reading: tabloids/classified ads
Outer-Directed: BELONGERS Members here conduct themselves in accordance with what others think.	Aging; traditional & conventional; contented; intensely patriotic; sentimental; deeply stable. Number: 57 million Age: median, 52 Income: median, $17,300 Education: median, high school graduate	Aging; need family & community; concerned about financial security, appearance, surroundings, health; able to cope with change, but avoid it. Number: 12 million	Two groups; one as in the U.S., with addition of wanting more satisfying work, the other, with traditional values, but more active, complaining, wanting improved quality of life; more concerned about education, creativity, emotions; this group younger, male. Number: 14 million	Active sports: none Spectator sports: none Outdoor rec: none The arts: none Cultural events: none Youth entertainment: none Table games: none Pleasure traveling: none TV: news particularly Movies: little Reading: newspaper Other: gardening, baking

Type				Activities
EMULATORS	Youthful and ambitious; macho; show-off, trying to break into the system, to make it big. Number: 16 million Age: median, 27 Sex: 53% male Income: median, $18,000 Education: high school graduate plus	Youthful, but older & quieter than in the U.S., better educated; entertain at home rather than outside; consider ideologies to be dangerous; concerned about health. Number: 4.4 million	Older than others; mostly females; more interested in social status than job status; sacrifice comfort & practicality for fashion. Number: 6.9 million	Active sports: bowling, billiards, pool Spectator sports: none Outdoor rec: none The arts: none Cultural events: none Youth entertainment: arcades, night clubs, amusement parks Pleasure traveling: none TV: comedies, movies Movies: some Reading: classified ads
Inner-Directed: **I-AM-ME** Although they came from outer-directed families, they live in ways dramatically opposite to their parents.	Transition state; exhibitionist & narcissistic; young; impulsive, dramatic; experimental; active; inventive. Number: 8 million Age: 91% under 25 Sex: 64% male Income: median, $8,800 Education: some college	Older (20–30); well educated; contemplative; little concern for financial security, social success, or materialism; enjoy their work. Number: 3.7 million	Too few to be statistically significant; exhibit self-expressive characteristics, but are more societally conscious. Number: 1 million	Active sports: bicycling, jogging, squash, swimming, bowling, billiards Spectator sports: pro, high school, college Outdoor rec: camping, hunting, backpacking, boating The arts: paint, sculpt, write poetry & fiction Cultural events: little Youth entertainment: pop/rock, night club, arcades, listen to music Table games: poker Pleasure traveling: often TV: weekend only Reading: comics
EXPERIENTIAL	Youthful; seek direct experience; person-centered; artistic; intensely oriented toward inner growth. Number: 8 million Age: median, 27 Sex: 55% females Income: median, $23,800 Education: 38% college graduates or more	Young; predominantly male; highly educated; not fulfilled by work but by leisure; enjoy the present; hedonistic. Number: 1.9 million	Highly educated; want excitement and adventure; risk-takers; creative & self-expressive; want to demonstrate abilities. Number: 5.2 million	Active sports: exercise, tennis, billiards, & bowling Spectator sports: some Outdoor rec: camping, backpacking, sailing, skiing The arts: little Cultural events: opera, ballet, museums Youth entertainment: pop/rock, night clubs, amusement park, arcades, list. music Table games: backgammon, chess, poker Pleasure traveling: always TV: seldom Movies: always Reading: heavy reader of books Other: own photographic & camping equipment & racing bicycles

Table 12.8 Comparison of European and U.S. life-style types and their pursuits

Bases	United States	France	United Kingdom	Leisure Pursuits
SOCIETALLY CONSCIOUS	Mission-oriented; leaders of single-issue groups; mature; successful; some live lives of voluntary simplicity. Number: 14 million Age: median, 39 Sex: 52% male Education: 58% college graduates, 39% some graduate school	Too few to be statistically significant, although most people have stronger societally conscious tendencies than in the U.S. Number: 1 million	Family-oriented; young; middle-class; more women well educated; want personal growth, self-expression, & spontaneity; creative; want meaningful, satisfying work; question authority & technology. Number: 6 million	Active sports: swimming Spectator sports: some Outdoor rec: sailing The arts: write poetry Cultural events: theater, opera, ballet, museums Youth entertainment: Table games: Pleasure traveling: by RV TV: most, particular early eve programs Movies: always Reading: heavy readers of books & magaz. Other: use library, own RV
INTEGRATED	Psychologically mature; large field of vision; tolerant & understanding; sense of fittingness. Number: 3.2 million	Psychologically mature; large field of vision; tolerant & understanding; sense of fittingness. Number: 1 million	Psychologically mature; large field of vision; tolerant & understanding; sense of fittingness. Number: 1.3 million	

Source: Mitchell, A., The Nine American Lifestyles: Who We Are and Where We're Going, 1983, p. 176-179. Macmillan Publishing Company. Reprinted with permission.

number of activities differs. The four-day, as opposed to the five-day, workers participate in experimental leisure, possibly to determine which are most enjoyable. As time passes, he or she devotes more time to fewer activities, settling into a pattern similar to that of the five-day worker.

Another attempt at comparing nations in their leisure pursuits was conducted by Ibrahim (1974:54–74) using Reisman's character typology. Reisman's theory of human behavior is based on the changes that have occurred and are occurring in the different populations in the world (1950). According to the theory, each human society manifests predominantly one of three social characters according to the particular phase of its population growth. The letter "S" represents this demographic orientation. The bottom horizontal line of the "S" represents the demographic phase of "high growth potential" when birthrates roughly equal death rates. Societies at this phase are tradition-directed. A phase of "transitional growth" occurs here when birthrates exceed death rates. This phase is represented by the vertical bar of the "S." Societies at this phase are inner-directed, producing an "inner-directed" social character. When demographers begin to detect a growing population of the middle-aged and aged, this signals the third phase of "incipient population decline" where both birth and death rates are low. These societies are "other-directed" and produce "other-directed" social character. This is represented by the top horizontal bar of the "S."

Economically speaking, Reisman's typology approximates Colin Clark's classification of primary, secondary, and tertiary economies. Primary refers to agriculture, hunting, fishing, and mining as the sources of economy; secondary refers to manufacturing; and tertiary refers to trade, communication, and services. In this sense, the tradition-directed society is at the primary level of economy, the inner-directed society at the secondary level, and the other-directed at the tertiary.

But economy is not the only variable that Reisman uses to differentiate among the three types of social character he delineates. Four agents of character formation were probed—parents, teachers, peers, and mass media—as well as activities such as politics, work, and play.

The theory utilizes worldwide examples, making it universal in orientation. At the same time it suggests the possibility of one social character overlying another in one society, like geologic strata. So, one society may show two, if not three, types of social character.

Leisure, play and recreation are given an important place in Reisman's theory as one of the areas where social character is reflected. Reisman uses the United States as an example of the shift in leisure inclination from inner-direction to other-direction. He does not discuss tradition-direction in detail, and proceeds to indicate, rather hurriedly, that the tradition-directed social character tends to make weak distinctions between work and leisure (play). Since inner-directed persons are trained to value production, their attitude toward consumption (including leisure) is slightly negative. Some inner-directed persons diminish attention to consumption and pleasure to a vanishing point. Others, perhaps the majority, are able to use the sphere of pleasure as an occasional escape from the sphere of work; yet they are consciously and sharply aware of the difference between work and leisure. Others turn consumption into work—the work of acquisition. Accordingly, sport and hobbies play an important role in the inner-directed character's life. With the rise of other-direction, one may see the passing both of the acquisitive consumers and the escapists. The passion for acquisition diminishes when property no longer has its old stability and objective validity; escape diminishes by the very fact that work and pleasure are interlaced. The other-directed becomes concerned with two things: popularity and consumption. Accordingly, social and communicative activities are important aspects of his or her leisure life.

The universality of the three typologies, the distinction among the three types, and the variation in leisure inclination were studied by Ibrahim (1974). He used a sample of 100 subjects from each of the following nations: United States, West Germany, Finland, and Egypt. He concludes that the three demographic variables suggested by Reisman (birthrate, death rate, and life expectancy) do not fit together to produce a society of one type of character or another. When empirically tested, Reisman's theory on social character is only supported in part. For instance, the Finnish sample was expected to show more interest in sport and hobbies, being inner-directed, as stipulated by Reisman, which it did. Also, the American sample was expected to show more interest in social and communicative activities, being other-directed, which it did.

But the results of the West German and Egyptian samples do not support Reisman's theory. In the case of the West German sample, the interest in social activities was higher than the interest in sport, which may be attributed to the movement of the country toward other-direction. The high mean in aesthetics and hobbies for the Egyptian sample is not surprising. Perhaps in the traditional societies there is more emphasis on aesthetic appreciation as a result of the emphasis on the past and its glory.

SUMMARY

Two main concentric social circles affect one's socialization. The first one includes two primary groups: family and school. Studies show that our leisure pursuits are most affected by these two groups. The second social group includes clubs, associations, and places of worship. These also have their impact on leisure choices. Moreover, demographic variables such as age, gender, occupation, income, and place of residence were found to have a relationship to the type of leisure activities in which the person participates. Personal traits such as physique and temperament may affect our choices, particularly the ones related to physical recreation. One's life-style and subculture have a direct bearing on these choices. The term *subculture* is favored over *ethnicity* since it describes groups that may not be outwardly different from the main population, yet whose members may follow a different set of values. *Life-style,* the term now being used by social scientists, incorporates most of the social variables that act on human behavior, including leisure pursuits.

REVIEW QUESTIONS

1. What is meant by primary groups? secondary groups? What does this mean to recreation?
2. Which of the eight demographic variables discussed in this chapter has greater impact on leisure choices?
3. In what way do personal traits affect leisure behavior?
4. How is life-style related to leisure? Describe some of the prevalent life-styles in the Western world.

SUGGESTED READINGS

Csikszentmihalyi, M., and R. Larson. 1984. *Being adolescent.* New York: Basic Books.

Kando, T. 1975. *Leisure and popular culture in transition.* St. Louis: Mosby.

Kelly, J. C. 1983. *Leisure, identities and interactions.* London: Allen & Unwin.

Mitchell, A. 1983. *The nine American lifestyles: Who we are and where we're going.* New York: MacMillan.

13

THE PHYSICAL CONTEXT OF LEISURE

Leisure pursuits are acquired through many agents. Home, school, the marketplace, youth clubs, and the local bar are but some of these agents. Some of these are both agents for and places of leisure. Others are basically places for leisure pursuits: the library, the museum, the beach, and the second home. In this chapter, agencies for and places of leisure are classified according to their location in relation to the participant. Home is the major center, concentrically spreading out into the neighborhood, city, county, state or province, the nation, and finally into the world. There is, of course, some overlap among agents and places.

HOME AND NEIGHBORHOOD

Most leisure pursuits take place at home or in places very close to it, such as schools and youth centers for the young and the local bar or coffeehouse for the adult.

Home

Glyptis and Chambers (1982:250) show that in Britain the family home remains the dominant setting for leisure. The attributes that fashion the home as a source for leisure are size, design, division of space, flexibility, and management. The authors add equipment as an important part of leisure at home and indicate that the list is increasing as new leisure equipment is marketed. British homes are equipped with radios, televisions, record players, tape and video players, books, magazines, musical instruments, sewing machines, bicycles, gardens, and cars. The new electronic gadgetry are also present: chess challengers, video games, sun lamps, and exercise machines. The garden is both a place for recreation and a focus of it.

In the United States, one would add computers and computerized games to the list above. Moreover, America's backyard, which is more of a yard than the British garden, is usually equipped with basketball backboards, playing apparatus, and with a patio for cooking, eating, and lounging. Estimates of the National Swimming Pool Institute show approximately half a million hot tubs and whirlpools and over 2 million swimming pools in America's backyards (MacLean et al. 1985:210). Data in table 8.1 show that among the samples from 13 nations used in that study, between 50% and 65% of free time is spent at home.

Playlots and Miniparks

Not too far from home, at least in most North American and West European cities, are playlots. Usually an acre in size, with an emphasis on the very young, playlots include sandboxes, swings, climbers, and slides. They are often attached to a minipark, which is equipped with shade trees, benches, and picnic tables for adults. Adventuresome equipment is sometimes included for older children. These areas are not seen in many cities of the world.

Neighborhood Park

The neighborhood park is intended to serve a neighborhood of about 5,000 people living within a one-mile radius, a standard observed more in

North America than anywhere else. It usually includes the features of a playlot and minipark and contains a basketball court, tennis courts, and a softball field. A wading pool and toilet facilities are sometimes provided. In a study of local parks, Cheek and Burch (1976:165) examined respondents' reports of the kind of activities they engaged in while in the park. They conclude that the local park is conducive to the development of social bonds among social groups.

The School

Schools in North America and Western Europe are adequately equipped for education and recreation, more so than in the developing countries of the Third World. Schools in the suburbs, particularly in North America, are provided with elaborate sport areas and recreational facilities. Despite the absence of this in the Third World and old urban centers of Western Europe and North America, the school presents itself as a place and agency for leisure pursuits. Yet according to Chubb and Chubb (1981:443), its potential for recreation is never realized because of bureaucratic red tape.

Day Camp

It was during the Depression years in the United States that many cities set aside sections of their parks to serve as day camps (Butler 1940:174). These are now intended to help in the socialization of the young and to provide him or her with nature experiences on a limited basis.

Community Center

The first community centers were actually social settlements such as the ones in London in 1885, New York in 1887, and Hull House in Chicago in 1889, which grew out of the humanitarian movement to help the poor. They became centers not only for welfare but for education and recreation (Neumeyer and Neumeyer 1949:66). Today, at least in the United States and Canada, community centers are dominated by recreational facilities and offerings. These include outdoor facilities, such as the ones seen in miniparks and neighborhood parks,

as well as indoor facilities such as gymnasia, multipurpose rooms, arts and crafts rooms, possibly a swimming pool, and a theater.

Parades and Festivities

Even in technologically advanced America and the West, parades are a technique for announcing the beginning of a major form of celebration, either for a religious occasion such as Christmas or a secular one such as the Fourth of July. What started as a festivity related to an agricultural season has become a reflection of technological advances. Using these technological advances, festivals are "rendered gigantically, with immense floats, the amplified size and sounds of the marching band, and the skyscraping balloons of animals and comic characters" (Abrahams 1982:175).

Bar and Cafe

Bars and cafes are very important agents for and places of leisure pursuits. In Great Britain (see chap. 9), the pub played, and still plays, an important role in the lives of the Britons. It is a place for socializing, entertainment, and involvement in leisure pursuits. The cafe had, and still has, similar impact on the leisure life of the French people, of whom 16% visit a cafe once a week or more (Dumazedier 1967:29). The atmosphere there has changed from mere socializing to the inclusion of all sorts of games. In Egypt, as in all eastern Mediterranean countries (Greece, Turkey, Syria, and Lebanon), the coffeehouse remains an important domain in the social life of men (Ibrahim et al. 1981:107–8).

Marketplace

The marketplace is an open area that is left in the center, and sometimes on the edge, of the village or town. The ancient Greeks believed that a town should be built around a marketplace. It became the origin of the Greek *agora* and the Roman *forum*. Although shops have replaced the market stall, the market square is kept as the hub around which these shops are built. A number of cities still have this arrangement, and the enlarged area became the stage for many entertainers and leisure providers. Movable mini-amusement parks are moved from one marketplace to another in Egypt and India.

Youth Centers

According to Neumeyer and Neumeyer, youth centers, often called "teen centers," or "teenage clubs," sprang up in the 1930s and 1940s in America in different places and under different auspices (1949:336). A study by Russell Sage Foundations in 1947 of 303 such centers in 34 states showed that they are chiefly for the age group 14–18 years. In the United States and Canada, the idea of a separate center for youth seems to have disappeared except for Boy's and Girl's Clubs (see chap. 12). Programs for youth are still sponsored in youth-oriented organizations such as the YMCA, YWCA, and Boy and Girl Scouts, and are found in schools, churches, and the local recreation departments. Separate youth centers are still seen in Great Britain, Egypt, India, and China.

CITY AND COUNTY

There are places in the city or county not too far from one's neighborhood where leisure is pursued. Except for the workplace, which is attended daily during the week, they are not frequented as often. All of these places affect one's leisure pursuits.

Squares and Plazas

The original function of squares and plazas was to serve as an open market, a civic gathering place, or a memorial. In North America and Europe, they are built with aesthetics in mind. They are usually studded with statues and fountains. The same is true of the rebuilt areas of the large cities of the Third World. In the old parts, there are other recreational outlets for many of the old city dwellers. In many of the towns and villages, the square is still used as a marketplace as it has been for hundreds of years. As an additional touch, street entertainment and children's rides have become a common feature.

City Park

In North America, the city park has become quite elaborate, measuring ten acres in size. City parks there include playfields and courts that go beyond the amenities listed under miniparks and neighborhood parks. The Third World suffers from a lack of open spaces in its congested urban centers and from a lack of funds.

Shopping Centers

The shopping center, a twentieth century feature, is emerging as a new kind of environment. It is increasingly seen as a leisure center as well as a retail center. Here, the idea is to separate the pedestrian and the vehicle (Whittick 1974:896). Europe and other countries are trying to build them at the same rate as the United States, which experienced a massive population shift to suburbia. Open space and ample private transportation allowed for growth in shopping centers. The American shopping center has a courtyard, which replaces the city plazas where people of all ages could congregate. Also, developers are interested in enhancing the leisure atmosphere of shopping centers. According to Chubb and Chubb, management arranges for special events, promotes jogging, and holds contests of all sorts inside the mall (1981:367). In addition, commercial recreation enterprises such as movie houses and legitimate theaters, hobby shops, bowling alleys, ice rinks, bookstores, pet stores, and restaurants are found there. Great Britain has followed suit (Martin and Mason 1987:79), keeping spatial, cultural, and business differences in mind. Some shopping centers are adding leisure centers onto their locations (table 13.1).

Health Spas

A health spa is looked upon as a health resort in most of the world. In North America, a spa may also be a place, not too far from home, that is oriented to health and fitness. It is usually equipped with more than a hot tub. It is a workout facility to which one goes two or three times a week after paying a membership fee. These places are dotting the urban centers as well as the suburban areas of North America.

Table 13.1 Some new UK shopping/leisure developments

Location/name	Retailing (square feet)	Leisure facilities
Bristol Cribbs Causeway	500,000	10-screen cinema; various leisure facilities; restaurants
Glasgow St. Enoch	50 shops	Ice rink; fast-food court
Gateshead Metrocentre	750,000	Funfair; 10-screen cinema; antiques market
Hatfield Park Plaza	450,000	Ice rink; garden center; hotel
Romford Mercury Gardens	94,000	Multi-screen cinema; disco; water slide; social clubs
Rotherham Parkgate Centre	1,500,000	10-screen cinema; bowling alley; ice rink; entertainment complex; fast-food court
Thurrock Dolphin Park	1,300,000	Multi-screen cinema; children's village; food court

Source: Martin, B., and S. Mason, "Current Trends in Leisure," Leisure Studies 6(1), 1987, p. 97. E. & F. N. Spon. Reprinted with permission.

The Private Club

Although the idea of a private, recreational club may have started with Saint Andrew's Golf Club in Scotland in the 1500s, the idea was not very acceptable in North America until 1888 when Brookline Country Club was established near Boston (Dulles 1965:242). It was estimated that there were 3,300 country clubs in the United States by the mid-1960s (Boyle 1962:69–74). According to Chubb and Chubb, there are hundreds of private clubs catering to every known sport, as well as hiking, traveling, cultural, and hobby clubs (1981:338–41). Kraus claims that "many country clubs, golf clubs, and tennis clubs discriminate against members of certain races or religions, although applications of their policies are often arbitrary and contradictory" (1984:242). He points to an investigation by the United States Senate Banking Committee that found women, blacks, and other ethnic minorities to be excluded from certain private clubs.

In some of the Third-World countries that were dominated by British Colonialism, the concept of private clubs was copied from the occupiers by the upper classes and became an important center of their leisure lives. This happened in India and Egypt. Eventually the middle classes began their own modest clubs. Because of the lack of open space in the ancient cities of these two countries, private clubs provide important leisure outlets for the middle and upper class, though leaving only much to wish for by the masses.

Fairs

Chapter 6 shows that the fair, although intended for trade, played an important role in the leisure life of a medieval European. Today, nations of the Third World still have the same type of fair with the same orientations to the past (see chap. 7). In North America, the agricultural fair has become much more leisure-oriented than in Europe. According to Chubb and Chubb (1981:504), 35 states have permanent state fairgrounds in their capitals. Also, many of the large counties in populated states such as California have permanent fairgrounds. The fair is no longer agricultural in its orientation. It has become a place of entertainment. Chubb and Chubb give as an example Ontario Place, which has a cinesphere (a spherical amphitheater), a children's village (a large area with unusual play equipment), and the pod (five structures with restaurants and boutiques) (1981:504).

The Workplace

The concept of having leisure pursuits at or provided by the workplace was unheard of in the industrial nations before the turn of the century. The Peacedale Company of Rhode Island offered a library to its employees as early as 1854, but it was a few decades until other American companies followed its lead (MacLean et al. 1985:216). According to Kraus (1984:221), *The Wall Street Journal* estimated that American business and industry spent about $800 million in 1953 on employee recreation, and *The New York Times* raised that estimate to $2 billion for 1975. In Eastern bloc nations, most of the recreational offerings are provided through work. According to Chubb and Chubb, about half of all Soviet citizens who go away for a vacation use tour buses operated by trade unions. Most of East Germany's 8,000 sport clubs are operated by enterprises or trade unions (1981:363). In Great Britain, the provision of recreational opportunities in the workplace seems to be very limited. Roberts (1983b:229) suggests the provisions there are sometimes anachronistic and should be handed over to the community, a voluntary organization, or a commercial enterprise. He recommends that British industry look at the United States, the USSR, or Scandinavia for examples.

The Library

The number of public libraries and their holdings in the 13 countries cited in this volume are shown in table 7.1. It seems that three Eastern bloc nations, Czechoslovakia, Poland, and East Germany, have better ratios of libraries and their holdings to persons than the Soviet Union, North American nations, West European countries, and the Third-World nations. The Soviet Union has a better ratio of libraries to persons (1:10,635) than the United States (1:28,253) and Canada (1:31,565). But the three countries have about the same ratio of book holdings in public libraries to persons (1.8:1; 1.9:1; 3:1 for the United States, Canada, and the Soviet Union, respectively). Libraries are becoming increasingly important in leisure pursuits all over the world.

The Museum

According to Chubb and Chubb, there are about 24,000 museums in the world today, 6,000 of which are in the United States (1981:590). This means that the United States, which represents about 6% of the world's population, has 25% of the world's museums. The authors list four types of museums:

Art museums. Modern, folk, primitive, and ethnic art.
Science museums. Aquatic, botanical, paleontological, and zoological museums.
History museums. National monuments and treasures, historical sites, anthropological and archaeological museums.
Specialized museums. Children's, military and ethnic museums, and private collections.

Statistics show that the number of museum visitors worldwide has recently increased dramatically (Chubb and Chubb 1981:593).

The Theater

Although the annual number of productions of plays by professionals declined in the United States, the number of amateur theatrical enterprises rose dramatically in the 1960s and the 1970s (Kando 1975:113). The drop may have resulted from increased television programming and movie production. In the meantime, the number of professional productions in other countries was increasing, perhaps due to government subsidy. But in the 1980s, theater in the United States and in all other countries is gaining ground. Broadway's 38 commercial theaters remain a premier attraction, totaling 9.8 million paid admissions in 1978–79. Also, London's West Side, the equivalent of New York's Broadway, has become extremely successful, attracting 50% of its theatergoers from abroad, including 25% from the United States alone (Chubb and Chubb 1981:574). Amateur theatrical groups numbered 25,000 in the United States in the mid-1970s: 5,000 were college groups, 5,000 belonged to nonprofit organizations, and 15,000 were affiliated with clubs, schools, and churches (Kando 1975:113).

The Movies

Movies represent an inexpensive form of amusive leisure, perhaps the first in history to democratize leisure and lead to its explosion. The technology spread extremely fast across the world, but its dominance was seen more in the United States. According to Kando (1975:197), there were 21,000 theaters showing 1,000 feature-length films in the 1920s United States. Sound was introduced in 1927. Attendance declined during the Depression, followed by another peak in the late 1940s. This was followed by a steep decline in favor of the new leisure pursuit, watching television. The number of commercial theaters then declined to 13,000. Today, there are about 10,000 movie theaters, both walk-in and drive-in, in the United States (table 11.4).

The Sports Arena

Across the world, spectator sport has increased dramatically in the last few decades. Although horse racing is the most attended sport in many countries as a result of the size of the racetrack and the frequency of the races, soccer is probably the most attended sport in the world today. For the 1950s World Cup, 200,000 spectators filled Maracana Stadium in Rio de Janeiro to watch the soccer finals. According to Baker (1982:246), the Soviets had a plan to build a 250,000 seat stadium, but it did not materialize. Growth in spectator sport in the United States is shown in table 11.10. Horse racing was the most attended sport in the last 15 years.

The Racetrack

Racetracks are the most attended sport arenas in many countries. Fans attend the day's program, which usually has eight or nine races for a specific distance and age of the horse. The courses themselves vary in size, type (soil or grass), and sharpness of the turns.

Theme Restaurants

In the sixteenth century, inns and taverns in England began to serve one meal at a fixed price at a common table called the *ordinary*. In 1765, a Paris establishment served a refreshment dish. *Restaurant* is the past participle of the verb *restaurer*, "to restore or fortify." Banquets moved from the home of the European aristocrats to restaurants and eating out became acceptable (Ibrahim 1978). Eating out was not part of the life-style of American pioneers. According to David Reisman and others (1950), as inner-directedness gave way to other-directedness in the United States (see chap. 12), a shift in leisure behavior took place and some Americans began to display their taste rather than their wealth or health, which led to the spread of gourmet cults. Although not totally responsible for the increase in the median weight of Americans, eating out comes to 50% of food expenditure in the United States. The theme restaurants' share is not exactly known, but data of the National Restaurant Association show that an increase of 153% was expected in total sales volume from 1970 to 1980 (Ibrahim 1978). The idea behind a theme restaurant is leisure dining accomplished by comfortable seating, displays, live entertainment, scenic views, revolving floors, unique settings, participatory and or spectator cooking, and stage performances. The increase in this type of dining is shown in the growth of dinner theaters in the United States, from 7 in 1969 to 500 in the early 1980s (Chubb and Chubb 1981:373).

Perusal through recent ads in Egypt's number one newspaper, *Al Ahram,* reveals an increasing number of ads for theme restaurants, a phenomenon of recent appearance.

The Beach

A sizable sandy area by the sea, ocean, lake, or river, with easy access, either privately or publicly owned, becomes a very attractive location for leisure pursuits, particularly in the summer. In warm climates, going to the beach becomes a matter of routine. While people may go to the park for social reasons (Cheek and Burch 1976), their reasons for going to the beach are different. Edgerton (1979) investigated the reasons for going to an urban public beach in southern California by spending three summers observing beach-goers, interviewing some of them, and recording various activities. He concluded that social order at the beach is not akin to the one in a small community, or in face-to-face primary groups. Nor is the interaction on the beach akin to the ones that take place in secondary groups. It is more or less like the interaction of a crowd in a sport event with one basic difference: there is no focal point other than the enjoyment of oneself and the elements. Beach-goers are together yet alone. Conflict is at a minimum because the aim is relaxed pleasure.

STATE AND PROVINCE

A wider circle of leisure agents and places exist under state, provincial, or governorate control. Naturally, this arrangement will vary with each society, but basically these facilities are not as numerous as the ones already discussed; yet they are somewhat larger.

Amusement Parks

In 1850 the pleasant, quiet summer resort on the southwestern end of Long Island saw a steady stream of people coming to be amused. Coney Island might well be called the first full-scale amusement park in the world, although a smaller one on Manhattan Island, Jones' Wood, was there already (Fazio 1979:186). An American exported the idea to France and built the world-famous Luna Park. The mild whirl of the "Loop the Loop" proved to be too much for customers, but other features compensated for its demise (Rearick (1985:204). Today there are amusement parks all over the world. Some are no more than movable rides that are mounted on chassis to be pulled from marketplace to marketplace; others are the gigantic amusement parks in the United States, such

as Disneyland or Magic Mountain. There are approximately 319 amusement parks in the United States, with annual revenues of close to $4 billion (Ulmer 1980:4, Grover 1987:38). Disneyland recorded its 250 millionth admission in August 1986 (Corliss 1986).

There are also now theme parks, which vary from the traditional amusement park where unrelated rides, games, and shows are put together. The theme park has a package of attractions revolving around one theme. Economic affluence and technology are bringing state-of-the-art equipment to leisure pursuits.

Camps and Campgrounds

Other than the day camp, which was discussed earlier, camps are of three types: resident, group, or travel camp. Resident camps, numbering almost 6,000 in the United States, are established camps where the campers stay for a session of one to two weeks. The camp usually has permanent features. Group camp consists of a pre-existing group, such as Boy Scouts. Groups go to an already existing camp. For travel camps the campers carry their own equipment.

Cerullo and Ewen (1982) suggest that there is a hierarchy of travel camps in the United States. At the top are national parks and forests, with a camping population who are decidedly upper class. In the middle are the elaborate and expensive private campgrounds. Below these are state parks and forests. At the bottom end of the social hierarchy are most of the private grounds. All of these campgrounds are divided into campsites that are equipped to receive individuals and groups wishing to camp in tents or recreational vehicles. Almost all of the campgrounds in Europe and Canada are publicly owned. But in the United States, 700,000 of its one million campsites are privately owned (Chubb and Chubb 1981:386). In Canada, there is evidence that camping is increasing (table 10.1). In the United States, camping is pursued by 21% of the 1,500 households investigated by the Gallup organization (table 11.7). In Great Britain, camping was practiced by only 2.1% of the participants in the four weeks prior to the administration of the General House Survey (Veal 1984). Camping may take place in other weeks in the year, but it seems that camping is not as popular in Great Britain as in North America (Canada, United States, and Mexico), possibly for the lack of both public and private campgrounds. On the other hand, Cerullo and Ewen claim that America's minorities—blacks, Jews, and Hispanics—barely exist in the camping world (1982:17).

College/University Campus

The concept of university campuses is a very recent one because the ancient universities were part of other institutions. Al-Azhar University, the oldest continuing university in the world, was conceived of as an integral part of the main mosque of Cairo in C.E. 969. The early Western universities in Bologna, Paris, Oxford, and Cambridge were initially single college buildings near the center of town. Additional buildings were acquired but were not adjacent enough to form a campus, as happened in the United States. According to Whittick, by the mid-twentieth century the grouping of university buildings followed a pattern of a central plaza surrounded by buildings generally used by students. Among these are an auditorium, a theater, and a student union—buildings that cater to the students' leisure pursuits (1974:1131). Since most American colleges and universities are residential, they must take the place of home and community (MacLean et al. 1985:154). A number of leisure activities are provided, including the many skills taught in the departments of music, drama, art, literature, and physical education. A complete set of intramural and extramural sport activities are provided for men and women, along with many spectator sports.

Second Homes

The concept of a second home for the purpose of relaxing, recreating, and contemplating is an old one. It was limited in intermediate societies to the rich aristocracy. This practice continued until very recently in China, Egypt, India, and Mexico. In Great Britain, the practice of acquiring a home in the country spread from the upper stratum to the middle class toward the end of the Victorian era (see chap. 9).

The concept gained popularity among the middle class of the United States and Canada. Ragatz (1974) estimated that 3 million families or 5% of American households have second homes. There is reason to believe that such numbers have not increased appreciably recently because the major provider of land for these homes, the United States Forest Service, has stopped the practice, started in 1915, of leasing sites in designated forest areas (Knudson 1984:129).

Most second homes are by water, in a forest, at the mountains, or in the country. A new idea has caught on rather recently, intended to cut cost: time-sharing property. The idea is that one partner occupies the home for a short period—a long weekend, a week, or a two-week vacation. The other partners will have their time also. This affordable idea is spreading into poorer countries, such as Egypt. An ad appeared in *Al Ahram,* the Cairo newspaper, for a time-sharing property. Despite its communistic orientation, some Soviet citizens own a *dasha,* or a cottage in the country, for one family's use only (see chap. 8).

Resorts

Resorts are self-contained facilities that cater to the demands of the recreationist. Accordingly, they not only provide room and board as hotels, motels, and inns do, but provide guests with activities for the period of time in which they are staying at the resort. According to Chubb and Chubb (1981:389–95), there are four main types of resorts. First are the warm weather resorts, ranging from primitive to luxurious, in which the guests have access to numerous leisure pursuits. Second, there are ski resorts, totaling 1,300 in the United States and catering to 14 million skiers (table 11.7). The purchasing power of skiers climbed from $379 million in 1980 to $650 million in 1986, a 70% increase in five years (table 11.2). There are major ski resorts in other parts of the world, mainly in Canada, but also in Australia, France, Germany, Italy, Yugoslavia, and Switzerland. Third, there are beauty and health resorts, which were originally founded around hot springs. We can credit the Romans for locating and using them. The concept is more dominant in Europe than in North America: in Czechoslovakia's Karlsbad, France's Vichy, and Germany's Bad Pyrmont. The Soviets are now providing resorts around the Black Sea, to be offered to workers who are recommended as good comrades (see chap. 8). Finally, sport resorts provide instruction and practice facilities. Tennis and golf resorts are particularly popular in the United States. As shown in table 11.8, the number of golfers increased from 13,036,000 in 1975 to 17,520,000 in 1985, an increase of 37%. The same table shows that the number of tennis players peaked in the late 1970s.

State and Provincial Parks

State and provincial parks fall between the small and limited local parks and the huge but inaccessible national parks. Inaccessibility here may be due to distance more than anything else. The provision of intermediate parks is seen more in Canada and the United States than in any other country. Although the total acreage of state parks in the United States does not exceed one-fifth of the national parks, nonetheless they are used three times as much. Foss suggests this is because they are closer to urban centers than national parks, and they provide easy access for tent camping (1971:255).

The Canadian provincial system of parks differs from the American system in that this system is expected to bridge the gap between the federal system and the total lack of park acreage in many areas of Canada. Also, as mentioned earlier, the Canadian province is much more autonomous than the American state. So it can act more independently on the Crown's land, the public domain's land, within its territory (Chubb and Chubb 1981:490).

State and Provincial Forests

In a manner similar to state and provincial parks, the state and provincial forests serve as intermediate recreational resources, between national forests and local areas. In the United States, state forests amount to 22 million acres disproportionately distributed around the country. Yet some are very accessible to persons living in the urban centers in the Northwest, northern New England, the middle and south Atlantic regions, and the mountain regions.

In Canada, the provinces control large areas of public lands. Although some of these lands are close to urban centers, there are choice areas that people "use air transportation to reach . . . for good hunting, fishing, or canoeing opportunities" (Chubb and Chubb 1981:501).

THE NATION AND THE WORLD

There are still other places for leisure and types of leisure to be considered. Some have national appeal and significance and others have a worldwide importance. Among these are national parks and forests, and travel and tourism.

National Parks

The concept of national parks is an American one, and was applied to Yellowstone in 1872. It is a permanent preservation of an area of exceptional qualities as a national reserve, protected and enjoyed by all people. In 1906, the National Park Service was established to oversee the many areas that are of exceptional quality and to be preserved for the future. Today the system has over 330 areas, bearing a variety of designations, for a total of 79 million acres, of which 54 million are in Alaska. Among the many designations are national monuments, historical, scientific, or archaeological sites, and national recreation areas. Table 11.11 shows that visitation in millions of visitor-hours peaked in 1983.

The Canadian national parks add up to 32 million acres, making them one of the largest systems in the world. The concept is spreading into many countries. New Zealand claims to be the second nation to establish a national park after the United States. Great Britain established its first national park in 1950 about the same time that the newly independent countries of Africa established theirs, Kenya's Nairobi National Park and Tanzania's Kilimanjaro and Serengeti national parks. Egypt has just declared part of the southern shore of Sinai a national park.

In order that the number of national parks be increased around the world, particularly in the Third World, Burnett and Butler (1984) suggest changing the old conservationist view that was originally used to establish European control over big game in Africa. They suggest that national parks become a tool of national development rather than a bastion of preservation. In some Third-World countries, national parks have become well managed resorts with a profitable tourist business. Others suffer from neglect due to lack of funds.

National Forests

National forests are areas with great potential for leisure pursuits. The United States has by far the most expansive national forest system in the world geared for such pursuits. According to Knudson (1984:267), the United States Forest Service offers the following: 100,000 miles of trails for hiking, skiing, and snowmobiling; 262 winter sport sites with over 2 million linear feet of ski lifts on 165 downhill ski areas; most of the National Wilderness Preservation Systems outside Alaska, with 128,000 miles of fishing streams and 2 million acres of lakes; one-third of the big game animals in the United States; 4,500 campgrounds with the capacity to handle more than 460,000 persons at one time; 1,500 picnic grounds; 600 interpretive sites, 52 of which are major interpretive centers; 1,500 recreational residence special use areas; and seven National Recreation areas.

Data show that visitations to United States national forests peaked in 1981 in both visiting hours (in billions) at 2,828 and visitor days (in thousands) at 235,709 (tables 11.11 and 13.2). Table 13.2 shows that camping and mechanized travel are by far the most dominant outdoor leisure pursuits in the United States national forests, followed by winter sport, fishing, and hunting.

Other than the United States, Great Britain became interested in national forests in 1919 because World War I showed that the country must rely on its own natural resources (Chubb and Chubb 1981:536). The British Forestry Commission was formed and today manages 3 million acres or about 5% of the British Isles. Most of these acres are open for pedestrian, but not vehicular, use. Orienteering, horseback riding, and pony trekking are the major leisure pursuits in the British national forests.

Wilderness Area

The wilderness area is an American idea advocated by such thinkers as Ralph Waldo Emerson, Henry David Thoreau, and George Catlin. The following represents their thinking:

> *A town is saved, not more by the righteous men in it than by the woods and swamps that surround it. A township where one primitive forest waves above while another primitive forest rots below—such a town is fitted to raise not only corn and potatoes, but poets and philosophers for the coming ages (Thoreau Excursions, 1893:280).*

A wilderness area is a primitive area and is to be kept that way. Most of these areas are within national forests. And since national forest regulations allow for multiple use such as timber, grazing, and mining, a wilderness area should be preserved in its natural state.

According to Cheek and Burch (1976:166), a wilderness area turns park notions inside out. The user of such areas is an inner-directed rather than

Table 13.2 National forest recreation use-summary, 1980–85, and by place and activity, 1985

Place where use occurred	Visitor days (1,000)	Percent
1980	233,549	x
1981	235,709	x
1982	233,438	x
1983	227,708	x
1984	227,554	x
1985 total	225,407	100.0
Developed sites	81,922	36.3
Observation sites	1,078	0.5
Boating and fishing sites	3,304	1.5
Swimming sites, playgrounds etc.	2,258	1.0
Campgrounds and trailheads	35,813	15.9
Picnic grounds	4,519	2.0
Hotels, lodges, and resorts	4,691	2.1
Organization sites	5,179	2.3
Recreation residence sites	6,128	2.7
Ski areas and winter sports sites	15,905	7.0
Documentary areas, concession sites, visitor centers	3,047	1.3
Dispersed areas	143,485	63.7
Roads (recreation)	52,059	23.1
Trails (recreation)	13,093	5.8
Airfields	20	z
Waters	27,037	12.0
General undeveloped country	51,276	22.8

Activity	Visitor days (1,000)	Percent
1985, total	225,407	100.0
Camping	53,142	23.6
Picnicking	7,725	3.4
Recreation travel (mechanized)	50,448	22.4
Water travel	8,489	3.7
Games and team sports	1,300	0.6
Water skiing and other water sports	535	0.2
Swimming and scuba diving	4,685	2.1
Winter sports	16,213	7.2
Fishing	15,845	7.0
Hunting	14,610	6.5
Hiking and mountain climbing	13,477	6.0
Horseback riding	3,599	1.6
Resort use	4,572	2.0
Organization camp use	3,621	1.6
Recreation cabin use	6,241	2.8
Gather forest products	4,927	2.2
Nature study	1,775	0.8
Viewing scenery, sports, and environment	10,319	4.6
Visitor information (exhibits, talks, etc.)	3,924	1.7

x = not applicable z = less than 0.5 percent
Source: U.S. Bureau of the Census, Statistical Abstracts of the United States: 1987 (107th Edition) Washington, DC, 1986, p. 210.

other-directed individual (see chap. 12). Inner-directed men and women, a vanishing breed in our contemporary consumer society, are serious-minded people who take their leisure pursuits seriously. As Cheek and Burch say, "something sociologically important is occurring when highly urbanized and industrial societies such as Canada and the United States devote so much media and legislative attention and such substantial research budgets to lands of no possible development potential." Perhaps this is because the small and select group of the national population who uses these areas is not only dedicated to their preservation but engages in a form of activity that the rest of us long for: the forgotten contemplative leisure, the highest form of leisure according to Aristotle.

> I do not count the hours I spend
> In wandering by the Sea;
> The forest is my loyal friend,
> Like God, it useth me.

Ralph Waldo Emerson
"Waldeinsamkeit (Forest Solitude)" 1858
(Whicher 1957:454)

Travel and Tourism

Between 1975 and 1980, international travel increased by 75%, an average of 15% per year, but international business did not increase by an equivalent amount during that period. The data indicates that a new age of tourism is upon us. An important point to consider in that trend is the increase in vacation days globally (Lerner and Abbott 1982:2). This is shown by the fact that more foreigners visited the United States in 1980, 1981, and 1983 than Americans visited foreign countries. The data show that most of these foreign visitors were from Canada and Mexico, followed by Western Europeans and Latin Americans. The ratio of almost 1:1 between Americans traveling abroad and foreigners visiting here changed again. In 1985, for each American that went abroad, 0.6 foreigners came to the United States. The ratio of 1:1 would have continued had the United States promoted tourism from abroad. Most countries have

governmental tourist offices to promote their country as a tourist spot. In fact, some provincial Canadian governments have offices abroad for that very purpose. Neither the federal government nor the state governments do that in the United States. There is interstate tourism promotion directed toward the American citizen, but not toward the international visitor. The efforts were basically by the business community. Becoming aware of the importance of promoting tourism, state campaign budgets totaled about $82.8 for 1985, an increase of 11.8% from the previous year. In 1985, 558.4 million trips were taken within the United States, about 30.2 million more than the previous year (Spandoni 1986:1).

Another factor to consider in increased travel and tourism is the Deregulation Bill of 1978, which allowed United States airlines to compete freely, reducing fares. These airlines had always faced and still face unfair competition from international airlines that are subsidized by their governments. A national airline is looked upon by many countries as a national symbol that should not be allowed to fail. Nonetheless, American carriers are faring well, carrying passengers from and to the United States as well as within the country.

Although air travel is the predominant mode of intercity travel within the United States (Lerner and Abbott 1982:9), other modes are used. For example, there is the recreational vehicle, whose sales peaked in 1972 at 540,000, leveled off, then dropped drastically to fewer than 200,000 in 1980. Sales picked up again to a little over 300,000 units in 1985 (Barker 1986:15). A 20% surge in attendance at RV shows was encouraging. According to MacLean and others (1985:258), there are 6 million trailers and motor homes in use in the United States, making camping a very popular activity, with almost one-fifth of the population participating in it (table 11.7).

In studying vacation travel patterns inside the United States, Smith (1985) suggests that while income, education, occupation, socialization, and other sociological variables affect travel patterns, geographic and environmental characteristics may be more important. These characteristics are more important as demand-shifters. In other words, a wild river that is within a reasonable distance will affect vacation travel more than the sociological variables.

SUMMARY

We consider leisure to be based on an attitude that allows people to participate in activity of their choice when they are freed from work, civic, or familial obligations. The question remains: where does this activity take place? Undoubtedly home is the main location for such activity. Within the first circle of the neighborhood, our leisure pursuits also take us to the playlot, the school, day camp, and youth community center. One may engage in leisure pursuits in the marketplace or in the local bar or coffeehouse. As our social circle widens, we engage in leisure pursuits in the city park, the health spa, the fairgrounds, and sometimes at the workplace. Our activities may take us to a movie or a theater; to a museum or to a library; to a sport arena or a beach; and, for the well-to-do, to a theme restaurant.

The circle of pursuits is enlarged further when one goes to a camp or an amusement park; and further when one visits a college campus. Having a second home, visiting a resort, a state forest and/or park adds to our leisure experiences. A wider circle is possible through travel and tourism to national parks and forests and wilderness areas within one's country, and to attractions in other countries.

REVIEW QUESTIONS

1. How can home and the neighborhood contribute to one's future leisure behavior?
2. What facilities in the city and county provide for recreation?
3. List the facilities in your state or province that have a recreational orientation.
4. How can travel and tourism, domestically and abroad, enhance leisure opportunities?

SUGGESTED READINGS

Cheek, N., and Wm. Burch. 1976. *Social organization of leisure in human society*. New York: Harper & Row.

Knudson, D. 1984. *Outdoor recreation*. New York: Macmillan.

Lerner, E., and C. B. Abbott. 1982. *The way we go*. New York: Warner Books.

14

CONCERNS AND CONSTRAINTS

This last chapter attempts to highlight some of the concerns and constraints for leisure in society. No attempt will be made to predict where leisure pursuits are heading or what agents for and places of leisure will emerge or disappear in the future. Prediction requires sophisticated research tools that are not yet available to leisure researchers.

UNEVEN DISTRIBUTION OF LEISURE

Leisure is predicated, in this work, on state of mind (a function of dominant values), on time freed from work (a function of the economic system), and civic/familial obligations (again a function of values). Leisure pursuits would be expected to vary significantly from society to society due to the differences in values, economics, political systems, and so on. Yet these pursuits vary, as well, within a given society, leading to an uneven distribution of free time and leisure pursuits. Two clear examples are gender and urban-rural differences within one society.

As seen in chapter 12, gender differences exist in play behavior in early life, in adolescence, and at a later age. These differences exist in a number of societies: American, Canadian, Egyptian, Norwegian, and Soviet. In general, married women seem to suffer the most when husbands do not help with housework. Details are discussed under each country in the earlier chapters.

The dichotomy between rural and urban residents in their leisure pursuits seems to be a function of both environment and income. The situation is improving in the Western nations but still needs improvement in the Eastern bloc nations. As to the Third World, the dichotomy is glaring, not only in leisure pursuits but in the life-styles of rural and urban residents. Urban residents in these countries have a life-style similar to that of any urban resident any place else, though on a more modest scale. But there is a great need to improve rural conditions.

Economic factors also lead to uneven distribution of leisure within a society. Income determines not only what leisure activity one pursues, but also simply whether one has the free time to pursue it. Mitchell's study of life-styles (1983) shows that those who are need-driven, whom he classifies as Survivors and Sustainers, have fewer leisure pursuits than others (table 12.8).

Uneven distribution of leisure is also seen cross-culturally. The amount of free time for the Egyptian and Peruvian samples is very close to that of the American samples (tables 8.1 and 7.2). This could be a reflection of underemployment in both Egypt and Peru. For in those two countries leisure pursuits that require discretionary income were participated in to a lesser degree. Both Egypt and Peru have a much lower per capita income, about $600 a year compared to over $6,000 for the United States. The Peruvians spent more time at home resting than all other nationals in the 12 nation study (Szalai 1972). The Egyptian sample spent more time going and returning from work than all other samples (table 7.2), having to use the inexpensive but inadequate public transportation systems.

Another factor that leads to the uneven distribution of leisure pursuits is the dominant value system. Some value systems frown on leisure pursuits altogether (e.g., the Puritan system); others may prohibit an activity that is universally acceptable today. A case in point is the prohibition of gambling and drinking in the Muslim world. Those two activities are becoming increasingly acceptable in most societies, under certain conditions. For example, in Egypt only foreign tourists are allowed to attend the casinos provided for them. Gambling is a good source of income for any government, including the Egyptian government, which tries to adhere to Islamic principles (in obvious appeasement to religious fundamentalists) by prohibiting bearers of Egyptian passports from gambling in their own country. As for drinking, there are a few bars in Egypt, most of whose customers are non-Muslims, but none at all in the strictly Muslim countries of Saudi Arabia and Iran.

Edgar Jackson (1980), in his study of the relationship between sociodemographic variables and recreation in Camrose, Alberta, concludes that age is the strongest and most consistent variable, although income, education, and family size are also important. These four variables determine three aspects of leisure behavior: participation in recreation in general, participation in specific activities, and the use of the local recreational resources. He claims that his findings substantiate previous research that if recreational opportunities are located approximately equally for all income groups, then the use of resources and facilities will be uniform for all segments of the population.

Jackson and Searle (1985) conclude that nonparticipation in leisure activities is a complex rather than a simple phenomenon. Earlier authors had identified five main reasons for nonparticipation: lack of interest, lack of time, lack of money, lack of facilities, and lack of required skills. But Jackson and Searle suggest that barriers to leisure should be looked upon as basically of two types: blocking and inhibiting. The status of each is not absolute, but rather relative to the individual and his or her circumstances.

Foley (1989) laments the decline of the "leisure rights" that entitle everyone to quality and affordable services. In Los Angeles, there has developed a "recreational apartheid" in which two systems are separated by income plus race. Since 1970, the city has practiced a market model, which assumes that if consumers desire services they will pay for them. One result has been the "dead parks," which the *Los Angeles Times* (3 September 1984) described as mostly cramped sites in neighborhoods, filled with gangs, drug dealers, and drunks. In 1985, the city's Parks and Recreation Department moved to rectify the situation.

In Chicago, a public interest group found it necessary to take the Park District to court, alleging inequitable allocation of public park and recreation resources. In 1984, after a four-year legal battle, the District agreed to spend 60 million dollars over the next six years to renovate and build parks and recreation programs in black and Hispanic neighborhoods.

Such problems are not limited to American society. According to Dawson (1988), scenic parks were established in middle-class areas and playing fields near working-class sections of England's cities. Fewer improvements and poorer maintenance were typical of the crowded working-class parks. He concludes that the park system helped maintain class distinction in leisure and supported the privileged status of the dominant class.

ANOMIE AND LEISURE

A social activity, such as lying on the beach, is allowed in a society if it serves a designated, acceptable social function. A whole interactive process may revolve around it, leading to an approved structure. In many instances, a society does not allow certain activities because they do not serve a needed social function. Activities allowed in a particular society are perceived to serve certain societal goals. For example, sport was, and still is, perceived in many societies as producing healthy and patriotic young citizens. Under certain conditions, a socially approved activity may become dysfunctional in that it fails to serve the goals expected of it, or it may come to serve additional goals that are eventually adopted as the intended goals of the activity. A case in point is American sport, which was adopted initially as a means of improving the health of the young. Now sport can be used as a means of providing economic assistance to aspiring college students, in the form of athletic scholarships.

But there are many cases in which an activity achieves unexpected or even undesirable results, such as when sport becomes a source of income for bookmakers. Such conditions are termed in sociology *anomie*. It happens when a disparity occurs between that which is expected and the actual social outcome of an activity. Anomie pervades a number of leisure pursuits.

How Much Television?

As mentioned before, the motto of French television is "to educate, to inform, and to entertain." Yet it seems television is doing much more entertaining than educating and informing, particularly in the United States. Most countries report less than 2 hours of television watching as a primary daily activity. But A. C. Neilsen, the watchdog of American television-watching patterns, reports that a television set in this country is left on for 7 hours and 49 minutes a day, on the average (Gertner 1986:14a). A household of four persons or more has the television set on for 9 hours, 42 minutes; and a household of one person has it on for 5 hours, 53 minutes, a day. For a single person, this is twice as much time as people report watching television as a primary activity (2 hours, 51 minutes, as per table 11.3 of the United Media Report on Leisure in America, 1983). Perhaps the set is watched only half the time it is on.

Amusive leisure permeates our lives through other means also. Videotapes and movies are good examples. Postman believes that America is engaged in the world's most ambitious experiment to accommodate itself to technological distractions made possible by the electric plug. While America and Americans are prepared to handle tyranny from the outside, they are not ready for the incursion from within (1985:156).

Although Esslin's work is based on television, his axioms describe entertainment in general. Television, states Esslin (1982:61), puts its emphasis on material with a dramatic, emotional, and personalized content. Therefore, it is received by its audience primarily as a medium of entertainment. Accordingly, all programming, including the news, documentaries, and even political broadcasts are ultimately judged by their entertainment value. Entertainment revolves around three cravings or desires. The first is amusement, laughter, light, glamour, and so on. The second is the craving for the cathartic effect of beautiful emotions: sadness, love, pride, and patriotism. These two cravings are harmless in themselves. But the third one, excitement, seems to have been exploited in the mass media in the countries that have greatest freedom of expression, including the United States.

The Media, Violence, and Sex

According to Esslin (1982:62), excitement comes in the form of surprise that makes the viewer forget the passing of time; the thrill arising from empathy with a hero facing danger; and relief from the victory of good over evil. But since excitement operates under the law of diminishing returns, the more accustomed a viewer becomes to violence, the greater the violence has to become to make an impact.

While there are no studies to show the relationship between violence on television and crime in general, there is an alarming increase in juvenile violence in the United States. Is the increase related to the fact that "violent incidents occur on American television on an average of five times per hour during prime time and eighteen times per hour during weekend daytime children's programming" (Esslin 1982:82)?

Television violence became an issue in a court case when a 15-year-old boy was arrested in Miami, Florida, for murdering an 85-year-old woman. His defense was that he was intoxicated by viewing television violence and committed the murder under its influence. The boy was found guilty by the court.

Another concern about television and the movies as the two dominant tools of entertainment all over the world is the overemphasis on sex. Kando (1975:262) suggests that the rock movement and the counterculture of the 1960s took it upon themselves to subvert the sexually repressive society and the value system upon which it has been based since the Enlightenment. The movement freed the libidinal, which could be disruptive. Many authorities today agree with this assessment.

Initially, sexual innuendos were considered harmless entertainment. But Cross asks: "Is entertainment really harmless? Is it possible for people to remain unaffected by the basic premises of such a program because they know its purpose is not to educate but to divert?" (1983:94). She concludes, after citing a number of studies, experiments, and historical events, that programs are subject to personal interpretation regardless of the intention of the producer and director (1983:238).

Spectatoritis

Aldous Huxley warned in *Brave New World* that a culture dominated by amusive leisure and entertainment is a culture at risk. One form of amusive leisure that has raised concerns is spectatoritis, which describes the condition of becoming vicariously involved in a physical activity in lieu of actually participating. It is a condition that has hit many a civilization in the past. Is the United States, and the whole world for that matter, moving toward a jaded sensationalism that will ultimately lead to the "Roman amphitheatre and the Spanish bullfight?" Kraus (1984:108).

It was 140 years ago, in 1850, when civic-minded leaders campaigned for sport as a deterrent to the "pale, pasty-faced, and narrow chested young Americans" (Dulles 1965:183). Young

Americans may not be suffering from these ailments anymore, thanks to the required, although inadequate, physical education in most of the 50 states. But adult Americans do not fare well in this department. Brooks assessed the leisure time physical activity of American adults through analysis of time diaries collected in 1981. She concluded that American adults, 25–65 years of age, were quite sedentary, with only 10%–17% meeting thresholds of physical activity thought to prevent cardiovascular disease (1987:455–60). Cardiovascular ailments are the leading cause of death in America.

ATYPICAL LEISURE BEHAVIOR

Typically, many laymen and professionals expect leisure behavior to take place in a camp, a gymnasium, or at home. In reality, there are many leisure activities that take place in bars, cafes, and the casinos. Pot parties and drag queen contests take place in the free hours of modern society. To ignore these places and events will not make them go away, but to study them will help us to understand them.

Alcohol and Leisure

Drinking alcoholic beverages has been part of many societies but is usually controlled in such a way that few, if any, members become alcoholics. When the drinking of alcohol is kept as part of meals or rituals, few problems arise. For example, Orthodox Jews drink alcohol as part of their religious ritual. The Italians drink wine exclusively with meals. The Cantonese Chinese drink as part of both ceremonials and meals. Yet drinking problems among these groups are few and no alcoholism is found among them (Trice 1966:23). On the other hand, there are societies that allow drinking as an activity *sui generis,* neither with meals nor on special occasions but as an activity in and of itself. Another phenomenon is the serving of alcohol in an establishment, the most famous of which is the English pub, described in chapter 9. The German beer hall also gained notoriety.

These two establishments, the pub and the beer hall, are agents for and places of leisure. Chubb and Chubb (1981:372) suggest that in smaller communities in Britain, public drinking seems to be under control because of the strong tradition in the community. At the other extreme are the large pubs in industrial cities where the mostly male clientele emphasizes hard drinking. In the United States, cocktail lounges became a part of many hotels and restaurants, and drinking became a way of whiling away the time.

According to de Grazia, since alcoholic drinking is banned on the job in the United States and drinking wine with meals is rare, alcoholic drinking takes place after work and after dinner, the hours of free time (1962:95). Drinking at home predominates over tavern and bar drinking. Home is the place for parties and ceremonials when drinking takes place. Drinking also takes place in the tavern, the present form of the old saloon and speakeasy. Taverns number in the hundreds of thousands, and rank among the most frequented recreation outlets (Trice 1966:16). Yet hardly a study exists on drinking and leisure, an oversight lamented by Cosper and others (1985). They assert that a study of the public drinking patterns of Canadians is not only of descriptive value, but is potentially of theoretical importance in understanding the place of leisure in contemporary society.

Cosper interviewed 1,706 Canadians age 18 and over representing the 10 Canadian provinces. The purpose of the investigation was to find out why people go to public drinking establishments, how often, and if they go to a regular place to drink. The investigator found that 22% of Canadians do not drink and 32% do not drink in public. Of the remaining 46%, 30% go to a lounge, 24% to a tavern or beverage room (beer and wine only), 27% to a private club, 8% to a night club, and 11% drink in sports facilities/outdoor locations. Their reasons for going to the drinking establishments are provided in table 14.1. Companionship, entertainment, and socializing, as well as eating, are the main reasons for going to drinking establishments in Canada.

Table 14.1 Reasons for going to regular public drinking establishments (%)

Reason	First given	Second given
To drink	2	3
To meet old friends	16	14
To make new friends	2	3
Accompany someone	24	21
Pass the time	2	5
Relax	8	16
Entertainment	20	24
Play games	1	1
Eat	20	10
Other	4	2
Total	99	100

Source: Cosper, R., et al., "Public Drinking in Canada," Society and Leisure 8(2) 1985, p. 712. Presses de Universite du Quebec. Reprinted with permission.

In Great Britain, a government survey found that nine out of ten adults drink alcohol at least occasionally, while 67% of all males and 76% of 18–24-year-olds visit a public house at least once a month (Roberts 1978:29). Gross claims that "social drinking may run second only to television watching as America's favorite pastime and the two habits are mutually reinforcing" (1983:3). Gross reports that some believe the concern expressed by temperance societies that increased free time would lead to destructive activities has been realized. Others do not feel that public drinking is a problem. In fact, Crompton asks the question "Why can't I get a beer when I go to the Recreation Center?" (1982:26). He suggests people in America drink anyway, and selling alcohol would be an income-generating proposition for the park and recreation departments.

The reaction to Crompton's proposal was swift, polarizing park and recreation personnel across the United States. Some were for selling alcohol on the premises, particularly the agencies with special provision for festive events. Others were against the sale of alcohol in a recreational facility on both moral and legal grounds (Kraus 1984:384).

Drugs and Leisure

Kando (1975:262) claims that the counterculture of the 1960s rejected substances such as alcohol and nicotine as belonging to the establishment and speed and amphetamines as belonging to the delinquent subculture. The hippies of the 1960s opened the door for recreational drugs as part of a new life-style.

Recreation was tied to drugs by the National Commission on Marijuana and Drug Abuse when it identified five different patterns of drug abuse (1973): (1) experimental drug use, (2) social or recreational drug use, (3) circumstantial-situational drug use, (4) intensified drug use, and (5) compulsive drug use (1973). The Commission suggested that recreational use of drugs assumes certain patterns, as in the ritualized pot parties of the 1960s. Such use is voluntary, thus recreational. While dependence and risk are low at this level of drug use, there is the possibility for greater dependence and risk.

Sociologically speaking, marijuana use in this country and in many other countries may have signaled a drastic shift in the ways human beings sought pleasure and reduced discomfort and distress. After all, that is what drugs do. With the decriminalization of the possession of marijuana that began with the state of Oregon in October 1973, a new phase in drug use was upon us. Nine other states followed suit. Was Snyder right when he wrote the following (1972)?

> *Marijuana is symbolic of a more passive,* contemplative, *and less competitive attitude toward life than has been traditional in the United States. It is usually denounced by people who like things the way they are. Whether society accepts or rejects the drug will undoubtedly have some influence on the evolution of our national character [emphasis added].*

Twenty years have passed and America is not passive, contemplative, or less competitive. Despite the decriminalization of marijuana in many states, the national mood is conservative, as shown by the election of a conservative president for two terms in the 1980s. The decriminalization acts were probably a reaction to the overcrowded prisons that were becoming increasingly packed with young Americans of good potential, not because the new way of achieving pleasure through drugs was becoming a universally acceptable practice in America.

Although a small portion of the population, basically young, still uses drugs, Americans are far from being hedonistic, as shown in the United Media study (1983). Today, drug testing is being required in many workplaces, and recently there has been a crackdown on its use by amateur and professional athletes. Lapchick (1986:276) estimates that recreational drug use is practiced by 5.6 million high school athletes. It is also widespread among college athletes. There is great concern over the use of hard drugs, particularly among professional athletes, who serve as role models for so many young Americans.

The year 1986 saw a number of cases of drug abuse among professional athletes in America. These involved not only marijuana and cocaine but the use of steroids, which are believed to increase strength and performance. W. O. Johnson estimated that 40% to 90% of professional football players were using them (1985). He also revealed that 32 football players from a major university were involved in these drugs and that the drugs are being widely used by high school athletes.

While there is no evidence of wide use of drugs among spectators of sport events, there is ample evidence that audiences at musical concerts, particularly rock and country music, are deeply committed to such use. Drugs are also used to enhance other leisure pursuits: "whether ballooning, motorcycling, concert-going, or driving a car, some participants like to season their perceptions with mind-bending substances" (Bammel and Bammel 1982:180).

The attitude of many young citizens toward drug use has troubled public recreation personnel in both the United States and Canada. They now have two battles on their hands, alcohol and drugs, which some believe should not be allowed in the supposedly wholesome recreational environment. "For some anxious prophets of doom, it is the symbol of the coming collapse" (Bammel and Bammel 1982:181). Others believe that drug use is a sign of an affluent society that is suffering from collective boredom. The organized recreational movement that started over eight decades ago was not prepared to handle this new situation, and it must adapt to it.

Public recreation professionals may find solace in the fact that marijuana's daily use among American high school students, though rising from 6% in 1975 to a high of 10.7% in 1978, declined to 9.1% in 1980 and was down to 7% in 1982 (Ray 1983:15).

Gambling and Leisure

Social scientists do not agree about why people gamble. Perhaps it is done for material gain, as suggested by some anthropologists. Or is it done to fulfill a psychological need? In a review of literature on gambling, Smith and Preston (1985:217) found that 11 motives were used to explain gambling: monetary gain, play, prestige, learned role, sociability, escape, intellectual exercise, luck, excitement, curiosity, and masochism. They interviewed 233 subjects in the greater Las Vegas metropolitan area, using questions derived from these 11 motives. Table 14.2 shows their responses, indicating that leisure, play, and recreation were selected by 91% (211) of the respondents as their reason for gambling. The investigators asked each respondent at the end of the interview to rank the 11 motives in order of importance. Table 14.3 shows that leisure, play, and recreation still ranked the highest, followed by boredom and excitement.

These findings corroborate the findings of the Michigan Survey Research Center for the United States Commission on National Policy toward Gambling (Kallick-Kauffmann 1979). The study showed that most gambling is done to have fun with friends, and for excitement, but not for monetary reasons. But when the respondents were asked why others gamble, an increased number suggested that

it was for monetary gain. Smith and Preston suggest that the respondents were probably trying to present their motives in a socially acceptable light to avoid the stigma attached to gambling, which is still perceived as creating social and psychological problems and associated with crime and vice.

Abt and others (1984) suggest that social scientists should adopt an alternative perspective of gambling. Rather than viewing it as a socially deviant activity, it should be viewed as a form of play that has many of the structural and functional components of acceptable sport activity. For instance, gambling has conventional rules for determining participation, for determining legitimate winning and losing, and for judging performance. Moreover, gambling has regulatory commissions, standardized equipment, and allows for sociability.

According to Kallick-Kauffmann (1979:14), there are three major avenues for gambling in the United States: legal-commercial gambling, gambling among friends, and illegal gambling. More men, blacks, and Hispanics are among the reported 16 million illegal gamblers in the United States. There are forty legal gambling activities, most of which are leisure pursuits as well. Gamblers, as a group, appear to desire more stimulation in their lives and their leisure pursuits. Kallick-Kauffmann found that nongamblers spend more time in passive and home-based activities, while gamblers spend more time in active pursuits outside the home. As a whole, gamblers spend more than nongamblers on recreation and vacations, and illegal gamblers more than regular gamblers (1979:22–23).

Does gambling constitute a social problem? To answer this question, Dielman (1979:36–42) tried to tie gambling to moral decay. He operationalized moral decay as a set of social problems, including marital and family disruptions, job dissatisfaction and absenteeism, garnishment of wages, and alcohol consumption. He related these variables to four levels of gambling activity: no betting at all, legal gambling with friends or commercially, legal and illegal gambling, and heavy betting on illegal

Table 14.2 Number of "Yes" responses to questions designed to indicate specific gambling motives

Categories of Motives	Total number of "Yes" responses	
Is one of the reasons you gamble . . .	Number	Percentage of total sample
to engage in play, leisure, and recreation?	211	91
to relieve boredom and generate excitement?	104	45
to gain monetary profit?	91	39
to have a new experience and out of curiosity?	73	32
to challenge decision-making skills?	70	30
as a result of a learned role?	66	29
to help escape frustrations?	62	27
as a result of your special luck?	55	24
to be sociable and gregarious?	49	21
to gain prestige from others?	45	20
a result of masochism and self-guilt?	36	16

Source: Smith, R., and F. Preston, "Expressed Gambling Motives: Accounts in Defense of Self." In B. Gunter, et. al. (Editors) Transition to Leisure: Conceptual and Human Issues, *1985, p. 224. University Press of America. Reprinted with permission.*

Table 14.3 Total number of times that respondents mentioned a category of motives as explaining their gambling behavior

Categories of motives	Total times that the category was mentioned	
	Number	Percentages of total sample
Play, leisure, and recreation	207	89
Boredom and excitement	103	45
Decision making	80	35
Sociability and gregariousness	74	32
Monetary profit	73	32
New experience and curiosity	71	31
Escape frustration	35	15
Learned role	31	14
Prestige	24	11
Belief in personal luck	23	10
Masochism and self-guilt	0	0

Source: Smith, R., and F. Preston, "Expressed Gambling Motives: Accounts in Defense of Self." In B. Gunter, et. al. (Editors) Transition to Leisure: Conceptual and Human Issues, *1985, p. 224. University Press of America. Reprinted with permission.*

activities. Dielman concluded that there is a relationship between unsatisfactory marital life and the level of gambling activities. Absenteeism and tardiness were also more prevalent among bettors than nonbettors, more so among those who use illegal channels. Garnishment of wages was significantly higher among illegal bettors. In addition, heavy and illegal bettors change their residences one-third more times than nonbettors or light bettors. Bettors reported consuming alcohol three times as many days per year as nonbettors.

Compulsive gamblers, those characterized by the preoccupation with and urge to gamble frequently, experience problems such as becoming financially insolvent and incapable of supporting themselves and their family. They may practice embezzlement and forgery and serve prison terms. While slightly over 1% of American males, and slightly less than 1% of American females are considered compulsive gamblers, their deleterious effects on society include loss of funds, loss of time, wounded emotions, and cost of imprisonment.

What about recreational gamblers, those whose gambling is a leisure pursuit? McGurrin and others (1982:88–97) conducted a survey of 155 items on 105 casino visitors, 90 racetrack gamblers, and 75 who use both establishments, as well as 325 nongamblers. They conclude that the stereotype of the gambler as a socially isolated, psychopathological deviant with a compulsive drive to destroy himself and others does not fit the picture of a recreational gambler. Gambling to him or her is play, and there seems to be an aspect of ritualism in both social and gambling behaviors.

In Frey's sociological review of gambling (1984:107–21), he suggests that if one is exposed to gambling as a child, and if opportunities are available and legal, one is more likely to gamble. Therefore, with the widespread legalization of gambling around the world, a greater proportion of the world population will gamble, either legally or illegally. The reason for legalization is financial. Plesser and others (1986) estimate that in the United States $177 billion was handled in both legal and illegal games in 1984 and produced an estimated $18.8 billion in gross revenues, or about an 11.6% increase over 1983. Lotteries, legal bookmaking, and slot machines showed the most growth in 1984. Figures on illegal gambling are unavailable. Total state lottery revenues increased by 37% in 1984 to $4.148 billion, basically because of new states entering the field. Slot machines in Nevada and New Jersey casinos took in $2.7 billion in the same year, an increase of 12.3% over 1983. Table games gained only 6.6%. Pari-mutuel betting in horse racing, on- and off-track revenues, rose by about 4.6%, but bingo games declined. Legal bookmaking showed an increase of 58% in 1983, but only 30% in 1984.

The number one form of illegal gambling in the United States is sport bookmaking. Plesser and others (1986:63) assert that radio and television, which have brought every type of sport into homes, account for the sport betting business. Most local newspapers make point-spreads readily available, and most make predictions about the outcome of the games. About one in four Americans bets either occasionally or frequently. Most of them are middle-aged men earning over $25,000 a year. The practice spread to college sport and is blamed for the point shaving that has plagued basketball, where it is easy to manipulate (shave or reduce) points to suit a particular party. Plesser suggests that the increased use of expensive drugs among the players leaves them vulnerable to gamblers (1986:67). In 1974, the United States Department of Justice estimated the level of illegal sport bidding at $35 billion annually. Nevada is the only state where sport betting is legal (Ibrahim and Cordes 1986:6).

Human Sexuality and Leisure

Nelson Foote (1958) suggests that by the nature of evolution, human sexuality is more than a mere biological function, indeed, that it might as well be a form of leisure. Such a stance is moot, but it points to the interactive relationship between leisure, whether amusive or recreational, and human sexuality.

Kando (1975:262) suggests that in America, the counterculture of the 1960s put its permanent stamp on the relationship between sex and leisure. In the January 1971 issue of *Playboy,* Allan Watts showed the numerous ways in which sex could be leisurely. He borrowed from the Kama Sutra (see leisure in ancient India, chap. 6).

Is sex a form of leisure? The United Media Enterprises report on leisure in America includes a section on the frequency of sexual activity in the respondents' lives (1983:35). The data do not reveal if indeed there is a relationship between leisure and sex; it only shows how many times the respondents engaged in sex.

Table 14.4 Lifetime and 1974 betting participation

	Lifetime		1974		
	Participation (%)	Share of betting activities (%)	Participation (%)	Share of betting activities (%)	Holding power (%)
Card games with friends	52.8	11	38.4	16	72
Lottery ticket	30.0	6	24.1	10	80
Professional football w/friends	25.8	5	20.2	8	77
Bingo	43.9	9	18.7	8	44
Professional baseball w/friends	25.7	5	17.7	7	70
Horse races	34.6	7	14.8	6	43
Miscellaneous events	22.1	5	14.8	6	68
Pool, billiards	18.3	4	11.3	7	61
Check pool	22	5	11.2	7	50
College football w/friends	17.8	4	11.1	7	61
Casinos	26.7	6	9.6	4	27
Fights or wrestling w/friends	13.7	3	7.7	3	57
Dice	20.8	4	7.6	3	38
Bowling	13.2	3	7.2	3	54
Professional basketball w/friends	8.3	2	6.3	3	66
Illegal card games	11.7	3	5.9	3	50
Pinball	14.6	3	5.6	2	40
College basketball w/friends	8.7	2	5.0	2	55
Tennis, golf w/friends	6.2	1.3	4.7	2	83
Auto racing	7.1	1.5	4.1	2	57
Dog tracks	14.4	3	3.9	2	29
Chess, checkers, dominoes	7.2	2	3.7	1.5	57
Sports cards	3.1	0.6	3.0	1.2	1.00
Numbers	7.2	1.5	3.0	1.2	43
Hockey w/friends	4.5	0.9	2.5	1.0	55
Jai alai	5.4	1.3	2.4	1.0	37
Horses w/bookies	7.3	1.5	2.4	1.0	33
Elections	9.1	2	2.3	1.0	22

Source: Kallick-Kaufmann, M., "The Micro and Macro Dimensions of Gambling in the United States," Journal of Social Issues 35(3) 1979, p. 17. The Society for the Psychological Study of Social Issues. Reprinted with permission.

But William Devall's study does attempt to show such a relationship. Devall wrote an exploratory essay on leisure and life-styles among gay men (1979). He argues that gay culture and gay life-styles are leisure life-styles and that these leisure life-styles are examples of emergent life-styles of many people in advanced industrial societies. Devall contends that for a growing number of gay men, avocational career is more important than a conventional work career or job because in the former they can express their gay social identity. This may be due to the fact that the people in North America tolerate gays but do not trust them, as shown by a Gallup poll of 1977 (Devall 1979:185).

It was a decade ago when Devall suggested that the kinds of leisure life-styles that many gay men in urban centers lead may be prototypical of the postmodern leisure life-style in other segments of the population. He suggested that if persons in advanced industrial societies become mobile, travel more, change residence more frequently, and have a series of partners rather than a lifelong marriage, are more affluent and more cosmopolitan in their attitudes, then gay men are the avant-garde of modernity. But such a life-style was not and still is not limited to gay men. It is a function of the change taking place among all social groups, and is not necessarily limited to gay men.

Moreover, Devall agrees that the gay men's life-style is hedonistic; yet this is not the case with the life-style of most Americans, as revealed in the United Media's findings. Only 15% of Americans go to the bars or nightclubs once or twice a week, and 36% say they have an alcoholic drink at least once or twice a week. While about half of the re-spondents (54%) engage in sexual activity at least once a week, 22% of the adult population say they never engage in sexual activity (1983). The survey was taken before the AIDS crisis had to be faced by the general American public, which indicates that the avant-garde life-style of the gay men was not that influential.

Perhaps the most important lesson from the gay community for leisure theory is that leisure became their main mode of expression as they were alien-ated from the work world. Such "privilege" is lim-ited to the leisure class, those who do not have to work, or do not need to identify with work or a career. Groups other than gay men may benefit from their experience and follow suit. In fact, a trend to find expression and meaning in leisure pursuits was reported by Hintereder in West Ger-many (1988:32).

DESTRUCTIVE LEISURE BEHAVIOR

This section presents three leisure behaviors that are destructive. Vandalism in the leisure place has plagued public and private recreational facilities all over the world. Violence in sport has grown out of control. Most gang activity and delinquent be-havior carries an element of play, yet leads to de-struction of life and property.

Vandalism in the Leisure Place

The term *vandalism* denotes deliberate, malicious destruction of property. The park is the place that suffers the most from vandalism. The problem is not a recent one. Sax (1976) quotes the following paragraph from a report written only a few years after the establishment of Yellowstone as Ameri-ca's first national park in 1872.

The visitors prowled around with shovels and axes, chopping and hacking and prying up great pieces of the most ornamental work they could find; women and men alike joining in the barbarous pastime.

In a later study, Campbell and others (1968) took three years to investigate undesirable behav-iors in three campgrounds: one in a national forest, another in a national park, and a third in a state park. The campgrounds were all large, water-oriented, well developed, and drew overflow crowds. Sixty percent of vandalism observed was directed at the facilities, 30% directed at the environment, and 10% at property. Vandalism toward the facil-ities was done mainly by children, and vandalism toward the environment mainly by adults. The acts were done more for entertainment than out of ig-norance of the rules. Campbell attributed the de-structive behavior to the way these offenders saw the park, not as a place of serenity and contem-plation but as a place of aggregation and enter-tainment. They had little direct contact with nature. They tended to stay close to their camp-sites, visit with friends, take short walks, and play structured games.

Knudson (1984:500–501) suggests that van-dalism can be looked upon in many different ways:

1. Overuse destruction, which often appears to be vandalism but is unintentional.
2. Conflict vandalism, the expression of a user doing what is most logical and natural, regardless of the designer's intent. There may be associated vandalism from nonusers who desire more facilities or changes in existing facilities to meet individual community needs and customs.
3. "No-other-way-to-do-it vandalism," such as sitting on a fence because there is no park bench or leaning a bicycle against a tree because there is no bike rack.
4. Inventive vandalism, such as borrowing a picnic table plank to make a springboard wedged into the jungle gym.

5. Curiosity vandalism, such as pulling up a tree to see what the roots look like—with infinite variations. An associated type stems from irresistible temptation or lack of personal discipline—picking flowers or riding motorbikes up and down a steep grassy hill, producing erosion.

6. Self-expression vandalism is the most common and the most exasperating to some—graffiti on walls and other public places. Somehow, a desperate attempt to be noticed in the anonymity of modern society is easily but pitifully expressed by writing one's name or message in a public place. More imaginative forms include doing seemingly impossible things such as placing big objects in an improbable place for the amazement of friends and other observers.

7. Spin-off vandalism sometimes occurs when other activities lead to the destruction of property, varying from the baseball through the window without apology to the damaging of facilities (and even bystanders) during a gang war in a park.

8. Slovenly vandalism is an expression of bad manners through littering and other carelessness. This may be the least destructive but most expensive form.

9. Malicious vandalism is usually the result of the individual wanting to get back at society or a particular agency or individual for real or imagined mistreatment.

10. Thrill or dare vandalism arises from the goading of friends or an individual desire for excitement and may be exceedingly dangerous to the individual and to the public.

Violence in Sport

An estimated 400 million viewers, about 10% of the world population, were tuned to Brussels for the European Cup final between Britain's Liverpool and Italy's Juventus of Turin, on 28 May 1985. Forty-five minutes before the scheduled 8:15 P.M. kick-off, a group of young Liverpool fans swarmed into adjoining sections of the Italians, throwing rocks and bottles and pushing the partition. In the process, 38 persons were crushed to death and 400 were injured. The blame was put squarely on the British and their soccer teams were banned from playing in many European countries. While spectators in many parts of the world have acted violently in the sport arena, the British suffer more from sports violence at home.

According to Guttmann (1986:160), British soccer has made a special contribution to spectator violence since the supporters of the Tottenham Spurs rioted in Rotterdam in 1974. Although British "football hooliganism" has acquired notoriety, the problem is hardly just British or European.

When a Uruguayan soccer referee disallowed a Peruvian goal against Argentina in 1964, which would have equalized the score, the Peruvian fans toppled the steel-link fence and set fire to the stadium. Unfortunately, the police fired tear gas and in the struggle to leave the burning stadium, 287 to 328 persons were crushed to death. In 1967, two rival clubs started a shooting battle in Turkey over a soccer match, ending in 42 dead. A year later, a group of hooligans in Buenos Aires, Argentina, threw burning newspapers on people exiting on a spiral stairway, leading to 71 deaths. In 1970, 2 million persons took to the streets of Rio de Janeiro to celebrate Brazil's winning of the World Cup, a riot erupted that ended with 1,800 injured and 44 dead. In 1974, when the Egyptian officials changed the location of a soccer match to a stadium that held 45,000 people after selling 100,000 tickets, 49 people were killed. An enthusiast waving the wrong flag was fatally stabbed in Milan, Italy, in 1984 (Guttmann 1986:160).

In comparison, the American fans seem to be very tame. There were only 312 sport-related riots in the United States between 1960 and 1972 and they have not accelerated to the level of soccer hooliganism. Few Americans have been killed in spectator violence and most of the disorders involved fist fights, the use of sticks, and throwing cans and bottles. There have been a few fights in the sport arena with racial overtones.

According to Guttmann, the Soviet bloc maintains that they have no spectator disorders, which is not true. Soviet tour guides warn tourists to stay away from soccer matches (1986:163).

Another problem related to sport violence is the phenomenal increase in sport injuries. According to Yeager (1979:17), there are 50,000 knee injuries a year in the United States alone requiring surgery. Most of the injuries involve boys 15 to 19 years old. He blames the American frantic pursuit of victory on the playing field for the increased level of injury. "Just as winning has become sacred, the perception of athletic foes as mortal enemies has become crucial to success in today's competition" (1979:10).

According to Yeager (1979:111–17), 30 young people a year have died playing football during most of this century. About 300,000 youth are treated annually for football injuries. Another study (Greenberg 1984) shows that while football has improved its safety records appreciably in recent years, catastrophic injuries that result in permanent disability are increasing in "new sport." The rate of catastrophic injuries per 100,000 participants in college sport in 1983–84 was 0.00 for baseball, cross-country, soccer, track, and wrestling, 3.55 for swimming, 6.63 for basketball, 6.83 for tennis, 9.33 for football, 14.27 for gymnastics, 12.73 for ice hockey, and 20.25 for lacrosse. Among high schoolers, the highest rates were in ice hockey, 4.16; lacrosse, 2.25; football, 2.28; and wrestling 1.96. During the same period there were 57 fatalities, most of which came from football.

Gangs, Delinquency and Leisure

About half a century ago, Butler (1940:20) wrote:

Since recreation helped to build character, it is obviously a potent agent in the prevention of crime and delinquency. Little wonder then that agencies directly concerned with this problem are turning to recreation as an effective ally! . . . Idle time is not an asset to any community. Most delinquent and criminal acts are committed during leisure time, and a large percentage of them are performed in order to get the means for the enjoyment of leisure.

A study on the relationship between recreation and delinquency was conducted by the Chicago Recreation Commission in 1942. It found that delinquent boys attended movies more frequently than nondelinquent boys and spent less time in supervised recreation. Nonetheless, the Commission recommended that to control delinquency more supervised recreation should be provided (Neumeyer and Neumeyer 1949:252).

Over thirty years ago, Meyer and Brightbill (1956:417–18) wrote,

Common sense indicated that using young people's idleness and free time for constructive recreation activities helps to forestall some delinquency . . . the role of recreation is not eliminating delinquency but rather holding the line against character disintegration through providing the chance for positive personal development.

The Gluecks (1968:194) compared delinquents and nondelinquents in their leisure tendencies and concluded that the homes of delinquent boys were so unattractive that they preferred the streets for their leisure activities. Moreover, the delinquents had no united family enjoyment of leisure. Outside the home, delinquents frequented taverns, barrooms, and nightclubs, usually with others of questionable character. The Gluecks conclude that there is a strong body of evidence that delinquents dislike the confinement of playgrounds, supervised recreation, or attendance at clubs, which they rarely join on their own initiative.

No wonder then, that MacLean and others (1985:13) suggest that although recreation may help to prevent antisocial behavior, it is not a panacea for social ills. Recreation programs do enrich the life of the majority. To deter a minority from delinquency is an important, but secondary, contribution of a recreation program. Kraus

(1984:358) suggests that recreation must be linked to other community services to become effective in combating delinquency.

That was attempted in Project Turn Around, a pilot project in Orange County, California, that was oriented to prevent delinquency (Bockelman 1973). It was designed to utilize 27 nonprofessional volunteers to provide counseling and guidance to 27 delinquents. The primary objectives of Project Turn Around were to offset factors such as school truancy, academic deficiency, incorrigibility, idleness, and unstable family environments. This author concludes that, when compared to the control group after an experimental period of one year, the pilot did not achieve the desired results in behavior changes. Like other delinquency reduction programs, community volunteer projects are not panaceas.

The British approach to the relationship between leisure and delinquency is different, but is still based on the notion that if a discrepancy exists between the goal toward which one aspires and the legitimate means to achieve it, deviant behavior will result. Vocational aspiration may be important to the deprived American youth, but British researchers found deprived British youth to be remarkably realistic and had reconciled themselves to their jobs with little difficulty. Their relevant aspirations have to do with the leisure life-style they want to adopt rather than educational certificates and jobs that they want to achieve (Roberts 1970:99). Downes (1966) found that the young Britons he studied possessed an urge to experience excitement and to engage in a variety of pursuits that cost money. When and if neither money nor excitement can be legitimately obtained, these young people resort to deviant methods for obtaining satisfaction.

SUMMARY

Provisions for free time, either economical (reduced work hours, more holidays, and more pay) or social (acceptable leisure behavior and socialization into it), have led to an expansion, and in many cases an explosion, in the sphere of leisure. Mass leisure may have come too soon. As seen in the section on West Germany, the term *leisure* itself is not a century old. Nonetheless, there is still uneven distribution of leisure, particularly in regard to gender, even in the most democratic of countries, the United States. Moreover, in many countries there is an uneven distribution between rural and urban areas. The contrast is glaring in the Third World countries, where urban residents enjoy most of the leisure pursuits of their urban counterparts in industrial nations.

Mass leisure creates a number of problems that may have social repercussions. For instance, are people the world over watching too much television? Is the amount of sex and violence depicted on television a danger to the public welfare? Has the world become nations of spectators rather than participants? Studies have been conducted to reveal the relationship between alcoholic consumption and drug use and leisure behavior. Many claim that sex has become more or less a leisure activity, not a mere biological function. Many a social scientist has warned that SAD, (sex, alcohol, and drugs) brings down mighty civilizations. Would today's mass leisure be accountable if such dreadful events took place? Will gambling's increasing legalization lead to unwanted social problems, fraud, marital conflicts, and alcoholism?

The above concerns have not materialized into social problems. But there are destructive elements of leisure behavior. Vandalism in the leisure place, violence in sport, and gangs and delinquency can be counted as outcomes of the contemporary mass leisure scene.

REVIEW QUESTIONS

1. In what way is leisure unevenly distributed?
2. What does the term *anomie* mean? How is it related to leisure?
3. List some atypical leisure behaviors and discuss their impact on society.
4. How destructive is destructive leisure behavior? Give examples.

SUGGESTED READINGS

Esslin, M. 1982. *The age of television.* San Francisco: W. H. Freeman.

Gross, L. 1983. *How much is too much?: The effects of social drinking.* New York: Random House.

Lapchick, R., ed. 1986. *Fractured focus: Sport as reflection of society.* Lexington, KY: Lexington Books.

Plesser, D. et al. 1986. *Gambling: Crime or recreation.* Plano, TX: Information Aids.

AN OVERVIEW OF PART FOUR

Part Four deals with the forces that shape leisure behavior, social and physical. The social forces include the family and other socializing agents. The impact of social forces is difficult to measure precisely. Yet there is enough evidence to show that the school as well as various secondary groups such as youth clubs, places of worship, and voluntary associations leave their marks on leisure behavior. The demographic factors of age, gender education, occupation, income, and residence determine to a great extent our leisure choices.

Besides the social forces listed above, certain personal traits such as physique, temperament, and personality traits affect leisure behavior. One's lifestyle shows a unique interplay between one's values on the one hand, and the social forces on the other. The concept of life-style is now being used by social scientists in lieu of social class or ethnic groups.

Social forces and personal traits alone do not shape leisure behavior. For leisure behavior takes place within physical settings. Besides one's home and the immediate vicinity, parks, schoolyards, community centers, and coffeehouses serve as recreational outlets. The circle of one's activity expands with age or wealth to include other physical settings such as plazas, shopping centers, health clubs, private clubs, and the fair. In many instances, one's workplace may become the main source of one's recreative leisure. The library, the museum, the theater, and the movies will play their part. The physical settings also include the beach, the racetrack, and the sports arena. As the circle of one's interaction widens even further, theme parks, camps and campgrounds, the college campus, resorts, regional parks and forests, and possibly a second home will be settings for recreation. Eventually, for many in today's world, a trip to a national park or forest at home or abroad may provide a recreational experience.

The expansion of leisure pursuits for the world's 5 billion inhabitants has not been without problems. Some of these problems are in the nature of restrictions. For despite expansion, there are those who suffer from a lack of leisure, some by choice, others because of circumstances beyond their control. In many cases, this lack is a product of the dominant value systems or economic conditions. In other cases, the mere location of the individual restricts his or her leisure choices.

Moreover, some leisure pursuits have become "destructive" in that they do not provide the expected outcome. For instance, sport as a healthy endeavor may have produced a nation, or nations, of sedentary spectators. Television too, may have concentrated on the amusive at the expense of the contemplative. Many social scientists are trying to show the correlation between the media and violence. Although hard evidence is lacking, the idea has some merit. Other social scientists suggest that many leisure choices have not been treated under the leisure rubric because they are not typical of what professional recreators promote and adopt as activities. Drinking alcoholic beverages, the partaking of drugs, and gambling have not been treated as leisure choices. To ignore them, however, does not render them nonrecreational. To try to understand the factors involved in selecting them would at least shed some light on the psychological and social motivations behind them. The same may be said of certain sexual behaviors that are, like alcohol consumption, drug use and gambling, leisurely oriented.

But most distressing is the rise of destructive leisure behavior, such as vandalism of the leisure place, violence in sport, and "playful" gang activities. In the well-publicized case of the four young men who attacked a jogger in New York City's Central Park in the spring of 1989, the motivational factor given by one of the youngsters was "wilding." When asked to explain, he added, to have "fun."

EPILOGUE

I began writing this epilogue on a desert island in the Red Sea off the Egyptian coast. A 20-passenger boat took a group of tourists from the main village to Gifton Island to spend the day. The main activities were to be shell-gathering and snorkeling. Five nationalities were represented on board. The American, British, German, Italian, and Japanese tourists did not seem to mind the 41° C (105° F) heat. They enjoyed the day and the lunch provided to them by the crew.

In fact, a few days earlier, other foreign tourists enjoyed visiting the famed 4,000-year-old monument of Abu Simbel, 600 miles south of Gifton, situated on Lake Nasser. This is a man-made lake created by the Aswan High Dam. Its building necessitated moving the monument 180 feet up a hill, at a cost of $40 million. Accordingly, the monument gained world-wide fame. There were additional foreign tourists at Abu Simbel—Australians, Canadians, French, and in fact an Ecuadorian group—all ignoring the 43° C (110° F) heat.

These foreign tourists have the time, and also the money, to pursue an activity for its own sake—either visiting monuments built 2,000 years before the birth of Christ or snorkeling around reefs and marine life in the Red Sea. One could venture to say that if the ancient Egyptians had not built the two colossal temples for Ramses the Great and his wife Nefertari at Abu Simbel, and if God had not endowed the Red Sea with reefs and exotic fish, these tourists, who came from thousands of miles away, would have found another activity to pursue—an activity done for its own sake during the time freed from work and civic/familial obligation.

This is the era of mass leisure. Not long ago, touring historical sites in exotic lands and snorkeling in far-away seas was limited to a certain class, a leisure class that was dominant in a previous era. But tourism and aquatics are only two vious era. But tourism and aquatics are only two among many activities that are pursued for their own sake. Watching television, participating in and watching sport, and attending cultural events are on the rise in almost all of today's societies. These activities, the motivation behind them, and the impact they may have on the individual and society are the central concerns of leisure studies. How some of these activities became dominant in a society and how they vary from society to society are the central concerns of this work.

A few more words on the conduct of both foreign and native tourists at the main village of Gifton, and a comparison of them, may help illustrate some of the changes that have taken place in human societies and their affect-effect relationship to the leisure sphere.

This work is predicated on Talcott Parson's notion that societies evolve from "primitive" to intermediate to modern when certain sociocultural conditions are met. A modern society is one that adopts a unified legal-behavioral code that, in general, is observed and followed by all members of the society. The 13 contemporary societies discussed in this work have evolved into modern societies, albeit at different times. The most recent entrants are the four Third-World societies of China, Egypt, India, and Mexico. The Eastern bloc nations of Czechoslovakia, East Germany, Poland, and the USSR and the Western nations of Canada, Great Britain, France, West Germany, and the United States entered that stage much earlier.

In the earlier, intermediate societies, there was more than one legal-behavioral code, which allowed for gaps and discrepancies in the conduct of the society's members. A distinct, elite group arose, conducted itself according to its own code and became a leisure class, with an abundance of discretionary time and surplus of funds. Accordingly, its members selected activities for their own sake and not for monetary gain. Among these activities was tourism, which at one point was limited to the wealthy. An example is the Mena House, a rest house built by the monarch of Egypt in 1870 for the dignitaries that came from Europe to visit the Giza Pyramids.

Today the Mena House is a 5-star hotel. Just meters from Mena House are 4, 3, 2, and no-star hotels that cater to the multitudes of foreign tourists visiting their new "Mecca." Visiting the Giza Pyramids is an activity that average Europeans before the turn of the century, at the time of the building of Mena House, would have never thought possible for themselves. They had neither the time nor the money to do so. One might add that they did not have an interest either. With the help of mass technology, and mass education, today's tourist is interested and is able to afford to visit these ancient relics.

Sport and cultural events were also not long ago limited to the wealthy and the privileged. These activities and more have become what is termed in this work *mass leisure.* Our era of mass leisure has its roots in the activities of the leisure class of the intermediate society and in the ritualized activities of the members of the "primitive" society that preceded it.

Although a society may evolve into a new stage, effects of the earlier stage may linger on. The leisure behavior of the native Egyptian tourist compared to the foreign ones at Gifton village provides an example of this. Egypt has only recently entered the stage of "modernism." As previously stated, the intermediate society allows for discrepancy in conduct, legal and personal, between groups. The gap extends beyond the poor-rich dichotomy to rural-urban, Bedouin-settler, or man-woman. Such was the case at Gifton. Not far from the American-European tourists sat a few native tourists under palm-leaf umbrellas. Almost all native women wore dresses, some at ankle's length. In fact, a few wore the *hijab,* a traditional headgear. Inches away, nonnative female tourists were in their scanty bikinis. While all nonnative men were in shorts or swimsuits, most native men were in pants and shirts. A few of the native men were wearing swimsuits. In other words, the same code was not applied equally to Egyptian men and women. Conservatism, a characteristic of an intermediate society, still hangs on.

Granted, leisure choices vary within a modern society. But the variation is due to personal taste once all other factors such as cost, location, accessibility, and so on are taken into consideration. In the case of an intermediate society, or a society recently emerging from that stage, that is, Egypt, the variation results from a restrictive value system rather than from personal taste, cost, location, accessibility, and so on. A case in point is the noticeable absence of "Arab" tourists either at Gifton or at the ancient monuments. Yet these tourists are found in droves at the local bazaars where shopping is a leisure activity. Here one sees the totally covered female, accompanied by her husband or male-escort who usually bargains on her behalf. To these women, the Egyptian woman has gone too far by sitting on the sandy beaches of Gifton. Money is available for her to stay in a 5-star hotel and for mass shopping, but not for a Gifton or a monument. This behavior is the outcome of the restrictive value system of intermediate society. A further example of this conservatism is that the Arab male may freely use the cafes at the 5-star hotels, while the female must content herself with room service. Mingling with strangers is not appropriate behavior for a female, but is acceptable for the male. It should be pointed out that there are now exceptions to this rule. It is only a matter of time for modernity to set in everywhere.

The intermediate society gave us, through its leisure class, a great number of leisure activities to be practiced in leisure places. The hunting estate of the British monarch and the enchanted gardens of the French royalty are good examples of leisure places that the common person now takes for granted. Table games and parades that were once limited to wealthy Indians and Chinese are now enjoyed by many. In fact, many of today's organized sports—badminton, bowling, croquet, and tennis to name a few—were limited to the aristocracy of the intermediate society.

Many a leisure activity can be traced to the predecessor of the intermediate society, the "primitive" society. The societies that remained at that stage lacked an important cultural element that would have helped them evolve into an intermediate society, that is, a written language. A written language allows for spatial and generational expansion of the dominant culture. Also, these societies are characterized by being simple as well as conservative. Nonetheless, they contributed to the leisure sphere through the activities that dominate the "primitive" society: rituals.

According to the theorists of ritual (Turner 1982a, Grimes 1982), this human activity is biologically based in that rhythmicity and formalization are important ingredients of ritualization. Rhythmicity occurs, for example, in the alternation of systole and diastole and formalization occurs in the tendency to impose order and repetition of body movement. Although ritualization describes the phylogenetically performed ceremonial acts of "animals," these theorists believe it to be the basis of ritual among humans. To Erikson (1977), the first signs of ritualization among humans occur between the newly born and its mother. The newly born awakens in the mother a repertoire of verbal and manipulative behaviors involving the limbic system of the human brain. Suzanne Langer (1972) believes that the bodily communion between mother and infant, which is seen in clinging, is gradually replaced by mental communion that evolves into symbolic collective acts—rituals.

Through rituals, humans may fulfill their need for affirmation and certification. But soon these rituals expand into ceremonies and celebrations, among other things. At this point certain activities are practiced in the rituals in which one may see an element of leisure behavior. There are plenty of examples from observers of "primitive" societies of the past, such as Wood (1871), and scholars of the present, such as Blanchard and Cheska (1985). During the ritual, these "primitive" people danced, sang, acted, and performed as a community, providing us with a good example of what Aristotle called recreative leisure. Eventually and only at a particular stage of societal evolution, certain performers, actors, or singers were pulled out and were asked to perform for an elite, wealthy group. This was the birth of the third form of leisure, amusive leisure, according to Aristotle. His first and most favored form is contemplative leisure. How recreative and amusive leisure emerged from ritual are explained by the following two theorists.

According to Gennep (1960), most rituals either segregate the person from two previous associations, incorporate him into a new experience, or prepare him for a marginal period. In all three cases, the person goes through *limen,* a term used by Turner (1982a) to describe a state of limbo not altogether negative. For to Turner, the sphere of liminality allows those who go through it to proceed between the established social structures in a betwixt-and-between, neither-this-nor-that domain. These are characteristics of leisure. The person selects activities to his liking—the making of a mask, the painting of the body, or the performing of an act. Rituals have the potential of turning into leisure activities. Some did; many did not and continued to be a source of affirmation and certification. But over the years an evolution was taking place. It was Turner who suggested that with industrialization and its concomitant outcomes, rituals are not limited to an activity of small congregation. Some have turned into mass activities, such as concert-going, sport-spectating, theatrical performances, parades, and the like. Thanksgiving is often no longer a quiet dinner with friends and family; it is the watching of a football game in person or on television. The scene is repeated, not only at Christmas in Europe and America, but all over the globe.

Mass leisure is here, but it is not without problems. Despite the gains, there is a lopsided distribution of leisure within each of the societies cited in this work and among them. Differences exist between the industrial societies of the West and the Third-World countries. Within societies, even the most democratic ones, there is an uneven distribution of leisure between rural and urban residents and between inner city and suburban dwellers.

Other vexing problems facing leisure are the negative outcomes of excessive television watching, increased violence in the media, and the dominance of spectating over participating in sport activities. These problems seem to be universal.

What the society should do about atypical leisure behavior—drinking alcoholic beverages, gambling (either legal or illegal), drug use and abuse, and nonconventional sexual conduct—remains a focus of debate between two groups. There are those who think they are leisure activities and deserve our attention, and there are those who would discard them as destructive activities.

Destructive leisure behavior, such as vandalism of the leisure place, violent behavior on the field and court, and gang delinquency, has caused some concern among leisure scientists. Yet, such behavior is not necessarily detrimental to the leisure sector in society. Although undesirable, these behaviors are tolerated by most members of the society.

On the whole, however, in today's society leisure is a welcome and beneficial addition to the lifestyles of most people. It is here to stay and will in fact expand. Leisure provides activities that have an affect-effect relationship with primary groups: family, school, and the neighborhood; and with secondary groups: clubs, places of worship, and voluntary associations. Age, gender, education, occupation, income, and residence play important roles in what leisure pursuits are selected by the individual. So do personal traits and life-style.

Because leisure is so pervasive in life, societies should exert great effort in providing the physical settings for leisure. First and most important is the home, where most leisure activities take place. Playlots, parks, camps, and community centers should be provided in the neighborhood. Each city should have enough parks, clubs, libraries, museums, theaters, and sport arenas to cater to its residents' needs. Campgrounds and larger parks and forests should be planned for regional use. National parks and forests should be provided for all the citizens. Travel and tourism should be looked upon as important ingredients of today's life-style. It goes without saying that providing the above leisure opportunities requires adequate funds. Naturally public support of these leisure opportunities will vary from one society to another depending on its economic status. Even in the very low status society, some support is better than none.

Another form of support in the leisure sphere is the provision of trained specialists in the area of leisure. Some societies have begun this task already; others have not. From all indications, many societies are discovering the need for such a specialist (D'Amours 1986).

BIBLIOGRAPHY

Abrahams, R. 1982. The language of festivals: Celebrating the economy. In *Celebration: Studies in festivity and ritual,* edited by V. Turner. Washington, D.C.: Smithsonian Institution Press.

Abt, V. et al. 1984. Gambling: The misunderstood sport—a problem in social definition. *Leisure Sciences* 6:205–19.

Adams, B., and R. Cromwell. 1978. Morning and night people in the family: A preliminary statement. *The Family Coordinator* 27:5–13.

Adams, J. 1856. *Works II.* Washington, D.C.: AMS Press.

Allen L. et al. 1987. The role of leisure: Satisfaction in rural communities. *Leisure Today* (April):5–8.

Armes, R. 1987. *Third-World film making and the West.* Berkeley: University of California Press.

Artiomov, V. A. et al. 1970. Free time: Problems and perspectives. *Leisure and Society,* 2 (3):18–36.

Attias-Donfut, C., and J. Dumazedier. 1975. The reduction of work time and the increase in leisure in France. *Society and Leisure* 7 (1):45–72.

Baily, D. A. 1975. The growing child and the need for physical activity. In *School-age children: Development and relationship,* edited by M. S. and R. C. Smart. New York: Macmillan.

Baker, Wm. 1982. *Sports in the Western world.* Totowa, NJ: Rowan and Littlefield.

Bammel, G. and L. L. 1982. *Leisure and human behavior.* Dubuque, IA: Wm. C. Brown.

Barker, R. 1986. On the road to recovery: RV makers rev up for a strong year. *Barrons* 24 February:15, 28–30.

Barnes, J. 1984. *The complete works of Aristotle.* Princeton, NJ: Princeton University Press.

Basham, A. L. 1963. *The wonder that was India.* New York: Hawthorn Books.

Beard, J. G., and M. G. Ragheb. 1980. Measuring leisure satisfaction. *Journal of Leisure Research* 12 (1):20–33.

Beck, D., and M. Jones. 1973. *Progress on family problems.* New York: Family Services Association.

Bensman, J., and A. Vidich. 1971. *The new American society.* New York: New York Times Books.

Berlyne, D. E. 1961. *Conflict, arousal and curiosity.* New York: McGraw-Hill.

Bernard, M. 1987. Leisure-rich and leisure-poor: Leisure lifestyles among young adults. *Leisure Sciences,* 10 (2):131–49.

Best, E. 1952. *The Maori as he was.* Wellington, Australia: A. E. Owen, Government Printer.

Betts, J. 1953. The technological revolution and the rise of sport. In *Sport, culture and society,* edited by J. Loy and G. Kenyon. Toronto: Collier-Macmillan.

Bialeschki, M., and K. Henderson. 1986. Leisure in the common world of women. *Leisure Studies,* 5 (3):299–308.

Blanchard, K., and A. Cheska. 1985. *The anthropology of sport: An introduction.* South Hadley, MA: Bergin and Garvey.

Blatt, S., and D. Quinlan. 1972. The psychological effects of rapid shifts in temporal referents. In *The study of time,* edited by J. T. Fraser, F. C. Haber, and G. H. Muller. New York: Springer-Verlag.

Bockelman, C. 1973. The impact of community volunteers on delinquency prevention: An exploratory investigation. *Sociology and Social Research* 57 (3):335–41.

Boothy, J. 1987. Self-reported participation rate: Further comment. *Leisure Studies* 6 (1):99–104.

Bosserman, P. 1975. The evolution of and trends in work and nonwork time in the United States society, (1920–1970). *Society and Leisure* 7 (1):89–132.

Boyle, R. 1962. The ways of life at the country club. *Sports Illustrated XVI* (26 February):69–74.

Boyle, R. 1963. *Sports: Mirror of American life.* Boston: Little, Brown.

Bradshaw, R., and J. Jackson. 1979. Socialization for leisure. In *Leisure: A psychological approach,* edited by H. Ibrahim and R. Crandall. Los Alamitos: Hwong.

Bradshaw, T. K. 1978. Life-styles in the advanced industrial societies. Institute for Governmental Study. Berkeley: University of California Press.

Brasch, R. 1967. *Mexico: A country of contrast.* New York: David McKay.

Brightbill, Ch. 1960. *The challenge of leisure.* Englewood Cliffs, NJ: Prentice-Hall.

Brine, J., M. Perrie, and A. Sutton, eds. 1980. *Home, school and leisure in the Soviet Union.* London: Allen & Unwin.

British Travel Association/University of Keele. 1967. *Pilot national recreation survey,* Report No. 2.

Brodda, H. 1971. Contemporary arts in the Federal Republic. In *Meet Germany.* 14th rev. ed. Hamburg: Atlantik-Brucke.

Brooks, C. M. 1987. Leisure time physical activity assessment of American adults through an analysis of time diaries collected in 1981. *Journal of Public Health* 77 (April):455–60.

Brown, J. D. 1961. *India.* New York: Time.

Bryant, A. 1970. *The Zulu people as they were before the white man came.* New York: Negro University Press.

Buck, P. 1949. *The coming of the Maori.* Wellington, Australia: Whitcombe and Tombs.

Bull, C. N. 1973. Comments on time panel discussion concerned with the future of the sociology of leisure. *Society and Leisure* 5 (1):145–48.

Burch, Wm. 1984. Much ado about nothing—Some reflections on the wider and wilder implications of social carrying capacity. *Leisure Sciences* 6 (4):487–501.

Burdge, R. J. 1969. Levels of occupational prestige and leisure activity. *Journal of Leisure Research* 1 (3):262–74.

Burdge, R. J. 1983. Making leisure and recreation research a scholarly topic: Views of a journal editor, 1972–1982. *Leisure Sciences* 6 (1):99–125.

Burdman, G. M. 1986. *Healthful aging.* Englewood Cliffs, NJ: Prentice-Hall.

Burke, P. 1978. *Popular culture in early modern Europe.* New York: New York University Press.

Burkert, W. 1983. Homo Necans: *The anthropology of ancient Greek sacrificial ritual and myth.* Berkeley: University of California Press.

Burnett, G., and L. Butler. 1987. National parks in the Third World and associated national characteristics. *Leisure Sciences* 9 (1):41–51.

Burns, T. 1973. Leisure in industrial society. In *Leisure and society in Britain,* edited by M. Smith, S. Parker, and C. Smith. London: Allen Lane.

Burton, T. 1979. The development of leisure research in Canada: An analogical tale. *Society and Leisure* 2 (1):13–32.

Burton, T., and T. Kyllo. 1974. *Federal-provincial responsibilities for leisure services in Alberta and Ontario.* Toronto: Ministry of Culture and Sport.

Butler, G. 1976. *Introduction to community recreation.* 5th ed. New York: McGraw-Hill. (First edition 1940.)

Butler, J. 1972. *The theatre and drama of Greece and Rome.* San Francisco: Chandler.

Campbell, F., J. Hendee, and R. Clark. 1968. Law and order in public parks. *Parks and Recreation* 3 (12):28–31, 51–55.

The Canadian Youth Commission. 1946. *Youth and recreation.* Toronto, Ontario: The Canadian Youth Commission.

Carlson, J. 1976. The recreation role. In *Role, structure and the family,* edited by F. L. Nye. New York: Sage.

Carlson, L. 1971. *Mexico: An extraordinary guide.* Chicago: Rand McNally.

Cerullo, M., and P. Ewen. 1982. Having a good time: The American family goes camping. *Radical America* 16 (1–2):13–43.

Chase, D., and G. Godbey. 1983. The accuracy of self reported participation rates. *Leisure Studies* 2(2):231–35.

Cheek, N., and Wm. Burch. 1976. *The social organization of leisure in human society.* New York: Harper & Row.

Cheek, N. H., D. Field, and R. J. Burdge. 1976. *Leisure and recreation places.* Ann Arbor, MI: Ann Arbor Science Publishers.

Chubb, M. and H. R. 1981. *One third of our time? An introduction to recreation behavior and resources.* New York: Wiley and Sons.

Churchill, S. P. 1899. Sports of the Samoans. *Outing* 33:562–68.

Ciepley, M. 1988. Weak dollar comes on strong for U.S. films shown in foreign markets. *Los Angeles Times* 5 January, sec. VI.

Cistriano, J. 1979. Amusement and entertainment. In *Leisure: Emergence and expansion,* edited by H. Ibrahim and J. Shivers. Los Alamitos: Hwong.

Clarke, A. C. 1956. The use of leisure and its relation to levels of occupational prestige. *American Sociological Review* 21:301–7.

Commission on the Reorganization of Secondary Education. 1918. *Cardinal Principles of Secondary Education.* Washington, D.C.: Bureau of Education.

Conner, K. A., and G. L. Bultena. 1979. The four-day workweek: An assessment of its effects on leisure participation. *Leisure Sciences* 2 (1):55–69.

Coppock, J. T. 1982. Geographical contributions to the study of leisure. *Leisure Studies* 1 (1):1–27.

Corbin, C. B., ed. 1980. *A textbook of motor development.* Dubuque, IA: Wm. C. Brown.

Corliss, A. 1986. If heaven ain't a lot like Disney. *Time* 127 (16 June):80.

Cortez, L. A. 1989. Leisure and recreation in Mexico. *Leisure Today* (April):12–13.

Cosper, R., and S. Shaw. 1985. The validity of time-budget studies. *Leisure Sciences* 7 (2):205–25.

Cosper, R., I. Okraku, and B. Neumann. 1985. Public drinking in Canada: A national study of a leisure activity. *Society and Leisure* 8 (2):709–15.

Cousins, N. 1977. The mysterious placebo. *Saturday Review* (1 October):16–18.

Crandall, R., and K. Slivken. 1979. Leisure attitudes and their measurement. In *Social psychological perspectives on leisure and recreation,* edited by S. Iso-Ahola. Springfield: Ch. Thomas.

Crompton, J. 1982. Why can't I get a beer when I go to the recreation center? *Parks and Recreation* 17(8):26.

Cross, D. W. 1983. *Mediaspeak: How television makes up your mind.* New York: Coward-McCann.

Cross, G. S. 1986. The political economy of leisure in retrospective: Britain, France, and the origin of the eight-hour day. *Leisure Studies* 5 (1):69–90.

Csikszentmihalyi, M., and R. Larson, 1984. *Being adolescent.* New York: Basic Books.

Cummings, E., and W. E. Henry. 1961. *Growing old: The process of disengagement.* New York: Basic Books.

Curtis, J. 1971. Voluntary association joining: A cross-national comparative note. *American Sociological Review* 36:872–80.

Cushman, H. B. 1899. *History of the Choctaw, Chickasaw and Natchez Indians.* Stillwater: Redlands Press. (1962 ed.).

D'Amours, M. 1986. *International directory of academic institutions in leisure, recreation and related fields.* New York: World Leisure and Recreation Association.

Dare, B., G. Welton, and Wm. Coe. 1987. *Leisure in Western thought.* Dubuque, IA: Kendall/Hunt.

Davis, F. 1986. *The Ottoman lady.* Westport, CT: Greenwood Press.

Davis, W. S. 1960. *A day in old Athens: A picture of Athenian life.* New York: Biblo and Tanner.

Dawson, D. 1988. Social class in leisure: Reproduction and resistance. *Leisure Sciences* 10 (3):193–202.

Debo, A. 1967. *The rise and fall of the Choctaw Republic.* Norman: University of Oklahoma Press.

de Grazia, S. 1962. *Of time, work and leisure.* New York: Anchor Books.

De Oreo, K., and J. Keogh. 1980. Performance of fundamental motor tasks. In *A textbook of motor development,* edited by C. B. Corbin. Dubuque, IA: Wm. C. Brown.

Department of Communications. 1987. *Marking time: Explorations in time use.* Ottawa: Department of Communications.

Devall, Wm. 1979. Leisure and lifestyles among gay men: An exploratory essay. *International Review of Modern Sociology* 9:179–95.

de Vore, I. 1965. *Primate behavior.* New York: Holt, Rinehart & Winston.

Dewey, J. 1966. *Democracy and education.* New York: Free Press.

Dickason, J. 1983. The origin of the playground: The role of the Boston women's clubs, 1885–1890. *Leisure Sciences* 6 (1):83–97.

Dielman, T. E. 1979. Gambling: A social problem? *Journal of Social Issues* 35 (3):36–42.

Dilts, M. M. 1938. *The pageant of Japanese history.* London: Longmans-Green.

Di Pietro J. 1981. Rough and tumble play: A function of gender. *Developmental Psychology* 17:50–58.

Doell, C., and C. Fitzgerald. 1954. *A brief history of parks and recreation in the United States.* Chicago: The Athletic Institute.

Donze, M. A., and C. Sauvageot. 1979. *China today.* Paris: Editions J. A.

Douville, R., and J. Casanova. 1967. *Daily life in early Canada.* New York: Macmillan.

Downes, D. M. 1966. *The delinquent solution: A study in subculture theory.* London: Routledge.

Dubois, A. J. A. 1906. *Hindu manners, customs and ceremonies.* Glasgow: Oxford University Press.

Dulles, F. R. 1965. *A history of recreation.* 2d ed. New York: Appleton-Century-Crofts.

Dumazedier, J. 1960. Current problems of the sociology of leisure. *International Social Science Journal* 4:522–31.

Dumazedier, J. 1967. *Toward a society of leisure.* New York: Free Press.

Duncan, O. 1964. Social organization and the ecosystem. In *Handbook of modern sociology,* edited by R. Ferris. Chicago: Rand McNally.

Durkheim, E. 1915. *The elementary forms of religious life.* London: Allen & Unwin.

Durkheim, E. 1938. *The role of the sociological method.* Chicago: University of Chicago Press.

Ebrey, P. B. 1981. *Chinese civilization and society: A source book.* New York: Free Press.

Edgerton, E. B. 1979. *Alone together: Social order on an urban beach.* Berkeley: University of California Press.

Edwards, P. K. 1981. Race, residence and leisure styles: Some policy implications. *Leisure Sciences* 4 (2):95–111.

Edwards, R. H. 1915. *Popular amusement.* New York: Association Press.

Eisen, G. 1988. Theories of Play. In *Understanding leisure,* edited by G. Gerson et al. Dubuque, IA: Kendall/Hunt.

Elton, L. B., and M. Messel. 1978. *Time and man.* Oxford: Pergman.

Ely, N. 1987. The power of music. *Scala* (29 December):38.

Encyclopedia of China. 1987. Beijing: Foreign Language Press.

Entwistle, H. 1970. *Education, work and leisure.* London: Routledge.

Epperson, A. 1983. Why people travel. *Leisure Today* (April):31.

Erikson, E. 1977. *Toys and reason: Stages in the ritualization of experience.* New York: Norton.

Esslin, M. 1982. *The age of television.* San Francisco: W. H. Freeman.

Farb, P. 1968. *Man's rise to civilization.* New York: Avon.

Farley, E. 1986. Coming soon to your neighborhood: More theatres. *Business Week* (14 July):31.

Fasting, K., and M. K. Sisjord. 1985. Gender roles and barriers to participation in sport. *Sociology of Sport Journal* 2 (4):345–51.

Fazio, J. R. 1979. Parks and other recreational resources. In *Leisure: Emergence and expansion,* edited by H. Ibrahim and J. Shivers. Los Alamitos: Hwong.

Feather, N. 1975. *Values in education and society.* New York: Free Press.

Ferguson, E. 1966. *Dancing gods: Indian ceremonials of New Mexico and Arizona.* Albuquerque: University of New Mexico Press.

Fitzgerald, C. P. 1933. *China: A short cultural history.* New York: Praeger.

Foley, J. 1989. Leisure rights: Policies for Los Angeles urban impact parks. A paper presented to the People for Parks Conference, Griffith Park.

Foote, N. 1958. Sex as play. In *Mass leisure,* edited by E. Larrabee and R. Meyershon. Glencoe, IL: Free Press.

Foret, C. M. 1985. Life satisfaction and leisure satisfaction among young-old and old-old adults with rural and urban residence. Ph.D. Diss., Texas Women's University.

Foss, P. D. 1971. Recreation. In *Conservation in the United States: A documentary history,* edited by F. Smith. New York: Chelsea House.

Fowler, W. W. 1925. *The Roman festivals.* London: Macmillan.

Frank, A. D. 1987. Leisure and recreation. *Forbes* 139:158–59.

Frey, J. 1984. Gambling: A sociological review. *Annals of the American Academy of Political and Social Sciences* 474 (July):107–20.

Fromm, E. 1973. *The anatomy of human destructiveness.* New York: Holt, Rinehart & Winston.

Galston, A., and J. Savage. 1973. *Daily life in People's China.* New York: Thomas Crowell.

Gastor, T. 1961. *Thespis: Ritual myth and drama in the ancient Near East.* New York: Harper & Row.

Gastor, T. 1962. Myth and mythology. In *The Interpreter's Dictionary of the Bible,* edited by G. Buttrik. New York: Abingdon.

Gattas, J. T. et al. 1986. Leisure and life-styles: Towards a research agenda. *Society and Leisure* 9 (2):529–37.

Geertz, C. 1973. *The Interpretation of Cultures.* New York: Basic Books.

Gennep, A. van. 1960. *The rites of passage.* London: Routledge & Kegan Paul.

Gernet, J. 1962. *Daily life in China.* Stanford, CA: Stanford University Press.

Gertner, R. 1986. *International television almanac.* New York: Quigley.

Gibbs, N. 1989. How America has run out of time. *Time* (24 April):58–67.

Giels, J. and F. 1974. *Life in a medieval castle.* New York: Thomas Crowell.

Gilson, E. 1960. *The Christian philosophy of Saint Augustine.* New York: Random House.

Ginsberg, B. 1983. Leisure patterns and leisure satisfaction of urban retired executives. *Leisure Studies* 2 (3):365–66.

Glassford, R. G. 1976. *Application of a theory of games to the transitional Eskimo culture.* New York: Arno Press.

Glueck, S. and E. 1968. *Delinquents and nondelinquents in perspective.* Cambridge: Harvard University Press.

Glyptis, S., and D. Chambers. 1982. No place like home. *Leisure Studies* 1 (2):247–62.

Godbey, G. 1980. *Leisure in your life.* Philadelphia: Saunders.

Goffman, E. 1959. *The presentation of self in everyday life.* New York: Doubleday.

Golby, J. M., and A. W. Purdue. 1984. *The civilization of the crowd: Popular culture in England 1750–1900.* New York: Schocken Books.

Goldschmidt, W. 1959. *Man's way: Preface to the understanding of human society.* New York: Holt, Rinehart & Winston.

Gray, D., and H. Ibrahim, eds. 1985. The nature of recreation experience. *Leisure Today* (October):1–32.

Greenberg, J. 1984. Inventory of sports fatalities and injuries yields some surprises. *Science News* 126 (28 July):53.

Grenier, A. 1926. *The Roman spirit in religion, thought and art.* New York: Knopf.

Grimes, R. 1982. *Beginnings in ritual studies.* Lanham, MD: University Press of America.

Groos, K. 1908. *Play of man.* Appleton: New York.

Gross, L. 1983. *How much is too much: The effects of social drinking.* New York: Random House.

Grover, R. 1987. Theme parks: This slugfist is no fantasy. *Business Week* (23 March):38.

Guillet, E. 1933. *Early life in upper Canada.* Toronto: University of Toronto Press.

Gurvitch, G. 1964. *The spectrum of social time.* Dordrecht, Holland: D. Peidel.

Guttmann, A. 1986. *Sports spectations.* New York: Columbia University Press.

Hafez, M. et al. 1957. *Leisure and recreation.* Cairo: Modern Press. (in Arabic)

Hammel, R., and C. Foster. 1986. A sporting chance: Relationships between technological change and concept of fair play in fishing. *Journal of Leisure Research* 18:40–52.

Hanstrais, L. 1984. Leisure Policy in France. *Leisure Studies* 3 (2):129–46.

Harney, W. E. 1952. Sport and play amidst the aborigines of the northern territory. *Mankind* 4 (9):377–79.

Harris, A., and S. Parker. 1973. Leisure and the elderly. In *Leisure and society in Great Britain,* edited by A. Smith et al. London: Allen Lane.

Haworth, J. T., and M. A. Smith. 1975. *Work and leisure.* London: Lepus Books.

Heider, K. 1977. From Javanese to Dani: The translation of a game. In *Studies in the anthropology of play,* edited by P. Stevens. West Point, NY: Leisure Press.

Hendee, J. 1969. Rural-urban differences reflected in outdoor recreation participation. *Journal of Leisure Research* 1:333–41.

Henderson, K. 1984. Volunteerism as leisure. *Journal of Voluntary Action Research* 13 (1):55–63.

Henderson, K. A., and J. L. Rannells. 1987. Farm women and the meaning of work and leisure: An oral history perspective. *Leisure Sciences* 10 (1):41–50.

Hendry, L. B. 1978. *School, sport and leisure.* London: Lepus Books.

Herchel, A. J. 1951. *Man is not alone: A philosophy of religion.* New York: Jewish Publication Society.

Higginson, T. W. 1858. Saints and their bodies. *Atlantic Monthly* 1:587.

Hintereder, P. 1988. Leisure: Boon or bane. *Scala* (November/December):28–38.

Hitti, Ph. 1970. *History of the Arabs.* New York: Macmillan.

Hjelte, G. 1940. *The administration of public recreation.* New York: Macmillan.

Hoberman, J. 1984. *Sport and political ideology.* Austin: University of Texas Press.

Hooper, J., and D. Teresi. 1986. *The three pound universe.* New York: Macmillan.

Horn, J. 1979. Leisure in Mexico. In *Leisure: Emergence and expansion,* edited by H. Ibrahim and J. Shivers. Los Alamitos: Hwong.

Horna, J., and E. Lupri. 1987. The family work and leisure interface: Gender asymmetry in parenting. Paper read at the 58th Annual Meeting of the Pacific Sociological Association, Eugene, Oregon, April 8–11.

Horna, J. L. A. 1988. Leisure studies in Czechoslovakia: Some East-West parallels and divergence. *Leisure Sciences* 10(2):79–94.

Huizinga, J. 1950. Homo ludens: *A study of the play element in culture.* Boston: Beacon Press.

Ibrahim, H. 1967. Comparison of temperament traits among intercollegiate athletes and PER majors. *Research Quarterly* 38:615–27.

Ibrahim, H. 1969. Recreation preference and personality. *Research Quarterly* 40:76–82.

Ibrahim, H. 1970. Recreation preference and temperament. *Research Quarterly* 41:145–54.

Ibrahim, H. 1974. Inner-other directedness, play and recreation: Cross-cultural validation. *International Review of Modern Sociology* 4:54–65.

Ibrahim, H. 1975. *Sport and society: An introduction to sport sociology.* Los Alamitos: Hwong.

Ibrahim, H. 1976. Education for leisure and the political system. *Leisure Today* (March):11–13.

Ibrahim H. 1978. Gastronomy: The new American pastime. *Leisure Today* (October):21–22.

Ibrahim, H. 1979. Leisure in the ancient world. In *Leisure: Emergence and expansion,* edited by H. Ibrahim and J. Shivers. Los Alamitos: Hwong.

Ibrahim, H. 1982a. Leisure and Islam. *Leisure Studies* 1 (2):197–210.

Ibrahim, H. 1982b. Leisure and recreation in Egypt. *Egypt* 1 (5):10–12. Washington, D.C., Embassy of Egypt.

Ibrahim, H. 1986. Leisure studies as a liberal arts. *Journal of Recreation and Leisure* (Winter): 52–58.

Ibrahim, H. 1988. Leisure, idleness, and Ibn Khaldun. *Leisure Studies* 7:51–58.

Ibrahim, H., and K. Cordes. 1986. Anomie and American sport. *Journal-Times* 49 (2):4–7.

Ibrahim, H., A. Sutton, and R. Stenius. 1972. Societal differentiation and recreational inclination. *Society and Leisure* 4:111–22.

Ibrahim, H., A. Mouti, and N. Touhami. 1981. Leisure behavior among contemporary Egyptians. *Journal of Leisure Research* 13 (2):89–104.

Ibrahim, H., R. Banes, and G. Gerson. 1987. *Effective parks and recreation boards and commissions.* Washington, D.C.: AAHPERD.

Ingham, R. 1986. Psychological contributions to the study of leisure—Part One. *Leisure Studies* 5 (3):255–79.

Isaacs, N. 1970. *Travels and adventures in Eastern Africa.* Capetown: C. Struick.

Jackson, E. L. 1980. Socio-demographic variables, recreation resource use, and attitudes toward development in Camrose, Alberta. *Leisure Sciences* 3 (2):189–211.

Jackson, E. L. 1988. Leisure constraints: A survey of past research. *Leisure Sciences* 10 (3):203–15.

Jackson, E. L., and M. S. Searle. 1985. Recreation non-participation and barriers to participation: Concepts and models. *Society and Leisure* 8 (2):693–705.

Jafari, J. 1983. Tourism today. *Leisure Today* (April):3–5.

Janisova, H. 1971. Leisure time and the recreation of the city resident. *Society and Leisure* (1):121–44.

Jary, D. 1973. Evenings at the ivory tower: Liberal adult education. In *Leisure and Society in Britain,* edited by M. Smith, S. Parker, and C. Smith. London: Allen Lane.

Jobes, P. C. 1984. Old timers and new mobile lifestyle. *Annuals of Tourism Research* 11 (2):181–98.

Johnson, R. 1979. Leisure in Canada. In *Leisure: Emergence and expansion,* edited by H. Ibrahim and J. Shivers. Los Alamitos: Hwong.

Johnson, W. O. 1985. Steroids: A problem of huge dimensions. *Sports Illustrated* (13 May):38–61.

Kahler, J. 1957. *The American class structure.* New York: Rinehart.

Kallick-Kauffmann, M. 1979. The micro and macro dimensions of gambling in the United States. *Journal of Social Issues* 35 (3):7–26.

Kando, T. 1975. *Leisure and popular culture in transition.* St. Louis: Mosby.

Kaplan, M. 1960. *Leisure in America: A social inquiry.* New York: Wiley.

Kaplan, M. 1975. *Leisure: Theory and policy.* New York: Wiley and Sons.

Kelly, J. R. 1974. Socialization toward leisure: A developmental approach. *Journal of Leisure Research* 6 (2):181–93.

Kelly, J. R. 1978a. Family leisure in three communities. *Journal of Leisure Research* 10 (1):47–60.

Kelly, J. R. 1978b. A revised paradigm of leisure choices. *Leisure Sciences* 1 (4):360.

Kelly, J. R. 1982. *Leisure.* Englewood Cliffs, NJ: Prentice-Hall.

Kelly, J. R. 1983a. *Leisure identities and interactions.* London: Allen & Unwin.

Kelly, J. R. 1983b. Leisure styles: A hidden core. *Leisure Sciences* 5 (4):321–37.

Kelly, J. R. 1987. *Freedom to be: A new sociology of leisure.* New York: Macmillan.

Kelly, J. R. et al. 1987. Later-life satisfaction: Does leisure contribute? *Leisure Sciences* 9 (3):189–200.

Kemp, W. B., and P. Jacobs. 1986. The tyranny of leisure. *Leisure and Science* 9 (1):193–201.

Klamus, H. 1981. Organic evolution and time. In *The voices of time,* edited by J. T. Fraser. Amherst: University of Massachusetts Press.

Kluchohn, C., and D. Leighton. 1974. *The Navajo.* Cambridge: Harvard University Press.

Knopp, T. 1972. Environmental determinants of recreation behavior. *Journal of Leisure Research* 4 (2):129–38.

Knudson, D. 1984. *Outdoor recreation.* New York: Macmillan.

Kramer, S. N. 1961. *Mythologies of the ancient world.* New York: Anchor Books.

Kraus, R. 1971. *Recreation and leisure in modern society.* New York: Appleton-Century-Crofts.

Kraus, R. 1984. *Recreation and leisure in modern society.* 3d ed. Glenview, IL: Scott, Foresman.

Kretzmann, N. et al. 1982. *The Cambridge history of later medieval philosophy.* Cambridge: Cambridge University Press.

Labarge, M. W. 1965. *A baronial household of the thirteenth century.* New York: Barnes & Noble.

Lancaster, J. B. 1975. *Primate behavior and the emergence of human culture.* New York: Holt, Rinehart & Winston.

Lane, E. W. [1836] (1973). *An account of the manners and customs of the modern Egyptians.* New York: Dover.

Langer, S. 1972. *Mind: An essay on human feeling.* Baltimore, MD: Johns Hopkins University Press.

Langlois, S. 1984. Consommation et activities de loisirs au Quebec. *Society and Leisure* 7 (2):327–49.

Lannoy, R. 1971. *The speaking tree: A study of Indian culture and society.* London: Oxford University Press.

Lapchick, R., ed. 1986. *Fractured focus: Sport as a reflection of society.* Lexington, MA: Lexington Books.

Larrabee, E., and R. Meyersohn. 1958. *Mass leisure.* Glencoe, IL: Free Press.

Larson, R. 1971. Television: A different system. In *Meet Germany.* 14th rev. ed. Hamburg: Atlantik-Brucke.

Laubin, R. and G. 1977. *Indian dances of North America.* Norman: University of Oklahoma Press.

Lauer, R. 1981. *Temporal man: The meaning and uses of social time.* New York: Praeger.

Leakey, R., and G. Isaac. 1972. Hominid fossils from the area east of Lake Rudolph, Kenya. In *Perspectives in human evolution,* edited by S. Washburn and P. Dolhihow. New York: Holt, Rinehart & Winston.

Lee, R. 1964. *Religion and leisure in America.* New York: Abingdon.

Lee, R., and I. de Vore. 1968. *Man the hunter.* Chicago: Aldine.

Le Goff, J. L. 1980. *Time, work and culture in the Middle Ages.* Chicago: University of Chicago Press.

Lerner, E., and C. B. Abbott. 1982. *The way to go.* New York: Warner Books.

Levine, D. 1984. The liberal arts and the martial arts. *Liberal Education* 13:23–28.

Lindeman, E. 1939. *Leisure: A national issue.* New York: Association Press.

Linhart, J., and J. Vitechova. 1975. The development of work time, nonwork time and leisure in socialist Czechoslovakia. *Society and Leisure* 7:133–54.

Lippold, G. 1972. *Annotated bibliography on leisure: German Democratic Republican.* Prague: European Centre for Leisure and Education.

Lloyd, A. 1981. *Timekeepers: An historical sketch.* In *The voices of time,* edited by J. T. Fraser. Amherst: University of Massachusetts Press.

Lornez, A. 1966. *On aggression.* New York: Harcourt, Brace & World.

Lowerson, J., and J. C. Meyerscough. 1977. *Time to spare in Victorian England.* Hassocks, Sussex: Harvester Press.

Lundberg, G. et al. 1934. *Leisure: A suburban study.* New York: Columbia University Press.

McCollum, R. 1979. Leisure from medieval times to colonial America. In *Leisure: Emergence and Expansion,* edited by H. Ibrahim and J. Shivers. Los Alamitos: Hwong.

McElroy, M. 1983. Parent-child relations and orientation toward sport. *Sex Roles* 9 (10):997–1004.

McFarland, E. 1970. *The development of public recreation in Canada.* Ottawa: Canadian Parks/Recreation Association.

McGuire, F. 1984. A factor analytic study of leisure constraints in advanced adulthood. *Leisure Science* 6 (3):313–25.

McGuire, F. A. et al. 1987. The relationship of early life experiences to later life leisure involvement. *Leisure Science* 9 (4):251–57.

McGurrin, M., V. Abt, and J. Smith. 1982. Play or pathology: A new look at the gambler and his world. In *The masks of play,* edited by B. Sutton-Smith and D. Kelly-Byrne. New York: Leisure Press.

MacLean, J., J. Peterson, and D. Martin. 1985. *Recreation and leisure: The changing scene.* New York: Macmillan.

McMillen, J. 1983. The social organization of leisure among Mexican Americans. *Journal of Leisure Research* 15 (2):164–73.

Magi, L. 1989. Recreation as seen by the Zulu of South Africa. *Leisure Today* (April):3.

Mahdi, M. 1964. *Ibn Khaldun's philosophy of history.* Chicago: Chicago University Press.

Mancini, J., and D. K. Orthner. 1978. Recreational sexuality preferences among husbands and wives. *Journal of Sex Research* 14:96–106.

Mandell, R. 1984. *Sport: A cultural history.* New York: Columbia University Press.

Mannell, R. C. 1984. Personality in leisure theory: The self-as-entertainment construct. *Society and Leisure* 7 (1):229–37.

Manz, G. 1976. Personality formation and time use—fundamental problem of their correlation. *Society and Leisure* 8 (3):199–208.

Marcus, J. 1961. Time and sense in history: West and East. *Comparative Studies in Society and History* 3:123–39.

Martin, B., and S. Mason. 1987. Current trends in leisure. *Leisure Studies* 6 1:93–97.

Mason, R. H. P., and J. G. Caiger. 1972. *A history of Japan.* New York: Free Press.

Mead, M. 1937. The Samoans. In *Cooperation and competition among primitive people,* edited by M. Mead. New York: Morrow.

Meier, G. M. 1989. *Leading issues in economic development.* New York: Oxford University Press.

Merton, R. K. 1957. Social structure and anomie. In *Social theory and social structure.* Rev. ed. Glencoe, IL: Free Press.

Metge, J. 1976. *The Maoris of New Zealand.* London: Routledge and Kegan Paul.

Meyer, H. D., and C. K. Brightbill. 1956. *Community recreation: A guide to its organization.* Englewood Cliffs, NJ: Prentice-Hall.

Mitchell, A. 1983. *The nine American lifestyles: Who we are and where we're going.* New York: Macmillan.

Monthly Labor Review 1926. (December):1162.

Moore, W. 1963. *Man, time and society.* New York: Wiley.

Morris, R. 1985. *Time's arrows: Scientific attitudes toward time.* New York: Simon & Schuster.

Morrison, S. E. 1965. *The Oxford history of the American people.* New York: Oxford University Press.

Morton, W. S. 1970. *Japan: Its history and culture.* New York: Thomas Crowell.

Moskoff, Wm. 1984. *Labour and leisure in the Soviet Union.* New York: St. Martin's Press.

Mundy, J., and L. Odum. 1979. *Leisure education: Theory and practice.* New York: Wiley.

Murray, M. 1963. *The splendor that was Egypt.* Hawthorn Books.

Nakahooda, Z. 1961. *Leisure and recreation in society.* Allahabad: Katab, Mahal.

Nakamura, H. 1981. Time in Indian and Japanese thought. In *The voices of time,* edited by J. T. Fraser. Amherst: University of Massachusetts Press.

Nash, J. B. 1953. *The philosophy of recreation and leisure.* Dubuque, IA: Wm. C. Brown.

National Commission on Marijuana and Drug Abuse. 1973. *Drug use in America: Problems in perspective.* Washington, D.C.: Government Printing Office.

Neumann, H. 1985. The healthiest of pastimes: Sports for everyone. *Scala* (November):18–30.

Neumeyer, M. and E. 1949. *Leisure and recreation.* New York: Roland Press.

Newman, B. 1973. Holidays and social class. In *Leisure and society in Britain,* edited by M. Smith, S. Parker, and C. Smith. London: Allen Lane.

Nikhilananda, S. 1949. *The Upanishads.* New York: Harper Brothers.

Odum, L., and R. Lancaster. 1976. Analysis of a national survey to determine the extent of leisure education programs in American public schools K–12. Arlington, VA: National Recreation and Park Association, unpublished paper.

O'Leary, J. T. et al. 1987. Age of first hunting experience: Results from a nationwide recreation survey. *Leisure Sciences* 9 (4):225–33.

Olszweska, A. 1979. Leisure in Poland. In *Leisure: Emergence and expansion,* edited by H. Ibrahim and J. Shivers. Los Alamitos: Hwong.

Oppenheim, L. 1964. *Ancient Mesopotamia: The portrait of a dead civilization.* Chicago: University of Chicago Press.

Ornestein, R., and R. Thompson. 1984. *The amazing brain.* Boston: Houghton Mifflin.

Orthner, D. 1980. *Families in blue.* Washington, D.C.: U.S. Air Force.

Orthner, D. 1985. Conflict and leisure interaction in families. In *Transitions to leisure: Conceptual and human issues,* edited by B. G. Gunter et al. Lanham, MD: University Press of America.

Orthner, D. K., and J. A. Mancini. 1978. Parental family sociability and marital leisure patterns. *Leisure Sciences* 1 (4):365–72.

Osgood, N. 1987. The middle-life leisure renaissance: A developmental perspective. *Leisure Today* (October):3–7.

Pachocinski, R., and J. Poturzycki. 1976. Adult education in people's Poland. *Society and Leisure* 8 (1):9–35.

Pack, A. N. 1934. *The challenge of leisure.* Washington, D.C.: McGrath.

Palisi, B., and H. Ibrahim. 1979. Voluntary associations. In *Leisure: Emergence and expansion,* edited by H. Ibrahim and J. Shivers. Los Alamitos: Hwong.

Parker, S. 1976. *Sociology of leisure.* New York: International Publication Service.

Parker, S. 1980. Leisure and leisure studies in the United States and Britain: A comparative survey. *Society and Leisure* 3 (2): 269–77.

Parker, S. 1983. *Leisure and work.* London: Allen & Unwin.

Parsons, T. 1966. *Societies: Evolutionary and comparative perspectives.* Englewood Cliffs, NJ: Prentice-Hall.

Parsons, T. 1971. *The system of modern societies.* Englewood Cliffs, NJ: Prentice-Hall.

Parten, M. 1932. Social play among preschool children. *Journal of Abnormal and Social Psychology* 27:243–69.

Petersson, T. 1920. *Cicero: A biography.* Berkeley: University of California Press.

Pieper, J. 1964. *Leisure: The basis of culture.* New York: Pantheon Press.

Plesser, D. et al. 1986. *Gambling: Crime or recreation.* Plano, TX: Information Aids.

Postman, N. 1985. *Amusing ourselves to death: Public discourse in the age of show business.* New York: Viking/Penguin Books.

Ragatz, R. 1974. *Recreation properties.* Springfield, VA: Council on Environmental Quality.

Ragnathan, I. R. 1954. *Education for leisure.* London: G. Blunt and Sons.

Rainwater, C. E. 1922. *The play movement in the United States.* Chicago: University of Chicago Press.

Rattray, R. 1969. *Religion and art in Ashanti.* London: Oxford University Press.

Ray, O. 1983. *Drugs, society and human behavior.* St. Louis: Mosby.

Reagan, A. 1932. Navajo sports. *Primitive Man* 5:68–71.

Rearick, C. 1985. *Pleasures of the Belle Epoque: Entertainment and festivity in turn-of-the-century France.* New Haven: Yale University Press.

Rehberg, R. A., and W. E. Schafer. 1968. Participation in interscholastic athletics and college aspirations. *American Journal of Sociology* 73:732–40.

Reisman, D. et al. 1950. *The lonely crowd: A study in the changing character.* New Haven: Yale University Press.

Restak, R. 1984. *The brain.* Toronto and London: Bantam.

Riordan, J. 1977. *Sport in Soviet society.* Cambridge: Cambridge University Press.

Riordan, J. 1982. Leisure, the State, and the Individual in the USSR. *Leisure Studies* 1 (1):65–79.

Riordan, J. 1989. The effects of glasnost: Leisure and recreation in the U.S.S.R. *Leisure Today* (April):27–29.

Roberts, J. M., M. M. Arth, and R. R. Bush. 1959. Games in culture. *American Anthropologist* 61:597–605.

Roberts, K. 1970. *Leisure.* London: Longman.

Roberts, K. 1978. *Contemporary society and the growth of leisure.* London: Longman.

Roberts, K. 1983a. *Youth and leisure.* London: Allen & Unwin.

Roberts, K. 1983b. Playing at work. *Leisure Studies* 2:217–29.

Roberts, V. M. 1962. *On stage: A history of theatre.* New York: Harper & Row.

Robinson, J. 1977. *Changes in Americans' use of time: 1965–1975.* Cleveland: Communication Research Center, Cleveland State University.

Robinson, J. 1981. Television and leisure time: A new scenario. *Journal of Communication* (Winter):120–30.

Rodnick, D. 1966. *An introduction to man and his development.* New York: Appleton-Century-Crofts.

Rokeach, M. 1973. *The nature of human values.* New York: Free Press.

Romer, J. 1984. *Ancient lives: Daily life in Egypt of the pharaohs.* New York: Holt, Rinehart & Winston.

Romsa, G. 1980. Recreation research and planning in the Federal Republic of Germany: A commentary. *Leisure Sciences* 3 (3):257–75.

Rostow, W. W. 1960. *The stages of economic growth.* Cambridge: Harvard University Press.

Roth, W. E. 1902. Games, sports, and amusements. *North Queensland Ethnography,* Bulletin No. 4, Brisbane: G. A. Vaughan, Government Printer.

Rowntree, B., and G. Lavers. 1951. *English life and leisure.* New York: Longman.

Royce, A. P. 1977. *The anthropology of dance.* Bloomington: Indiana University Press.

Rubenstein, C. 1980. Vacations. *Psychology Today* (May):62–67.

Rubin, K. H., G. Kein, and D. Vanenberg. 1983. Play. In *Handbook of child psychology,* edited by P. H. Mussen. New York: Wiley and Sons.

Russell, J. T. 1981. Time in Christian thought. In *The voices of time,* edited by J. T. Fraser. Amherst: University of Massachusetts.

Samuel, N. 1986. Free time in France: A historical and sociological survey. *International Social Science Journal* 38:49–63.

Sansom, G. B. 1936. *Japan: A short cultural history.* New York: Appleton-Century.

Sax, J. 1976. America's national parks. *Natural History* 85 (8):57–89.

Scheys, M. 1987. The power of life-style. *Society and Leisure* 10 (2):249–61.

Schierwater, H. V. 1971. The young generation. In *Meet Germany*. 14th rev. ed. Hamburg: Atlantik-Brucke.

Schlesinger, A. 1944. Biography of a nation of joiners. *American Historical Review* (October)50:1–25.

Searle, M., and E. Jackson. 1985. Socioeconomic variations in perceived barriers to recreation participation among would-be participants. *Leisure Sciences* 7 (2):227–49.

Seib, W., and P. Hintereder. 1986. The undying past. *Scala* (March):18–21.

Service, E. 1963. *Profiles in ethnology*. New York: Harper & Row.

Service, E. 1975. *Origins of the state and civilization: The process of cultural evolution*. New York: Norton.

Shallis, M. 1981. *On time: An investigation into scientific knowledge and human experience*. New York: Schocken Books.

Shamir, B., and H. Ruskin. 1983. Sex differences in recreational sport behavior and attitudes: A study of married couples in Israel. *Leisure Studies* 2 (3):253–68.

Shaw, D. 1980. Achievements and problems in Soviet recreational planning. In *Home, school and leisure in the Soviet Union*, edited by J. Brine et al. London: Allen & Unwin.

Shaw, S. 1985. Gender and leisure: Inequality in the distribution of leisure time. *Journal of Leisure Research* 17 (4):266–82.

Sheldon, Wm. 1954. *Atlas of men*. New York: Harper & Row.

Shivers, J. 1979. The origin of man, culture, and leisure. In *Leisure: Emergence and expansion*, edited by H. Ibrahim and J. Shivers. Los Alamitos: Hwong.

Singer, M. 1965. *Krishna: Myths, rites and attitudes*. Honolulu: East-West Center Press.

Skorzynski, Z. 1972. The use of free time in Torun, Maribor, and Jackson. In *The use of time: Daily activities of urban and suburban populations in twelve countries*, edited by A. Szalai. The Hague: Mouton.

Small, C. 1977. *Music, society, education*. New York: Schirmer Books.

Smith, A. 1894. *Chinese characteristics*. New York: Fleming Revell.

Smith, M., S. Parker, and C. Smith, eds. 1973. *Leisure and society in Britain*. London: Allen Lane.

Smith, P., ed. 1984. *Play in animal and humans*. London: Basil Blackwell.

Smith, R., and F. Preston. 1985. Expressed gambling motives: Accounts in defense of self. In *Transitions to leisure: Conceptual and human issues*, edited by B. Gunter et al. Lunham, MD: University Press of America.

Smith, S. 1985. U.S. vacation travel patterns: Correlates of distance decay and the willingness to travel. *Leisure Sciences* 7 (2):151–73.

Snyder, S. H. 1972. *Uses of marijuana*. New York: Oxford University Press.

Sorokin, P., and R. Merton. 1937. Social time: A methodological and functional analysis. *The American Journal of Sociology*. 42:618–28.

Soustelle, J. 1962. *The daily life of the Aztecs on the eve of the Spanish conquest*. New York: Macmillan.

Spandoni, M. 1986. Special report: Travel and tourism. *Advertising Age* (14 July):6.

Spencer, H. 1873. *Principles of psychology*. New York: Appleton.

Statistical Abstracts of the United States. 1987. Washington, D.C.: Bureau of the Census.

Statistics Canada. 1983. *Cultural statistics: Performing arts*. Ottawa: Ministry of Supplies and Services.

Statistics Canada. 1986a. *Tourism and recreation*. Ottawa: Ministry of Supplies and Services.

Statistics Canada. 1986b. *Touriscope: 1986 international travel*. Ottawa: Ministry of Supplies and Services.

Statistics Canada. 1987. *Travel log*. Ottawa: Ministry of Supplies and Services.

Statistics Canada. 1988. *Year book, 1988*. Ottawa: Ministry of Supplies and Services.

Stewart, D. 1967. *Early Islam*. New York: Time.

Stone, C. L. 1963. Family recreation: A parental dilemma. *The Family Life Coordinator* 12:85–87.

Straus, M., R. Gellis, and S. Steinmets. 1980. *Behind closed doors*. New York: Anchor Books.

Strutt, J. [1801] (1970). *The sports and pastime of the people of England*. New York: Augustus Kelly.

Sutton-Smith, B., and B. C. Rosenberg. 1971. Sixty years of historical change in the game preference of American children. In *Child's play*, edited by R. E. Herron and B. Sutton-Smith. New York: Wiley and Sons.

Szalai, A., ed. 1972. *The use of time: Daily activities of urban and suburban population in twelve countries*. The Hague: Mouton.

Theobald, Wm. 1978. Discrimination in public recreation: Attitudes toward and participation of females. *Leisure Sciences* 1 (3):231–39.

Thomas, K. 1960. Work and leisure in pre-industrial society. *Past and Present* 29:50–62.

Thoreau, H. D. 1893. Walking. In *Excursions*. Boston: Houghton Mifflin.

Thorndike, E. 1905. *The elements of psychology*. New York: Seiler.

Tinsley, H. E. et al. 1987. The relationship of age, gender, health and economic status to the psychological benefits older persons report from participation in leisure activities. *Leisure Science* 9 (1):53–65.

Trice, H. M. 1966. *Alcoholism in America*. New York: McGraw-Hill.

Truby, J. 1987. Whatever you may like. *Scala* (November):18–24.

Turner, V. 1969. *The ritual process: Structure and antistructure*. Chicago: Aldine.

Turner, V. 1977. Variations on a theme of limenality. In *Secular ritual*, edited by S. Moore and B. Meyerhoff. Amsterdam: Ban Gorcum-Assen.

Turner, V. 1982a. *From ritual to theatre: The Human seriousness of play*. New York: Performing Arts Journal Publications.

Turner, V., ed. 1982b. *Celebration: Study in festivity and ritual*. Washington, D.C.: Smithsonian Institute Press.

Ulmer, J. 1980. *Amusement parks of America*. New York: Dial Press.

United Media Enterprises. 1983. *Where does the time go.* New York: Newspaper Enterprise Association.

United Nations. 1985. *Statistical yearbook.* Paris: U.N.

Veal, A. J. 1984. Leisure in England and Wales: A research note. *Leisure Studies* 3 (2):221–29.

Veblen, T. [1899] 1953. *The theory of the leisure class.* New York: New American Library.

Viau, J. 1939. *Hours and wages in American organized labor.* New York: George Putnam and Sons.

Von Hagen, V. W. 1967. *The ancient sun kingdoms of the Americas.* London: Panther Books.

Wade, M., ed. 1985. Introduction: Aspect of a biology of leisure. In *Constraints on leisure,* edited by M. Wade. Springfield, IL: Ch. Thomas.

Wall Street Journal. 1987. Tourism in China. (18 August):47.

Weber, M. 1930. *The Protestant ethics and the spirit of capitalism.* New York: Charles Scribners and Sons.

Weber, M. 1955. *The religion of China.* Glencoe, IL: Free Press.

Weber, M. 1958. *The religion of India.* Glencoe, IL: Free Press.

Welton, G. 1979. Leisure in the formative years. In *Leisure: Emergence and expansion,* edited by H. Ibrahim and J. Shivers. Los Alamitos: Hwong.

Whicher, S. 1957. *Selections from Ralph Waldo Emerson.* Boston: Houghton Mifflin.

White, C. 1955. Social class difference in the uses of leisure. *American Journal of Sociology* 61:145–50.

White, T. H. 1975. The relative importance of education and income as predictors in outdoor recreation participation. *Journal of Leisure Research* 7 (3):191–99.

Whittick, A. 1974. *Encyclopedia of urban planning.* New York: McGraw-Hill.

Willgoose, C. E. 1956. Body types and physical fitness. *Journal of Health, Physical Education and Recreation* 27:26–32.

Witt, P. A., and T. L. Goodale. 1981. The relationships between barriers to leisure enjoyment and family stages. *Leisure Sciences* 4 (1):29–49.

Wolf, D. P. 1984. Repertoire, style and format: Notions worth borrowing from children's play. In *Play in animal and humans,* edited by P. Smith. London: Basil Blackwell.

Wolfe, R. I. 1978. Vacation homes as social indicators: Observations from Canadian census data. *Leisure Sciences* 1 (4):327–43.

Wood, J. 1871. *The uncivilized races of men.* Hartford, CT: J. B. Burr.

Wyman, S. 1975. *The mountainway of the Navajo.* Tucson, AZ: University of Arizona Press.

Yeager, R. 1979. *Seasons of shame.* New York: McGraw-Hill.

Yoesting, D., and D. Burkhead. 1973. Significance of childhood recreation experience on adult leisure behavior. *Journal of Leisure Research* 5 (1):25–36.

Yoesting, D. R., and J. E. Christensen, 1978. Reexamining the significance of childhood recreation patterns on adult leisure behavior. *Leisure Sciences* 1 (3):219–29.

Young, R. A., and R. Crandall. 1984. Wilderness use and self-actualization. *Journal of Leisure Research* 16 (2):149–60.

Young, T. R. 1964. Recreation and family stress: An essay in institutional conflict. *Journal of Marriage and the Family* 26 (1):95–96.

AUTHOR INDEX

SUBJECT INDEX